CW00662917

Sanctions and Dominion

Other Books by Gary North

Marx's Religion of Revolution (1968, 1989)
An Introduction to Christian Economics (1973)
Puritan Economic Experiments (1974, 1988)
How You Can Profit From The Coming Price Controls (1974, 1976, 1977, 1978)
Unconditional Surrender (1981, 1988, 1994)
Successful Investing in an Age of Envy (1981)
The Dominion Covenant: Genesis (1982, 1987)
Government by Emergency (1983, 1991)
Last Train Out (1983)
Backward, Christian Soldiers? (1984)
75 Bible Questions Your Instructors Pray You Won't Ask (1984, 1988, 1996)
Coined Freedom (1984)
Moses and Pharaoh (1985)
The Sinai Strategy (1986)
Conspiracy: A Biblical View (1986, 1996)
Honest Money (1986)
Fighting Chance (1986), with Arthur Robinson
Unholy Spirits: Occultism & New Age Humanism (1986, 1988, 1994)
Dominion and Common Grace (1987)
Inherit the Earth (1987)
Liberating Planet Earth (1987)
Healer of the Nations (1987)
The Pirate Economy (1987)
Is the World Running Down? (1988)
When Justice Is Aborted (1989)
Political Polytheism (1989)
The Hoax of Higher Criticism (1990)
Tools of Dominion: The Case Laws of Exodus (1990)
Victim's Rights (1990)
Judeo-Christian Tradition (1990)
Westminster's Confession (1991)
Christian Reconstruction (1991), with Gary DeMar
The Coase Theorem (1992)
Politically Incorrect (1993)
Salvation Through Inflation (1993)
Rapture Fever (1993)
Tithing and the Church (1994)
Leviticus: An Economic Commentary (1994)
Baptized Patriarchalism (1995)
Lone Gunners For Jesus (1995)
Crossed Fingers: How the Liberals Captured the Presbyterian Church (1996)

SANCTIONS AND DOMINION
An Economic Commentary on Numbers

Gary North

Institute for Christian Economics
Tyler, Texas

Library of Congress Cataloging-in-Publication Data

North, Gary.
Sanctions and dominion : an economic commentary on Numbers / Gary North.
p. cm.
Includes bibliographical references and index.
ISBN 0-930464-76-1
1. Dominion theology. 2. Bible. O.T. Numbers--Criticism, interpretation, etc. 3. Economics--Religious aspects--Christianity. 4. Law (Theology)--Biblical teaching. 5. Economics in the Bible. 6. Jewish law. 7. Church and state--Biblical teaching. I. Title.
BT82.25.N677 1996
222'.1407--DC20 96-9229
CIP

Institute for Christian Economics
P.O. Box 8000
Tyler, Texas 75711

This book is dedicated to

Gary DeMar

who has proven that there
is life beyond shot-putting

TABLE OF CONTENTS

PREFACE

I began writing my economic commentary on Genesis in the spring of 1973. I wrote one chapter per month for the *Chalcedon Report*, beginning in May, 1973. I accelerated the process in August of 1977: ten hours a week, 50 weeks a year. Even so, it took me until 1982 to publish *The Dominion Covenant: Genesis*. I immediately began working on Exodus. That project occupied eight years and three volumes of commentary, plus four books that served as appendixes to the third volume.[1] *Moses and Pharaoh: Dominion Religion vs. Power Religion* took three years (1982–85); *The Sinai Strategy: The Economics of the Ten Commandments* took a year (1985–86); and *Tools of Dominion: The Case Laws of Exodus* took four years (1986–90). *Leviticus: An Economic Commentary*, a short version (about 800 pages) of *Boundaries and Dominion*, took almost five years (1990–94). Yet when I began Leviticus, I had thought that I might do Leviticus and Numbers in one volume.

It took me about six months to write the first draft of this book. I began in January of 1995. I completed the first draft in late June. It took another six months to revise, correct, typeset, and proofread it. By that time, I had finished Chapter 29 of my commentary on Deuteronomy, which went through Deuteronomy 12. The Deuteronomy manuscript was already longer

1. *Dominion and Common Grace* (1987), *Is the World Running Down?* (1988), *Political Polytheism* (1989), *Millennialism and Social Theory* (1990).

than the entire commentary on Numbers. I had not expected much trouble in writing *Sanctions and Dominion*, but I had not expected it to be as easy as it turned out to be, not counting the appendix, which was a challenge. I do not expect any future volume in this series to be equally easy.

My next assignment will be far more difficult to achieve. Deuteronomy repeats many of the laws of Exodus and Leviticus. I shall have to write it while looking over my shoulder at what I have already written. New readers who have not read my commentary on Leviticus will expect full discussions; readers who have read it will want mainly new material. It is difficult to please everyone and still keep a book short enough to be read by anyone. It will not be a short book.

The Five-Point Covenant Model

Deuteronomy completes book five of the Pentateuch, which in turn follows the five-point structure of the biblical covenant model.[2] When I began writing this economic commentary on the Bible, I was unaware of this structure's all-pervasive importance for understanding the Pentateuch. I had read Meredith G. Kline's *Treaty of the Great King* (1963) years earlier, but I had forgotten its thesis regarding the precise number of points in the covenant. I did not recognize its implications for this project until late 1985, when Ray Sutton first presented his version of the model, based on the earlier research by Kline. Sutton's version was more precise – exactly five points, not five or six – and it was more explicitly judicial. Most important, he brought the covenant model into the New Testament era, unlike Kline, who had relegated it to the Mosaic economy only. Kline's goal was to seal off the Mosaic law from the New Testament era. Sutton's goal was to demonstrate the continuity of the covenant's structure in both testaments.

---

2. Ray R. Sutton, *That You May Prosper: Dominion By Covenant* (2nd ed.; Tyler, Texas: Institute for Christian Economics, 1992).

First, I saw that the Ten Commandments are structured in terms of two parallel sets of five points each, priestly (1–5) and kingly (6–10).[3] This verifies the Protestant version of the numbering of the Decalogue, in contrast to the Roman Catholic and Lutheran[4] arrangement. It also lays to rest Calvin's peculiar 4–6 structuring of what he regarded as the two tables of the law: 1–4 (piety) and 5–10 (justice).[5] The traditional 5–5 structuring had been suggested as early as Josephus' first-century history of the Jews.[6] That structuring is correct, although Josephus' thesis that the two tablets had five commandments written on each of them probably is not.[7] Second, I realized that the Pentateuch itself is structured in terms of the same five points: Genesis (God's transcendence/presence), Exodus (God's authority and Israel's deliverance), Leviticus (God's law), Numbers (God's historical sanctions), and Deuteronomy (Israel's inheritance). On these points, I have gone into greater detail in the General Introduction in the second edition of *The Dominion Covenant: Genesis* (1987) and in the Preface to *Leviticus: An Economic Commentary*. There is no need to repeat myself here.

The Book of Numbers extends the Bible's covenant model through a consideration of Israel's post-exodus, pre-conquest wilderness history. As the fourth book in the Pentateuch, its overarching theme is sanctions: point four of the biblical covenant model.[8] God brought negative sanctions on the exodus

3. Preface, Gary North, *The Sinai Strategy: Economics and the Ten Commandments* (Tyler, Texas: Institute for Christian Economics, 1986), pp. xiv–xxi.

4. Conservative Lutherans do not like to be referred to as "Protestants," which they equate with the Swiss Calvinistic Reformers. Their version of the Decalogue reinforces this preference. Their view of justification by faith does not.

5. John Calvin, *Commentaries on the Four Last Books of Moses Arranged in the Form of a Harmony*, 4 vols. (Grand Rapids, Michigan: Baker, [1563] 1979), III, p. 6.

6. Josephus, *Antiquities of the Jews*, III:v:5.

7. *Ibid.*, III:v:8. I accept Kline's thesis: there were two complete sets of ten commandments each that were placed inside the Ark of the Covenant as testimonies: one was God's receipt; the other was Israel's. Meredith G. Kline, *The Structure of Biblical Authority* (rev. ed.; Grand Rapids, Michigan: Eerdmans, 1975), Pt. II, ch. 1.

8. Milgrom refers to "the difficulties of finding the book's inner cohesion." Jacob

generation because that generation had refused to bring negative sanctions against Canaan immediately after the return of the spies. When the next generation brought negative sanctions against cities on the wilderness side of the Jordan River, its members proved that they were covenantally ready to escape from the wilderness. The historical events of the wilderness era were, above all, a manifestation of God's corporate covenantal sanctions in history: negative against Israel.

New Heavens and New Earth: Prophesied Sanctions

We come now to the passage of the Bible that amillennialists resist commenting on, the passage that categorically and forever testifies against amillennialism. The crucial issue is sanctions: specifically, the historical sanction of extremely long life. Isaiah wrote of God's work in his day:

> For, behold, I create new heavens and a new earth: and the former shall not be remembered, nor come into mind. But be ye glad and rejoice for ever in that which I create: for, behold, I create Jerusalem a rejoicing, and her people a joy. And I will rejoice in Jerusalem, and joy in my people: and the voice of weeping shall be no more heard in her, nor the voice of crying. There shall be no more thence an infant of days, nor an old man that hath not filled his days: for the child shall die an hundred years old; but the sinner being an hundred years old shall be accursed (Isa. 65:17–20).

Consider these highly specific words: "There shall be no more thence an infant of days, nor an old man that hath not filled his days: for the child shall die an hundred years old; but the sinner being an hundred years old shall be accursed." These words are clear; they are also prophetically binding. They tell us that in this sin-cursed world, where death still

---

Milgrom, *The JPS Torah Commentary: Numbers* (New York: Jewish Publication Society, 1990), p. xiii. This inner cohesion becomes obvious when it is seen as book four in the Pentateuch, with the Pentateuch structured by the covenant model.

reigns, the reign of death will someday be challenged by a revolutionary increase of life expectancy. This has not happened yet; it must be in the future. This prophecy cannot possibly apply to the post-resurrection world of eternity, for death will still exist, the text says. This passage is literal and eschatological. The promised blessings are both literal and future. These blessings are the kinds of blessings that postmillennialists and premillennialists[9] expect during a literal, future era of millennial blessings. These historical blessings cannot be allegorized away without compromising the text, yet allegorizing is the only exegetical option for an amillennialist. This passage unquestionably destroys the case for amillennialism. No wonder amillennial Bible commentators and theologians grow hyperbolic and allegorical on those exceedingly rare occasions when they deign to offer comments on this, their position's exegetical Achilles' heel.[10] The positive sanction of long life is just too positive for their would-be future realm of Satanic persecution of the church. Sinners who die at age one hundred will be accounted as children: early death. Covenant-keepers will live much longer than this. But these demographic conditions reverse the prophesied amillennial future, where evil always increases in strength and receives external blessings, while righteousness is increasingly confined to the persecuted ghettos of life.

The historical sanctions of God during the final phase of the New Heaven and New Earth, as described by Isaiah, conform to the postmillennial system: righteousness is rewarded with

9. What destroys the premillennial system is Matthew 13, the chapter on historical continuity between the first advent of Christ and His second advent.

10. Amillennialist Archibald Hughes, in a book titled *A New Heaven and a New Earth* (Philadelphia: Presbyterian & Reformed, 1958), refuses to comment directly on this passage, despite the fact that the phrase "New Heaven and New Earth" first appears here. He mentions the passage only in passing, along with other verses, saying that it refers to eternal life, despite the fact that it discusses long life, not eternal life (pp. 138–39). There is no other comment anywhere in his book on this, the key problem passage in the Bible for amillennialists. This sort of evasive scholarship reveals a deep-seated weakness of the amillennial position.

greater wealth and power in the long run, while evil becomes increasingly impotent. Such a view of the future, we are assured by amillennialists, is heretical. It is obvious who ought to be the chief heretic in the canon of amillennialism: the prophet Isaiah.[11]

My main point here is that God's historical sanctions are indissolubly connected to the process of corporate inheritance and disinheritance in history. That is, *eschatology and historical sanctions are indissoluble covenantally*. To discuss either without reference to the other is to commit a major exegetical error.

Covenantal Sanctions and the Protestant Reformation

The issue of oath-bound sanctions served as the great dividing issue theologically in the Western church from the Protestant Reformation until the late nineteenth century, when eschatology replaced sanctions as the primary dividing issue within the Protestant community.[12] Martin Luther broke with Rome over the practical question of the sale of indulgences. He asked: Does the Papacy possess the authority to annul God's eternal sanctions in exchange for cash? The underlying theological issue here was salvation from hell's negative sanctions: By faith or by works? But the theoretical issue of the judicial basis of salvation came as a spin-off of the practical question of the sale

---

11. For a detailed study of the eschatological and social implications of Isaiah 65:17–20, see Gary North, *Millennialism and Social Theory* (Tyler, Texas: Institute for Christian Economics, 1990), ch. 5.

12. In the early church, the initial divisive issue was sovereignty: the doctrine of God. This was settled by the great Trinitarian creeds of the early church councils. It was the only issue that ever was settled. Then the debate moved to authority: church vs. State. The Eastern Church placed the State at the top of the hierarchy in history. The Western Church proclaimed the equal ultimacy of church and State under God. That issue came to the forefront in the West in 1076: the Papal Revolution. The next dividing issue in the West began immediately: the doctrine of law. The Scholastics attempted to fuse Roman law and canon law into one theoretical system. They failed; the two legal orders separated: rational law (State) vs. spiritual law (church). The modern world has inherited this ethical dualism.

of indulgences. It was Tetzel's sales program that led to Luther's 95 theses.

There were two other covenantally related issues that came to the forefront in the Reformation, neither of which has ever been settled: vows and sacraments. The Roman Church accused Luther and his allies of being vow-breakers, which indeed they were. This accusation was reasserted eloquently as recently as 1993 by E. Michael Jones in his study of the sexual debauchery of modern art, *Degenerate Moderns*.[13] He traces the degeneracy of modern art to the sexual debauchery of the artists. Then, without warning in the final chapter, and without offering any historical evidence for subsequent connections, he identifies the origin of modern sexual debauchery in Western art and culture as Luther's undermining of priestly and monastic vows. Jones argues that Luther wanted sex; the priests and nuns wanted sex; they broke their vows to get sex; and that led to Picasso. This line of reasoning may seem a bit tenuous to Protestants, but so ingrained is the centrality of the vow of celibacy in the thinking of traditionalist Roman Catholics that the emptying of Northern European nunneries and monasteries, 1520 to 1540, constitutes for some of them the crucial turning point in Western civilization. Everything evil in Western male-female relations stems from that event. They believe that it did more than merely undermine the church's ministry; it destroyed Christendom. The monstrous evil that Renaissance humanism's Papacy had become by 1517 is somehow beside the point; better the Borgias than Luther, we are still implicitly (though never explicitly) assured. The Borgias bribed people, poisoned people, and led totally debauched lives, but Luther broke his vow of celibacy. The latter act is seen as the essence of the great rebellion, not the former.

The other issue, the sacraments, was also the issue of covenantal sanctions. Luther asked: How many sacraments are

---

13. San Francisco: Ignatius Press.

there? Who has the authority to admit laymen to these sacraments? Who has the right to excommunicate whom? All of these sacramental issues were tied to the overriding issue of oath-bound ecclesiastical sanctions. A series of excommunications and counter-excommunications began in Northern Europe in the 1520's; they led to civil wars over the next century.

Because the West was Christian, the entire social order was oath-bound in 1517: church, State, and family. Only the Jews lived outside rule of law established by covenantal Trinitarian oaths, and they lived in separate ghettos with their own legal order. In the West, these ghettos were literally sealed off at night. In Poland, Jews lived in enclaves in the cities owned by the nobility, exempt from many gentile urban economic laws. This ghetto system benefitted the rabbis, for it transferred civil power to them over other Jews.[14] But Jews were the great exception; everyone else was under Trinitarian covenantal oaths. Thus, the Reformation's schism over the legitimacy of existing oaths led in the sixteenth century to dynastic persecutions, burnings at the stake, and wars in Northern Europe, followed by a series of civil wars in the seventeenth century. The devastating Thirty Years War in Germany (1618–48), the English-Scottish war (1638–41), the English Civil War (1642–49), Cromwell's Lord Protectorship (1652–58), the restoration of Charles II in 1660, were all struggles over the content of the civil oath.

The theoretical reconciliation of this covenantal issue in civil affairs after 1700 marks the triumph of Enlightenment political pluralism over a pietistic Protestantism. Newtonian natural law theory replaced the Bible and Scholastic natural law theory as the new basis of social ethics and civil law. Protestants abandoned civil institutions to what they believed was a legitimate common-ground morality. Today, almost all Protestant theolo-

---

14. Israel Shahak, *Jewish History, Jewish Religion: The Weight of Three Thousand Years* (London: Pluto, 1994), pp. 54, 60–63.

gians defend this dualism between revealed religion and civil authority. According to Enlightenment political theory, civil authority is not governed by Trinitarian oaths; it is governed by common-ground confessions of loyalty to a religiously neutral State. This confession of faith is accepted by Protestant theology, though with increasing doubts regarding the underlying myth of neutrality. As the myth of neutrality fades, so does the theoretical foundation of modern political pluralism.

The Renunciation of God's Historical Sanctions

To maintain the legitimacy of civil oaths without Trinitarian content, pluralism's Christian defenders have had to renounce the concept of predictable supernatural sanctions in history, i.e., sanctions invoked by corporate covenantal oath. This denial of the presence in the New Testament era of God's predictable covenantal sanctions has left Protestantism without any means of defending the ideal of Christendom. Lutheranism was always dualistic, but Calvinism was originally cultural-civilizational. Unofficially after 1700, and formally after 1787, American Calvinism adopted Lutheranism's dualistic view of society.[15]

Without the concept of covenantal sanctions in history, original Calvinism's comprehensive world-and-life view has been truncated to encompass little or nothing outside church and family. Attempts to revive Calvinism's once confident worldview, but on a pluralistic basis, most notably Abraham Kuyper's attempt in the late nineteenth century Netherlands, and more recently Francis Schaeffer's in the United States, have all failed, and for the same three reasons. First, without an appeal to a uniquely biblical law-order that encompasses politics, there is no way to distinguish Christendom from common-ethics En-

15. The Reformed Presbyterian Church of North America ("Covenanters") long resisted this, but how much of the older view is shared today in this tiny denomination is questionable. Much depends on the theological commitment of the faculty of its denominational college, Geneva College.

lightenment humanism. Second, without the threat of God's predictable direct sanctions in history – sanctions lawfully invoked by covenantal oath – Christians cannot provide a biblically grounded defense of the right of the State to enforce the Bible-mandated sanctions attached to biblical law. The State imposes its sanctions as God's minister (Rom. 13:4). If God does not bring sanctions in history in terms of His covenant law, neither should the State. Civil law then becomes humanistic law. Third, without a predictable historical separation of cultural inheritance and disinheritance in terms of God's law and biblical sanctions, the meek cannot inherit the earth. Covenant-breakers will. Modern pluralistic Calvinism denies all three.[16] Thus, it cannot suggest a uniquely Calvinist or even vaguely Trinitarian social theory. It merely baptizes the reigning humanist pluralist worldview and then rushes to embrace some crackpot liberal economic reform scheme that the liberals abandoned as hopelessly out of date ten years earlier.

The Lutherans have always been ethical dualists. Luther defended a theory of two completely separate legal orders, one for Christians and the other for the inherently non-Christian State.[17] For Luther, there was no possibility of Christendom.[18] The Anabaptists have also remained consistent: they renounced the ideal of Christendom and its mandated Trinitarian civil oaths in the aftermath of the failed Münster communist rebellion in 1535. In both views, Christian passive resistance to State tyranny is all that is allowed by God. This quietism was not Northern American Presbyterianism's view until after the de-frocking of J. Gresham Machen in 1936 and his death six

---

16. Gary Scott Smith, *The Seeds of Secularization: Calvinism, Culture, and Pluralism in America, 1870–1915* (Grand Rapids, Michigan: Christian University Press, 1985). This publishing house is a subsidiary of William B. Eerdmans.

17. Martin Luther, "Temporal Authority: To What Extent It Should Be Obeyed" (1523), in *Luther's Works* (Philadelphia: Fortress Press, 1962), vol. XLV.

18. Charles Trinkaus, "The Religious Foundations of Luther's Social Views," in John H. Mundy, *et al.*, *Essays in Medieval Life* (Cheshire, Connecticut: Biblo & Tannen, 1955), pp. 71–87.

months later, when Presbyterianism finally succumbed to eschatologies analogous to Lutheranism's amillennialism[19] and Anabaptism's premillennialism.[20] Quietism was not Southern Presbyterianism's view until after the Civil War, when the denomination went pietistic-fundamentalist on the few social issues it formally discussed: gambling, liquor, and prostitution, but not tobacco.[21] American Presbyterianism in the twentieth century has abandoned its Scottish roots, thereby becoming either Lutheran-amillennial or pietist-premillennial in its social outlook. Pessimillennialism, when coupled with the ethical dualism of modern political pluralism, has transformed Calvinism into something barely distinguishable from its old Protestant rivals: Lutheranism and Anabaptism.

Sanctions and Eschatology: Calvin vs. Kline

John Calvin believed that God enforces His law in history through the imposition of predictable sanctions. This was basic to his worldview. Without this faith in historical sanctions, Calvinism would have become another version of Lutheran dualism or Anabaptist quietism. Calvin's comments on the fifth commandment's promise of long life and blessings to those who obey their parents is indicative of his outlook. He knew, as David knew (Ps. 73), that bad things happen to good people, and good things happen to bad people. But this does not negate the law of God and its attached sanctions, Calvin insisted. There are times "where God works variously and unequally," Calvin said, but this does not make His promises void. There are always compensating rewards in heaven. More important for our understanding of his outlook, however, is what he adds: "Truly experience in all ages has shown that God has not in

19. Westminster Seminary was dominated by Dutch theologians after 1936.

20. Carl McIntire's Faith Seminary after 1936 and the Bible Presbyterian Church after 1938.

21. The Virginia and Carolina economies were closely tied to tobacco.

vain promised long life to all who have faithfully discharged the duties of true piety towards their parents. Still, from the principle already stated, it is to be understood that this Commandment extends further than the words imply; and this we infer from the following sound argument, viz., that otherwise God's Law would be imperfect, and would not instruct us in the perfect rule of a just and holy life."[22] In other words, the sanctions of the fifth commandment are still in force. God's visible sanctions in history in general are not random; they reflect His commitment to defend and extend His law in history.

Calvin's comments on the fifth commandment were put into final form by the author in 1563, the year before his death, and therefore represent the culmination of his thinking. A century later, in the aftermath of the Restoration of Charles II, his spiritual heirs began to abandon this outlook. They began to lose faith in the covenantal predictability of God's sanctions in history, especially positive sanctions for covenant-keepers.[23] In our day, Meredith Kline has devoted his academic career to persuading Calvinists to abandon Calvin on this point. If Calvin was correct here, then Kline's denial of the continuing New Covenant authority of the Mosaic law-covenant[24] would represent the abandonment of Calvinism in the name of Lutheranism, which I contend is exactly what Kline's theology represents.[25]

---

22. Calvin, *Harmonies*, III, p. 11.

23. The turning point in New England was marked by the publication in 1662 of Michael Wigglesworth's two poems, *The Day of Doom* and *God's Controversie With New England*. In England, the imposition of the Act of Uniformity (1662) and the expulsion of some two thousand Calvinist pastors from their pulpits were equally devastating to older Calvinism's faith in the future and in God's positive sanctions in history.

24. Kline, *Structure of Biblical Authority*, Pt. 2, ch. 3: "The Intrusion and the Decalogue."

25. Kline's former student and full-time disciple Michael Horton is far more open regarding this quest for a Lutheran-Calvinist reconciliation. The judicial basis of such a reconciliation is Calvinism's acceptance of Lutheranism's ethical dualism, which Horton seems to accept. In a letter to *Christian News* (Nov. 13, 1995), a conser-

Both European Calvinist traditions – Dutch and Scottish – produced their formative documents in an era in which civil sanctions were assumed mandatory in the protection of church doctrine and liturgy. Two centuries later, Anglo-American Calvinism officially renounced the ideal of Christendom in the revision of the Westminster Confession of 1787–88. It adopted the Enlightenment's ideal of political pluralism. The Synod was timed to match the Constitutional Convention of May, 1787. The two meetings overlapped briefly in Philadelphia; the Synod was ending on a Monday as the Convention was beginning.[26] Meanwhile, Continental Calvinism had almost no influence outside of Holland after 1700. After 1800, right-wing Enlightenment social theory was substituted by the theologians for the older theocratic ideal. Calvinist social theory after 1800 has been indistinguishable from conservative humanism's social theory. It has been some variant of Whig political theory.

Kline has offered a dualistic theology in the name of Calvin. Kline's theology rests openly on his denial of the presence of humanly predictable covenantal sanctions in New Testament times. According to Kline, ethical cause and effect in history are, humanly speaking, essentially random. In this, he has challenged Calvin at the very core of Calvin's ethical theory. He writes: "And meanwhile it [the common grace order] must run its course within the uncertainties of the mutually conditioning principles of common grace and common curse, prosperity and adversity being experienced in a manner largely unpredictable because of the inscrutable sovereignty of the divine will that dispenses them in mysterious ways."[27] Calvin, in stark contrast,

---

vative Lutheran publication, he wrote of his organization, CURE, that "we are building a cooperative effort between the Reformed and Lutheran Christians in an effort to restore a Reformation witness." Horton left the Reformed Episcopal Church and joined the Christian Reformed Church in 1995.

26. Gary North, *Political Polytheism: The Myth of Pluralism* (Tyler, Texas: Institute for Christian Economics, 1989), pp. 543–48.

27. Meredith G. Kline, "Comments on an Old-New Error," *Westminster Theological Journal*, XLI (Fall 1978), p. 184.

dismissed such a view of historical causation as pagan to the core. Yes, he said, following David, good things sometimes happen to bad people and bad things to good people, but this is merely Satanic deception. "When such is the state of matters, where shall we find the person who is not sometimes tempted and importuned by the unholy suggestion, that the affairs of the world roll on at random, and as we say, are governed by chance?"[28] With respect to his theory of visible cause and effect in history, Kline succumbed to the temptation.

The theological contrast between Kline and Calvin could not be sharper. In the name of Calvin, Kline has abandoned Calvinism and has substituted an ethical dualism consistent with Lutheranism, Anabaptism, and, for that matter, Enlightenment humanism. His theory boils down to this: in this world, God does not defend or extend His law by means of humanly predictable corporate sanctions. On this point, covenant-breakers are in full agreement with Kline. (So, from what I can see, are most of his colleagues at Westminster Seminary.)[29]

The Christian Ghetto: Living Under Humanism's Sanctions

Couple Kline's view of God's unpredictable corporate sanctions in history with the amillennialism of sixteenth-century Calvinism, and the result is ghetto Christianity: the mentality of a defensive community of besieged and culturally doomed Christians – "cannon fodder for Christ." Its unofficial slogan is: "Of the ghetto, by the ghetto, for the ghetto!" With respect to Christian civilization, these ghetto theologians deeply believe, "Once lost, always lost." Christianity must remain a strictly defensive operation culturally. Although Christians created Western civilization, once the humanists conquered it in the

---

28. John Calvin, *Commentary on the Book of Psalms* (Grand Rapids, Michigan: Baker, [1557] 1979), III, p. 122.

29. Gary North, *Westminster's Confession: The Abandonment of Van Til's Legacy* (Tyler, Texas: Institute for Christian Economics, 1991).

eighteenth century, this supposedly set in historical concrete humanism's position as the reigning covenant-breaking social order. Any attempt to re-conquer culture for Christ is heretical, we are assured.

It is true that sixteenth-century Calvinists were hostile to the idea that the gospel would eventually convert most of mankind. On this point, they adhered strictly to the dominant tradition of Roman Catholic eschatology. Calvin himself was ambivalent on the issue; there were elements of what would later become postmillennialism in his thinking.[30] The others were outright hostile. (So were the Lutherans.) But Calvinists also believed that Protestant Christians, although a permanent minority group worldwide, had the right and moral obligation to defend their local majority positions in sections of Northern Europe by means of the sword. They were all theocrats in the traditional meaning of the word. They believed in the imposition of civil sanctions in the name of Jesus Christ and His earthly kingdom.

Not so today. Their spiritual heirs, as Enlightenment pluralists, have abandoned sixteenth-century Calvinism's theocratic ideal, but not its amillennialism. Today, Christians are in the minority everywhere. So it must stay forever, announce the theologians of the Protestant ghetto. So it was always intended to be. Writes Protestant Reformed Church theologian-editor, David J. Engelsma: "The ungodly always dominate. The world's rulers always condemn the cause of the true church. The wicked always oppress the saints. The only hope of the church in the world, and their full deliverance, is the Second Coming of Christ and the final judgment. This is Reformed doctrine."[31] On the contrary, this is merely ghetto theology's doctrine.

---

30. North, *Millennialism and Social Theory*, Appendix D: "Calvin's Millennial Confession." Cf. Gary North, "The Economic Thought of Luther and Calvin," *Journal of Christian Reconstruction*, II (Summer 1975), pp. 104–106.

31. Editorial, "A Defense of (Reformed) Amillennialism. 3. Apostasy and Persecution," *The Standard Bearer* (May 1, 1995), p. 365.

The sixteenth-century Reformers believed no such thing regarding the perpetual subordination of Christians to covenant-breakers, which was why Calvin consented to the execution of Servetus. Christians, the Calvinist Reformers universally believed, are not to accept as final any temporary triumph of their enemies in the social order. This is why the Calvinist Reformers all invoked the sword as a means of preserving the hegemony of Protestant Christianity in the West. Every Calvinist theologian agreed on this, right down to the days of Oliver Cromwell. Nor did Calvin teach that Protestant rule in all parts of Northern Europe was necessarily doomed eschatologically. Yet his spiritual heirs have substituted the political doctrines of the Enlightenment's common-ground humanism for Calvin's theocratic worldview. They defend cultural surrender and ghetto living as Calvinism in action, i.e., *inaction*. They have interpreted Calvin's doubts concerning a future, universal, worldwide rule of Christianity in every society as if Calvin had in some way affirmed the universal, worldwide rule of covenant-breakers over covenant-keepers in every society. Let me put it as clearly as I can: *modern Calvinists have adopted Servetus' view of the political order, and they have done so in the name of Calvin.* This ought to be regarded as the greatest irony in the history of applied Calvinism. Meanwhile, Calvinist defenders of the permanent cultural ghetto are ready, figuratively speaking, to burn at the academic stake any postmillennial Calvinist who calls attention to this remarkable irony.

Permit me to invoke a familiar phrase: it is never a question of civil sanctions vs. no civil sanctions. It is always a question of *whose* civil sanctions. It is a question of who imposes sanctions against which public evils. It is a question of whose laws define the public evils for which civil sanctions are legitimately imposed. In short, there is no neutrality.

Second, let me restate the obvious: the history of man is a war between covenant-keepers and covenant-breakers. Marx was wrong: history is not the history of the class struggle. It is the history of the covenantal struggle. Thus, there are two possible choices for building a civilization: Christendom or anti-Christendom. We now get to the famous bottom line: "He that is not with me is against me; and he that gathereth not with me scattereth abroad" (Matt. 12:30). There are Christians who want to limit this two-fold distinction to individual souls, families, and churches. They categorically deny that this division applies to the civil covenant. They do so because they are opposed to the ideal of Christian civilization. Officially, they affirm the existence of a freedom-enhancing, creedally neutral civil law. Unofficially, they either prefer to live under anti-Christian civil laws rather than biblical law, or else they seek a peace treaty with humanism because they are convinced that the only alternative to this is the open persecution of the church and the nearly total destruction of all traces of Christian culture. They believe that their unofficial peace treaty with covenant-breakers can gain Christians limited zones of neutral freedom under "mild" anti-Christian civil sanctions. They prefer life in a Christian cultural and emotional ghetto to the comprehensive responsibilities associated with the Great Commission.[32] To put it in historical terms, their theory of civil government borders on the Amish view. In this sense, Protestant political theory has become Anabaptist, beginning with Roger Williams and continuing in Westminster Seminary's faculty.[33] It relies on some combination of natural law, natural revelation, natural rights theory, and common grace to protect Christians from tyranny.

The issue here is sanctions. Anti-Christendom Christians believe that anti-Christians will not impose harsh civil sanctions on Christians if Christians agree publicly not to impose any civil sanctions on anti-Christians. They have adopted as a New Testament theological doctrine Sam Rayburn's political dictum:

---

32. Kenneth L. Gentry, Jr., *The Greatness of the Great Commission: The Christian Enterprise in a Fallen World* (Tyler, Texas: Institute for Christian Economics, 1990).

33. North, *Westminster's Confession*. See also North, "'I've Been Framed!' A Study in Academic Positioning" (Dec. 1995), published by the ICE.

"You've got to go along to get along."[34] More to the point, they have adopted the strategy of pre-emptive surrender. They think they can settle for Finlandization: a degree of independence from a powerful neighbor. They forget that Finland achieved Finlandization in 1940 only by fighting Stalin's forces and inflicting so much havoc on his troops that it paid Stalin to settle with them. The Finns did not start out with a policy of Finlandization; otherwise, they would have wound up like Latvia, Estonia, and Lithuania.

But it is even worse than this. Christian defenders of neutral politics, neutral civil law, and the pre-emptive surrender of Christians, as Christians, in the political order do not believe that Stalin, Mao, Hitler, Khomeini, and Saddam Hussein are representative of consistent covenant-breaking in operation. They think loveable old Ben Franklin is.

D. J. Engelsma vs. the Mosaic Sanctions

As I argue in this book and will argue in greater detail in my commentary on Deuteronomy, the issue of covenantal sanctions cannot be separated theologically from the issue of eschatology. Positive and negative sanctions in eternity – heaven vs. hell, the New Heavens and New Earth vs. the lake of fire – are reflected in history: kingdom of God vs. kingdom of Satan. What divides most conservative Christian expositors today is their assessment of which kingdom visibly reflects God's positive corporate sanctions in history: God's or Satan's. The vast majority of those who call themselves Christians today believe that the answer is clearly "Satan's." God's positive corporate sanctions in history are showered on covenant-breakers, we are told. God's negative corporate sanctions in history are progressively imposed on the

34. Rayburn was Speaker of the U.S. House of Representatives longer than anyone in history, 17 years, 1940 to 1961, excepting only 1948–49 and 1953–55, when the Republicans were in power. He was America's second most powerful politician after the President. He was a House member from 1912 to his death in 1961, also a record.

church, we are also told. Only one view of eschatology denies this with respect to the New Covenant church age: postmillennialism. This view is dismissed as heretical by premillennialists and amillennialists.

Consider the inflamatory rhetoric of amillennialist Engelsma. He dismisses "the carnal kingdom of postmillennialism" as "injurious, if not disastrous." Postmillennialism raises "practical nightmares." He invokes a code word of the pietist-Anabaptist tradition: "worldly." He goes on: "Reformed men and churches make strange, forbidden, wicked alliances in order, by hook or by crook, to build the earthly kingdom of Christ."[35] Christian Reconstruction introduces the "fundamental heresy of Judaizing" by calling for "a vast array of Old Testament laws. . . ."[36] As for J. Marcellus Kik's book, *An Eschatology of Victory* (1971), it is heretical, as is Christian Reconstructionism. "By heresy, I mean not only a serious departure from the teaching of the Scriptures but a grievous corruption of the gospel. The error is that the spiritual kingdom revealed and realized by the gospel is changed into a carnal kingdom, and the spiritual triumph of the exalted Christ in history is changed into an earthly triumph."[37] This is very strong judicial language. Is he correct?

Here I must offer the reader an explanation. I devote the remainder of this Preface to answering Rev. Engelsma. Yet he is not a well-known critic of Christian Reconstruction. He is a leader in a small Dutch-American denomination, the Protestant Reformed Church.[38] Then why single him out? First, because

---

35. David J. Engelsma, "Jewish Dreams," *The Standard Bearer* (Jan. 15, 1995), pp. 173–74.

36. *Ibid.*, p. 174.

37. *Ibid.* (March 15, 1995), p. 295.

38. It was founded in 1923 in reaction to the Christian Reformed Church's position on common grace, namely, that God shows some degree of favor and love to all men. The PRC has denied the very existence of God's common grace, thereby abandoning Calvin and the entire history of Reformed theology. Their theologians cannot easily explain I Timothy 4:10: "For therefore we both labour and suffer reproach, because we trust in the living God, who is the Saviour of all men, specially

he keeps singling me out in his denominational magazine, calling me one of America's most dangerous heretics. But this accusation does not mean too much. To identify me as a heretic requires only that you get at the tail end of a long line. Hal Lindsey, Dave Hunt, and Constance Cumbey (the *Hidden Dangers of the Raindow* lady) are up at the front; Rev. Engelsma is a comparative late-comer with a very limited readership.

Second is the fact that Rev. Engelsma and his colleague Rev. Hanko[39] are among the very few remaining Dutch-American Calvinist defenders of traditional amillennialism who are willing to go into print on the topic. I have previously referred to their eschatology (and to premillennialism) as ghetto eschatology.[40] Rev. Engelsma admits that there are not many defenders of the Dutch amillennial tradition: "DeMar may well be right when he says that the number of Reformed and Presbyterian amillennialists 'is steadily declining.' The reason, in part, is the great apostasy now fulfilling the apostle's prophecy in II Thessalonians 2:3. This falling away is due, in part, to the failure of Presbyterian and Reformed churches, ministers, theologians, and editors of religious periodicals" – he is a minister, theologian, and editor of a religious periodical – "vigorously to defend amillennialism and equally vigorously to expose and condemn postmillennialism."[41] He and Rev. Hanko believe that the church is now in the end times, a belief which they share with most dispensational premillennialists.

---

of those that believe." What did Paul mean, *specially*, if special grace does not contrast with common grace? Salvation in this general context of God's universal salvation means healing, not eternal life. See Gary North, *Dominion and Common Grace: The Biblical Basis of Progress* (Tyler, Texas: Institute for Christian Economics, 1987), p. 57.

39. For an intellectually devastating refutation of Rev. Hanko's writings on eschatology, see Kenneth L. Gentry, Jr., *He Shall Have Dominion: A Postmillennial Eschatology* (Tyler, Texas: Institute for Christian Economics, 1992), Appendix B.

40. Gary North, "Ghetto Eschatologies," *Biblical Economics Today*, XIV (April/May 1992).

41. Engelsma, "Another Letter and Response on 'Jewish Dreams'," *The Standard Bearer* (March 15, 1995), p. 296.

In recent years, a growing number of Calvinistic amillennialists have preferred to identify themselves as "optimistic amillennialists." I think this repositioning has had something to do with the Reconstructionists' success in identifying amillennialism as a philosophy of self-conscious historical retreat and psychological paralysis: a permanent remnant psychology.[42] No one likes to be tarred and feathered with this kind of imagery, even if it happens to fit. The amillennialist, like the premillennialist, seeks a cultural stalemate today, since he sees the only eschatological alternative as persecution for the church.[43] For an amillennialist or a premillennialist, a cultural stalemate would constitute a major victory, however temporary, for the church. In earlier versions of amillennialism, its defenders were perfectly content to accept cultural defeat and persecution, in order to assure the imminent return of Jesus Christ in final judgment. "The worse things get, the better we feel: our deliverance draweth nigh!" No one so far has set forth an exegetical case for optimistic amillennialism, i.e., an eschatology of permanently stalemated forces, good vs. evil. But so few theologians today are ready to defend with real conviction and enthusiasm the original amillennial pessimism, that Rev. Engelsma and Rev. Hanko have staked out a kind of operational monopoly: the last really enthusiastic defenders of the older Dutch amillennial tradition. I think they correctly perceive that they face declining public interest in their message of inevitable defeat and persecution for God's church: no victory and no secret rapture. This is not what most people would call an inspiring message.

As we shall see, one thing that bothers Rev. Engelsma is the inescapable reality of the Old Testament's mandated civil sanctions against adultery and homosexuality. *The issue is sanctions.*

---

42. R. J. Rushdoony, *Van Til* (Philadelphia: Presbyterian & Reformed, 1960), p. 13.

43. Gary North, *Backward, Christian Soldiers? An Action Manual for Christian Reconstruction* (Tyler, Texas: Institute for Christian Economics, 1984), ch. 11: "The Stalemate Mentality."

He argues that there is supposed to be no trace of the Old Testament's legal order in New Testament era civil law. "The New Testament reality of the nation of Israel, the real kingdom of God in the world, does not legislate and execute the civil laws of the Old Testament. It has no use for the civil laws of the shadow-nation."[44] This means one of two things: 1) the real New Testament kingdom of God has no civil aspect, and hence does not legislate, or 2) the real New Testament kingdom does have a civil aspect, but some other source of civil law has been substituted by God. What other source, he refuses to say.

Reconstructionists ask: "Where should Christians seek accurate definitions of law and crime?" Engelsma prudently remains silent on this point, except to say where we should not search: the Old Testament. He and Rev. Hanko have remained silent on this matter for the last decade and a half in their intermittent attacks on Christian Reconstruction. In this respect, they share a great deal with all of Reconstructionism's critics. Reconstructionists have offered a comprehensive ethical system in the name of Christ; meanwhile, our critics resort to rhetoric. They yell, "Heretics!" This is not a legitimate substitute for detailed biblical exegesis: criticism based on biblical texts. This is why I have devoted almost a quarter of a century to writing detailed commentaries on the economics of the Pentateuch. Our critics have yet to respond with an equally detailed series of commentaries on any aspect of the Pentateuch. As time goes on, the disparity between our commentaries and our critics' rhetoric will become more pronounced.

Kingdom Sanctions

Notice that Rev. Engelsma speaks of "the real kingdom of God in the world." He does not say exactly what this phrase means. I need to make two additional observations. *First*, if he

---

44. Engelsma, "Jewish Dreams," *op. cit.*, pp. 174–75.

is defining this "real kingdom" strictly and solely as the institutional church, he has abandoned a fundamental tenet of the Protestant Reformation, which denied that the institutional church constitutes the whole of the kingdom of God in history. The New Testament kingdom encompasses the institutional church, but it is far more. On this issue, I appeal to Geerhardus Vos, a respected theologian in the Dutch Reformed tradition, who also held a faculty position for over four decades at Princeton Theological Seminary. He wrote of the kingdom of God: "There is a sphere of science, a sphere of art, a sphere of the family and the state, a sphere of commerce and industry. Whenever one of these spheres comes under the controlling influence of the principle of the divine supremacy and glory, and this outwardly reveals itself, there we can truly say that the kingdom of God has become manifest. . . . On the one hand, his [Christ's] doctrine of the kingdom was founded on such a profound and broad conviction of the absolute supremacy of God in all things, that he could not but look upon every normal and legitimate province of human life as intended to form part of God's kingdom. On the other hand, it was not his intention that this result should be reached by making human life in all its spheres subject to the visible church."[45] *The institutional church is narrower than God's kingdom.* This has always been the Reconstructionists' view of the kingdom.[46] It is quite conventional in Reformed circles, contrary to Rev. Engelsma's suggestion.

Second, if Rev. Engelsma is not defining the kingdom as the institutional church alone, then he needs to offer reasons why the Mosaic civil laws governing adultery and homosexuality are no longer valid. It is not enough for him merely to say that they are not valid; he must show us why. He refuses to do this,

---

45. Geerhardus Vos, *The Teachings of Jesus Concerning The Kingdom and the Church* (Grand Rapids, Michigan: Eerdmans, 1958), p. 88.

46. See R. J. Rushdoony, *The Institutes of Biblical Law* (Nutley, New Jersey: Craig Press, 1973), pp. 69–70, for a discussion of this point which relies on Vos.

however. He immediately moves from the question of civil law to the church, calling on the church to exercise only the power of excommunication. This is an illegitimate line of argument. The two systems of covenantal sanctions are judicially separate: State vs. church. Any discussion of church sanctions as if these in some way constitute the whole of the kingdom's earthly sanctions is in error. If the kingdom is more than the institutional church, which it is, then a covenant theologian must discuss civil sanctions in terms of covenantal law. But Rev. Engelsma, whose theology becomes pietistic at this point, prefers to discuss only church sanctions. He wants his readers to imagine that only church sanctions possess the legitimate designation of kingdom sanctions in history. He writes: "For the church is a spiritual realm. She does not, e.g., put adulterers and homosexuals to death. Where there is public, impenitent practice of these sins, the church exercises discipline, which is a spiritual key of the kingdom of heaven. Her purpose is the repentance of the sinner, so that she may again receive him into her fellowship."[47]

This logically irrelevant comment deflects the reader's attention from the crucial judicial issue: *the function of civil sanctions in a Christian commonwealth*.[48] No author in the Reconstructionist camp has suggested or implied that the institutional church has the authority to impose civil sanctions.[49] *The issue of criminal sanctions is a State matter*. It is here that Christians, as Christians, are required by God to suggest explicitly biblical definitions of crime. But Rev. Engelsma has already ruled out any appeal to the Mosaic law as a possible standard for definitions of crime. Why? He offers no exegetical or hermeneutical reasons; he apparently just does not like the Mosaic law.

---

47. Engelsma, "Jewish Dreams," *op. cit.*, p. 175.

48. Kenneth L. Gentry, "Civil Sanctions in the New Testament," in *Theonomy: An Informed Response*, edited by Gary North (Tyler, Texas: Institute for Christian Economics, 1991), ch. 6.

49. Gentry, "Church Sanctions in the Epistle to the Hebrews," *ibid.*, ch. 7.

Notice: if we substitute the words "sexual molestation of children" or "murder" or any other crime for "adultery" and "homosexuality," Rev. Engelsma's subtle shift from a discussion of Mosaic civil sanctions (supposedly annulled in our era) to ecclesiastical excommunication (always open to removal upon repentance) would strip Christians of the biblical authority to call for biblically defined State sanctions against crime. The twin issues here are *definition* and *sanctions*. Definitions of criminal behavior and the appropriate legal sanctions are found in the Mosaic law. But Rev. Engelsma rejects the Mosaic law. His theological position leads, step by step, to the necessary acceptance by Christians of humanist definitions of crime. His open and defiant rejection of the Mosaic law and its civil sanctions in principle delivers Christians into the tender mercies of covenant-breaking man, which is exactly where Rev. Engelsma says Calvinism teaches that we must be until Christ comes again. For those of us who think that we are not morally obligated or eschatologically condemned to such a state of affairs, Rev. Engelsma has a description: "heretics."

What is the kingdom of God? In this book and throughout my writings, I offer this simple definition: *the civilization of God*, i.e., **Christendom**. God's kingdom comprises redeemed hearts and redeemed institutions. It is neither exclusively spiritual nor exclusively material-social, neither exclusively eternal nor exclusively temporal. The kingdom of God is parallelled by the kingdom of Satan. What are the former's boundaries? Wherever sin presently operates, there Christians should seek to extend the boundaries of the kingdom of God. Its definitive boundaries are the whole creation. "And Jesus came and spake unto them, saying, All power is given unto me in heaven and in earth" (Matt. 28:18). Its operational boundaries are being extended through time, but not in a straight line. Territory is gained; then it gets surrendered. The question is: Can the whole world be subdued to God's glory? Not perfectly, but progressively, the postmillennialist says. Not in history, the amillennialist says.

Only after Jesus comes with His angels to rule the earth in person, the premillennialist says.

The pessimillennialist, whether premillennial or amillennial, resists my definition of the kingdom, for it extends long-abandoned and long-denied areas of responsibility to Christians. It announces the need for comprehensive evangelism as part of God's mandated program of comprehensive redemption.[50] Pessimillennialists seek to escape these added kingdom responsibilities. It is all that the pietistic theologian can do to maintain biblical relevance inside the narrow confines of the Christian ghetto. Defending the Bible's relevance in the frightening world outside this ghetto is more than he chooses to bear.

Orwellian Newspeak

Rev. Engelsma's eschatology denies the transforming power of the gospel in history. It does not present Christianity a world-transforming, evangelizing, spiritual leaven (Matt. 13:33). It implies that the presence of the Holy Spirit will not transform our world. He sees Satan's earthly kingdom as possessing the only comprehensive, world-changing program in history. His implicitly humanistic social theory and his defeatist eschatology justify life in a defensive Christian ghetto.

For Rev. Engelsma and theologians who share his views, the doctrine of Christ's bodily ascension in history to the right hand of God remains an irrelevant doctrine for social theory. In fact, these men deny the very possibility of Christian social theory, precisely because of their ghetto eschatology. They spend their careers re-writing the plain meaning of the Great Commission: the discipling of all nations.[51] The Great Commission cannot mean this, Rev. Engelsma's theology implicitly insists; therefore,

50. Gary North, *Is the World Running Down? Crisis in the Christian Worldview* (Tyler, Texas: Institute for Christian Economics, 1988), Appendix C: "Comprehensive Redemption: A Theology for Social Action."

51. Gentry, *The Greatness of the Great Commission.*

it must mean gathering the elect out of these nations, not placing them over these nations through successful evangelism. The promised victory of Christ is re-defined as Satan's permanent defeat of the Great Commission in history.

Rev. Engelsma understands that Christians resist being labeled pessimists and retreatists, especially when they really are pessimists and retreatists. He therefore adopts the language of postmillennial optimism to describe the amillennial defeat of Christ's Great Commission in history. In this sense, he is a faithful practitioner of what George Orwell called "newspeak" in his novel, *1984*. "Freedom is tyranny. Peace is war." For Rev. Engelsma, *defeat is victory*. Christ supposedly has predestined that His church must fail in fulfilling the terms of the Great Commission. This failure must be regarded by Christians as a great victory, he believes, since the church has and will continue to participate in its cultural suicide mission.

> Amillennialism believes that the gospel is now, will be, and always has been "successful" (we prefer to say, "victorious") on earth. Its triumph on earth is its accomplishment of the purposes of the risen Christ with the gospel. These purposes are the gathering of the elect out of all nations and thus the saving of the nations in them; the preservation of the elect in faith and holiness; the empowering of the elect believers and their children to live obedient lives to the Lord Christ in all spheres of earthly life; the building of the church; and the hardening of the reprobate. This victory is worldwide.[52]

So, he says, Christ empowers His people "to live obedient lives to the Lord Christ in all spheres of earthly life." I ask: "What constitutes Christian obedience to Christ in the realm of politics?" Political reform? He answers emphatically, *no*; rather, we must retreat more deeply into our Christian ghetto, self-consciously and openly abandoning the entire social and politi-

---

52. Engelsma, "An Open Letter to Gary North (Part One)," *The Standard Bearer* (March 1, 1996), p. 246.

cal world to the devil. This is God's plan for the ages, he says. "But Satan *does* have 'complete control over the nations of the world.' Of course, he is not the almighty sovereign. The triune God is sovereign. But Satan controls the nations of the world as to their spiritual condition."[53] This is not merely a temporary condition that Christians must work to reverse. On the contrary, we must learn to live with it. "Until the personal return of Christ, the nations under the government of the kings of the earth make war against Him as He is present in His church by His Word."[54] The old phrase that Ben Franklin recommended as America's national slogan – "Resistance to tyrants is obedience to God!" – has been in effect reworked by Rev. Engelsma: "Resistance to tyrants is disobedience to God!" Our goal is to be let alone by the humanists in our little ghettos. Otherwise, our task is to serve as martyrs. There is no legitimate hope in Christian social transformation. We are little more than sheep for the slaughter. He calls this theology "victorious." Indeed, it is . . . for Satan.

Conclusion

The seventeenth century brought the beginnings of postmillennial optimism to Protestantism, and accompanying this postmillennialism, for the first time in man's history, came the ideal of long-term economic growth, compounded. This economic growth ideal eventually transformed England; it was in England that the Industrial Revolution began in the late eighteenth century. What was first believed to be possible in the seventeenth century began to take place a century later: long-term growth without permanent reversal.

---

53. Engelsma, "A Defense of (Reformed) Amillennialism. 3. Apostasy and Persecution," *ibid.* (May 1, 1995), p. 343.

54. Engelsma, "A Defense of (Reformed) Amillennialism. 2. Revelation 20," *ibid.* (April 15, 1995), p. 366. April 15 is tax-filing day in the United States: appropriate for Dr. Engelsma's tirade against all Christian political reform.

Anglo-Scottish-American Presbyterianism was postmillennial right down to the late nineteenth century. Only with the spread of liberalism and pietism in the Northern Church and pietism in the Southern Church after 1900 did conservative American Presbyterianism move into premillennialism and amillennialism, when Scofield in the South and Westminster Seminary's mostly Dutch faculty in the North after 1936 replaced the postmillennial tradition of the Hodges, Warfield, Thornwell, Dabney, and Machen. But all of them, on the question of sanctions, agreed with the Anabaptists: God does not bring predictable corporate sanctions in history in terms of societies' adherence to or defiance of His Bible-revealed law. They were right-wing Enlightenment Whig humanists on the question of civil oaths.[55]

To maintain such a Whig worldview, you must abandon the Book of Numbers. The Book of Numbers is the Pentateuch's book of sanctions. The refusal of the Israelites of the exodus generation to impose negative military sanctions against Canaan brought God's negative sanctions against them: death in the wilderness. This indicates that sanctions are an inescapable concept. It is never a question of sanctions vs. no sanctions. It is always a question of whose sanctions. As Lenin so graphically put it, "Who, whom?" There is no escape from this question in eternity; there is also no escape from it in history, as the exodus generation learned to their great discomfort.

55. Gary North, *Crossed Fingers: How the Liberals Captured the Presbyterian Church* (Tyler, Texas: Institute for Christian Economics, 1996).

INTRODUCTION

Behold, the days come, saith the Lord, *that I will make a new covenant with the house of Israel, and with the house of Judah: Not according to the covenant that I made with their fathers in the day that I took them by the hand to bring them out of the land of Egypt; which my covenant they brake, although I was an husband unto them, saith the* Lord *(Jer. 31:31–32).*

Harden not your heart, as in the provocation, and as in the day of temptation in the wilderness: When your fathers tempted me, proved me, and saw my work. Forty years long was I grieved with this generation, and said, It is a people that do err in their heart, and they have not known my ways: Unto whom I sware in my wrath that they should not enter into my rest (Ps. 95:8–11).

The Psalmist offers as a warning the Israelites' wilderness experience, which is the central focus of the Book of Numbers. The wilderness experience was a curse: a negative sanction. This curse was announced in God's wrathful oath that the exodus generation would not inherit the Promised Land. They would die in the wilderness. Thus, what might have been a temporary transition period in the lives of the exodus generation became their lifetime experience. The Promised Land was associated with rest from their labors. Israel would not gain this rest during their lifetimes. "So I sware in my wrath, They shall not enter into my rest."

This passage offers important information for a correct assessment of the primary theme of the Book of Numbers: oath/sanctions. This theme is point four of the biblical covenant model.[1] The Book of Numbers is the Pentateuch's book of sanctions. Had the exodus generation been faithful to God, this book would have been the book of conquest: the victory of Israel (positive sanctions) over Canaan (negative sanctions). Instead, it is the book which chronicles Israel's rebellion against God through rebellion against Moses, and of God's negative sanctions imposed in response to their rebellion.

Actually, this is an overstatement. Numbers does not chronicle most of the wilderness period. It chronicles about four years: two at the beginning of the wandering and two at the end.[2] It provides historical information on the reasons for God's imposition of corporate negative sanctions on the exodus generation (1–17); then it provides more historical information regarding the removal of these sanctions from their children, (21–36). Two chapters are devoted to certain priestly laws (18, 19). The central passage is chapter 20, which records the death of Miriam, the sin of Moses in striking the rock, God's judgment against Moses – he shall not enter the land – and Aaron's death. This marks the great transition: from wrath to grace for Israel.

Numbers reveals the covenantal basis of historical progress: positive sanctions for covenant-keeping and negative sanctions for covenant-breaking. This covenantal cause-and-effect relationship serves as the foundation of the theory of economic growth. Profits (positive sanctions for accurate forecasting),[3]

---

1. Ray R. Sutton, *That You May Prosper: Dominion By Covenant* (2nd ed.; Tyler, Texas: Institute for Christian Economics, 1992), ch. 4.

2. R. K. Harrison, *Numbers: An Exegetical Commentary* (Grand Rapids, Michigan: Baker, 1992), p. 431.

3. Frank H. Knight, *Risk, Uncertainty and Profit* (New York: Harper Torchbooks, [1921] 1965).

wages, and interest-rent[4] can be invested. If these investments are based on accurate forecasts of the future, and if they are implemented on a cost-effective basis, they produce an expansion of capital, which is a tool of dominion. With greater capital, more of the earth can be brought under mankind's dominion. The positive feedback of compound growth, if extended over time, becomes the basis of economic transformation and the conquest of nature, or as economic historian John U. Nef put it, the conquest of the material world.[5]

We conclude that one of the foundations of mankind's fulfillment of the dominion covenant (Gen. 1:26–28) is long-term economic growth. Without the possibility of reinvested earnings and the growth of capital – above all, accurate information and the social means of implementing it – there would be no way for mankind to extend God's kingdom across the face of the earth, transforming nature to reflect the covenantal, hierarchical rule of God in history through His ordained agent, man. The idea of an "unspoiled nature" that has not been influenced by man and reshaped by man in terms of man's desires and needs is an anti-biblical concept. God made it plain to Israel: better the rule of covenant-breaking Canaanites than the rule of nature. "And I will send hornets before thee, which shall drive out the Hivite, the Canaanite, and the Hittite, from before thee. I will not drive them out from before thee in one year; lest the land become desolate, and the beast of the field multiply against thee. By little and little I will drive them out from before thee, until thou be increased, and inherit the land" (Ex. 23:28–30). In other words, God's negative sanctions against Canaan were to be delayed so that the land would not fall

---

4. Rent is another word for interest. It arises from the same phenomenon: the discount which all men apply always in the present to the value of expected future income. See Ludwig von Mises, *Human Action: A Treatise on Economics* (New Haven, Connecticut: Yale University Press, 1949), ch. 19.

5. John U. Nef, *The Conquest of the Material World: Essays on the Coming of Industrialism* (Cleveland, Ohio: Meridian, [1964] 1967).

under the negative sanctions of the animals. The reappearance of autonomous nature was regarded by God as being a more fearful negative sanction against the land than continuing dominion by covenant-breaking mankind.

The late twentieth-century environmental movement denies this view of nature by elevating the supposed needs of impersonal, autonomous nature over the goals of man.[6] Such a view of nature is pagan to the core. Increasingly, environmentalism has become pantheistic and even occult: earth as "Gaia" – a living spirit.[7]

The Covenantal Structure of the Exodus-Wilderness Books

The Book of Exodus presents the story of God's deliverance of the Israelites. The true king delivered them out of their former bondage to a false king. God intervened in history to demonstrate His power in history. "For I will at this time send all my plagues upon thine heart, and upon thy servants, and upon thy people; that thou mayest know that there is none like me in all the earth. For now I will stretch out my hand, that I may smite thee and thy people with pestilence; and thou shalt be cut off from the earth. And in very deed for this cause have I raised thee up, for to shew in thee my power; and that my name may be declared throughout all the earth" (Ex. 9:14–16). This is point two of the biblical covenant model: hierarchy.[8] The evidence of God's power was His ability to impose negative sanctions on Pharaoh and those whom he represented. The

---

6. A manifesto of such a view of autonomous nature is Bill McKibben's book, *The End of Nature* (New York: Random House, 1989).

7. Even when cloaked in scientific terminology, any attempt to revive the name of the Greek goddess Gaia in relation to "mother nature" is indicative of an anti-biblical religious impulse. See *Gaia: An Atlas of Planet Management*, edited by Norman Myers (New York: Doubleday/Anchor, 1984); *The Gaia Peace Atlas: Survival into the Third Millennium*, edited by Frank Barnaby (New York: Doubleday, 1988). For a detailed critique of the politics and religion of environmentalism, see Michael S. Coffman, *Saviors of the Earth?* (Chicago: Northfield Publishing, 1994).

8. Sutton, *That You May Prosper*, ch. 2.

deliverance of Israel began with sanctions that led to a transfer of inheritance. "And the LORD gave the people favour in the sight of the Egyptians, so that they lent unto them such things as they required. And they spoiled the Egyptians" (Ex. 12:36). This structure of redemption in history was to serve as a model for the exodus generation and all succeeding generations. Inheritance and disinheritance are linked by sanctions: positive for the inheritors, negative for the disinherited.

From Exodus we move to Leviticus: the book of holiness, where the laws of holiness appear. This is point three of the biblical covenant model: ethics.[9] The goal of God's deliverance is the restoration of covenantal obedience on the part of those delivered. This message was to become part of the Passover's ritual, an opportunity to teach respect for God's law to each successive generation. "Then thou shalt say unto thy son, We were Pharaoh's bondmen in Egypt; and the LORD brought us out of Egypt with a mighty hand: And the LORD shewed signs and wonders, great and sore, upon Egypt, upon Pharaoh, and upon all his household, before our eyes: And he brought us out from thence, that he might bring us in, to give us the land which he sware unto our fathers. And the LORD commanded us to do all these statutes, to fear the LORD our God, for our good always, that he might preserve us alive, as it is at this day. And it shall be our righteousness, if we observe to do all these commandments before the LORD our God, as he hath commanded us" (Deut. 6:21–25).

The Book of Numbers is clearly concerned with point four of the covenant model: sanctions. The Israelites repeatedly rebelled against Moses in the wilderness. Moses was God's representative. God therefore repeatedly brought corporate negative sanctions against the generation of the exodus. Their rebellion ultimately cost them their inheritance. Godly inheri-

---

9. *Ibid.*, ch. 3.

tance – point five[10] – is based on faithfulness to the stipulations of the covenant. The sons of the rebellious generation lawfully claimed the inheritance. The Epistle to the Hebrews extends the theme of the Psalmist by describing this inheritance in terms of rest. "But with whom was he grieved forty years? was it not with them that had sinned, whose carcases fell in the wilderness? And to whom sware he that they should not enter into his rest, but to them that believed not? So we see that they could not enter in because of unbelief" (Heb. 3:17–19). The transfer of the right of inheritance was based on sanctions: negative against the generation of the exodus, positive for the generation of the conquest. The actual transfer was also based on sanctions: positive for the Israelites, negative against the Canaanites. The preliminary phase of this transfer began in Numbers 21: the disinheritance of King Arad.

From Point Four to Point Five

The Book of Numbers has relatively little to say about the details of economics, at least when compared to the other four books of the Pentateuch. Numbers is concerned with sanctions, but always in terms of the promised inheritance. The main sanctions the book discusses are military and liturgical. The book begins with a numbering of the people, which was in fact a mustering of God's holy army. Excluded from this initial mustering was the tribe of Levi. This tribe was the priestly tribe, i.e., the tribe that was in charge of the sacrificial system. The sacrificial system was a system of sanctions.

The economic issues dealt with in the Book of Numbers mainly have to do with the distribution of the spoils of war. Military spoils were an important topic because Israel was preparing for the conquest of Canaan. The military victory of Israel would constitute the disinheritance of Canaan's nations. That is, the disinheritance of Canaan by Israel was to be the

---

10. *Ibid.*, ch. 5.

basis of Israel's inheritance. The sanctions were simultaneously positive and negative. This God-mandated disinheritance would be an extension of what Israel had already experienced in Egypt. God's disinheritance of Egypt's firstborn sons had been the historical basis of Israel's initial inheritance: "Speak now in the ears of the people, and let every man borrow of his neighbour, and every woman of her neighbour, jewels of silver, and jewels of gold" (Ex. 11:2). The Egyptians were ready to surrender what would have been the inheritance of the firstborn because of the trauma of the final plague.

The promise of military spoils was designed to motivate the Israelites to greater fervor (Num. 32:17–18; Josh. 17:13–18). The promise of victory[11] was insufficient to motivate the exodus generation. The Book of Numbers provides a grim history of that generation. The book's Hebrew title is *bemidbar*, "in the wilderness": the fourth word in the first verse.[12] Israel's wilderness experience was the product of Israel's refusal to believe God, obey God, and become the sanctions-bringing agent of God. The long-promised inheritance began only when all the members of the exodus generation except Moses had died (Num. 20). At that point, the conquest generation began the process of *disinheritance through conquest* on the wilderness side of the Jordan River (Num. 21).

The Promised Land

The promise given to Abraham was that in the fourth generation after the descent into Egypt, Israel would conquer the inhabitants of Canaan (Gen. 15:16). This promise was conditional: the Israelites had to remain a people. The visible covenantal mark of this unity was circumcision. The failure of the

---

11. "By little and little I will drive them out from before thee, until thou be increased, and inherit the land" (Ex. 23:30).

12. Timothy R. Ashley, *The Book of Numbers* (Grand Rapids, Michigan: Eerdmans, 1993), p. 1.

Israelites of the exodus generation to circumcise their sons required the mass circumcision of Israel at Gilgal after they had crossed the Jordan (Josh. 5:5). Israel had to experience the negative sanction of shed blood before the nation could lawfully shed the blood of the Canaanites who occupied the Promised Land. The negative sanction of circumcision preceded the negative sanction of disinheriting Canaan militarily. Military disinheritance, in turn, had to precede the positive sanction of national inheritance: "But we ourselves will go ready armed before the children of Israel, until we have brought them unto their place: and our little ones shall dwell in the fenced cities because of the inhabitants of the land. We will not return unto our houses, until the children of Israel have inherited every man his inheritance" (Num. 32:17–18).

This should alert us to the two-fold nature of covenantal sanctions: positive and negative. It should also alert us to the two-fold nature of covenantal inheritance: inheritance through disinheritance.

The exodus generation wanted their inheritance without the obligation of disinheriting others. They wanted the benefits of the covenant without the costs: circumcision, obedience, and risk. They died in the wilderness because they refused to accept the risk of negative sanctions. Because they feared death more than they desired the inheritance on God's terms, God gave them death without the inheritance. They sought God's positive sanctions apart from the threat of negative sanctions. This had been Adam's desire, too: to be as God without the threat of death. The result in both cases was death.

Military Sanctions

The Book of Numbers has less to say about economics because it is concerned with military sanctions. In war, the winners gain victory at the expense of the losers. The winners gain spoils at the expense of the losers. This is what economists call a *zero-sum game*. There is no increase in total wealth; the gains of the winners are paid for by the losers.

The free market allows mutual benefits through voluntary exchange. Each party to a transaction seeks to better himself by exchanging one set of circumstances for another. Market exchange is not based on the military principle of "beggar thy neighbor." It is based on the principle of mutual benefit.[13]

Because Canaan was to be placed under God's total ban – *hormah* – Israel's inheritance had to be based on violence: specifically, military conquest. The mandated process of inheritance could not be a market process. There had to be a forcible disinheritance. Canaanites were not to gain by Israel's presence in the land. They were not to be allowed to enter into a mutually profitable economic relationship with Israel. This is why the Book of Numbers is not much concerned with economics. Its focus is military sanctions: a system of "winner take all."

Israel was not to expand its borders through conquest after the Canaanites had been expropriated. The boundaries of the Promised Land were fixed by the original distribution of land. The sacrificial system prevented any extensive growth in Israel's geography, since the men of Israel who dwelt in the land had to walk to a central location three times a year, minimum, in order to participate in the national feasts and sacrifices. Vio-

---

13. An exception is a futures contract, in which two parties agree with each other either to buy or sell a specified quantity of goods in the future at a fixed price. Whatever profit one party gains is supplied by the other party. The benefit to each party is the freedom of each to affirm his assessment of the economic future by means of an investment tied to that assessment. There are also benefits for the society in general: the best assessments of participants with capital are brought to bear on pricing scarce resources. The presence of the various futures markets brings valuable information into play in the economy. Prices respond faster to the expected conditions of supply and demand. That is, the most accurate information is assimilated faster into the economy by means of the price system. This information transfer costs nothing to the vast majority of the participants in the economy. These costs are born by the participants in the futures markets. What is a zero sum game for the two parties to the contract has positive benefits for the economy as a social system. The futures market, when considered in the context of society's quest for better information at low prices, is not a zero sum game.

lence was not to become the basis of wealth creation in Israel. The military conquest of Canaan was to be a one-time event.

A Fool in His Folly

Martin Noth, who died as he was completing his commentary on Numbers, was (and remains) one of the most respected academic commentators on the Old Testament. Yet any normal person who picks up his Numbers commentary and reads two pages will think to himself: "This book is utterly incoherent. No one in his right mind would waste his life writing something as useless as this. Noth must have been a German." Indeed, he was. He was a German's German: enormously learned, enormously liberal, and enormously unreadable. His commentary on Numbers does not bother with the mundane task of explaining what any passage means. Instead, it goes on and on about which traditions or late-date authors' interpolations found expression in Numbers, producing a definitively chaotic book. The Book of Numbers is a jumble without any integrating theme, Noth argued, because of these later insertions. Noth wrote:

> From the point of view of its contents, the book lacks unity, and it is difficult to see any pattern in its construction.[14]

> There can be no question of the unity of the book of Numbers, nor of its originating from the hand of a single author. This is already clear from the confusion and lack of order in its contents.[15]

> Numbers participates only marginally in the great themes of the Pentateuchal tradition.[16]

---

14. Martin Noth, *Numbers: A Commentary* (Philadelphia: Westminster Press, 1968), p. 1.

15. *Ibid.*, p. 4.

16. *Ibid.*, p. 5.

Martin Noth was a liberal higher critic who denied that the Pentateuch is the inspired, authoritative, morally binding word of God. Put more biblically, Martin Noth was a fool. "The wise in heart will receive commandments: but a prating fool shall fall" (Prov. 10:8). "He that trusteth in his own heart is a fool: but whoso walketh wisely, he shall be delivered" (Prov. 28:26). He adopted and applied the hermeneutic of higher criticism, namely, that many people wrote the Pentateuch a millennium after it says it was written. He invoked the evidence offered by higher criticism: the alleged chaos of the Pentateuchal texts. Then he assured his readers that Numbers is incoherent and without unity. But his conclusion had nothing to do with Numbers; it had everything to do with Noth's blindness. Noth and his academic peers are blind.

And in that day shall the deaf hear the words of the book, and the eyes of the blind shall see out of obscurity, and out of darkness (Isa. 29:18).

His watchmen are blind: they are all ignorant, they are all dumb dogs, they cannot bark; sleeping, lying down, loving to slumber (Isa. 56:10).

Let them alone: they be blind leaders of the blind. And if the blind lead the blind, both shall fall into the ditch (Matt. 15:14).

Contrary to Noth, the Book of Numbers is integral to the Pentateuch, and its overriding theme reflects this: sanctions. The book is placed exactly where it should be: book four, which corresponds to point four of the biblical covenant model. Had Noth understood the covenant, respected it, and paid attention to it, he might not have concluded that Numbers possesses no unity and "participates only marginally in the great themes of the Pentateuchal tradition." But Noth was a fool who did not heed Solomon's counsel: "Even a fool, when he holdeth his peace, is counted wise: and he that shutteth his lips is esteemed a man of understanding" (Prov. 17:28) He went into print to be hailed around the academic world by less notable fools who have shared his hermeneutic.

What is disheartening is to read a supposedly conservative commentator – a Dutchman who, like so many Dutch theologians, feels compelled to imitate German scholarship – who spouts the same Party Line: ". . . Numbers is not a literary unit but acquired its present form over a period of time."[17] Or Timothy Ashley, who does his best to avoid the most blatant theses of the higher critics, especially the incoherent-text theory, who writes: "Moses may be seen as having a key role in the origin of some of the material in Numbers, though we have no way of knowing how much of it goes back to him."[18] I suggest this percentage of the Book of Numbers that was written by Moses: one hundred. "And Moses wrote their goings out according to their journeys by the commandment of the LORD: and these are their journeys according to their goings out" (Num. 33:2).

Conclusion

The Book of Numbers, book four in the Pentateuch, conforms to point four of the biblical covenant model: oath/sanctions. The message of the book is clear: when covenant-keepers rebel against God in history, the blessings – positive sanctions – associated judicially with covenantal faithfulness will be removed; God's negative corporate sanctions will be imposed. This does not mean that the heirs of covenant-keepers are permanently disinherited. On the contrary, their heirs will surely inherit. The negative corporate sanctions are not permanent down through the generations. The promise will be fulfilled. The structure of the covenant cannot be broken. "For evildoers shall be cut off: but those that wait upon the LORD, they shall inherit the earth. For yet a little while, and the wick-

17. A. Noordtzij, *Numbers* (Grand Rapids, Michigan: Zondervan, 1983), p. 13.

18. Ashley, *Numbers*, p. 7.

ed shall not be: yea, thou shalt diligently consider his place, and it shall not be. But the meek shall inherit the earth; and shall delight themselves in the abundance of peace" (Ps. 37:9–11).

The New Covenant in no way reverses this structure of inheritance. On the contrary, the New Covenant reaffirms it. "Blessed are the meek: for they shall inherit the earth" (Matt. 5:5). The New Covenant was marked by a transfer of inheritance from Israel to the church. "Therefore say I unto you, The kingdom of God shall be taken from you, and given to a nation bringing forth the fruits thereof" (Matt. 21:43). This transfer was visibly imposed by God through Rome's destruction of the temple in A.D. 70.[19]

The Book of Numbers has stood as a warning down through the ages: the basis of covenantal inheritance is corporate covenant-keeping. Numbers calls on men and nations to repent, to turn back to God in search of the standards of righteousness. If God was willing to disinherit the exodus generation because of their constant complaining and their lack of courage, how much more should the spiritual heirs of the Canaanites take heed!

---

19. David Chilton, *The Days of Vengeance: An Exposition of the Book of Revelation* (Ft. Worth, Texas: Dominion Press, 1987).

1

MUSTERING THE ARMY OF THE LORD

And the L*ORD* *spake unto Moses in the wilderness of Sinai, in the tabernacle of the congregation, on the first day of the second month, in the second year after they were come out of the land of Egypt, saying, Take ye the sum of all the congregation of the children of Israel, after their families, by the house of their fathers, with the number of their names, every male by their polls; From twenty years old and upward, all that are able to go forth to war in Israel: thou and Aaron shall number them by their armies. And with you there shall be a man of every tribe; every one head of the house of his fathers (Num. 1:1–4).*

God told Moses to number the fighting men of Israel. This message came to Moses in the wilderness. "In the wilderness" (*bemidbar*) was the original Hebrew title of the fourth book of the Pentateuch. The title of this book in the Septuagint, the Greek translation of the Hebrew Scriptures (275 to 100 B.C.), was *Arithmoi*,[1] from which we get the English word, arithmetic. The English title, Numbers, is related to *arithmoi*. The book begins with God's command to number the people. This was a military numbering, i.e. a mustering of troops.[2] Every man

---

1. Jacob Milgrom, *The JPS Torah Commentary: Numbers* (New York: Jewish Publication Society, 1990), p. xi.

2. Milgrom, Excursus 2, "The Census and Its Totals," *ibid.*, p. 336.

above age 19 was mustered, even though some were physically unfit for duty, e.g., the aged. The principle here was that the army of Israel was a holy army of all the men of the nation. Those who could not fight were represented by those who could. This was analogous to the distinction between front-line troops and those on duty far from the battlefield. All were in the army, but some did the fighting. All were "in uniform," but not all carried weapons. All were under the chain of command.

What may seem astounding in today's world of bureaucratic delays, Moses and Aaron assembled the congregation, and the designated tribal leaders then mustered the entire nation, on the same day that God ordered the mustering: the first day of the second month. "And they assembled all the congregation together on the first day of the second month, and they declared their pedigrees after their families, by the house of their fathers, according to the number of the names, from twenty years old and upward, by their polls" (Num. 1:18).[3] That was a remarkable chain of command.

The Israelites had departed from Egypt a little over a year earlier: on the fifteenth day of the first month, the day after Passover (Ex. 12:18). Exactly one month later, they arrived in the wilderness at Sin (Ex. 16:1). In the third month, they came to Sinai (Ex. 19:1).[4] There they ratified their national covenant with God. God recounted verbally what He had done for them in delivering them from Egypt; then He demanded an oath of obedience.

---

3. Milgrom cites Numbers 10:11 in his attempt to prove that it took 20 days. "And it came to pass on the twentieth day of the second month, in the second year, that the cloud was taken up from off the tabernacle of the testimony." I see no connection between this event and the mustering. *Ibid.*, p. 337.

4. Jewish tradition says that this was 50 days after the Passover, i.e., on the very first day of Pentecost, which was formalized ritually in Mosaic Israel as the firstfruits feast. Alfred Edersheim, *The Temple: Its Ministry and Services As They Were in the Time of Jesus Christ* (Grand Rapids, Michigan: Eerdmans, [1874] 1983), p. 261.

> Ye have seen what I did unto the Egyptians, and how I bare you on eagles' wings, and brought you unto myself. Now therefore, if ye will obey my voice indeed, and keep my covenant, then ye shall be a peculiar treasure unto me above all people: for all the earth is mine: And ye shall be unto me a kingdom of priests, and an holy nation. These are the words which thou shalt speak unto the children of Israel. And Moses came and called for the elders of the people, and laid before their faces all these words which the LORD commanded him. And all the people answered together, and said, All that the LORD hath spoken we will do. And Moses returned the words of the people unto the LORD (Ex. 19:4–8).

God had imposed negative corporate sanctions on Egypt. This was the basis of the Israelites' deliverance. There was a message here: negative corporate sanctions are the concomitant of positive corporate sanctions in the struggle for covenantal supremacy in history. In this sense, the struggle is analogous to a military struggle, not a free market transaction in which both parties benefit. God's grace preceded His law. Now He called the nation to obedience. He set forth a conditional promise: if they obeyed Him, He would make them a kingdom of priests. Moses informed the elders and the people of what God had said, and they swore allegiance to Him. The Book of Numbers is a history of how they repeatedly broke their agreement, and the consequences thereof.

The Exodus Numbering

Approximately nine months after this corporate act of national covenant renewal, Israel had completed the construction of the tabernacle: "And it came to pass in the first month in the second year, on the first day of the month, that the tabernacle was reared up" (Ex. 40:17).[5] We are not told how long it took

---

5. In 1611, "reared" referred to buildings, while "raised" referred to children (Gen. 38:8; Ex. 9:16; Josh 5:7). By 1900, American grammar had reversed the usage. Hardly anyone except English teachers in the United States says "reared" these days.

them to construct the tabernacle, although it could not have been much more than three months. Construction did not begin until after Moses returned with the second writing of the tables of the law (Ex. 34:29). He had been on Mt. Sinai the first time for 40 days (Ex. 24:18) and 40 days the second time (Ex. 34:28). In between was another 40-day period in which he fasted without water. This fast took place after he cast down the original tablets of the law (Deut. 9:18).[6] We are not told how much time separated his second return from Sinai and the beginning of construction, but it seems to have been brief. The nation's voluntary offering for the construction of the tabernacle followed his second return (Ex. 35). Then construction began (Ex. 36). Subtracting 120 days (40 X 3 = 6 months) from nine months leaves three months for the construction of the tabernacle.

To build the tabernacle, the people had donated gold and silver that they had taken from the Egyptians (Ex. 33:4–6; 38:24–25). This voluntary mass donation was accompanied by a mustering of Israel: "A bekah for every man, that is, half a shekel, after the shekel of the sanctuary, for every one that went to be numbered, from twenty years old and upward, for six hundred thousand and three thousand and five hundred and fifty men" (Ex. 38:26).

Mustering was an aspect of priestly atonement (Ex. 30:15). The nation was supposed to be numbered – literally: *mustered* – prior to holy warfare. There is an element of negative sanctions associated with the Hebrew word for numbering used here: *paqad*. It does not mean mere counting.[7] "When thou takest the sum [count] of the children of Israel after their number [*paqad*], then shall they give every man a ransom for his soul

6. Moses went without food and water for a total of 120 days, or four months: on Sinai the first time (Deut. 9:9), after the golden calf incident (Deut. 9:18), and on Sinai the second time (Ex. 34:28).

7. James B. Jordan, *The Law of the Covenant: An Exposition of Exodus 21–23* (Tyler, Texas: Institute for Christian Economics, 1984), p. 227.

unto the LORD, when thou numberest [*paqad*] them; that there be no plague among them, when thou numberest them" (Ex. 30:12). The same word is sometimes translated as *visit*. "Thou shalt not bow down thyself to them, nor serve them: for I the LORD thy God am a jealous God, visiting the iniquity of the fathers upon the children unto the third and fourth generation of them that hate me" (Ex. 20:5). This visitation implies negative sanctions: "Thus saith the LORD unto this people, Thus have they loved to wander, they have not refrained their feet, therefore the LORD doth not accept them; he will now remember their iniquity, and visit [*paqad*] their sins" (Jer. 14:10). The word can mean *punish*. "And I will punish [*paqad*] the world for their evil, and the wicked for their iniquity; and I will cause the arrogancy of the proud to cease, and will lay low the haughtiness of the terrible" (Isa. 13:11).

The nation faced no military enemy at the time of the Exodus mustering. No one is said to have ordered this mustering, yet the nation voluntarily consented to it: "And the silver of them that were mustered of the congregation was an hundred talents, and a thousand seven hundred and threescore and fifteen shekels, after the shekel of the sanctuary: A bekah for every man, that is, half a shekel, after the shekel of the sanctuary, for every one that went to be numbered, from twenty years old and upward, for six hundred thousand and three thousand and five hundred and fifty men" (Ex. 38:25–26). This corresponded to the required payment of half a shekel of silver per man (Ex. 30:14–15). This was in addition to their voluntary offerings of gold and brass, which they brought in such abundance that God ordered Moses to tell them to stop (Ex. 36:5–7).[8] While the final accounting appears in Exodus 38, it was recorded here after the construction of the tabernacle had begun. The donations had come at the time of the mass presen-

8. Gary North, *Tools of Dominion: The Case Laws of Exodus* (Tyler, Texas: Institute for Christian Economics, 1990), ch. 30.

tation (Ex. 35:20–29). The same tally lists the gold (Ex. 38:24), yet this gold would not have been donated after God had told them to stop. So, the donations must have come in prior to the prohibition.

These numbers reinforce the text's estimates of the size of the Israelite population. The Babylonian system of monetary units roughly parallelled the Israelite system. The Babylonians used a hexadecimal system: 60 shekels to a mina, 60 minas to a talent. The Israelite system was based on 50 shekels to the mina, 60 minas to the talent.[9] The same system was still in force in the Israel of Christ's day.[10] The scholars' estimate of the Israelite shekel as one-3,000th of a talent is derived from Exodus 38. Thus, to avoid relying heavily on circular logic, I argue only that this account provides a rough confirmation of size of the Israelite population. What can be said with confidence is that the monetary units of Israel and Babylon were similar, so the account of the money collected reinforces the picture of a large Israelite population. At 50 shekels per mina, there were 3000 shekels to the talent. The 100 talents of silver totalled 300,000 shekels, plus 1,775 additional shekels, or 301,775 shekels. Multiplied by two, this totals 603,550, the number of those mustered. Conceivably, these estimates could have been inserted by a later forger, but there is internal consistency of the account. Had there been an inconsistency, the higher critics would have pounced on it centuries ago.

God had told Moses: "Speak unto the children of Israel, that they bring me an offering: of every man that giveth it willingly with his heart ye shall take my offering. And this is the offering which ye shall take of them; gold, and silver, and brass" (Ex. 25:2–3). He did not tell Moses to muster them. The tally in

---

9. "Money," *A Dictionary of the Bible*, edited by James Hastings, 5 vols. (New York: Charles Scribner's Sons, 1900), vol. III, p. 419; "Weights and Measures," *The International Standard Bible Encyclopaedia*, edited by James Orr, 5 vols. (Grand Rapids, Michigan: Eerdmans, [1929] 1943), vol. V, p. 3080.

10. Josephus, *Antiquities of the Jews*, XIV:vii:1, III:viii:10; cited in "Money," *idem*.

Exodus 38 specifies that they gave silver in terms of the mustering requirements. So, with respect to silver, they donated in terms of the mustering requirement; with respect to gold and brass, there were no required amounts. The gold and brass constituted their voluntary excessive giving.

As we learn from the Book of Numbers, every adult fighting man of Israel must have participated in this first mustering, since exactly the same number of men were mustered at this time as were mustered about four months later: 603,550 (Num. 1:46).[11] So, no eligible male refused to participate. This identical number indicates that Israel was in a condition of zero population growth: as many men had entered the ranks of those eligible to be mustered as those who had died.

Joshua and Caleb soon served as spies who entered Canaan (Num. 13:6, 8). This means that they had been mustered, since they were part of a military reconnaissance unit. Caleb was 40 years old at the time (Josh. 14:7). Toward the end of the conquest, he spoke of being 85 yet physically strong (Josh. 14:10–11). This strength was some sort of special miracle – an aspect of God's promise to him (Num. 14:24) – or so he seemed to indicate. But he was not Moses' age, who was 120 at the time of his death just before the conquest (Deut. 34:7), when Caleb was almost 80. He must have been in the generation that followed Moses. Surely Joshua was, for Joshua died an old man "a long time after that the LORD had given rest unto Israel from all their enemies" (Josh. 23:1). So, God's promise to Caleb and Joshua should not be interpreted as having singled them out as unique survivors among Moses' generation, but as survivors of the wilderness experience in general.

---

11. If the Exodus mustering took place immediately before the beginning of the tabernacle's construction, then it took no more than three months for the tabernacle to be completed. The tabernacle was completed on the first day of the first month of the second year (Ex. 40:17). The second mustering (the first Numbers mustering) took place a month later: the first day of the second month of the second year (Num. 1:1, 18).

Why the Exodus Mustering?

The mustering in Exodus was judicially unique: Israel faced no imminent military confrontation, and no judicial compulsion is mentioned in the text. The tabernacle was not uniquely associated with warfare, i.e., Israel in its judicial capacity as God's holy army. Each man presented a half shekel of silver (Ex. 38:26). This silver had been required for making the implements of the tabernacle (Ex. 26:19, 25, 32; 27:17), and was so used (Ex. 38:27–31). Some of the offerings were voluntary (Ex. 25:2), but with respect to silver, the offerings were tied to the mustering. Why was the nation numbered?

Perhaps this first mustering had nothing to do with atonement. In such a case, they did not plan to bring exactly the amount of silver per person that God required whenever they made atonement at a mustering. This possibility seems farfetched. Why didn't they bring more silver than what was required to make atonement? They brought so much wealth that God told Moses to tell them to stop. But with respect to silver, they brought exactly the amount required to make atonement.

For what action were they making atonement? This mass donation of money took place after the golden calf incident (Ex. 32). Perhaps the people were making retroactive atonement payments for themselves. They had gone to war with God. They had lost. The Levites had become the enforcing army of the Lord, killing 3,000 men (Ex. 32:28). This was what had changed Levi's judicial status from a family under a curse (Gen. 49:5–7)[12] to God's firstborn, priestly family (Num. 3:12); no other judicially relevant act on their part is mentioned. The text does not say that the golden calf incident was the cause of the mustering; the context only suggests that this was the case. All we know for sure is this: the half shekel paid at a mustering was atonement money. Atonement was a ransom or a judicial

---

12. The cause was the illegitimate negative sanction of war that Levi and Simeon had imposed on the Shechemites after they had been circumcised (Gen. 34:25–30).

covering for some infraction. The most obvious infraction even remotely associated with war's bloodshed was the golden calf incident.

The number of men slain was not a large percentage of the total male population, if the Israelites numbered 600,000 fighting-age males: about one-half of one percent. But if the number of Israelites was a fraction of 600,000, the death toll was more significant. This point becomes important in the Appendix, where I discuss the possibility that the bulk of those mustered in Exodus 38 were adoptees out of the mixed multitude that had fled with Israel. If they were adopted after the sanctions were applied because of the golden calf incident, then the 3,000 deaths constituted a significant fraction of the Israelite nation. As I show in the Appendix, this conceivably may have been close to 10 percent of the adult male population.

Numbers' Two Musterings

God required Moses to muster the men of Israel twice in the wilderness: once at the beginning of the wilderness period and once at the end (Num. 26). There were three musterings: these two and the prior one in Exodus.[13] The problem here is to discover a judicial link among the three events. I think it is associated with the shedding of man's blood.

The mandatory mustering in Numbers 1 took place just before the nation was ready to begin its march toward Canaan. Had they not sinned subsequently by refusing to listen to Joshua and Caleb (Num. 14), they would have begun the war of conquest in Canaan. Thus, the mustering in Numbers 1 was preparatory for war.

Mustering required the payment of atonement money (Ex. 30:15–16). No reason for the need for atonement is stated. Jordan believes that it was God's presence that mandated the

---

13. Gordon J. Wenham, *Numbers: An Introduction and Commentary* (Downers Grove, Illinois: Inter-Varsity Press, 1981), pp. 57, 59.

payment.[14] I would add that it was God's presence in His covenantal capacity as sanctions-bringer. When God is present in His office as sanctions-bringer, the unholy man is profane: a boundary violator.[15] Prior to holy warfare, God approached the nation of Israel as the sanctions-bringer: positive and negative. "For the LORD thy God walketh in the midst of thy camp, to deliver thee, and to give up thine enemies before thee; therefore shall thy camp be holy: that he see no unclean thing in thee, and turn away from thee" (Deut. 23:14). God would then bring sanctions against whichever army was not holy. The payment of atonement money judicially set apart God's assembled army as the holy army. This is why the Israelites of Joshua's day had to be circumcised before they could begin the conquest (Josh. 5:5). They could not be covenantally holy inside the boundaries of the holy land apart from circumcision. God's presence in their midst in his capacity as sanctions-bringer would destroy them, just as the angel of the Lord had almost destroyed Moses' uncircumcised son Gershom when Moses brought him across the border into Egypt (Ex. 4:24–26).[16]

The second mustering came after a series of successful wars outside of Canaan (Num. 21). Why didn't God muster the nation prior to these wars? Because they were defensive wars. The Canaanites had initiated them. After the treachery of the Midiantites, however, God told Moses to vex them (Num. 25:17). Then the mustering took place. The conquest of Midian and then Canaan were offensive wars for Israel. They were holy wars in God's name. They involved violating the national boundaries of societies that had been set apart by God for judgment.

14. Jordan, *Law of the Covenant*, pp. 228–29.

15. On the distinction between common and profane, see Gary North, *Leviticus: An Economic Commentary* (Tyler, Texas: Institute for Christian Economics, 1994), ch. 6.

16. On the angel's attack on Gershom rather than Moses, see Gary North, "The Marriage Supper of the Lamb," *Christianity and Civilization*, 4 (1984), p. 220. See also George Bush, *Notes on Exodus* (Minneapolis, Minnesota: James & Klock, [1852] 1976), I, p. 67.

No Population Growth

One month after the tabernacle's completion, the size of Israel's militarily eligible male population was exactly the same as it had been approximately four months earlier at the Exodus mustering: 603,550 men (Ex. 38:26; Num. 1:46). This indicates that Israel's population had reached zero growth. Thirty-nine years later, God ordered another mustering. The population was essentially unchanged at this second compulsory mustering: 601,730 (Num. 26:51); so was the number of Levites (Num. 3:39: 22,000; Num. 26:62: 23,000). Israel suffered from zero population growth in the wilderness.

The approximately 600,000 fighting-age males in the first two musterings comprised two generations: Moses' and Joshua's. The conquest generation and their adult-age sons replaced the 600,000 men who had been over age 19 at the time of the first mustering. If the top two generations were 300,000 each (population replacement-rate mode), then a family of Joshua's generation produced on average one son and grandson age 20 or older by the time of the second Numbers mustering. But should we assume a stagnant population prior to the exodus? The textual evidence is against this: families with more than two children. If population was growing, then Joshua's generation was larger than Moses'. This growth process was reversed in the wilderness, where most Israelites had even smaller families than two children. The nation moved from grace to curse. Why?

Time Perspective

The early chapters of the Book of Numbers record a series of complaints and rebellions on the part of the Israelites. They afflicted Moses with their murmering. The exodus generation was continually looking backward longingly at Egypt, despite the fact that they had been in bondage there. They were a present-oriented people who looked to the past with nostalgia. They had short memories.

God had delivered them, not to dwell in the wilderness, but to dwell in Canaan. He expected them to be future-oriented. But these ex-slaves could not shake off their mental chains. They looked backward to their lives of bondage and saw only prosperity and security. They resented freedom because they resented responsibility. They were not an operational army; they were a psychologically dependent assembly.

God had to raise up a new army. He had to wait for the children of Joshua's generation and their children to mature. Joshua's generation had to learn patience. They would grow up in a wilderness, not an empire. They would have no illusions regarding the wonders of life in the wilderness. They would not look backward to Egypt, where they had lived only as children or not at all. They would look forward to Canaan.

The ex-slaves did not multiply in the wilderness. They stagnated. One by one, they died; one by one, they were replaced. The army of the Lord was not short on numbers; it was short on leadership, courage, and faith. Its failure was not based on its lack of size. God did not honor them by expanding the army's size, which would have retroactively affirmed the legitimacy of their fears in refusing to invade Canaan. The next generation would conquer the land with the same size army.

Population stagnation is a curse in the Bible, though not so great a curse as population reduction. There was a slight reduction in the wilderness era. The nation was under a curse. We could say that He placed the nation "on hold." The exodus generation would have to content themselves with being nomads rather than pilgrims. Pilgrims have a destination; nomads simply wander in circles. Only to the extent that members of the exodus generation could look forward covenantally to victory through their children could they become pilgrims. They had been told that they would die in the wilderness. To the extent that they were mentally bound to a time horizon no longer than their own lifetimes, they became nomads.

These nomads were not ready to fight a war with the Canaanites. Their pilgrim children would be. The pilgrim wants rest in the place of his dreams. His life's walk is linear even though he may wander in circles for a time. He has a goal, so the fact of his circular wandering is not a disaster. He knows that he will eventually break out of his familiar pattern.

The stagnation of Israel's population matched the stagnation of vision of the exodus generation. Present-oriented people discount the future at a higher interest rate than future-oriented people do. The present value of a future achievement is lower for a present-oriented person than for a future-oriented person. The estimated payoff for thrift and sacrifice in the present is lower. The present-oriented person wants immediate gratification. The conquest generation had no choice but to defer their gratification. They were under the authority of present-oriented people. Their deliverance was still in the future; their parents' deliverance had been in the past. In the interim, the nation stagnated.

For those members of the conquest generation who longed for deliverance from the stagnation of the wilderness, God's curse was real. But it offered hope. In the fourth generation, they would gain their promised inheritance. In the meantime, the governing principle of their existence was the army's rule: "Hurry up and wait."

Conclusion

The three musterings of Israel were military actions. They were aspects of holy warfare. The mustered Israelites had to pay the priests atonement money in preparation for the shedding of blood. This bloodshed was covenantal: an aspect of God's negative sanctions against covenant-breaking nations. The Exodus mustering probably was a retroactive payment for the Levites' sanctions in God's name and the nation's name against

3,000 representative Israelites for the golden calf. The first Numbers mustering was in preparation for the conquest of Canaan, which was postponed because of Israel's rebellion (Num. 14). The second Numbers mustering took place just before the holy war against Midian.

The conquest generation had to learn patience for 39 years. They had to learn about deferred gratification. They would conquer Canaan, but only after their parents and grandparents had died in the wilderness. Their inheritance would have to wait. This was the result of the present-oriented, fear-driven rebellion of the exodus generation. The army of the Lord was a defeated army psychologically. Until this changed through generational attrition and replacement, the holy army wandered in the wilderness.

2

MILITARY PLANNING VS. CENTRAL PLANNING

Take ye the sum of all the congregation of the children of Israel, after their families, by the house of their fathers, with the number of their names, every male by their polls; From twenty years old and upward, all that are able to go forth to war in Israel: thou and Aaron shall number them by their armies (Num. 1:2–3).

This commandment was theocentric. God was the military head of Israel. He gave them victories as well as defeats, as they would learn after their rejection of the testimony of Joshua and Caleb (Num. 14:45). He was in no need of a military census. Why did He require one? The first reason was that He delegates authority to creatures who are not omniscient. They must find substitutes for omniscience. Number is one of the most useful substitutes for comprehensive knowledge – an extraordinary tool.[1] Second, there was the matter of an atonement payment. This also required a census.

---

1. Eugene Wigner, "The Unreasonable Effectiveness of Mathematics in the Natural Sciences," *Communications on Pure and Applied Mathematics*, XIII (1960), pp. 1–14. Wigner was a Nobel Prize-winning physicist.

Church and State in Wartime

Man is not God. No numerical census will ever equal God's omniscience. No substitute for omniscience will ever approach God's omniscience as a statistical limit. No expenditure of economic resources in data-gathering will ever replace reliance on God's covenantal sanctions in history. The creature will remain a creature. The quest for omniscience is therefore an unholy quest. Omniscience is an illegitimate goal. This is one reason why God placed strict limits on mustering. It was not a normal event. It was done only prior to holy warfare, except for the instance of the mustering in Exodus 38, which may have been a retroactive atonement for the golden calf.

God told Moses and Aaron to muster the entire adult male population, family by family. Aaron's presence was mandatory. Mustering in Mosaic Israel was an act preparatory to holy war. No holy war could be called without the consent of the high priest, for the Aaronic priests had to blow the silver trumpets that assembled the nation (Num. 10:2, 8). Blowing only one trumpet gathered the princes (v. 4). Both trumpets had to be blown to assemble the whole nation at the tabernacle (v. 3). This twin trumpet signal sounded the alarm. A second blowing of both trumpets by the priests launched the army on its march (vv. 5–6). Without the participation of the priests, no holy war could be launched. *This gave the priesthood a veto over national military action.* No military mustering was legal without their participation.

Moses was present in his capacity as a civil ruler. He was the representative of the nation in its judicial capacity. So, in the case of holy warfare, the supreme civil commander functioned in a priestly capacity, even though he was not a priest. We might call this quasi-priestly authority: legitimate power over life and death. The entire nation is at risk. In wartime, the senior military commander lawfully possesses such quasi-priestly authority. He does not possess it in peacetime, except in preparation for war.

The armies were tribal affairs, and under them, family affairs. This meant that warfare was intensely personal. If a section of the army was overrun, whole families would die, whole communities would be emptied of men. This happened in the American Civil War (1861–65), where the fighting-age male population of entire towns sometimes disappeared. Town regiments signed up as units and were kept as units throughout the war. This built a closeness of spirit, but it involved great risk to the community. Enlistment policies were changed in subsequent wars to prevent this. In World War II, brothers were allowed to enlist together, but when all five Sullivan brothers died on a sinking ship, the rule was changed. A modern army is far less personal, with senior officers required to rotate regularly through various commands. The bureaucratic impulse has replaced the personal impulse as warfare has become more rationalized. Such was not the case in Mosaic Israel. The localism of Mosaic Israel was reflected in their military formations.

The army was a federation. Each tribe supplied warriors. In mustering the armed forces, a tribe might refuse to participate, as was the case when Deborah called the army together to fight Sisera: several tribes refused to send anyone (Judg. 5:16–17).

Mustering and Atonement

There was an exemption in this tribal mustering: Levi. This was the priestly tribe. The rules governing tribal mustering seem to be in conflict. At first, God forbade Moses to number the Levites. "For the LORD had spoken unto Moses, saying, Only thou shalt not number the tribe of Levi, neither take the sum of them among the children of Israel" (Num. 1:48–49). "But the Levites were not numbered among the children of Israel; as the LORD commanded Moses" (Num. 2:33). God later told Moses to number them (Num. 3:15). "All that were numbered of the Levites, which Moses and Aaron numbered at the commandment of the LORD, throughout their families, all the males from a month old and upward, were twenty and two thousand" (Num. 3:39). Children were numbered. Why were the Levites numbered differently from the other tribes?

God gave this as His explanation for not mustering them: "But thou shalt appoint the Levites over the tabernacle of testimony, and over all the vessels thereof, and over all things that belong to it: they shall bear the tabernacle, and all the vessels thereof; and they shall minister unto it, and shall encamp round about the tabernacle" (Num. 1:50). They possessed a unique geographical responsibility; it was a capital crime for non-Levites[2] to approach the tabernacle while the Levites assembled and disassembled it whenever the nation moved (v. 51).

Furthermore, when the fighting men paid their half shekel at the time of their mustering, they paid it as atonement money (Ex. 30:15). This was an ecclesiastical payment. "And thou shalt take the atonement money of the children of Israel, and shalt appoint it for the service of the tabernacle of the congregation; that it may be a memorial unto the children of Israel before the LORD, to make an atonement for your souls" (Ex. 30:16). This money must have been paid to the tribe of Levi, for they alone served in the tabernacle. They did not pay atonement money; they received it. Thus, when they counted the money, they did not declare a shortfall when money from the tribe of Levi did not appear in the total. The mustering process referred to in Numbers 1 was related to the Levites' collection of the atone-

2. The Hebrew word is transliterated *zoor*. The same root is translated "strange" in the case of the strange fire offered by Nadab and Abihu (Num. 3:4). A stranger (*zoor*) was any person who could not lawfully cross an ecclesiastical boundary. "There shall no stranger [*zoor*] eat of the holy thing: a sojourner of the priest, or an hired servant, shall not eat of the holy thing" (Lev. 22:10). A hired servant could be an Israelite, yet he was kept away. The boundary around the priest's table included even his married daughter, though not if she was no longer married and without a child. "But if the priest's daughter be a widow, or divorced, and have no child, and is returned unto her father's house, as in her youth, she shall eat of her father's meat: but there shall no stranger [*zoor*] eat thereof" (Lev. 22:13). Her child made her part of her husband's family, even though he was no longer her husband.

ment money: a half shekel per warrior. But the Levites were not to be mustered in this way; they did not owe the atonement money.

Banners and Battles

Each of the other tribes had a standard, meaning a military identification banner. The other tribes were required to pitch their tents around their respective banners (Num. 1:52). The Levites had no such standard around which to pitch their tents. "But the Levites shall pitch round about the tabernacle of testimony, that there be no wrath upon the congregation of the children of Israel: and the Levites shall keep the charge of the tabernacle of testimony" (v. 53).

The Hebrew word for standard is translated "banner" only once in the King James Version – oddly enough, in the Song of Solomon: "He brought me to the banqueting house, and his banner over me was love" (Song 2:4). This was meant to be hyperbolic: not a battle flag but a love flag. The banners are mentioned in Numbers 2 and 10, both cases when the Israelites marched. "On the west side shall be the standard of the camp of Ephraim according to their armies: and the captain of the sons of Ephraim shall be Elishama the son of Ammihud" (Num. 2:18). "In the first place went the standard of the camp of the children of Judah according to their armies: and over his host was Nahshon the son of Amminadab" (Num. 10:14). These identifying flags are common in infantry maneuvers. A general in the field can see from a high emplacement where his armies are located on the battlefield.

The Levites had no battle flag. They were not to be placed in the field as a separate tribe. Their job was to guard the tabernacle and the Ark of the Covenant.[3] Their battle marker

---

3. Milgrom writes: "The most important function of the Levites, one that invests their entire adult life, is to guard the sanctuary against encroachers. In fact, they are identified by this function – 'guardians of the tabernacle of the Lord' (31:30,47)."

was the Ark of the Covenant. When the nation moved, it moved in military formation. The Levites carried the portable tabernacle and the Ark. They were guarded on all four sides by the other tribes. Military commanders knew exactly where the Levites were during battle: in the middle of the formation. James Jordan provided a diagram in *Through New Eyes*.[4] This diagram is found in Wenham's commentary.[5] It is reprinted exactly in Milgrom's commentary, right down to its typography: which tribal names to place in capital letters.[6]

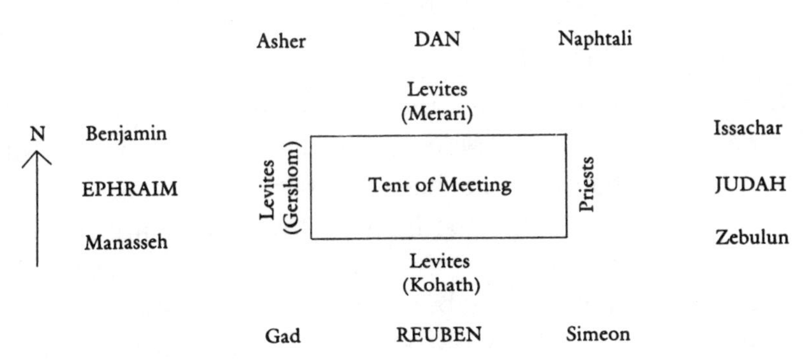

(Jordan has revamped it; he now believes that the corners were symbolically the most important. He places the lead tribes there rather than the center.)

The Ark of the Covenant had to be separated from the other tribes by 2,000 cubits in Joshua's day (Josh. 3:4), or about 1,000 yards (914 meters). Numbers 2 describes the peacetime formation. Judah led it in wartime (Num. 10:14). The priests were protected by the other tribes; they in turn defended the tabernacle from enemies, including invaders from the other tribes.

Jacob Milgrom, *The JPS Torah Commentary: Numbers* (New York: Jewish Publication Society, 1990), p. xl. Cf. Milgrom, p. 341.

4. James B. Jordan, *Through New Eyes: Developing a Biblical View of the World* (Brentwood, Tennessee: Wolgemuth & Hyatt, 1988), p. 205.

5. Gordon J. Wenham, *Numbers: An Introduction and Commentary* (Downers Grove, Illinois: Inter-Varsity, 1981), p. 67.

6. Milgrom, *Numbers*, p. 340.

In other words, at the very center of the formation was the Ark of the Covenant, the dwelling place of God. This had to be protected by the nation, at the cost of their lives. The last defensive barrier was the tribe of Levi.

This meant that the Levites did not put themselves at risk as a tribe in the initial confrontation with the enemy. Only if the enemy broke through the lines did the Levites go into battle. From the point of view of military risk, the Levites were protected by the structure of the army's formation.

Defending the Tabernacle

Because members of the other tribes could not approach the tabernacle when it was being moved by the Levites (Num. 1:51), they probably would have hesitated to pursue invaders who had broken through the lines and who were approaching the tabernacle. It is not said that God held non-Levites responsible for approaching the tabernacle as its would-be defenders, but this silence would have produced psychological hesitancy – often fatal to military defenders. In all likelihood, they were not allowed to approach the tabernacle in wartime, even for the sake of defending the Ark. The later example of Uzzah, who reached out to steady the Ark as it was being moved, indicates that this was the case: when he touched it, he was killed by God on the spot (II Sam. 6:6–7). So, once the outer lines were breached by the enemy, the Levites would have fought alone. This made them even more dependent on the other tribes. The Levites were warriors, but their task was different: to defend the tabernacle, not to defend the land.

A military commander has the obligation to estimate what his forces are. Mustering was a pre-war event. Because they were warriors with a defensive assignment, to protect the tabernacle, it was lawful for the Levites' commander to number them. The list of mustered tribes does not include the Levites in either instance in Numbers; this population figure is always given separately. "But the Levites after the tribe of their fathers were not numbered among them" (Num. 1:47). Moses and Aaron later numbered them (Num. 3:39). As the senior representative of the tribe, Aaron had the right to know the number of warriors under his command.

This does not mean that Israel's senior military commander possessed this authority over Levites. The Levites were not part of his forces. They could not be called into military service for the defense of the land. They were called into ecclesiastical service by the high priest to defend the tabernacle. They lawfully bore the sword, not as civil agents but as ecclesiastical agents. They were the anointed defenders of God's house.

The Levites were not the first line of military defense. They were at lower risk in battle. They did not pay atonement money. They seemed to have all the advantages. So, God imposed a disadvantage: they had no inheritance in the land. "At that time the LORD separated the tribe of Levi, to bear the ark of the covenant of the LORD, to stand before the LORD to minister unto him, and to bless in his name, unto this day. Wherefore Levi hath no part nor inheritance with his brethren; the LORD is his inheritance, according as the LORD thy God promised him" (Deut. 10:8–9). This disadvantage would have had the effect of reducing any murmuring against the Levites by those who were at greater risk, since the potential critics would inherit rural land.

Landed Inheritance

There was a relationship between ministering to God and landed inheritance. The Levites had no rural landed inheritance. Their immediate commitment was not to land but to God. They did not guard the land; they guarded the dwelling place of God. They were not to spend the bulk of their time improving the land. This is why they were entitled to the tithes of the other Israelites. "The priests the Levites, and all the tribe of Levi, shall have no part nor inheritance with Israel: they shall eat the offerings of the LORD made by fire, and his inheritance" (Deut. 18:1). The other tribes were guardians of the land; hence, they had a landed inheritance.

The Levites were numbered in the sense of merely counting them. They were not numbered in the sense of collecting atonement money from them. They were numbered as defenders of the tabernacle. They were not numbered as defenders of the land. They had no battle flag. They had no landed inheritance as a tribe. Grammatically, the numbering process was the same: mustering. Covenantally, there were two separate numbering processes: one for those who possessed a landed inheritance and who owed atonement money prior to national battle; the other for those who did not have a landed inheritance and did not owe atonement money.

If the payment of Exodus 30 had been a civil head tax, then there is no reason why the Levites should not have paid it, since it would have gone to the State. But it did not go to the State for civil purposes; it went to the Levites for the service of the tabernacle.[7] The obligatory payment or non-payment of this money was central to the numbering (counting) and yet non-numbering (civil mustering) of Levi.

Levites were citizens. They paid civil taxes, whatever these taxes were and however they were collected. Levites did not pay atonement money. They were not to inflict offensive military sanctions against Israel's enemies; rather, they were to inflict defensive ecclesiastical sanctions against invaders who might break through the lines of the other tribes. Their task was to keep boundary violators from profaning the sacred space of the tabernacle, whether Israelites or non-Israelites.

---

7. My target here is Rushdoony, who argues that the atonement money of Exodus 30 was in fact the only civil tax in Mosaic Israel. He argues specifically that the temple collection was a civil tax. R. J. Rushdoony, *The Institutes of Biblical Law* (Nutley, New Jersey: Craig Press, 1973), p. 281–82. For my previous rebuttal, see *Tools of Dominion: The Case Laws of Exodus* (Tyler, Texas: Institute for Christian Economics, 1990), ch. 32.

Citizenship and Military Service

Citizenship in Mosaic Israel was tribal. Each of the 12 non-priestly tribes was required to supply a representative to monitor the numbering process. The Levites were represented by Aaron. Each of the dozen representatives had to be the head of his father's household, i.e., the senior patriarch or most respected officer. "These were the renowned of the congregation, princes of the tribes of their fathers, heads of thousands in Israel" (v. 16). For example, the representative of Judah was Nashon (v. 7). His son Salmon would marry Rahab; his descendants included Boaz and David (Ruth 4:20).

Citizenship was by a dual oath: civil and ecclesiastical. The judicial issue was two-fold: hierarchy (point two of the covenant) and sanctions (point four).[8] There was a hierarchy of civil appeals courts (Ex. 18). A person who was not bound by oath under covenantal sanctions could not lawfully impose these sanctions on others. A citizen was a civil judge. A judge could impose civil sanctions as a lawful agent of the State. Every citizen was under the stipulations of two of God's covenants: civil and ecclesiastical. Apart from being bound by a pair of self-maledictory oaths under these two covenantal institutions, a person did not possess lawful authority to impose civil sanctions in Mosaic Israel.

Mosaic civil sanctions were exclusively negative. They were defensive: discouraging evil acts. The results were positive – a reduction in public evil – but the sanctions were negative. The model for civil sanctions was military defense: imposing physical sanctions against invaders. Those who were outside the national covenant and also outside the holy land were to be kept from invading, which would have been a boundary violation: a profane act. God's holy army was supposed to keep a rival army from transgressing the nation's geographical boundaries, i.e,

---

8. Ray R. Sutton, *That You May Prosper: Dominion By Covenant* (2nd ed.; Tyler, Texas: Institute for Christian Economics, 1992), chaps. 2, 4.

profaning the land. The mandatory mark of citizenship was eligibility for service in God's holy army.[9] Keeping out unauthorized, non-sanctioned invaders from outside the land and from outside the national covenant was central to citizenship.

Does this mean that the Levites were not citizens? An expositor could argue this way, since they were not numbered as civil warriors. Their assignment was ecclesiastical: defending the tabernacle at the center of the military formation. I argue that they were members of their tribe, and they had judicial authority within their tribe. They did not have civil judicial authority in their place of residence if they were not living in a Levitical city. In a Levitical city, they possessed permanent legal claims on family-owned real estate that was part of the jubilee (Lev. 25:32–33), so they must have had civil authority there. They were the only permanent residents. I see the Levites as citizens who were not numbered for military service as warriors. They were the exception to the rule governing citizenship because of their special legal situation: defenders of the tabernacle rather than defenders of the land.

Citizen Warriors

What about an old man who was no longer capable of fighting? Did his physical incapacity disqualify him as a judge? The Mosaic law did not mandate this. There were old men who served as judges. Barzillai, who was 80 years old, pleaded that he could no longer discern good from evil, and therefore should not accompany David on his triumphal journey back to Jerusalem (II Sam. 19:34–35). Yet he had fed the king and his men when they fled from Jerusalem during Absalom's revolt (II Sam. 17:27). While in Barzillai's house, David had numbered those fighting men still with him. Barzillai was not numbered

9. Gary North, *Leviticus: An Economic Commentary* (Tyler, Texas: Institute for Christian Economics, 1994), ch. 30, section on "Holy War, Citizenship, and Liberty." Deborah was a judge; she also led God's holy army.

by David (II Sam. 18:1). Yet David later regarded him as fit to travel at his side in a place of honor. Barzillai had pleaded age, not with respect to his fighting ability, which was obviously nil, but with respect to his powers of judicial discernment. David granted him his request; he stayed behind. That he had been a loyal citizen was obvious. He had aided David in the latter's capacity as supreme civil judge. Yet he was no longer fit for military service. This in no way restrained David from asking him to accompany him after the defeat of Absalom. The issue was Barzillai's powers of judgment.

Similarly, Joshua in his old age called the judges of Israel to hear his final words. He instructed them as Moses had instructed him before the conquest, invoking a similar message. Moses had said: "Be strong and of a good courage: for thou shalt bring the children of Israel into the land which I sware unto them: and I will be with thee" (Deut. 31:23). Joshua told the judges: "Be ye therefore very courageous to keep and to do all that is written in the book of the law of Moses, that ye turn not aside therefrom to the right hand or to the left" (Josh. 23:6). Both invoked military imagery with respect to the law of God. Yet Moses was no longer fit to serve in the military, and neither was Joshua. Both were judges when they delivered their final addresses.

I conclude that citizenship for all but Levites was based on eligibility for service in the military at some point in life, but not in old age. Moses and Joshua had served in the military, yet were still judges in their old age. Barzillai had once been eligible for the military, and his decision to aid David at the risk of his life was clearly a military act. Only his self-declared mental incapacity kept him from serving as an honored judge at David's side.

Military Sanctions

Mustering was an act preparatory to the imposition of God's legitimate covenantal sanctions in history. It was an act under priestly sanctions. Those who were not under priestly sanctions in Mosaic Israel were not allowed to impose holy sanctions. They could not become members of the army. The biblical principle of covenant membership is this: those who impose sanctions must be under them. This is the principle of the rule of law. These holy military sanctions were positive for the winners and negative for the losers. The primary historical sanction of war is death. To begin preparing for a war is to begin preparing for someone's death, possibly one's own. Death stalks every battlefield.

Mustering was part of military planning. It was mandatory prior to a war. More than this: *the military census is the biblical model for all other forms of planning.*

> For which of you, intending to build a tower, sitteth not down first, and counteth the cost, whether he have sufficient to finish it? Lest haply [it happen], after he hath laid the foundation, and is not able to finish it, all that behold it begin to mock him, Saying, This man began to build, and was not able to finish. Or what king, going to make war against another king, sitteth not down first, and consulteth whether he be able with ten thousand to meet him that cometh against him with twenty thousand? Or else, while the other is yet a great way off, he sendeth an ambassage, and desireth conditions of peace (Luke 14:28–32).

There is more to military planning than numbering the army. There is also the question of the army's willingness to fight: mental preparedness. This applied both to the army and the civilian population. Moses sent spies into the land and awaited their reports (Num. 13–14). God did not order this (Num. 13:2) in order to evaluate the strength of the enemy; He did this in order to test the spies' willingness to evaluate the land's blessings and military strength in terms of the Israelites' willingness to fight. A fearful man was not to fight, for his fear might spread to those around him (Deut. 20:8). Gideon dismissed 22,000 people who admitted that they were afraid to fight (Judg. 7:3).

In Mosaic Israel prior to the Babylonian captivity, the male civilian population above the age of 19 was the army (Num. 1:20). The Book of Numbers records the history of the wilderness period in terms of a central theme: military preparedness, i.e., the ability of God's covenant people to impose military sanctions. God brought the holy nation/army under a series of sanctions in the wilderness, including military sanctions, in order to enable Moses to evaluate the military preparedness of the nation prior to the conquest of Canaan.

Moses began with a rag-tag army of civilians. In every sense of the word, this was an army of conscripts. They had been thrown out of Egypt by the Egyptians (Ex. 12:33). Moses had not taken them out by way of Philistia for fear that they would turn back toward Egypt in the face of war (Ex. 13:17). They had never fought a battle prior to the war with Amalek, and Moses had to stand with his arms above his head for them to win (Ex. 17:8–13). They had been placed in bondage by the Pharaoh of the oppression because he was fearful that they might someday fight a battle alongside Egypt's invading enemies (Ex. 1:10). They had been bullied for a generation by Egyptian taskmasters, as well as taught submissiveness by their own civil representatives. In Egypt, they had been fearful of any confrontation with authority (Ex. 5:20–21), let alone a war. This Egyptian training had been remarkably successful. Except for Moses' slaying of the taskmaster, during the entire era only the Hebrew midwives had been courageous enough to resist. Their non-violent actions of self-conscious deception of the civil authorities had saved the nation (Ex. 1:19–20). They lied to a false god (Pharaoh) in the name of the true God, and God blessed them for this, dwelling specially with them (Ex. 1:20a). Israel had been delivered by women. This had taken place 80 years before the exodus – a distant memory testifying to the long-term submission of Israel's males to pagan military power.

A Strictly Civil Census

God required Moses to muster the people shortly after the exodus, before the nation had sinned by bringing negative sanctions against Joshua and Caleb (Num. 14). God had not yet forbade this generation from entering the Promised Land. The second mustering took place just prior to the next generation's invasion of the land. Mustering was related to the payment of blood money to the priests (Ex. 30:13); both were religiously holy acts. The ritual payment of atonement money ceased with the demise of the Mosaic priesthood. Mustering was associated strictly with that priesthood. Abram had not been required to make such a payment to Melchizedek prior to his battle with Chedorlaomer (Gen. 14).

Such mustering was not lawful apart from the threat of war and a payment to the Levites. When God was angry with the people of Israel, He caused David to muster the nation, so that He could bring judgment against them. "And again the anger of the LORD was kindled against Israel, and he moved David against them to say, Go, number Israel and Judah" (II Sam, 24:1). This mustering was illegal, as Joab understood:

> For the king said to Joab the captain of the host, which was with him, Go now through all the tribes of Israel, from Dan even to Beer-sheba, and number ye the people, that I may know the number of the people. And Joab said unto the king, Now the LORD thy God add unto the people, how many soever they be, an hundredfold, and that the eyes of my lord the king may see it: but why doth my lord the king delight in this thing? Notwithstanding the king's word prevailed against Joab, and against the captains of the host. And Joab and the captains of the host went out from the presence of the king, to number the people of Israel (II Sam. 24:2–4).

God did this to David, and through his representative covenantal leadership, to Israel, by way of Satan, who acts as an intermediary in such matters.

> And Satan stood up against Israel, and provoked David to number Israel. And David said to Joab and to the rulers of the people, Go, number Israel from Beer-sheba even to Dan; and bring the number of them to me, that I may know it. And Joab answered, The LORD make his people an hundred times so many more as they be: but, my lord the king, are they not all my lord's servants? why then doth my lord require this thing? why will he be a cause of trespass to Israel? Nevertheless the king's word prevailed against Joab. Wherefore Joab departed, and went throughout all Israel, and came to Jerusalem (I Chron. 21:1–4).[10]

I have reproduced both passages in full so there can be no doubt: they describe the same incident.

Joab falsified his report by refusing to number the tribes of Benjamin and Levi (I Chron. 21:5–6). No military agent of the nation was ever allowed to number Levi (Num. 1:49). By refusing to muster Benjamin, Saul's tribe, the smallest tribe in Israel (I Sam. 9:21), Joab made certain that the mustering was not of the entire nation. By not mustering all of the non-priestly tribes, Joab silently declared that this was not a holy war, for the priesthood had not authorized it by blowing the twin trumpets, nor had the entire nation been mustered.

---

10. May we legitimately say that Satan and his followers sometimes do God's work of deception? The Bible repeatedly affirms that this is the case. "And the LORD said, Who shall entice Ahab king of Israel, that he may go up and fall at Ramoth-gilead? And one spake saying after this manner, and another saying after that manner. Then there came out a spirit, and stood before the LORD, and said, I will entice him. And the LORD said unto him, Wherewith? And he said, I will go out, and be a lying spirit in the mouth of all his prophets. And the LORD said, Thou shalt entice him, and thou shalt also prevail: go out, and do even so. Now therefore, behold, the LORD hath put a lying spirit in the mouth of these thy prophets, and the LORD hath spoken evil against thee" (II Chron. 18:19–22). "And for this cause God shall send them strong delusion, that they should believe a lie: That they all might be damned who believed not the truth, but had pleasure in unrighteousness" (II Thess. 2:11–12). Nevertheless, we must not blame God for what God uses Satan to do. This is illogical by the standards of autonomous man (meaning also the standards of Gordon Clark), but it is required that we hold both positions – God's absolute sovereignty and Satan's full responsibility – in order to avoid making God the author of sin. On this point, see Romans 9:14–23.

Immediately upon receiving Joab's report, David knew he had done a sinful thing. "And David said unto God, I have sinned greatly, because I have done this thing: but now, I beseech thee, do away the iniquity of thy servant; for I have done very foolishly" (I Chron. 21:8). God then gave David three terrible choices (v. 12). David told God to decide (v. 13); so, God brought a plague against the people, killing 70,000 of them (v. 14). This was consistent with the law of mustering. "When thou takest the sum of the children of Israel after their number, then shall they give every man a ransom for his soul unto the LORD, when thou numberest them; that there be no plague among them, when thou numberest them" (Ex. 30:12). Plague came because David mustered the people without collecting the mandatory atonement money for the priests. This mustering invited God into their midst as the sanctions-bringer, but they made no payment. They thereby became profane.

Why did Joab know that the mustering was wrong? Because no priest had consented to it. No blood money had been paid to the priesthood. The act was clearly sacrilegious: a profane act because it violated a sacred boundary. But what could that boundary have been? It had something to do with the non-payment of blood money. It had something to do with the priesthood. Mustering was to precede a holy war. David was not facing a holy war, yet he mustered Israel's fighting men. This was an assertion of a priestly authority that he possessed only as the national military leader in a time of war. David was the senior military commander, the one under whom blood would be shed. He was the senior priest of the military, under the authority of the high priest. He did not possess this mustering authority as senior civil magistrate. This authority was priestly, not kingly. Thus, it was illegal for the civil government to conduct this census. It was an assertion of priestly authority that was legitimate only prior to a holy war.

Joab told the king: "Now the LORD thy God add unto the people, how many soever they be, an hundredfold, and that the eyes of my lord the king may see it." It would be a blessing for God to multiply the military might of the nation, he said, so that David could see this. Spoken like a true soldier. The cost of supporting an army a hundred times larger, however, would have to be borne by someone. In a war, a large army is a clear blessing; in peacetime, it isn't. Joab's point was that David should not be counting the nation on his own authority. To experience an increase in the army large enough for its commander to see is a fine goal in wartime, but to muster the nation apart from a looming battle was wrong.

The New Covenant

The issue was ecclesiastical: atonement money and the shedding of blood. Under the New Covenant, the Mosaic priesthood is gone forever, as the Epistle to the Hebrews teaches. Numbering prior to a war is no longer mandatory. The question is this: Is such numbering (counting) legitimate?

Taking a careful accounting of one's assets is legitimate for an individual, and was compared by Jesus with taking a military census. Should the State be prohibited from doing what an individual should do and the senior military commander had to do under Mosaic law prior to a war? Can it lawfully number its fighting forces even though no war is imminent? I see no reason not to allow this. Maintaining defensive forces is designed to prevent war, i.e., prevent the shedding of blood. This is a valid goal of the State, which has a legal monopoly on imposing physical negative sanctions.

But what about other forms of census-taking? Has God given the State lawful authority over planning except with respect to planning for a war, i.e., the legitimate imposition of God's physical sanctions against covenant-breakers who have violated the law? There is no biblical warrant for such indiscriminate data collection. The State may lawfully count the policemen under its authority, since the State is God's designated covenantal agent in a war against crime. But the State is not given the authority to conduct prying investigations into the lives of law-abiding private citizens.

Wherever the State asserts authority which is not warranted by the Bible, it imitates David's illegal mustering. It asserts for itself power that God has not delegated to it. Such an unlawful arrogation of power is the mark of a Pharaonic State. It claims ownership – legal control – over the allocation of assets not lawfully under its sphere of legitimate authority. One of the marks of State control is its census-taking activity. Whenever the State numbers things not lawfully under its legitimate authority, it becomes Pharaonic.

Jesus was born in Bethlehem because Joseph had travelled there to be enrolled in a census conducted by Augustus Caesar (Luke 2:1–5). This was not a tax, as the King James Version misleadingly says; it was a census. Augustus was following the lead of Julius Caesar, who had compiled a detailed statistical record of the empire, the *descriptio orbis*. Augustus had sent 20 trained agents throughout the empire to compile a similar work, which he wrote in his own hand, *Breviarium totius imperii*.[11] To manage a centrally planned empire, the emperor needed statistical data.

Statistics and Government Planning

One of the great evils of an income tax is that it mandates reporting to the State of a family's income, capital, and financial dealings. The State assembles huge, detailed dossiers on individuals, families, and businesses, which only tax officials are allowed to inspect for accuracy.[12] The income tax has been the great engine of statistics-gathering by the modern State. The

11. Frederick Louis Godet, *Commentary on the Gospel of Luke*, 2 vols. (Grand Rapids, Michigan: Zondervan, [1887]), I, pp. 120–21.

12. "IRS to expand secret data base on people's lives," *Dallas Morning News* (Jan. 20, 1995), p. 1. This data base will be closed to the general public. It is being set up in order to facilitate more efficient tax collection.

census is the other. Both are compulsory in the United States. A resident can be fined for refusing to cooperate with the census-taker. Statistics pour into the U.S. Department of Commerce, the Department of Labor, the Internal Revenue Service, and many other agencies: federal, state, and local.

Some of these statistics are sold to the public on computer disks or in printed government reports. But only rarely are they used by businesses for strategic planning, especially small businesses. They are rarely delivered in a useful form. They do not tell most businesses what business managers need to know. In any case, they are old; they are at best snapshots of past behavior. Nonexistent is the firm that goes bankrupt or sustains a major loss because of its heavy reliance on faulty government statistics. This is because no business management team would be so foolish as to rely on government statistics for making major decisions. They hire specialized market testing organizations that seek out and analyze the highly specific and narrow information needed by business managers.

Each year in the United States, the government releases a 1000-page book, *Statistical Abstract of the United States*. It is jointly produced by the Department of Commerce, the Bureau of the Census, and the Economics and Statistics Administration. It is a convenient government subsidy to such professional groups as historians, economists looking for factual support for almost any theory, editorial writers, and students writing term papers. Politicians' assistants use it to ghostwrite speeches and reports.

Statistics are records of the past that have been summarized in the form of numbers. Economist Ludwig von Mises writes: "Statistics provides numerical information about historical facts, that is, about events that happened at a definite period of time to definite people in a definite era. It deals with the past and not with the future. Like any other past experience, it can occasionally render important services in planning for the future, but it does not say anything directly valid about the future."[13] Furthermore, "what the statistics of human action really show is not regularity but irregularity. The number of crimes, suicides, and acts of forgetfulness . . . varies from year to year."[14] The biologist, writes sociologist-historian Robert Nisbet, can predict future changes in some environmentally controlled population, but "It is very different with studies of change in human society. Here the Random Event, the Maniac, the Prophet, and the Genius have to be reckoned with. We have absolutely no way of escaping them. The future-predicters don't suggest that we can avoid or escape them – or ever be able to predict or forecast them. What the future-predicters, the change-analysts, and trend-tenders say in effect is that with the aid of institute resources, computers, linear programming, etc. they will deal with the kinds of change that are *not* the consequence of the Random Event, the Genius, the Maniac, and the Prophet. To which I can only say: there really aren't any; not any worth looking at anyhow."[15]

Government statistics are used by economic planners, including the central bank, to regulate the national economy. Not that these statistics are accurate or even useful. Older data are constantly being revised. But they create the illusion that government planners are capable of making effective representative decisions for consumers on the basis of an overall economic plan. The planners supposedly are capable of devising comprehensive, scientific, economic input-output grids, inserting the latest data, and presto: an accurate picture of the economy emerges. This picture then supposedly enables them to forecast the future effects of their official decisions. This is a politically convenient myth. Academic studies of government forecasting

13. Ludwig von Mises, *The Ultimate Foundation of Economic Science* (Princeton, New Jersey: Van Nostrand, 1962), p. 56.

14. Ludwig von Mises, *Theory and History: An Interpretation of Social and Economic Evolution* (New Haven, Connecticut: Yale University Press, 1957), pp. 84–85.

15. Robert A. Nisbet, "The Year 2000 and All That," *Commentary* (June 1968), p. 66.

repeatedly conclude that flipping a coin would be as accurate (perhaps more accurate) as the forecasts of government economists; so would making the simple assumption that this year will be pretty much the same as last year.

Faith in the power of statistics to convey relevant economic information to government planners is visible in a statement by Eugene Rostow. He assumes that it is an altruistic civil government, not the profit-seeking decisions of consumers and producers in a free market, which is truly rational. Government planners alone can see the big picture and rationally guide the overall economy for the benefit of others, or so we are told. "The policy of maintaining high levels of employment therefore implies a policy of seeking to make the current output of the economy a maximum – that is, to obtain as valuable a yield as possible from the intelligent current use of the nation's capital resources, and its inheritance of capital, organization, skill, and habit. This goal is the first economic problem of any responsible government."[16] This faith lodges initiatory and final economic sovereignty in the State, and in those who are ordained by the State to conduct its planning activities.

In contrast to the god of socialism, this god of the mixed economy is not an earthly version of Calvin's predestinating God, but it is surely an immanent Arminian kind of god. It does not predestinate, but it makes incentives available to those who conform to its laws. It nudges history along its orderly path. But a blind god is not much of a god (Deut. 4:28), so this immanent god must be said to be able to see clearly. He must be given eyes. Samuel Ruggles, the American delegate to the International Statistical Congress of 1863, was an early prophet of the statistical millennium: "Statistics are the very eyes of the statesman, enabling him to survey and scan with clear and comprehensive vision the whole structure and economy of the

---

16. Eugene V. Rostow, *Planning for Freedom: The Public Law of American Capitalism* (New Haven, Connecticut: Yale University Press, 1959), p. 69.

body politic."[17] Such confident rhetoric is not so evident today, but the underlying faith is still widespread. Rostow asserts that "the development of the statistical series which provide rough tools of accounting for the current economic performance of the economy has improved our opportunities for studying the behavior of the economy, and for making both private and public policy decisions more rational and effective."[18] He was a professor of law, not an economist, but his faith in the planned economy was very great. Freedom through State compulsion: here is the twentieth-century liberal's number-one official economic goal. (His number-one goal, unofficially, is the quest for power: a very ancient goal.)

Apart from coercively collected, tax-funded statistics, the government planning priesthood and their academic allies could not easily maintain the myth of their ability to predict the economic future and then create incentives through tax policy and monetary policy to overcome the supposed inefficiency of voluntary economic exchange, i.e., the free market social order. Rothbard is correct: "If the government received no railroad statistics, for example, how in the world could it even start to regulate railroad rates, finances, and other affairs? How could the government impose price controls if it didn't even know *what* goods have been sold on the market, and what prices were prevailing? Statistics, to repeat, are the eyes and ears of the interventionists; of the intellectual reformer, the politician, and the government bureaucrat. Cut off those eyes and ears, destroy those crucial guidelines to knowledge, and the whole threat of government intervention is almost completely eliminated."[19]

---

17. Cited in Murray N. Rothbard, "Fact-finding is a proper function of government," *Clichés of Politics*, edited by Mark Spangler (Irvington, New York: Foundation for Economic Education, 1994), p. 93n. The essay was first published in *The Freeman* in June, 1961: "Statistics: Achilles' Heel of Government."

18. Rostow, *Planning for Freedom*, p. 69.

19. Rothbard, "Fact-finding," p. 92.

In a 1960 article, Rothbard surveyed the history of economists' opinions on the collection of government statistics since the mid-nineteenth century. In case after case, the economists who praised such statistical work had as a motive the creation of a planned economy. The Fabian socialists in England in the late nineteenth century are the models.[20] Richard T. Ely, one of the founders of the American Economic Association, and Lester Frank Ward – sociologist, government bureaucrat, and the first major apologist for central planning in the U.S. – both defended the collection of such data.[21] Wesley C. Mitchell, one of the pioneers in statistical inquiry in economics in the early twentieth century, said that "the type of social invention most needed today is one that offers definite techniques through which the social system can be controlled and operated to the optimum advantage of its members."[22] His wife wrote of his work at mid-century that "he envisaged the great contribution that government could make to the understanding of economic and social problems if the statistical data gathered independently by various Federal agencies were systematized and planned so that the interrelationships among them could be studied. The idea of developing social statistics, not merely as a record but as a basis for planning, emerged early in his own work."[23] The Bureau of the Budget in 1954 announced: "National growth and prosperity demanded an enlightened conduct of public affairs with the aid of factual information. The ultimate responsibility of the Federal Government for underwriting the health of the national economy has always been implicit in the American system. . . ."[24] The accelerating growth of U.S. gov-

---

20. Murray N. Rothbard, "The Politics of Political Economists: Comment," *Quarterly Journal of Economics*, 74 (Nov. 1960), p. 660.

21. *Ibid.*, pp. 660–61.

22. *Ibid.*, p. 662.

23. Lucy Sprague Mitchell, *Two Lives* (New York: Simon & Schuster, 1953), p. 363. Cited in *idem.*

24. *Economic Statistics*, Hearings Before the Subcommittee on Economic Statistics

ernment data collection came, the Bureau said, during the Great Depression of the 1930's, as a means for the government to combat the Great Depression.[25]

It is not just that statistics require constant tinkering, both theoretically[26] and in terms of their proper collection.[27] It is also that they establish the indispensable theoretical foundation for coercive government intervention into the economy. The Bible is unalterably opposed to such coercive intervention. It is therefore opposed to the collection of statistics that are not part of its war-making authority, including the war against crime.

Rothbard noted in 1960 that the collection of statistics by the government leads to greater intervention: ". . . the growth of statistics, often developed originally for its own sake, ends by multiplying the avenues of government intervention and planning."[28] Furthermore, when pragmatic social reformers go looking for problems to solve by government action, they use statistics. "The pragmatist looks for areas where the economy and society fall short of the Garden of Eden, and these, of course, abound."[29]

---

of the Joint Economic Committee on the Economic Report, 83rd Congress, July 12, 1954 (Washington, D.C.: Government Printing Office, 1954), p. 10; *ibid.*, p. 663.

25. *Idem.*

26. North, *Leviticus*, ch. 19, section on "Intuition and Measurement." Cf. Oskar Morgenstern, *On the Accuracy of Economic Observations* (2nd ed.; Princeton, New Jersey: Princeton University Press, 1963). Morgenstern wrote a book on game theory with John von Neumann, one of the most gifted mathematicians of the twentieth century. Morgenstern was aware of the limits of mathematics as a tool of economic analysis. A more recent treatment of the problem is Andrew M. Kamarck's *Economics and the Real World* (Philadelphia: University of Pennsylvania Press, 1983). See also Thomas Mayer, *Truth versus Precision in Economics* (Hampshire, England: Elgar, 1993).

27. Examples taken from my files in 1989 – a small sample of two decades of my files on the topic: "America Counts on Its Numbers," *Insight on the News* (May 22, 1989); Richard Lipkin, "Painting policy by the numbers: Imprecise art?" *Washington Times* (May 23, 1989); "Getting Physical," *The Economist* (Aug. 26, 1989); Jonathan Fuerbringer, "Rusty Statistical Compass for U.S. Policy Makers," *New York Times* (Oct. 30, 1989).

28. Rothbard, "Comment," p. 663.

29. *Ibid.*, p. 664.

Conclusion

The Book of Numbers begins with the mandated mustering of the fighting men of Israel. This was an aspect of Israel as the holy army of the Lord. It was an aspect of negative civil and ecclesiastical sanctions – specifically, the military conquest of Canaan. It was a priestly activity. The priesthood had to sanction every holy war that involved the whole nation.

God is omniscient. Man is not. God allows men to pay for data-gathering in order to make better private decisions, but mankind cannot become omniscient. The State, as the most powerful covenantal agency, is not allowed by God to pursue data-gathering in an unholy quest of God-like omniscience or omnipotence.

When David mustered the people when no war was being contemplated, God judged him by killing 70,000 Israelite males by a plague. This indicates that legitimate mustering by the civil government was regarded by God as a unique event, something associated with authorized combat and the threat of death in battle: the shedding of blood.

Those who were eligible for mustering, and hence for battle, were citizens in Mosaic Israel. Prior to the Babylonian captivity, their eligibility to serve in the army of the Lord was their primary proof of citizenship.

The rise of the modern planning State was associated with the rise of government statistics. The two developments were intimately and necessarily associated. Governments began collecting statistics before the ideology of central planning was widespread. Once begun, however, coercive data gathering became part of the larger process of extending State authority over the decision-making of all those under its authority. The quest for ever more detailed, accurate, and recent statistical data is an aspect of man's attempt to become God. The messianic State, if it is to bring its promised healing, must imitate God. It must pursue omniscience, which in turn becomes the supposed basis of its representative (statistically significant) omnipresence and, ultimately, its omnipotence. Because Mosaic Israel was founded on a public repudiation of Egypt's messianic State, its legal order made impossible the civil government's collecting of statistics that were unrelated to the defense of the nation against covenant-breakers. There is nothing in the New Covenant that altered the Old Covenant's view of the messianic State. Thus, there is no reason to believe that government data-gathering is legitimate except in the specified areas of national defense and crime prevention. It can lawfully collect taxes, but taxes that mandate the collection of information on private citizens are inherently suspect. Such data must not be used for manipulating the economy; they are to be used only for legal purposes, to prove that someone has or has not paid his taxes.

3

THE HIERARCHY OF SERVICE/SANCTIONS

And the LORD *spake unto Moses, saying, Bring the tribe of Levi near, and present them before Aaron the priest, that they may minister unto him. And they shall keep his charge, and the charge of the whole congregation before the tabernacle of the congregation, to do the service of the tabernacle. And they shall keep all the instruments of the tabernacle of the congregation, and the charge of the children of Israel, to do the service of the tabernacle. And thou shalt give the Levites unto Aaron and to his sons: they are wholly given unto him out of the children of Israel. And thou shalt appoint Aaron and his sons, and they shall wait on their priest's office: and the stranger that cometh nigh shall be put to death (Num. 3:5–10).*

The English word "hierarchy" comes from the Greek word for priest (*hierus*). We think of a hierarchy of command in terms of an image: a vertical chain. This hierarchy may be judicial; it may be merely functional. It is associated with point two of the biblical covenant model: hierarchy or representation.[1]

This law, as with all the other Mosaic laws, was theocentric. In this case, however, the theocentric character of the law was

1. Ray R. Sutton, *That You May Prosper: Dominion By Covenant* (2nd ed.; Tyler, Texas: Institute for Christian Economics, 1992), ch. 2.

manifested geographically. This law governed the Aaronic priesthood. The central – literal and figurative – service of the Aaronic priesthood was associated with the holy of holies. The holy of holies marked the central focus of Israel: the earthly dwelling place of God, the place of His name. The holy of holies was the geographical link between heaven and earth. In it rested the Ark of the Covenant.

Guardians

The Mosaic priesthood guarded the boundaries associated with the holy of holies. The priests in the narrow sense were those who officiated in the sacrifices: the sons of Aaron. In a broader sense, the priesthood was the tribe of Levi. In the broadest sense, Israel was a nation of priests (Ex. 19:6). They all were to guard the tabernacle by imposing physical sanctions on those who violated a series of concentric boundary markers: from the holy of holies to the nation's boundaries.

Priests were the assigned agents of bloodshed inside the sacrosanct boundaries associated with the holy of holies. The narrowly defined priests shed the blood of animals to placate God. The more broadly defined priesthood defended the tabernacle from profane invaders who had no lawful access. The most broadly defined priesthood was the army of the Lord, a holy army, which defended the nation because the nation was God's sanctified dwelling place.

The legal basis of the Levitical priesthood of pre-exilic Mosaic Israel had begun in the wilderness with the golden calf incident (Ex. 32). First, there was an act of corporate rebellion in which the high priest, Aaron, had participated. Aaron's act of rebellion had been a re-capitulation of the original sin of Adam, who ate a forbidden covenantal meal as mankind's representative high priest. This corporate act of rebellion involved the whole nation. God required a bloody sacrifice to atone for it. There is no atonement apart from the shedding of blood (Heb. 9:22).

Second, the Levites gained their tribal office as the Mosaic priesthood because they had atoned for their sin by wielding the sword without mercy (Ex. 32:26–29). This atonement extended retroactively to their earlier sin, which had been a merciless wielding of the sword: the slaying of the Shechemites and the looting of their assets (Gen. 34:25–27), an act cursed by Jacob (Gen. 49:5). Imposing mortal sanctions on their biological brothers brought their sanctification, thereby offsetting their curse for having imposed the same sanctions against the Shechemites, their newly adopted brothers. *The covenant is far more important than brotherhood.* Levi had violated this principle with Shechem; his heirs honored it in the wilderness.

The golden calf incident was a prelude to the next act of priestly rebellion, the strange fire incident (Lev. 10:1–2). The first incident led to the elevation of the Levites to priestly office when they joined Moses and executed 3,000 Israelites. The second incident led to the substitution of a new pair of priests due to the deaths of the two original officers. *Bloodshed marked the Mosaic priesthood from the beginning.*

The priestly office was sacrificial before God, meaning that it involved the imposition of the negative sanction of death. The threat of sanctions was hierarchical: on the animals as representatives, on those whom they represented if the nation continued in their rebellion, and directly on those who acted as the mediatorial agents of sacrifice.

Because the priests performed the ritual acts of substitutionary atonement – judicially representative deaths – they were under the threat of more immediate and more direct negative sanctions than the people were. They stood on holy ground. The closer that men came to the most comprehensive act of representative sacrifice – the yearly sprinkling of blood inside the holy of holies – the more dangerous was the ground. *Holy ground was bloody ground, judicially speaking.* It was the place of negative sanctions.

Hierarchy and Inner Circles

The old rule governing the organization of a workshop applied to priestly service: "a place for everything, and everything in its place." At the center of Israel were the contents of the Ark of the Covenant: two tables of the law, a golden pot of manna, and Aaron's rod (Heb. 9:4). The manifestation of God's law and the implements of His sanctions were linked spatially: the tablets (law), the manna (bread), and the rod (sanctions). Man needs law and bread in order to live. "And he humbled thee, and suffered thee to hunger, and fed thee with manna, which thou knewest not, neither did thy fathers know; that he might make thee know that man doth not live by bread only, but by every word that proceedeth out of the mouth of the LORD doth man live" (Deut. 8:3). The rod served as a warning: violate the boundaries of the Ark, and negative sanctions will be applied, just as they were applied on Pharaoh by means of this rod.[2] These three items were encased inside the Ark and were never supposed to be viewed by any person in history.[3] This was the ultimate inner sanctum of Israel: "For God's eyes only." It was closed to man, just as the tree of the knowledge of good

2. Exodus 7:9–10, 19; 8:5, 16. There has been a long debate among the Jewish commentators as to whether this rod was Moses' or Aaron's. The twentieth-century editor and Chief Rabbi of the British Empire J. H. Hertz includes a gloss by David Levi and Isaac Delgado, late eighteenth-century commentators: ". . . the rod of Moses used by Aaron at the bidding of Moses." Hertz (ed.), *The Pentateuch and Haftorahs* (2nd ed.; London: Soncino, [1937] 1987), p. 236. The mid-nineteenth-century Orthodox Jewish commentator Samson Raphael Hirsch wrote: "There is absolutely no necessity to believe that this was Moses' staff and not Aaron's. (Some of the commentators put themselves to considerable effort to try and prove it must have been Moses' staff). It is much more reasonable to take it, as the verse clearly says, as Aaron's staff." Hirsch, *The Pentateuch*, 5 vols. (Gateshead, London: Judaica, 1989), II, p. 78. I believe that the same rod was used by both men, even as Aaron spoke for Moses.

3. I am assuming here that the mercy seat which sat above the Ark was a lid (Ex. 25:21). The Hebrew word used for "mercy seat," *kapporeth*, comes from *kaphar*, meaning "covering."

and evil had been closed to man. A boundary protected this inner sanctum: the walls of the Ark.

A series of concentric circles of holiness encased the Ark. The Ark was placed behind a curtain, creating the holy of holies, into which only the high priest came once a year to offer sacrifice (Lev. 16:14–15). The high priest had this job; no one else did (v. 17). "Now when these things were thus ordained, the priests went always into the first tabernacle, accomplishing the service of God. But into the second went the high priest alone once every year, not without blood, which he offered for himself, and for the errors of the people" (Heb. 9:6–7). This annual event conformed to the five-point biblical covenant model. The requirement mandating judicial representation (point two) in the offering of one representative annual sacrifice of blood (point four) overcame the otherwise absolute sanctity (point three) of the holy of holies, the dwelling place of God (point one), thereby enabling the Israelites to survive as a nation (point five).

Like the garden of Eden, where only the tree of the knowledge of good and evil was declared off-limits to man, so was Mosaic Israel. Only the interior of the Ark was declared completely off-limits. But Adam had proven that man does not honor God's verbal boundaries, so God placed a series of "No Trespassing" signs in front of men as they approached the Ark's sacred space. He placed swords – not flaming – into the hands of the Levites to guard the last few hundred feet (Num. 1:51). The basis of this authority was their previous willingness to use the sword against their brothers (Ex. 32:27).

The closer to the inner circle of holiness in Mosaic Israel – the implements inside the Ark of the Covenant – the higher the level of ecclesiastical authority. The greater the danger was of violating a sacred boundary, the higher the ecclesiastical authority. With respect to the sacred, *inner* meant *higher*. This relationship was unique to the church covenant. It did not apply to the civil hierarchy. There was no other place that was geographically sacrosanct outside of the areas associated with the throne room of God. The holy of holies housed the highest of highs, associated with God's mountain.[4] Like Mt. Sinai, where God gave the law to Moses, so was the tabernacle. Jordan writes: "The boundary around the mountain correlates to the boundary inside the courtyard that kept the people from approaching the altar. In this way, then, the Tabernacle (and later the Temple) were models of the ladder to heaven, of the holy mountain. . . . The Tabernacle was God's portable mountain."[5]

Circles of Authority

The association of the inner circles of the tabernacle with hierarchy, secrecy, and authority was to make the sacred space of the tabernacle foreboding to outsiders. The sense of power was inescapable. The circles of authority grew more diffuse as they moved away from the tabernacle. Hierarchy meant access to power; centralization meant access to power. To be a part of the inner circle meant access to power.

God closed access to these inner circles to those not part of specific families: Aaron, Kohath, Gershon, and Merari. Apart from adoption into one of these families, which involved the surrender of a man's inheritance in the land, and also involved the payment of an entry fee,[6] access to these inner circles was closed. There could be no competition for such access between excluded families.

The Levites lived in a camp separated from the other tribes by 2,000 cubits[7] (Josh. 3:4). Non-priestly Israelites were to be kept away from the inner courts of the tabernacle by the Le-

---

4. James B. Jordan, *Through New Eyes: Developing a Biblical View of the World* (Brentwood, Tennessee: Wolgemuth & Hyatt, 1988), pp. 85, 155–163, 212–13.

5. *Ibid.*, p. 213.

6. Gary North, *Leviticus: An Economic Commentary* (Tyler, Texas: Institute for Christian Economics, 1994), ch. 36.

7. About 1,000 yards (914 meters).

vites, who were to kill intruders. The Mosaic law clearly separated land ownership from sacred space. During wartime, it kept political authority at arm's length – at least 1,000 yards – from the sanctuary of the highest ecclesiastical hierarchy. After all of the copies of the Mosaic law had disappeared for generations, a copy was found in the temple (II Ki. 22:8). The oppression of covenant-breaking kings had not stripped the land of every copy. The temple's inner sanctuary had provided a safe hiding place for the lost copy. The symbolic point was this: *God's law is beyond the authority of kings to re-write.* The hierarchy that declared the law was not under the king, nor did the king have lawful access to the inner sanctum where the law rested. God's law was higher than the king. The tablets representing God's law were housed in the inner sanctum of the tabernacle, not in the king's household. There should be no mistake about this: *the church was the central institution in pre-exilic Mosaic Israel because the Ark of God was guarded by the church.*[8] The swords of the Levites took precedence over the sword of the king.

Hierarchy and the Division of Labor

There was a Levitical division of labor established by family membership. This division of labor was associated with tasks that were performed separately in a series of concentric circles with the Ark at their center.

Aaron was the high priest of Israel. On his shoulders rested the responsibility of performing those rituals that only the high priest was allowed to perform as a judicial representative of the nation. His yearly entrance into the holy of holies was the primary ritual (Ex. 30:10). The high priest was closest to the inner circle.

8. After the exile, despite the absence of the Ark, the church no longer had any serious competition from the State with respect to its social centrality. The State in Israel was part of a foreign hierarchy: Medo-Persian, Hellenic, or Roman.

To perform his duties successfully, he needed assistance. Under him were his two sons, Eleazar and Ithamar, who had replaced the two older sons, Nadab and Abihu (Lev. 10:12; Num. 3:4), who had been burned by fire from the altar when they offered strange fire (Lev. 10:1–2; Num. 3:4). "And to the office of Eleazar the son of Aaron the priest pertaineth the oil for the light, and the sweet incense, and the daily meat offering, and the anointing oil, and the oversight of all the tabernacle, and of all that therein is, in the sanctuary, and in the vessels thereof" (Num. 4:16). The sons of Aaron had access to areas that were off-limits to the other Kohathites: "But they shall not go in to see when the holy things are covered, lest they die" (Num. 4:20).

The Kohathites were required to tend to the implements that were inside the boundaries of these outer coverings but outside the inner coverings of the structure, i.e., outside of the holy of holies (Num. 3:31). They were allowed to minister closer to the inner circle than the Gershonites were. The Gershonites were required to tend to the hanging coverings of the tabernacle (Num. 3:25–26). These were the *implements of separation*: boundary markers inside the structure. The sons of Merari were required to tend to the outer structure itself (Num. 3:36–37). All the Levites were under Eleazar's supervision whenever they performed ritual activities inside the sanctuary (Num. 3:32). Otherwise, they were under Ithamar's authority (Num. 4:28, 33; 7:8).

The next set of differentiating tasks was associated with moving the tabernacle. The corporate job of Aaron's sons in times of travel was to cover the Ark of the Covenant (or Testimony) with the veil of the tabernacle (Num. 4:5), and then cover the other holy implements (Num. 4:6–14). This was the task of separation: *preserving the boundaries of holiness associated with the sacrifices*.

Once these vessels were covered, the Kohathites came to assist the sons of Aaron by moving the covered vessels (Num.

4:15). The coverings preserved the visual sanctification of the objects. The Kohathites were warned not to touch any holy object (v. 15b). The objects were carried on poles ("staves")[9] inserted through rings[10] or carried on top of bars (vv. 10, 12). God also warned the sons of Aaron not to do this task. "And the LORD spake unto Moses and unto Aaron, saying, Cut ye not off the tribe of the families of the Kohathites from among the Levites: But thus do unto them, that they may live, and not die, when they approach unto the most holy things: Aaron and his sons shall go in, and appoint them every one to his service and to his burden: But they shall not go in to see when the holy things are covered, lest they die" (Num. 4:17–20). Kohathites were to be kept away from these objects until the sons of Aaron took down the hanging walls of separation, so that there was no longer any "in" to go into.

The Gershonites were prohibited from doing the work of the Kohathites. Their assignments related to the next circle outward: bearing the curtains of the tabernacle. They disassembled and reassembled the tabernacle's coverings and the associated furnishings (Num. 4:22–28). They were under the jurisdiction of Ithamar (v. 28).

Similarly, the sons of Merari had their tasks associated with the next outward circle: bearing the boards and pillars (Num. 4:29–33). They were required to do the same with the outer support structure of the tabernacle (Num. 4:29–33). Each item was assigned to one man by name (v. 32). They, too, were under the jurisdiction of Ithamar (v. 33). The Hebrew word, *massaw*, indicates carrying or portering. They used oxcarts to transport the various materials (Num. 7:7).

The Levites transported the Ark on a cart in David's day, which was clearly in violation of the law. They were supposed

---

9. Numbers 4:6, 8, 11.

10. "And thou shalt put the staves into the rings by the sides of the ark, that the ark may be borne with them. The staves shall be in the rings of the ark: they shall not be taken from it" (Ex. 25:14–15).

to carry the Ark on poles. This infraction led to the death of Uzzah, who reached out and touched the Ark in order to steady it, and God killed him (II Sam. 6).

If we were to draw a map of authority within the tribe of Levi, it would look like this: the high priest at the center; Eleazar as his servant, in charge of ritual; Ithamar in charge of supervising the other families in non-ritual affairs; followed by Kohath, Gershon, and Merari. Because the Merari family guarded the outer boundaries of the temple, its members bore the sword against intruders. With respect to hierarchy, we can understand this through the analogy of a military chain of command: commanding officer, chaplains, general staff, field grade officers, officers, and enlisted men. All would be in uniform, and only they could lawfully wear these uniforms.

These tasks did not require all of the family members of each of the three Levitical families to serve at the central place of worship all of the time. Presumably, the Aaronic families of Eleazar and Ithamar did remain at the tabernacle full time. Those Levites who were not employed full-time at the tabernacle dwelt in the Levitical cities and in other cities. During wartime, all of the Levites would have returned to the tabernacle to guard it as the last line of defense against foreign invaders.

The Mosaic law did not assign special tasks to those Levites who lived away from the tabernacle. In other words, when outside the sacred boundaries of the tabernacle, the Levites could do whatever they wanted to do. They might teach, provide legal counsel for elders in the gates, farm, engage in trade, or whatever else they had the skills to do. They were not permitted to buy rural farmland, but they could lease it.

The Hierarchical Flow of Funds and Service

The language of the texts indicates the subordination of service. The high priest ruled. The sons of Aaron were to serve the high priest; the Kohathites were to serve the sons of Aaron; the Gershonites served the Kohathites; and the sons of Merari were the Levites who served the other families by protecting the perimeter. They bore the sword. The imagery is that of an upward flow of service.

This upward flow of service was paralleled by an upward flow of funds. The Levites collected the tithes of the people; the priests collected the tithes of the Levites. The separation of the family of Levi from any normal inheritance in the land established its moral claim on income from those who enjoyed landed inheritance (Num. 18:20–30). Levi became Israel's substitute for the firstborn son, and therefore he was entitled to the double portion (Deut. 21:17): automatic income. But this double portion eliminated their inheritance in the land.

Authority flowed outward from the throne room in which the tables of the law were housed to the borders of the nation and beyond (Jonah). Funds flowed inward toward that inner circle. The judicial declaration of the law and the ritual purification of the nation had to be paid for. Priestly service was ultimately representative service to God. God dwelt in the inner circles of Israel. He was the highest authority.

Tithe of the Tithe

The law established that Levites paid a tithe to Aaron. This referred to the high priest. I find it difficult to believe that one percent of the nation's net increase went each year to one man to cover his basic living expenses. Did this money go only to the sons of Aaron, namely, the priests who offered the sacrifices? The text does not say.

To find the answer, we must ask ourselves: Is the laborer worthy of his hire (Luke 10:7)? If he is, then those Levites who were in full-time service at the tabernacle must have been paid by the high priest. We do not get something for nothing; there are no free lunches. The Mosaic law does not indicate that these servants were self-funded or funded as some sort of family obligation. This is indicated by the text in Nehemiah: "And the priest the son of Aaron shall be with the Levites, when the

Levites take tithes: and the Levites shall bring up the tithe of the tithes unto the house of our God, to the chambers, into the treasure house. For the children of Israel and the children of Levi shall bring the offering of the corn, of the new wine, and the oil, unto the chambers, where are the vessels of the sanctuary, and the priests that minister, and the porters, and the singers: and we will not forsake the house of our God" (Neh. 10:38–39). Again, we read: "And all Israel in the days of Zerubbabel, and in the days of Nehemiah, gave the portions of the singers and the porters, every day his portion: and they sanctified holy things unto the Levites; and the Levites sanctified them unto the children of Aaron" (Neh. 12:47).

Who were the priests who received the tithe of the Levites in pre-exilic times?[11] Answer: those who were serving God full-time in sacramental activities at the tabernacle. This included those Levites who were serving their tour of duty at the tabernacle. In the tribal division of labor, they could not spend time working at other jobs.

Tithe-Exempt

The Levites' tithe to Aaron is specified as a tithe of everything they collected from the other tribes. "Thus speak unto the Levites, and say unto them, When ye take of the children of Israel the tithes which I have given you from them for your inheritance, then ye shall offer up an heave offering of it for the LORD, even a tenth part of the tithe. And this your heave offering shall be reckoned unto you, as though it were the corn

11. This changed in post-exilic times because so few Levites returned and so many priests did. Accompanying Zerubbabel were 4,289 priests (Ezra 2:36–39) and 341 Levites (Ezra 2:40–42). Extra-biblical evidence, mainly from Josephus, indicates that the tithe was divided so that the priests were supported more directly by the fruits of the people. See *Life of Flavius Josephus*, 15; *Antiquities of the Jews*, XI:v:8; XX:viii:8; ix:2. *Against Apion* I:22; cited in "Tithe," in *Cyclopaedia of Biblical, Theological, and Ecclesiastical Literature*, edited by John M'Clintock and James Strong, 12 vols. (New York: Harper & Bros, 1894), X, p. 436.

of the threshingfloor, and as the fulness of the winepress" (Num. 18:26–27). The phrase, "as though it were the corn of the threshingfloor," indicates that those Levites who made incomes from non-sacramental services paid a tithe on this increase to the priests.

Those at the top of the hierarchy did not pay a tithe. They paid in full-time service to God and to the other tribes. They were judicial intermediaries. Because they devoted all of their time to the service of God and the other tribes, they were not required to pay a tithe to themselves. This indicates that they were not to spend time in commercial ventures, agriculture, and other income-generating activities. If they did, then they would have owed a tithe on any increase to those full-time priests who did not. Full-time service was defined as sacramental service that was associated with sacrifices and cleansing. It was tied geographically to the tabernacle and/or the holy of holies (when the Ark of the Covenant was not inside the tabernacle, as it was not in the era after Eli and before David brought it back to Jerusalem, the city of David).[12] Such service was closed to those who were not ordained to it. It was explicitly ecclesiastical service. The mark of full-time service was personal exemption from the tithe. It was therefore a mark of total dependence on the tithes of others. *The greater the degree of service, the greater the degree of economic dependence*. The most authoritative ruler in Israel – the high priest – was the most dependent servant: dependent on God's grace with respect to the correct performance of his duties and the duties of those priests under his jurisdiction,[13] and dependent on the people to pay their tithes.

This principle has not changed. Ministers do not owe a tithe to the church on their income gained from the church. There

---

12. Jerusalem was known as the city of David (II Sam. 5:6–7). David brought the Ark back to his city (II Sam. 6:12).

13. North, *Leviticus*, ch. 4.

is no need for an accounting game of "pay the minister's tithe," with the church paying him a larger salary so that he has enough money to live on after the tithe, which goes back to the church. Those working in what is euphemistically called full-time Christian service owe a tithe to the local church unless they are employed by the church. Salaries received from the church in exchange for services to the church are not to be tithed. This, of course, does not apply to profit-seeking businesses that sell goods or services to the church. This rule applies to individuals who are paid by a local church to perform services associated with that church's official tasks, if they are also members of this church. If they are members of another local church, then their tithe goes to the other church.

This exemption from the tithe applies only to employment by the church, which possesses a lawful sacerdotal monopoly. It does not apply to employment by parachurch organizations. For example, a person who is employed by a parachurch organization who then tithes his income back to this organization is doing more than playing economically meaningless accounting games; he is rebelling against God. He owes the tithe to his local church.

Holiness and the Division of Labor

The priesthood was hierarchical. Different branches within Levi performed different tasks. This separated authority hierarchically within the tribe of Levi, and it separated Levitical authority to declare the law hierarchically to the other tribes.

Korah was a member of the family of Kohath. He was Moses' cousin: the son of Moses' uncle, Izhar (Ex. 6:18–21). He led a democratic revolt against Moses. "Now Korah, the son of Izhar, the son of Kohath, the son of Levi, and Dathan and Abiram, the sons of Eliab, and On, the son of Peleth, sons of Reuben, took men: And they rose up before Moses, with certain of the children of Israel, two hundred and fifty princes of the assembly, famous in the congregation, men of renown: And they gathered themselves together against Moses and against Aaron, and said unto them, Ye take too much upon you, seeing all the congregation are holy, every one of them, and the LORD is among them: wherefore then lift ye up yourselves above the congregation of the LORD?" (Num. 16:1–3). Korah's revolt rested judicially on the basis of the supposed equality of authority within Israel. God disposed of them appropriately: by causing the earth to open up beneath them (Num. 16:31–33). They had lifted themselves up; God would pull them down. But not immediately.

For Korah to make such a democratic claim, he had to enlist the cooperation of members of at least one other tribe. His claim would have made no sense had he limited his recruiting to the tribe of Levi. To have done so would have pointed to the existence of hierarchy in Israel: Levi over all the others. This would have undermined his claim. Therefore, Korah had to approach the sacred center of Israel accompanied by non-Levites. He also had to participate in a profane act: the transgressing of a sacred boundary.

Moses' prophetic test of equality was both geographical and liturgical: to have all claimants to priestly authority light fires. Those who did not possess lawful hierarchical authority to perform such a liturgical act would be placed under God's direct negative sanctions. Their fire would be declared strange fire. Moses proposed a test based on sacrilege, which in turn was based on the division of labor. "And he spake unto Korah and unto all his company, saying, Even to morrow the LORD will shew who are his, and who is holy; and will cause him to come near unto him: even him whom he hath chosen will he cause to come near unto him. This do; Take you censers, Korah, and all his company; And put fire therein, and put incense in them before the LORD to morrow: and it shall be that the man whom the LORD doth choose, he shall be holy: ye take too much upon you, ye sons of Levi" (Num. 16:5–7). The holiness of separation would soon prove to be total.

Moses criticized Korah for the latter's refusal to be content with the high degree of authority that God had given to the Levites: "And Moses said unto Korah, Hear, I pray you, ye sons of Levi: Seemeth it but a small thing unto you, that the God of Israel hath separated you from the congregation of Israel, to bring you near to himself to do the service of the tabernacle of the LORD, and to stand before the congregation to minister unto them? And he hath brought thee near to him, and all thy brethren the sons of Levi with thee: and seek ye the priesthood also?" (Num. 16:8–10). But Korah wanted even more authority.

Moses declared himself to be a prophet in terms of God's immediate application of negative sanctions: "And Moses said, Hereby ye shall know that the LORD hath sent me to do all these works; for I have not done them of mine own mind. If these men die the common death of all men, or if they be visited after the visitation of all men; then the LORD hath not sent me. But if the LORD make a new thing, and the earth open her mouth, and swallow them up, with all that appertain unto them, and they go down quick into the pit; then ye shall understand that these men have provoked the LORD" (Num. 16:28–30). The Old Covenant prophet was a prophet because God's negative sanctions predictably followed the prophet's declaration of a covenant lawsuit. This is why the office no longer exists under the New Covenant, and also why the negative civil sanction of capital punishment for false prophecy (Deut. 18: 20–21) no longer applies. The Old Covenant's rigorous temporal predictability no longer exists.

God's visible judgment against Korah made it clear that the Mosaic Covenant's hierarchy of priestly authority was a *hierarchy of power*. This is because it was a *hierarchy of sacramental holiness*. This hierarchy of holiness was the basis of a division of labor in the service of God. Not everyone had the authority to approach God's inner sanctum by passing through the concentric circles of holiness that surrounded it. Korah had proclaimed the doctrine of equal holiness. God pronounced visible judgment against this doctrine by destroying him and those allied with him. The division of labor in Israel would be retained.

These concentric circles ended definitively at the crucifixion, when the veil of the temple was rent, top to bottom (Matt. 27:51). That this tearing began at the top of the veil indicated that God had initiated it. Nevertheless, what was definitive judicially took a generation to fulfill. The high priest still possessed a sacrosanct position, which Paul acknowledged when he apologized for having berated him, not knowing that he was the high priest (Acts 23:4–5). Not until the fall of Jerusalem and the burning of the temple by the Romans did the Mosaic law's degrees of priestly holiness finally cease. The fires of the altar ended forever when God burned the temple. The altar's fire had become strange fire through Old Covenant Israel's rebellion. The priesthood ended, thereby ending the influence of the Sadducee party. The Pharisees – defenders of the oral law, unlike the Sadducees[14] – replaced them as the leaders of the new religion of Judaism.[15]

Monopoly Services and Economic Dependence

The Levites provided teaching services and judgment to the nation. They also carried the tabernacle from place to place. Both forms of service involved holiness. The Levites had been set aside by God for these purposes. These services were tribal monopolies. As monopolies, they could have become opportunities for economic oppression. God placed economic limits on the Levites in order to limit their economic return from the possession of these monopolies: a limit of ten percent of any increase in wealth by the people and the Levites' requirement

14. Herbert Danby, "Introduction," *The Mishnah* (New York: Oxford University Press, [1933] 1987), pp. xviii–xix.

15. The key figure in this transition was Johanan ben Zakkei. *Ibid.*, pp. xix–xx. On Judaism as a post-A.D. 70 religion, see Jacob Neusner, *Judaism and Scripture: The Evidence of Leviticus Rabbah* (University of Chicago Press, 1986), Preface.

to provide free freight hauling services. Those who were involved in transporting the tabernacle became priests for the duration of the journey: full-time priestly servants of God. The free market's pricing principle – high bid wins – did not apply to the ecclesiastical services performed by the Levites. The tithe did.

The Mosaic Covenant clearly established the principle of tribal interdependence. In Mosaic Israel, the tribes other than Levi were covenantally incapable of serving God sacramentally by themselves. They became covenantally dependent on members of the tribe of Levi to serve as intermediaries between them and God. The inter-tribal link among the other dozen tribes was the tribe of Levi, which served all the others and collected tithes from them.

The Levites were heavily (though not exclusively) dependent economically on the other tribes for their income. They were more dependent in the early stages of Mosaic Israel's history than God intended them to be as time went on. God made them economically dependent initially by way of the laws of landed inheritance: they did not participate in the original distribution, nor could they buy up rural land or inherit it.[16] As the nation grew in numbers and wealth, however, this economic dependence would have been reduced by the increasing value of urban property in relation to rural land. Mosaic law was biased against capital in rural land, for the law favored population growth: fewer miscarriages (Ex. 23:26) and longer life spans (Ex. 20:12) for covenantal obedience. Population growth in the context of a fixed supply of rural land, with all male heirs inheriting, leads to ever-smaller family allotments.[17] Under such conditions of covenantal blessing, the Levites, who

---

16. With this exception: "And if he will not redeem the field, or if he have sold the field to another man, it shall not be redeemed any more. But the field, when it goeth out in the jubile, shall be holy unto the LORD, as a field devoted; the possession thereof shall be the priest's" (Lev. 27:20–21). See North, *Leviticus*, ch. 37.

17. *Ibid.*, ch. 34.

could own inheritable real estate in the cities, would have seen their income sources less dependent on tithes based on the agricultural productivity of the other tribes.

Levites were not prohibited from owning urban businesses, so their economic dependence on the other tribes would have been reduced over time, at least when the nation was covenantally faithful to God. This was an economic incentive for the Levites to teach and enforce God's law. God's positive corporate sanction to Israel – urban growth – would have served as a subsidy to the Levites, who would have been more likely to buy urban real estate prior to this demographic shift. They were more likely to be early residents of cities, since they could not lawfully inherit rural land.

There could have been another factor in the decreasing economic dependence of Levi: the growing size of the tribe in comparison to the numbers involved in full-time priestly service. When the need to transport the tabernacle ended with the completion of the temple, this reduced an important aspect of priestly service. This Levitical service was replaced by singing (I Chron. 15:15–16). Also, it is possible that the number of priests required for the sacrifices would not have grown proportionately to the tribe of Levi. That would have depended on the demand for sacrifices by the general population. It is possible that the growth in demand for sacrifices would have required many more priests. We do not know. We do know that far more priests returned from the exile than Levites (Ezra 2:36–42).

There was a dual monopoly in Mosaic Israel: control over sacrifice by the Levites and control over rural land by the other tribes. Members of the other tribes had no hope of obtaining the guaranteed income of the tithe unless they were adopted into a Levite family (Lev. 27:2–8). The Levites had no hope in agricultural inheritance. The dozen other tribes had to be fed spiritually by the Levites. The Levites were to be fed literally by the other tribes. Each of the monopolists knew that what he possessed was incomplete, that he would have to supply services to others in order to prosper.

Mobility at Some Price

As men approached the holy of holies, there was increasingly limited lawful geographical mobility. This limited mobility was based on the presence of sacred boundaries. Transgression of these boundaries was not a violation of etiquette; it was a violation of sacred space: profanity.

Israelite society was not characterized by a fixed hierarchy, especially a hierarchy of inheritance. The sacred hierarchy was confined to a single tribe. This opened the possibility of social mobility for those outside the tribe of Levi. There were no economic guarantees outside of Levi, but there were also no significant restraints on what a free man could earn or do with his capital, including time. There was the jubilee law (Lev. 25), but this law was to be applied infrequently. Economically speaking, its effects would have become decreasingly significant over time in a covenantally faithful society, as a result of the decreasing economic relevance of agricultural landed property.

The sacred boundaries for Israelites were limited to the area close to the tabernacle. Beyond this geographical limit, men could go where they would. They could rise as high as their talents would allow when God's law was enforced. There was no caste system that specified that a man, family, or tribe had to perform this or that service. Service was contractual. With the exception of those services identified by God's law as inherently immoral, each person could offer his services for sale without restriction. Because Israelite society was not sacred, service was not fixed. *Sacred boundaries applied only to the sacramental realm of the sacrifices.* Had Mosaic society been universally sacred, these sacred boundaries would have encased men and their talents within tight legal and geographical boundaries.

Beyond the sacred space of the tabernacle, and outside of any sacred services performed by local Levites, men were free to move. So, they were free to choose. They could offer to buy their way into whatever position was for sale, whether they used their labor or their money as the appropriate currency of access. Every hierarchy other than the hierarchy of ecclesiastical service, which included the king's office as military priest in times of holy warfare, was temporary. Because men possessed the legal right of mobility, upward and downward, the hierarchies that existed at any point in time were mobile.

The covenantal hierarchy of the priesthood was sacred: a matter of life and death. The covenantal hierarchy in the army was quasi-priestly: control over life and death. The respective chains of command were necessary for the performance of oath-bound service. The hierarchical structure of both of these hierarchies could lawfully be defended by the threat of violence. Outsiders could not gain lawful access apart from adoption and/or oath. The same is true in a family, another oath-bound institution. But there is no fourth institution lawfully established by means of a covenantal oath.

With the annulment of the Mosaic priesthood, neither birth nor family adoption is necessary to gain access to the mediatorial ecclesiastical office of minister. Only a wife[18] and a ministerial oath is mandated. Even in the case of the military services, access to the top positions has generally been open to men of lower classes during wartime. The man who repeatedly wins battles "buys" his way into senior military positions normally closed in times of peace. The currency of upward mobility during wartime is victory. This is why, in Tocqueville's opinion, the non-commissioned officer in a democratic army favors war.[19] Exemplary service in battle, coupled with the high

---

18. "This is a true saying, If a man desire the office of a bishop, he desireth a good work. A bishop then must be blameless, the husband of one wife, vigilant, sober, of good behaviour, given to hospitality, apt to teach" (I Tim. 3:1–2).

19. Alexis de Tocqueville, *Democracy in America*, J. P. Meyer, editor, 2 vols. (Garden City, New York: Anchor, [1966] 1969), II (1840), ch. 23, p. 654.

death rate of officers, are his ways of gaining permanent promotion.

This stands as a warning: in a non-covenantal hierarchy, those who seek to use violence against others in order to maintain their places against those who wish to compete lawfully for office, income, or position have violated God's law. If they invoke the State as their agent of coercion, they have sinned. The free market principle of "high bid wins" must be honored. *The right to bid for place is fundamental to biblical liberty*. Others must be allowed to buy their way into any non-covenantal hierarchy if access is for sale – and access is almost always for sale, although the terms may be unofficial and concealed.

In modern democracy, political incumbents establish new layers of bureaucracy and reinforce old layers in order to seal off outsiders from access to civil authority. The Italian theorist Robert Michels called this the iron law of oligarchy.[20] This sociological law may be iron-like, but any use of force to preserve the benefits of an oligarchy is biblically illegitimate. A society that allows such acts to become widespread and then endemic will eventually come under God's judgment in history. The nearly bloodless collapse of Communism's bureaucracies in the Union of Soviet Socialist Republics and its satellites, 1989 to 1991, is the most graphic display in modern history of the reality of this cause-and-effect relationship. Communism literally went bankrupt.[21] This economic bankruptcy after seven decades had caught up with Communism's theoretical bankruptcy,[22] which in turn had created moral bankruptcy.[23] The So-

---

20. Robert Michels, *Political Parties: A Sociological Study of Oligarchical Tendencies of Modern Democracy* (New York: Free Press, [1908] 1949).

21. Judy Shelton, *The Coming Soviet Crash: Gorbachev's Desperate Pursuit of Credit in Western Financial Markets* (New York: Free Press, 1989).

22. Gary North, *Marx's Religion of Revolution: Regeneration Through Chaos* (Tyler, Texas: Institute for Christian Economics, [1968] 1989).

23. Konstantin Simis, *USSR: The Corrupt Society: The Secret World of Soviet Capitalism* (New York: Simon & Schuster, 1982).

viet hierarchy, established by force,[24] collapsed. Or better put, its members found new ways of imposing force and surviving, but without the ideology of international Communism to justify the use of force.

The Inevitability of Hierarchy

Hierarchy is an inescapable concept, built into the creation through the dominion covenant: man's exercise of dominion over the creation. God acts through intermediaries. The husband exercises headship over his wife and children, for whom he is responsible. The general exercises authority over his troops, for whom he is responsible. Hierarchy is an outworking of representative responsibility: God holds leaders more responsible than followers for the outcome of events, even though followers, corporately, are the intermediate source of a leader's authority. Authority is distributed by God from the top down and from the bottom up simultaneously.[25] Nevertheless, God holds leaders more responsible than followers: with greater authority comes greater responsibility (Luke 12:47–48).

Hierarchy in Mosaic Israel was based on the sacrosanct yet limited extent of the sacred. The sacred did not encompass everything in Israel; on the contrary, it encompassed very little, and the narrow boundaries of sacred space were evidence of this. While ethical transgression was common, necessitating sacred sacrifices, profaning sacred boundaries was rare, for profanation was frequently fatal. It was rarely repeated by the same person. Fear of sacred space was widespread.

The fixed hierarchical boundaries of the Levites were tied to the fixed concentric structure of sacred boundaries. When these boundaries were annulled by the New Covenant, the old tribal

---

24. Michael Voslensky, *Nomenklatura: The Soviet Ruling Class* (Garden City, New York: Doubleday, 1984); Davis K. Willis, *KLASS: How Russians Really Live* (New York: St. Martin's, 1985).

25. North, *Leviticus*, ch. 4.

hierarchy was annulled with it. The torn veil of the temple pointed to the torn condition of tribal boundaries. The Mosaic priesthood ended, and with it, the tribal separations.

What the Bible denies is the legitimacy of judicially fixed hierarchies in non-covenantal institutions. The Bible does not promote equality. There is no equality in heaven (I Cor. 3:14), nor is there equality in hell (Luke 12:47–48). There is a bedrock individualism in biblical sociology because there is an inescapable individualism in final judgment. No person can transfer responsibility to another person and thereby escape the consequences of his actions (Gen. 3:12–13). Yet there is also a bedrock corporate element in biblical sociology: final judgment is announced to two great collectives: sheep and goats, saved and lost (Matt. 25).

I mention this because, as a late twentieth-century social theorist, I am well aware of the conflict between liberalism and conservatism, a conflict that cannot be mediated by radicalism. Conservative sociologist Robert Nisbet has described it well: "If the central ethos of liberalism is individual emancipation, and that of radicalism the expansion of political power in the service of social and moral zeal, the ethos of conservatism is tradition, essentially medieval tradition. From conservatism's defense of social tradition sprang its emphasis on the values of community, kinship, hierarchy, authority, and religion, and also its premonitions of social chaos surmounted by absolute power once individuals had become wrenched from the contexts of these values by the forces of liberalism and radicalism."[26] The twentieth century has seen the fruition of conservatism's fears: two world wars, Communism, Nazism, and the alienation and despair produced by individual moral debauchery. Yet we should not ignore an insight of the mischievous libertarian humorist, P.

---

26. Robert A. Nisbet, *The Sociological Tradition* (New York: Basic Books, 1966), p. 11.

J. O'Rourke. If you think the good old days were good, think of one word: dentistry.

In opposition to the individualism of liberalism, the collectivism of radicalism, and the traditionalism of conservatism, I offer biblical covenantalism: a sovereign God whose decree governs history, who has been revealed in history by the Bible and Jesus Christ, both called the word of God, who have announced God's unchanging standards. I proclaim God's predictable visible corporate sanctions in history, leading to the progressive triumph of His elect representatives in history. Covenantal social theory has a place for the conservative ideals of community (church), kinship (family), hierarchy, and authority. But it also has a place for the liberal ideals of individualism, progress, science, peaceful political change (democracy), and economic growth. What is needed today, and will be needed in a thousand years, is a theoretically coherent and practical integration of these ideals which preserves personal liberty without sacrificing the bonds of community, and also preserves sufficient political power to repel military invaders and suppress domestic disturbers of the peace. Without sanctions, there is no hierarchy; there is only opinion. Point four and point two of the biblical covenant model are intimately linked.

Conclusion

The hierarchy of sacred service in Mosaic Israel involved a hierarchy of authority. The high priest was at the pinnacle of this hierarchy. He had far greater responsibility than those under him. Below him came the sons of Aaron. Then came the other Levites: Kohath, Gershon, and Merari. Below them came the other tribes. The closer that a man's service came to the Ark of the Covenant, the more dangerous it was. This system of geographical holiness kept each man in his place. As a man approached Israel's central holy place, he in effect approached God's holy mountain, and like Mt. Sinai, where God met with Moses to establish the covenant and deliver the law, it was a capital offense for insufficiently holy Israelites to cross its boundary (Ex. 19:12–13).

Participants in Israel's holy commonwealth knew that they could not operate alone. They knew also that services had to be paid for. There were no free lunches in Israel, although the presence of the manna in the Ark at the very center of the nation testified that there had been partially subsidized lunches in the wilderness. The curse of the ground had been removed for a season.

There was no possibility of equality in Israel; the society was hierarchical. The closer to the Ark that a man operated lawfully, the greater his sacerdotal authority and responsibility, and also the greater his economic dependance on the economic success of others and their obedience to the law. While the high priest in Israel would probably never go hungry, he risked God's sanctions every time he performed a mandated ritual. The fiery testimony of Nadab and Abihu was sufficient warning. No one could lawfully trade places with him, and no one who wanted to live would have tried.

Priestly service was governed by the workshop rule: a place for everything, and everything in its place. But the farther away from the holy of holies, the less that Israel was governed by this narrowly circumscribed law. The office of high priest was unique. There could only be one high priest at a time. The farther away from the Ark, the less that any man had a specific mandated service or required place. Put differently, priestly service is judicially more specific than non-priestly service.

Let us consider the most successful of all the non-biblical systems of sacred hierarchy in man's history: Hinduism. The Hindu system of permanent religious castes is the product of a religious worldview that extends the principle of priestly service to all of life. A man born into one caste cannot advance himself or his family if such advancement is dependent upon his performing services that are monopolies of another caste. Social stagnation in Hindu society is correlative to its vision of the proper maintenance of religious tradition, even to the point of denying the cosmic reality of linear change.

Life is religious. It is also judicially protected by God. There is a right to life under God's law, but this is not a sacred right, for life is not a sacred rite. To argue otherwise is to move in the direction of Hinduism's caste society.

By confining sacred service within narrow geographical and tribal boundaries, God opened Mosaic society to the possibility of upward social mobility and progress. Sacred hierarchy there was, but it was tightly bounded, both for its own protection and the protection of the society around it.

4

THE FIRSTBORN AND NEGATIVE ECONOMIC SANCTIONS

And the Lord *spake unto Moses, saying, And I, behold, I have taken the Levites from among the children of Israel instead of all the firstborn that openeth the matrix among the children of Israel: therefore the Levites shall be mine; Because all the firstborn are mine; for on the day that I smote all the firstborn in the land of Egypt I hallowed unto me all the firstborn in Israel, both man and beast: mine shall they be: I am the* Lord *(Num. 3:11–13).*

The theocentric focus of this law is God's ownership. This passage announced God's unique proprietary claim on the Levites because of their position as the sacrificial substitutes for the firstborn sons of Israel. As Creator, God owns everything, but He established here a special claim on the firstborn, including animals. This special claim had its origin in God's execution of the firstborn sons of Egypt.

God hallowed (*kawdash*) the firstborn. The Hebrew word *kawdash* means holy or sanctified. The word is also used with respect to the sabbath. "And God blessed the seventh day, and sanctified [*kawdash*] it: because that in it he had rested from all his work which God created and made" (Gen. 2:3). "Remember the sabbath day, to keep [*kawdash*] it holy [*kawdash*]" (Ex. 20:8).

"For in six days the LORD made heaven and earth, the sea, and all that in them is, and rested the seventh day: wherefore the LORD blessed the sabbath day, and hallowed [*kawdash*] it" (Ex. 20:11). The word means *set apart*. God is the Lord of each day of the week (general claim), yet He has set apart one day as His special holy day (special claim). There are six common days and one holy day. This distinction between common and holy applied to the Levites' position among the tribes of Mosaic Israel. The law of the firstborn's redemption appears immediately prior to the law of the sabbath (Ex. 34:20–21).

Firstborn Sons

Did *firstborn* refer only to a son? Both text and context indicate that it did. First, in relationship to covenantal inheritance, God designated the nation of Israel as His firstborn son. God told Moses: "And thou shalt say unto Pharaoh, Thus saith the LORD, Israel is my son, even my firstborn: And I say unto thee, Let my son go, that he may serve me: and if thou refuse to let him go, behold, I will slay thy son, even thy firstborn" (Ex. 4:22–23).

Second, the subsequent system of sacrifice mandated sacrifices for firstborn sons, not daughters. "But the firstling of an ass thou shalt redeem with a lamb: and if thou redeem him not, then shalt thou break his neck. All the firstborn of thy *sons* thou shalt redeem. And none shall appear before me empty" (Ex. 34:20; emphasis added). The interpretation of biblical passages that are less specific should be governed by passages that are more specific. This one is less specific: "Sanctify unto me all the firstborn, whatsoever openeth the womb among the children of Israel, both of man and of beast: it is mine" (Ex. 13:2). This one is more specific: the Israelite father's words to his inquiring son. "And it came to pass, when Pharaoh would hardly let us go, that the LORD slew all the firstborn in the land of Egypt, both the firstborn of man, and the firstborn of beast: therefore I sacrifice to the LORD all that openeth the matrix, *being males*; but all the firstborn of my children I redeem" (Ex. 13:15; emphasis added). The father acts as God did: slaying firstborn male animals (reflecting Egypt's loss) and redeeming his firstborn son (reflecting Israel's gain).

Third, when requiring the substitution of Levites for first-born Israelites, God specified firstborn sons: "And the LORD said unto Moses, Number all the firstborn of the males of the children of Israel from a month old and upward, and take the number of their names" (Num. 3:40). When the sex of the firstborn child is not specified, the Bible assumes the child is masculine: "And it shall be, that the firstborn which she beareth shall succeed in the name of his *brother* which is dead, that his name be not put out of Israel" (Deut. 25:6; emphasis added). This is how the Book of Nehemiah interpreted firstborn: "Also the firstborn of our sons, and of our cattle, as it is written in the law, and the firstlings of our herds and of our flocks, to bring to the house of our God, unto the priests that minister in the house of our God" (Neh. 10:36).

Fourth, when the judgment came on Egypt, it was a judgment against the nation's strength: "He smote also all the first-born in their land, the chief of all their strength" (Ps. 105:36). This corresponds to Jacob's identification of firstborn Reuben as his might, strength, and power (Gen. 49:3). This was what made David's position unique: the eighth son of Jesse was the heir who became the strong man and king (I Sam. 17:12, 14).

Fifth, prior to the substitution of the Levites for the firstborn sons of the other tribes, the nature of the redemption system was unstated. "Thou shalt not delay to offer the first of thy ripe fruits, and of thy liquors [vintage]: the firstborn of thy sons shalt thou give unto me" (Ex. 22:29). This involved some sort of formal dedication, but God did not say what this dedication was. This law pointed to the nation's need of a system of re-demption, but it did not offer specifics. Israelites were to look forward to the establishment of a redemption system; until then, they were mentally to set apart their firstborn sons. Having set apart (made holy) their firstborn sons, the parents had to wait upon God to tell them what to do next, just as Abraham had to wait upon God for further details in the sacrifice of Isaac. They were to set apart their firstborn; then they were to wait for God to tell them what to do next. But they were not willing to wait on God; instead, they "rose up to play" (Ex. 32:6). In response, God had Levi impose the negative sanction of death on their representatives (Ex. 32:28).

Sixth, only firstborn sons were entitled to a double inheritance (Deut. 21:15–17). There was no similar provision for firstborn daughters when all of the children were girls. Daughters in such a household had a right of landed inheritance in Israel, so long as they did not marry outside their tribe (Num. 36). But the absence of any reference to double inheritance indicates that the double portion was related to the extension of a man's name and strength in Israel. Not being entitled to the unique covenantal blessing, the firstborn daughter was not under the unique covenantal burden.

Passover, Sanctions, and Succession

God said, "for on the day that I smote all the firstborn in the land of Egypt I hallowed unto me all the firstborn in Israel, both man and beast: mine shall they be: I am the LORD" (v. 13). Something had happened on the first Passover night to change the previous legal relationship between God and the firstborn. The question is: What?

The firstborn prior to the first Passover had been exclusively a positive sanction from God. The firstborn was entitled to a special blessing from his father, which is why Jacob deceived Isaac regarding his identity: he wanted the blessing that would have gone to Esau (Gen. 27:19), had God not revealed to Rebekah that Jacob was the chosen son (Gen. 25:23), and had not Esau sold his birthright to Jacob (Gen. 25:33). The firstborn was the extension of the father's might, dignity, and power. The firstborn was God's sign that through succession, the father's name and rule would extend into the future. After the Passover, however, there was a negative sanction associated with the firstborn, both of sons and male animals. "And the LORD spake unto Moses, saying, Sanctify unto me all the firstborn, whatsoever openeth the womb among the children of Israel, both of man and of beast: it is mine" (Ex. 13:1–2). Why was there the imposition of a negative economic sanction?

This had something to do with the judicially representative character of the firstborn. The firstborn represented the future: a family's future and, corporately, a nation's future. God placed a unique claim on this inheritance after the death of the firstborn of Egypt. He called the firstborn *His*. He did not limit this to humans; it included the animals, too. To enforce His claim of ownership after the first Passover, God imposed a system of negative sanctions. As we shall see, clean animals had to be slain, unclean animals redeemed with a money payment, and sons redeemed with a money payment.

Sanctions and Inheritance

No Egyptian family escaped the negative sanction of the death of the firstborn (Ex. 12:29–30). When Israel departed, the Israelites took with them much of the wealth of Egypt (Ex. 12:35).[1] All the firstborn sons of Egypt were dead. Israel, God's firstborn son, therefore inherited what would have been the inheritance of the firstborn Egyptians. This transfer of inheritance, family by family, was the result of God's negative sanctions against the original heirs. The spoils of Egypt repaid Israel for decades of slavery – the kidnapping of God's firstborn – but in a unique form: wealth gained as a direct result of the death of the firstborn sons of Egypt. What is important here is the link between negative sanctions – the death of Egypt's firstborn – and disinheritance. God's provision of an inheritance for

1. This wealth was sufficient to enable 600,000 men to pay the half shekel of silver three times in the wilderness.

Israel (positive) was based on His disinheritance of Egypt (negative). The historical means of Egypt's disinheritance was the death of Egypt's firstborn. In short, the sanction of death was the historic basis of the subsequent disinheritance-inheritance. This covenantal process of sanctions/inheritance-disinheritance was to be repeated in the conquest of Canaan a generation later.

The Mosaic penalty for kidnapping was death: "And he that stealeth a man, and selleth him, or if he be found in his hand, he shall surely be put to death" (Ex. 21:16). God found His son in the hands of the representative agent of the kidnappers: Pharaoh. Pharaoh's accomplices were given an opportunity to renounce the crime and escape bloodguilt by placing the blood of a lamb on their doorposts, but no Egyptian family complied. This led to the comprehensive disinheritance of Egypt: "And it came to pass, that at midnight the LORD smote all the firstborn in the land of Egypt, from the firstborn of Pharaoh that sat on his throne unto the firstborn of the captive that was in the dungeon; and all the firstborn of cattle" (Ex. 12:29).

The Passover was required of the Israelites to remind them of the night in which God's wrath passed over the families of Israel. The shedding of a lamb's blood had protected each family. But Israel was not to forget the negative sanction imposed on Egypt: "That ye shall say, It is the sacrifice of the LORD'S passover, who passed over the houses of the children of Israel in Egypt, when he smote the Egyptians, and delivered our houses. And the people bowed the head and worshipped" (Ex. 12:27). The positive sanction of national deliverance was accomplished through the negative sanction of corporate execution. The shedding of blood preceded this deliverance: the shedding of the lambs' blood. Either a lamb's blood was shed or else the firstborn son perished in the households of Israel and Egypt.[2]

---

2. I do not think lambs' blood was necessarily mandatory for the non-Egyptian,

At the first Passover, firstborn sons became uniquely representative of the future: the future of Egypt and the future of Israel. So representative was the firstborn son at the first Passover that he died unless he had a blood covering: firstborn animals and firstborn sons. The Passover brought the imposition of a negative sanction: death. The outcome of this sanction determined succession and inheritance in Egypt: the Egyptians' second-born sons (if any) were disinherited by the departing Israelites. This indicates that point four of the biblical covenant model – sanctions – is judicially bound up with point five: succession.

Firstborn Rites

Immediately following the recapitulation of the law of the Passover (Ex. 13:3–10), we read:

> And it shall be when the LORD shall bring thee into the land of the Canaanites, as he sware unto thee and to thy fathers, and shall give it thee, That thou shalt set apart unto the LORD all that openeth the matrix, and every firstling that cometh of a beast which thou hast; the males shall be the LORD'S. And every firstling of an ass thou shalt redeem with a lamb; and if thou wilt not redeem it, then thou shalt break his neck: and all the firstborn of man among thy children shalt thou redeem. And it shall be when thy son asketh thee in time to come, saying, What is this? that thou shalt say unto him, By strength of hand the LORD brought us out from Egypt, from the house of bondage: And it came to pass, when Pharaoh would hardly let us go, that the LORD slew all the firstborn in the land of Egypt, both the firstborn of man, and the firstborn of beast: therefore I sacrifice to the LORD all that openeth the matrix, being males; but all the firstborn of my children I redeem. And it shall be for a token upon thine hand, and for frontlets between thine eyes: for by strength of hand the LORD brought us forth out of Egypt (Ex. 13:11–16).

---

non-Israelite slaves. See Appendix, below: pp. 362–63.

As in the case of the Passover, they were to do this as a means of instructing each generation in the story of their deliverance from Egypt. Firstborn animals were either to be slain or redeemed with money. Leviticus 27 specified that the firstborn of clean animals had to be sacrificed: ". . . no man shall sanctify it; whether it be ox, or sheep: it is the LORD'S" (v. 26b). That meant that it had to die. The firstborn of an unclean animal had to be redeemed by paying their market value plus one-fifth (v. 27).

The one exception was the donkey: it had to be slain by breaking its neck, or else it could be redeemed by the sacrifice of a lamb. We shall consider the reason for this exception later in this chapter. The donkey and the horse were unclean animals. They had hooves, but these hooves were not cloven. To be a clean beast with hooves, it had to have cloven hooves and also chew the cud (Lev. 11:3–7). Horses were comparatively rare in Israel; the donkey was the commonly used beast of transport for man.

As in the case of the Passover feast (Ex. 12:26–27), sons were expected to ask what the meaning of this practice was. The meaning here was the same as the meaning of Passover: 1) the family's deliverance (positive sanction) through the shedding of a lamb's blood (negative sanction); 2) collecting the inheritance of Egypt (positive sanction) through the death of Egypt's firstborn (negative sanction).

As already mentioned, unclean animals were not to be killed; they were instead redeemed by a payment. "Every thing that openeth the matrix in all flesh, which they bring unto the LORD, whether it be of men or beasts, shall be thine: nevertheless the firstborn of man shalt thou surely redeem, and the firstling of unclean beasts shalt thou redeem" (Num. 18:15). A money payment had to be substituted for Israelite firstborn males and unclean animals. Was the link here based on Israelite firstborn as judicially unclean? No, but they, like unclean beasts, were not eligible to serve as literal sacrifices. So, a substitute payment was mandatory. After the rebellion of the golden calf incident, the required sacrifice was specified by God as economic. It had not been specified prior to this incident.

The firstborn son, who before the revolt was the son who extended the father's strength, became an economic liability compared to his brothers. The rejoicing of fathers was reduced by the expense of this sacrifice. God had delivered His firstborn son on the night of the first Passover. After the rebellion at Sinai, something associated retroactively with the deliverance from Egypt led to God's imposition of a cost associated with the firstborn.[3] The close association of this law with the Passover regulations (Ex. 13:2–3) pointed to the Passover as the definitive event.

The Levites as Substitutes

When Israel in the wilderness abandoned the God of their deliverance and pressured Aaron to construct a golden calf, the nation allied itself spiritually with a false god. The Levites subsequently came to the defense of God's name by joining Moses in imposing the sanction of blood. They executed 3,000 men (Ex. 32:28). This became the basis of their blessing from God: "For Moses had said, Consecrate yourselves to day to the LORD, even every man upon his son, and upon his brother; that he may bestow upon you a blessing this day" (Ex. 32:29). Their deliverance from the curse of Jacob (Gen. 49:7) was made possible by their participation in the shedding of blood. The 3,000 executions were representative sacrifices that placated God's wrath against the nation. The Levites became the nation's priestly tribe because of their willingness to participate in what

3. This points to a fundamental biblical principle: God must sacrifice something when He delivers His people. He sacrifices what Abraham was asked to sacrifice: His son. Abraham was offered a substitute to save his son: a ram (Gen. 22:13). Israel on Passover night was offered a substitute to save a firstborn son: a lamb. These substitutions were possible only because God did not substitute a lesser sacrifice for His son.

was in part an atoning sacrifice and in part a defense of God's name.

They gained a unique inheritance because of this. They would henceforth receive redemption money from the other tribes. This substitute payment benefitted the other tribes, who were released from an obligation that would otherwise have bound firstborn sons. The theological debate is over what that obligation was, as we shall see. What is clear is that the Levites did not pay this redemption money to themselves or to the priests, since they had been chosen by God to serve Him as representatives of the nation. They did not make a substitute payment, for they had become the substitute payment.

Firstborn Sons as Sacrifices

The Levites became the priestly tribe after the golden calf incident. They also became substitutes for the firstborn sons. The question is: Why did the firstborn sons need substitutes? The traditional Jewish answer is that firstborn sons would have had to become priests if the Levites had not replaced them. Rashi,[4] the eleventh-century commentator, argued along these lines.[5] Samson Raphael Hirsch, the intellectual founder of what in his day came to be called Orthodox Judaism, wrote in the nineteenth century: "By the transference of the service of the Sanctuary from the firstborn to the Levites, the consecration of the firstborn is not removed. They remain, unaffected by the transference, consecrated to God."[6]

The problem with this argument is that the context does not indicate sacrifice in the sense of personal service to God. The context indicates sacrifice in the sense of execution. The first-

4. Rabbi Solomon (Shlomo) Yizchaki.

5. Rashi, *Chumash with Targum Onkelos, Haphtaroth and Rashi's Commentary*, A. M. Silbermann and M. Rosenbaum, translators, 5 vols. (Jerusalem: Silbermann Family, [1934] 1985 [Jewish year: 5745]), IV, p. 11 (Num. 3:12–15).

6. Samson Raphael Hirsch, *The Pentateuch*, 5 vols. (Gateshead, London: Judaica Press, [1875?] 1989), IV, *Numbers*, p. 29 (Num. 3:13).

born animals were not given to the priests for their use; on the contrary, they were either killed or redeemed. Unclean animals had to be redeemed with money. Why? Because they could not serve as sacrificial substitutes.

There is nothing in the texts governing the firstborn to indicate that the firstborn son had some unique claim on priestly service. The Bible never says that a firstborn son under the Old Covenant would automatically have become a family priest in the household of his father. Both Cain and Abel offered priestly sacrifices, not just Cain (Gen. 4:3–4). By the time a man reached 30 years old, the age of Mosaic priestly service (Num. 4:47), he would probably have been the head of his own family.

Someone had to serve as a priest, but this office was not said to be a monopoly of firstborn sons. Prior to the golden calf incident, Moses used young men of Israel as assistants: "And Moses wrote all the words of the LORD, and rose up early in the morning, and builded an altar under the hill, and twelve pillars, according to the twelve tribes of Israel. And he sent young men of the children of Israel, which offered burnt offerings, and sacrificed peace offerings of oxen unto the LORD" (Ex. 24:4–5). Non-Levites originally had duties associated with offering sacrifices.

The rabbis are correct about one thing: the firstborn sons were indeed consecrated by God. They were consecrated in the same way that firstborn sons in Egypt had been consecrated: as *covenantal representatives of the nation's future*. The mark of their unique status was their inheritance of a double portion. Their judicially consecrated status became an enormous threat to them at the golden calf incident. Because of the rebellion of their parents, the firstborn sons of Israel became the judicial equivalent of the firstborn sons of Egypt: under a curse. These sons were in need of another blood atonement: the judicial equivalent of Passover lambs.

God substituted others in order to save the firstborn sons: 3,000 of their fathers. The Levites served as the priests in this atoning sacrifice. *They slew 3,000 men, who became the judicial equivalent of Passover lambs.* The Levites became executioners because the men had become idolaters, just as the Egyptians had been. Had the Levites not acted to execute 3,000 representatives of Israel, God would have slain the firstborn sons. The firstborn sons of Israel, apart from the bloody service of the Levites, were as deserving of death as the firstborn sons of Egypt had been. God substituted the Levites and the redemption payment system, not for the sake of some hypothetical, God-consecrated priestly role for Israel's firstborn, but for the sake of *the firstborn sons' judicial status as condemned representatives of the nation's future*: point four of the biblical covenant – sanctions – in relation to point five, succession.

As in the case of Egypt, Israel's inheritance would have been cut off had God imposed this negative sanction. If the Israelites on the pre-adoption Passover night were in replacement-rate mode, then the future of the nation would have been completely cut short apart from a program of adoption. Only daughters would have remained. They would have had to marry adopted sons of the mixed multitude. But more to the point covenantally, the destruction of firstborn sons would have left the Ark of the Covenant undefended in the next generation.

Bloodless Execution

A redemption payment was mandatory for the firstborn sons. It was also mandatory for unclean animals. The exceptional case was the donkey. Here, the owner had a choice: *break its neck or redeem it with a slain lamb.* This is repeated twice in Exodus. "And every firstling of an ass thou shalt redeem with a lamb; and if thou wilt not redeem it, then thou shalt break his neck: and all the firstborn of man among thy children shalt thou redeem" (Ex. 13:13). "But the firstling of an ass thou shalt redeem with a lamb: and if thou redeem him not, then shalt thou break his neck. All the firstborn of thy sons thou shalt redeem. And none shall appear before me empty" (Ex. 34:20).

What was the reason for the link between a redemption payment for donkeys and men?

First, consider the fact that the donkey had to be killed in a special way: a broken neck. No other sacrifice in the Mosaic Covenant was by broken neck. What was the relevance of a broken neck? *It was execution without bloodshed.* Every other animal sacrifice involved the knife. The sacrificed animal's blood was used in the ceremony as a sign of atonement. But this animal sacrifice was unique: no blood. It was therefore not a means of atonement. It was a sacrifice strictly in the sense of an economic loss.

Second, this law was given prior to the Mosaic dietary laws. But there was an earlier dietary law in force. If an animal remained in a bloodless condition, its carcass became valueless; its flesh could not be eaten. *No animal could be eaten lawfully with its blood still in it.* The context of this dietary law was God's covenant with Noah – specifically, the provision dealing with the killing of men. "But flesh with the life thereof, which is the blood thereof, shall ye not eat. And surely your blood of your lives will I require; at the hand of every beast will I require it, and at the hand of man; at the hand of every man's brother will I require the life of man. Whoso sheddeth man's blood, by man shall his blood be shed: for in the image of God made he man" (Gen. 9:4–6). So, the sacrifice of the firstborn donkey was exclusively a negative economic sanction. Neither the owner nor the priest could eat it or use its carcass if it remained in an uncut state. The implication was that it could not be skinned after its death, for it was to be killed with its blood intact.

Third, the substitute for the firstborn donkey was a lamb. *This is the only case in the Mosaic law of an animal's substituting for the firstborn.* Clean animals had to be slain; firstborn sons had to be redeemed by a payment of five shekels; unclean animals had to be redeemed by a money payment of its market value plus one-fifth – the payment associated with the Levitical redemption payments.[7] But the donkey was unique: its redemption required the sacrifice of a lamb.

Fourth, the sacrifice of the donkey was *symbolic of the Passover* in two ways. First, the death of the firstborn sons of Egypt was bloodless. God executed them directly without the use of any implement. This was not a ritual execution in the normal sacrificial sense, for there had been no knife. It was also not warfare in the traditional sense, for there had been no weapons. It was uniquely the intervention of God. Second, without the covering of a lamb's blood on the doorposts, the firstborn of Egypt perished. But so would the firstborn of Israel. The life of the firstborn sons of Israel on the Passover night in Egypt was spared only by shedding a lamb's blood.

Fifth, *the slain lamb could be eaten by the priest*. This substitution converted an unmitigated economic loss (slain donkey) into a benefit for the priest (slain lamb).

All this leads me to a conclusion. *Any firstborn son who was not redeemed by a money payment was considered to be the judicial equivalent of a donkey with a broken neck*. But the firstborn Egyptians had also been the judicial equivalent of donkeys with broken necks: bloodless victims of God's wrath. This symbolism pointed to an unredeemed firstborn son as the judicial equivalent of a firstborn Egyptian: under God's wrath. He would therefore not have been entitled to be circumcised. He would have become a *disinherited son*. If his father circumcised him anyway, the son would thereby have been placed under the negative sanctions of the covenant. He would then have had his ecclesiastical membership taken away: excommunication. This would have left him without citizenship in Israel.[8] He would not have been allowed to inherit his share of his father's land – the double portion (Deut. 21:17).

---

7. Leviticus 5:16; 6:5; 27:9–15, 19, 27, 31.

8. Gary North, *Tools of Dominion: The Case Laws of Exodus* (Tyler, Texas: Institute for Christian Economics, 1990), pp. 841–45.

The Firstborn Sons of Levi

The firstborn son received a special inheritance (Deut. 21: 17). The presence of such an inheritance is what identified the recipient as a firstborn son. Because of their firstborn legal status, the Levites were entitled to payments from the other tribes for every firstborn son (Num. 3:47). Because of their firstborn legal status as God's firstborn (Ex. 4:22), the Israelites were entitled to restitution payments for their forced servitude in Egypt, which they collected from inheritances that would otherwise have gone to the dead firstborn sons of Egypt (Ex. 12:35–36). It is in this context that we should interpret Numbers 5:5–8:

> And the LORD spake unto Moses, saying, Speak unto the children of Israel, When a man or woman shall commit any sin that men commit, to do a trespass against the LORD, and that person be guilty; Then they shall confess their sin which they have done: and he shall recompense his trespass with the principal thereof, and add unto it the fifth part thereof, and give it unto him against whom he hath trespassed. But if the man have no kinsman to recompense the trespass unto, let the trespass be recompensed unto the LORD, even to the priest; beside the ram of the atonement, whereby an atonement shall be made for him.

This law was an extension of the law of restitution found in Leviticus 6:5. It was a law that penalized sin by requiring a restitution payment of 20 percent. But it also rewarded voluntary confession, since the penalty for theft was normally double restitution (Ex. 22:4), and could be four-fold (dead or sold sheep) or five-fold (dead or sold ox) (Ex. 22:1).[9]

This extension of the law specified the priest as the final claimant to both the replacement and restitution payments. If the victim could not be located or was dead, then his relative would receive the payment. If the relative could not be located,

---

9. Gary North, *Leviticus: An Economic Commentary* (Tyler, Texas: Institute for Christian Economics, 1994), ch. 6.

then the priest received it. There was no escape from the trespasser's liability. By identifying the priest as a person with a final claim on the property, the Mosaic law made clear the legal status of the priests: God's firstborn sons among the Levites. *Their responsibility before God was greater than that of any other judicially representative group in Israel.*[10]

There is no New Covenant principle that would remove this firstborn legal status of the institutional church. As the guardian of the civil oath, the institutional church still performs a judicial function of the Mosaic priesthood. It is this function that entitles the church to payments from convicted criminals.[11]

Monetary Policy

In Numbers, God specified the firstborn son's redemption price: five shekels of the sanctuary (Num. 3:47). Five shekels of silver was also the entry price for a male child adopted into the tribe of Levi (Lev. 27:6).[12] Because the judicial intent in both cases was related to Levitical inheritance, the shekels must have been of the same value.

A currency unit could be called a shekel, but the priestly shekel was mandatory for making payments to God's ecclesiastical agents. In times of widespread monetary debasement (Isa. 1:22), God could not be lawfully cheated by those who would have offered a shekel of lower value, even if both currency units were called "shekel." It would have been a profane act to offer such a debased payment to the Levites.[13] Every time the shekel of the sanctuary is mentioned, the text says that it weighs 20 gerahs.[14] This informed the nation what the sanctuary's shekel weighed. People could then compare the market's shekel

10. *Ibid.*, ch. 4, section on "The Priestly Office."

11. *Ibid.*, ch. 6.

12. On the entry price system, see *ibid.*, ch. 36.

13. This would explain the presence of money-changers in the temple area (John 2:14–15).

14. Exodus 30:13; Leviticus 27:25; Numbers 3:47; 18:16; Ezekiel 45:12.

with the sanctuary shekel. This would keep the moneychangers more honest. The priesthood also would have greater difficulty debasing their shekel. If this judicial connection is correct, then the priestly shekel was originally intended by God to become the standard for the weight and fineness of silver for the other currency units specified as shekels.

Conclusion

God's slaying of Egypt's firstborn identified Him as the nation's blood avenger – the kinsman-redeemer – on their behalf. Only a slain lamb would have protected the Egyptians. God executed the firstborn of Egypt in a bloodless manner, just as Israelites were subsequently required to kill every firstborn donkey that they chose not to redeem with a slain lamb. The firstborn male donkey was symbolic of the firstborn sons in Egypt, whether Egyptian or Israelite. Only the shed blood of a lamb could save them.

The Israelites owed the Levites payment because the Levites had shed blood on their behalf. The Levites had saved Israel from the judgment of God (Ex. 32). God separated them from the other tribes because they were His agents of wrath as well as His agents of sacrificial substitution: blood avengers and kinsman-redeemers. They were the agents of sacrifice, both as recipients of the sacrificial funds and as guardians of the place of sacrifice. They were holy.

God brought sanctions on Passover night: positive for Israel and negative for Egypt. This changed the judicial status of firstborn sons in Israel. Before the first Passover night, the birth of the firstborn son was exclusively a positive event: the extension of a man's strength. After the first Passover night, the firstborn sons of Israel were set apart by God. They were His. They were His, not in the sense of priestly servants, but in the sense of being destined for execution, yet unfit as altar sacrifices. This was the symbolic negative sanction hanging over the head of every family: the threat of disinheritance by execution.

To save the firstborn son's double inheritance after the golden calf incident, each family had to redeem the firstborn son with a payment of five shekels to the Levites. Without this, the firstborn son forfeited his inheritance in Israel: a mark of God's curse on the family. This law was imposed only after the construction of the tabernacle. This sanctified the Levites as permanent substitutes for the firstborn sons.

The specification of five shekels of silver paid to the Levites as the Levitical adoption entry price, as well as the redemption price for firstborn sons, indicates that the shekel of the sanctuary was to serve as a standard for Israel's money payment system. The five shekels referred to silver. Any debasing of the currency would be detected. The shekel of the sanctuary was to remain a monetary standard that was free from political control. This unit of exchange was not to be tampered with by the priests; thus, it would condemn any other currency that was called a shekel but which did not contain 20 gerahs of silver.

The New Covenant has substituted baptism for circumcision. There is no longer any difference between sons and daughters with respect to their required subjection to a covenant sign. The annulment of Passover and the transfer of covenantal sanctions to the Lord's Supper ended the judicial discontinuity in Israel's history that Passover imposed on Israel. This law was unique to Mosaic Israel. The unique covenantal threat to firstborn sons no longer exists.

5

BLESSING AND NAMING

And the LORD *spake unto Moses, saying, Speak unto Aaron and unto his sons, saying, On this wise [in this way] ye shall bless the children of Israel, saying unto them, The* LORD *bless thee, and keep thee: The* LORD *make his face shine upon thee, and be gracious unto thee: The* LORD *lift up his countenance upon thee, and give thee peace. And they shall put my name upon the children of Israel; and I will bless them (Num. 6:22–27).*

The theocentric focus of this law is obvious: God is the source of predictable covenantal blessings in history, i.e., positive sanctions. The Israelites were required to accept God's name as marking their family status among the nations: God's firstborn son (Ex. 4:22–23). Aaron and his sons publicly placed (invoked: NASB) God's name on the people of Israel. This invocation of the blessing was linked to their authority to invoke God's name on the sons of Israel. If the people remained faithful to God's covenant law, they would receive the positive sanctions that God promised to bring upon them (Lev. 26:3–12). Naming them placed them formally under the sanctions.

The sanctions listed here were positive. The specific one was peace (v. 26). This was the exodus generation's number-one goal. They did not want to fight. They wanted peace. God told them how to attain it: not by avoiding the conquest of Canaan but by avoiding evil. They viewed peace as the absence of negative sanctions. This was wrong. *Peace is the extension of God's kingdom in history*. "For unto us a child is born, unto us a son is given: and the government shall be upon his shoulder: and his name shall be called Wonderful, Counsellor, The mighty God, The everlasting Father, The Prince of Peace. Of the increase of his government and peace there shall be no end, upon the throne of David, and upon his kingdom, to order it, and to establish it with judgment and with justice from henceforth even for ever. The zeal of the LORD of hosts will perform this" (Isa. 9:6–7). Peace therefore necessarily involves *the imposition of negative sanctions on evil*: Satan's kingdom of man.

Peace with God comes through covenantal faithfulness. By explicitly invoking positive sanctions, the priests were implicitly also invoking negative sanctions. Presumably, the main one was war: the absence of peace for God's enemies. There is no escape from the two-fold nature of God's covenantal sanctions. To place yourself under His blessings, you must also place yourself under His cursings. Both blessing and cursing come in terms of His law (Lev. 26; Deut. 28).

The sanction of peace was visible. It was important for this sanction to be universally respected and sought after, for it was to serve as a testimony to pagan nations. The Psalmist wrote: "God be merciful unto us, and bless us; and cause his face to shine upon us; Selah. That thy way may be known upon earth, thy saving health among all nations. Let the people praise thee, O God; let all the people praise thee. O let the nations be glad and sing for joy: for thou shalt judge the people righteously, and govern the nations upon earth. Selah" (Ps. 67:1–4). The positive covenantal sanction – "saving health" or "salvation" (*yeshuw'ah*) – was to remind men of the reality of God's covenantal stipulations: "thy way." God judges the nations of the earth; they are all bound by the cross-boundary stipulations[1] of His covenant; He brings predictable corporate sanctions in terms of these stipulations.

Who was under God's special covenantal sanctions, as distinguished from His common-grace, cross-boundary sanctions (e.g., Nineveh in Jonah's day)? That person who was under oath-bound covenantal authority and who therefore bore God's name. Who invoked the name of God and the name of the person? The sons of Aaron and those with priestly authority who were operating under their jurisdiction. Had their invocation of God's blessings not been followed by covenantal blessings, this would have called into question their authority to name the people. This is why one sign of forfeited authority by the priesthood was the failure of the blessings to appear. This surely was what the drought in Elijah's day was all about: the failure of the gods invoked by the priests of Ahab's Israel to bring corporate blessings.

Why did these blessings have to be invoked publicly by the sons of Aaron? First, because Aaron's sons were the guardians of the four covenantal oaths of society: marital (Num. 5), personal (Num. 6), civil,[2] and ecclesiastical. Second, they were God's highest judicial representatives between God and man, which is why they conducted the altar's sacrifices, and why their family representative, the high priest, alone had lawful access to the inner sanctum of the tabernacle: the holy of holies (Ex. 30:10). As such, they interpreted God's word authoritatively. The ordained representatives of a society serve as the interpreters of the law. They possess lawful authority to enforce the law. Enforcement involves the imposition of sanctions. Without sanctions, their interpretations are mere opinion.

---

1. On cross-boundary laws, see Gary North, *Leviticus: An Economic Commentary* (Tyler, Texas: Institute for Christian Economics, 1994), pp. 643–45.

2. *Ibid.*, ch. 6: "Guardian of the Civil Oath."

Sanctions and Law

The sons of Aaron could lawfully invoke God's positive covenantal sanctions in history because they possessed priestly authority. The biblical State lawfully imposes only negative sanctions. It bears the sword, but it is not a God-designated agency of healing.[3] The church, however, is an agency of positive sanctions. It does not possess the sword; it cannot lawfully impose punishment on all those living within specified geographical boundaries. It cannot lawfully impose physical punishment. It imposes its judgments judicially and verbally: speaking in God's name as His agent.

Here is a fundamental judicial principle: *no sanctions–no law.* If the State cannot lawfully impose sanctions on those who have violated a civil law, then this law is nothing more than one opinion among many. It is not a civil law.

He who speaks officially in the name of the law must be able either to impose or invoke predictable sanctions in terms of this law. If he cannot do this, then his authority is compromised. If there are no sanctions attached to his interpretation of the law, then his authority is specious. He is not to be taken seriously as a representative; at best he is an insightful commentator.

Invocation is verbal. The invocation calls forth God's sanctions, either in history or eternity. If God has not authorized this invocation, then the invoker is either a charlatan or very confused about his authority in this instance. We can see this most clearly in the two Mosaic laws governing prophets.

If there arise among you a prophet, or a dreamer of dreams, and giveth thee a sign or a wonder, And the sign or the wonder come to pass, whereof he spake unto thee, saying, Let us go after other gods,

3. A State that claims the right to impose positive sanctions has become messianic. Its healing comes from its exercise of monopolistic power: the sword and wealth collected by means of the sword. The messiah's healing power does not come from confiscated wealth. This is why the messianic State is a pretender. It exercises power in the name of healing through coercion.

which thou hast not known, and let us serve them; Thou shalt not hearken unto the words of that prophet, or that dreamer of dreams: for the LORD your God proveth you, to know whether ye love the LORD your God with all your heart and with all your soul. Ye shall walk after the LORD your God, and fear him, and keep his commandments, and obey his voice, and ye shall serve him, and cleave unto him. And that prophet, or that dreamer of dreams, shall be put to death; because he hath spoken to turn you away from the LORD your God, which brought you out of the land of Egypt, and redeemed you out of the house of bondage, to thrust thee out of the way which the LORD thy God commanded thee to walk in. So shalt thou put the evil away from the midst of thee (Deut. 13:1–5).

But the prophet, which shall presume to speak a word in my name, which I have not commanded him to speak, or that shall speak in the name of other gods, even that prophet shall die. And if thou say in thine heart, How shall we know the word which the LORD hath not spoken? When a prophet speaketh in the name of the LORD, if the thing follow not, nor come to pass, that is the thing which the LORD hath not spoken, but the prophet hath spoken it presumptuously: thou shalt not be afraid of him (Deut. 18:20–22).

The false prophet was marked by either of two ways: 1) he prophesied an event, it came to pass, and then he told people to worship another god; 2) he foretold the future in God's name, but the event did not come to pass. A false prophet had to be executed. This is why the false priests on Mt. Carmel were executed by Elijah (I Ki. 18:40): they had prophesied the falling of fire on the sacrifice, but nothing happened; they had also called people to worship false gods. The agent of the sanction of execution, Elijah, had prophesied that the fire would fall on the sacrifice when he invoked God's name; it did. He had called on the people to decide: worship God or Baal (I Ki. 18:21).

The reason why these two Mosaic laws no longer apply under the New Covenant is that the special office of prophet no longer exists. Men can lawfully speak prophetically in God's name of sanctions in general following sins in general, but they are not given accurate insights into the future. We see the future as through a glass darkly today (I Cor. 13:12). Because no one can legitimately claim the lawful prophetic authority to direct the imposition of negative civil sanctions under the New Covenant, which was not the case in Elijah's day, the Mosaic Covenant's negative civil sanctions against false prophets no longer apply. Because the Old Covenant office of prophet has been annulled with the completed text of the Bible, the civil laws governing false prophecy have also been annulled. Excommunication by the church has replaced execution by the State in the matter of false prophecy. If there were still prophets among us, then we would still need the negative sanction of capital punishment to protect society from false prophecy.

Under the Mosaic Covenant, God's sanctions visibly followed the spoken word of a true prophet. This was the basis of his authority to demand the imposition of civil sanctions: to deflect God's corporate negative sanctions. (The same justification undergirds civil sanctions everywhere, in every era.) A false prophet was under the threat of execution: his invoked heavenly sanctions might not come to pass. He who claimed the authority to invoke heavenly sanctions also could invoke civil sanctions; he was therefore under these sanctions. As a false prophet, he was also a false witness. The penalty for being a false prophetic witness in God's name was death, for such testimony invoked God's name in an evil cause: a violation of the third commandment (Ex. 20:7). If there had been no covenantal correlation between sanctions invoked and sanctions perceived, the Mosaic civil law governing the false prophet (Deut. 18:20–22) would not have been enforceable. Guilt or innocence was determined by the presence of cause and effect: verbal cause followed by visible effect. This is no longer the case in the New Covenant because the New Covenant has not retained the covenantal connection between heavenly sanctions invoked and heavenly sanctions imposed. This is because covenantally authoritative revelation ceased with the closing of the canon of Scripture.[4]

Numbers 5 established the law of the accused wife. Her husband accused her of sexual immorality; under oath she denied it. She took a loyalty oath before her husband, the priest, and God. The priest then subjected her to a rite. If she was guilty, there would be visible manifestations in her body. If she was innocent, nothing would happen. The visible results testified to her guilt or innocence. She and her husband had to accept these results as judicially binding. This jealousy testing had meaning only within the context of a covenantally predictable cause-and-effect relationship binding the oath, rite, and visible sanctions.

Natural Law, Random Events, and Dialecticism

There are three ways of denying the covenantal relationship that unites God's Bible-revealed law, man's formal oath, and God's predictable historical sanctions. One is to appeal to an unbreakable natural law which admits no deviations and therefore no miracles. Second, appeal to a realm of chance in which every event is infused with an element of randomness. Third, appeal to law and chance simultaneously. The twentieth century has seen all three approaches, with the third becoming more popular since the discovery of quantum physics in the late 1920's. But the theoretical conflict between impersonal fate and impersonal chance has always been with mankind. So have attempts to put the two together in a dialectical relationship.

Throughout history, men have asked themselves at key points in history: Is this God's special intervention or merely causes familiar to man? Under the Old Covenant, men devised tests that would tell them whether God was specially involved.

---

4. Revelation from God in the sense of unique personal insights still exists because the Holy Spirit guides individual men into truth, but such revelation is not covenantally authoritative.

The most famous incident in the Bible was Gideon's testing of the fleece: wet fleece, dry ground; dry fleece, wet ground (Jud. 6:37–40). But there were others. Moses' challenge to Korah and Dathan was one. "And Moses said, Hereby ye shall know that the LORD hath sent me to do all these works; for I have not done them of mine own mind. If these men die the common death of all men, or if they be visited after the visitation of all men; then the LORD hath not sent me. But if the LORD make a new thing, and the earth open her mouth, and swallow them up, with all that appertain unto them, and they go down quick into the pit; then ye shall understand that these men have provoked the LORD" (Num. 16:28–30).

There were times when God's intervention in history was understood even by covenant-breakers. When the inhabitants of each successive Philistine city in which the stolen Ark of the Covenant resided came down with boils, the civil rulers recognized their problem. They came to the priests for counsel. The priests recommended a test: "Now therefore make a new cart, and take two milch kine, on which there hath come no yoke, and tie the kine to the cart, and bring their calves home from them: And take the ark of the LORD, and lay it upon the cart; and put the jewels of gold, which ye return him for a trespass offering, in a coffer by the side thereof; and send it away, that it may go. And see, if it goeth up by the way of his own coast to Beth-shemesh, then he hath done us this great evil: but if not, then we shall know that it is not his hand that smote us; it was a chance that happened to us" (I Sam. 6:7–9). It was not chance; it was God. The oxen walked into Israel (v. 12).

In the depths of philosophical despair, the author of Ecclesiastes wrote: "All things come alike to all: there is one event to the righteous, and to the wicked; to the good and to the clean, and to the unclean; to him that sacrificeth, and to him that sacrificeth not: as is the good, so is the sinner; and he that sweareth, as he that feareth an oath. This is an evil among all things that are done under the sun, that there is one event unto all: yea, also the heart of the sons of men is full of evil, and madness is in their heart while they live, and after that they go to the dead" (Eccl. 9:2–3). This way lies madness, as he understood. He returned to law and sanctions at the end: "Let us hear the conclusion of the whole matter: Fear God, and keep his commandments: for this is the whole duty of man. For God shall bring every work into judgment, with every secret thing, whether it be good, or whether it be evil" (Eccl. 12:13–14).

The Place of God's Name

To name a thing is to assert authority over it. Adam named the animals; he also named Eve. The sons of Aaron placed God's name on the Israelites: "And they shall put my name upon the children of Israel; and I will bless them" (Num. 6:27). *They were asserting their authority over the people.* As those who were lawfully invested by God with this authority, they could lawfully invoke God's blessings in history on those under their authority, which meant under God's authority.

The sons of Aaron could lawfully draw close to the dwelling place of God. This was their special authority. The dwelling place of God was the dwelling place of God's holy name. "Then there shall be a place which the LORD your God shall choose to cause his name to dwell there; thither shall ye bring all that I command you; your burnt offerings, and your sacrifices, your tithes, and the heave offering of your hand, and all your choice vows which ye vow unto the LORD" (Deut. 12:11). King Darius also recognized this: "And the God that hath caused his name to dwell there destroy all kings and people, that shall put to their hand to alter and to destroy this house of God which is at Jerusalem. I Darius have made a decree; let it be done with speed" (Ezra 6:12).

Proximity to the heavenly throne of God is proximity to His sanctions, both heavenly and earthly (Job 2; Rev. 6:10). Proximity to His earthly dwelling place means proximity to His earthly sanctions. The sons of Aaron were in closest proximity to God's earthly throne: the Ark of the Covenant. Thus, they were closest to His earthly sanctions. They could lawfully invoke His positive sanctions because they lived in proper fear of His negative sanctions. They knew what had happened to Nadab and Abihu: strange fire had brought consuming fire (Lev. 10:1–2). Those who submitted themselves to the authority of the sons of Aaron submitted themselves to God's name. This was the judicial basis of their participation in the predictable corporate blessings of God under the Mosaic Covenant. What was this name? With respect to His general authority over history, His is the self-existent name: "And Moses said unto God, Behold, when I come unto the children of Israel, and shall say unto them, The God of your fathers hath sent me unto you; and they shall say to me, What is his name? what shall I say unto them? And God said unto Moses, I AM THAT I AM: and he said, Thus shalt thou say unto the children of Israel, I AM hath sent me unto you" (Ex. 3:13–14). With respect to His special manifestations within Israel's history, He was the God of Abraham, Isaac, and Jacob. He was, judicially speaking, the God of the covenant. This covenant extends across time. At the close of his life, Moses told the generation of the conquest:

> That thou shouldest enter into covenant with the LORD thy God, and into his oath, which the LORD thy God maketh with thee this day: That he may establish thee to day for a people unto himself, and that he may be unto thee a God, as he hath said unto thee, and as he hath sworn unto thy fathers, to Abraham, to Isaac, and to Jacob. Neither with you only do I make this covenant and this oath; But with him that standeth here with us this day before the LORD our God, and also with him that is not here with us this day (Deut. 29:12–15). . . . Lest there should be among you man, or woman, or family, or tribe, whose heart turneth away this day from the LORD our God, to go and serve the gods of these nations; lest there should be among you a root that beareth gall and wormwood; And it come to pass, when he heareth the words of this curse, that he bless himself in his heart, saying, I shall have

peace, though I walk in the imagination of mine heart, to add drunkenness to thirst: The LORD will not spare him, but then the anger of the LORD and his jealousy shall smoke against that man, and all the curses that are written in this book shall lie upon him, and the LORD shall blot out his name from under heaven (Deut. 29:18–20).

When a person under the oath-bound covenant has God's name removed from him, his name is blotted out in history. The curses will come on him if he fails to repent and take up God's name again. This is the structure of biblical law. But who formally removed God's name from a person under the Mosaic Covenant? The final earthly authority to do this was the priesthood, with the sons of Aaron comprising the high court prior to the exile.

When the sons of Aaron departed into apostasy under Eli, the nation lost the war with the Philistines. The Ark was lawfully removed from the tabernacle in times of war. But in Eli's day, it was captured on the battlefield by the Philistines (I Sam. 4). After the Philistines sent the Ark back by cart, it was not immediately returned to the tabernacle. The sons of Aaron no longer offered sacrifices in the presence of the Ark. Only under David's kingship was the Ark returned to Jerusalem (II Sam. 6:17).

Good News from False Prophets

For the priests to have blessed Israel when Israel was in rebellion would itself have been an act of rebellion. This would have been a public manifestation of the nation's covenant rebellion. To call down God's blessings on rebellious people is to break covenant with God. The mark of a false priesthood was the invocation of God's blessing of peace on a nation in ethical rebellion. Even Ahab, the consummate evil king of Israel, understood this. He knew the difference between a prophet who told him what he wanted to hear and a prophet who told him the truth. He just refused to listen to the truth.

And all the prophets prophesied so, saying, Go up to Ramoth-gilead, and prosper: for the LORD shall deliver it into the king's hand. And the messenger that was gone to call Micaiah spake unto him, saying, Behold now, the words of the prophets declare good unto the king with one mouth: let thy word, I pray thee, be like the word of one of them, and speak that which is good. And Micaiah said, As the LORD liveth, what the LORD saith unto me, that will I speak. So he came to the king. And the king said unto him, Micaiah, shall we go against Ramoth-gilead to battle, or shall we forbear? And he answered him, Go, and prosper: for the LORD shall deliver it into the hand of the king. And the king said unto him, How many times shall I adjure thee that thou tell me nothing but that which is true in the name of the LORD? And he said, I saw all Israel scattered upon the hills, as sheep that have not a shepherd: and the LORD said, These have no master: let them return every man to his house in peace. And the king of Israel said unto Jehoshaphat, Did I not tell thee that he would prophesy no good concerning me, but evil? (I Ki. 22:12–18).

Micaiah then went on to warn the king regarding the supernatural source of the good news announced by the king's official prophets:

And he said, Hear thou therefore the word of the LORD: I saw the LORD sitting on his throne, and all the host of heaven standing by him on his right hand and on his left. And the LORD said, Who shall persuade Ahab, that he may go up and fall at Ramoth-gilead? And one said on this manner, and another said on that manner. And there came forth a spirit, and stood before the LORD, and said, I will persuade him. And the LORD said unto him, Wherewith? And he said, I will go forth, and I will be a lying spirit in the mouth of all his prophets. And he said, Thou shalt persuade him, and prevail also: go forth, and do so. Now therefore, behold, the LORD hath put a lying spirit in the mouth of all these thy prophets, and the LORD hath spoken evil concerning thee (I Ki. 22:19–23).[5]

---

5. That this spirit was evil is clear from the context. Prior to Christ's ministry, Satan had access to the court of heaven (Job 2). After the crucifixion, he no longer had such access. "And there was war in heaven: Michael and his angels fought

The true prophet announced that God had sent a lying spirit to deceive both the false prophets and the king. God did this to false prophets under the Mosaic Covenant, in order to destroy them publicly as testimonies to the nation. "And if the prophet be deceived when he hath spoken a thing, I the LORD have deceived that prophet, and I will stretch out my hand upon him, and will destroy him from the midst of my people Israel" (Ezek. 14:9). Not every false prophet was a lying prophet; some reported accurately the messages of lying spirits. They were deceived prophets. Micaiah graciously revealed the true source of the false prophecy to the king. One of the prophets struck him (I Ki. 22:24). Micaiah pronounced a curse on him (v. 25). Then the king brought the negative sanction of imprisonment against Micaiah (vv. 26–27). The truth of the matter would be revealed in terms of whose negative sanctions prevailed.

There had been sufficient covenantal awareness on the part of the king to know that he needed another opinion. He had also recognized that Micaiah had been lying to him by giving him the initial good news. Micaiah had deliberately uttered false words to him, just as God had lied to Ahab's new set of priests – the first set had perished on Mt. Carmel (I Ki. 18:40) – through the lying spirit. Micaiah at first told him what he wanted to hear. But the king knew better. He recognized false words when he heard them in the mouth of a prophet of God. This was no court prophet hired by the king and his wife. Ahab knew what Micaiah's God was planning for him; he had been

---

against the dragon; and the dragon fought and his angels, And prevailed not; neither was their place found any more in heaven. And the great dragon was cast out, that old serpent, called the Devil, and Satan, which deceiveth the whole world: he was cast out into the earth, and his angels were cast out with him. And I heard a loud voice saying in heaven, Now is come salvation, and strength, and the kingdom of our God, and the power of his Christ: for the accuser of our brethren is cast down, which accused them before our God day and night. And they overcame him by the blood of the Lamb, and by the word of their testimony; and they loved not their lives unto the death. Therefore rejoice, ye heavens, and ye that dwell in them. Woe to the inhabiters of the earth and of the sea! for the devil is come down unto you, having great wrath, because he knoweth that he hath but a short time" (Rev. 12:7–12).

warned by Elijah: "And thou shalt speak unto him, saying, Thus saith the LORD, Hast thou killed, and also taken possession? And thou shalt speak unto him, saying, Thus saith the LORD, In the place where dogs licked the blood of Naboth shall dogs lick thy blood, even thine" (I Ki. 21:19). He was determined to prove Elijah and Micaiah wrong.

Ahab commanded his guards to imprison Micaiah. Micaiah then offered another word of prophecy, also connected to God's visible sanctions in history: "And Micaiah said, If thou return at all in peace, the LORD hath not spoken by me. And he said, Hearken, O people, every one of you" (I Ki. 22:28). The positive sanction of peace would be the public test. If peace came to Israel, Micaiah was the false prophet and therefore had to be executed (Deut. 18:20–22). If peace did not come, then the court prophets were deserving of execution.

Ahab took the prophet's words seriously enough to disguise himself before going into battle (I Ki. 22:30). This did him no good. He did not return alive. "And a certain man drew a bow at a venture [in his simplicity], and smote the king of Israel between the joints of the harness: wherefore he said unto the driver of his chariot, Turn thine hand, and carry me out of the host; for I am wounded" (v. 34). There was nothing random about this event, despite the bowman's lack of knowledge regarding the identity of his target. Ahab died. "And one washed the chariot in the pool of Samaria; and the dogs licked up his blood; and they washed his armour; according unto the word of the LORD which he spake" (I Ki. 22:38). Three prophecies had come to Ahab regarding his end; two were true and one was official. He knew the difference. He sought to kill the first unofficial prophet (Elijah) and imprisoned the second (Micaiah). But he knew the difference. He sought to bring negative sanctions against those true prophets who invoked God's name and His curses. He listened – i.e., decided his course of action – to false prophets who invoked God's name and His blessings.

God then brought negative sanctions against him, as prophesied.

Conclusion

Aaron and his sons invoked God's name and God's positive sanctions on the nation. They could do this lawfully only because they were the highest anointed ecclesiastical representatives between God and Israel. This invocation of God's name publicly placed Israel under the terms of God's covenant: His law. This was an act of corporate covenant renewal, for Israel as a nation had already covenanted with God in Exodus 19. God's name was already on them. They were supposed to understand that when the blessing of peace came, this was not an impersonal event, either random or by the nation's military power. It was God's gift to the nation, either in response to their covenantal faithfulness or as a prelude to His negative sanctions against their pretended autonomy: "And thou say in thine heart, My power and the might of mine hand hath gotten me this wealth" (Deut. 8:17).

6

THE ALTAR OFFERING

And it came to pass on the day that Moses had fully set up the tabernacle, and had anointed it, and sanctified it, and all the instruments thereof, both the altar and all the vessels thereof, and had anointed them, and sanctified them; That the princes of Israel, heads of the house of their fathers, who were the princes of the tribes, and were over them that were numbered, offered: And they brought their offering before the LORD, *six covered wagons, and twelve oxen; a wagon for two of the princes, and for each one an ox: and they brought them before the tabernacle (Num. 7:1–3).*

The builders completed the tabernacle on the first day of the first month (Ex. 40:17). Moses then finished the interior (Ex. 40:18–30). Numbers 7 begins with the completion of the tabernacle. There can be no doubt: this is the same event.[1] So,

---

1. Milgrom sees a major problem here. If the text is taken at face value, the donations began on the day the tabernacle was completed. This was the first day of the first month (Ex. 40:17). Passover began on the 14th day (Ex. 12:18). This means that if the offerings brought by the chieftains were actually sacrificed on the day they were presented to the priests, the priests had to do the work. But they had not yet been consecrated. Thus, he concludes, the phrase "in the day" is mistranslated. It should be merely "when" – an indeterminate timing. The sacrifices were made after Passover. Jacob Milgrom, *The JPS Torah Commentary: Numbers* (New York: Jewish Publication Society, 1990), pp. 362–64. A simpler way to solve this problem is to say that the offerings were not immediately sacrificed when presented. They were kept

Numbers 7 backtracks 30 days, for the events of Numbers 1 took place on the first day of the second month (Num. 1:18).

The princes or chieftains of Israel delivered the offering to Moses. God instructed Moses to distribute the carts and oxen to the families of Gershon and Merari, but not to Kohath, which was Moses' family. Kohath was closest to the Ark of the Covenant. This created a special holiness burden. "But unto the sons of Kohath he gave none: because the service of the sanctuary belonging unto them was that they should bear upon their shoulders" (Num. 7:9). The closer to the inner circle, the greater the ritual responsibility, the greater the danger of profanity, and the greater the holiness of those serving. In contrast, the closer a Levite was to the non-Levitical tribes, the larger the required physical burden of sacrifice on behalf of these tribes.

Levite families that were closer to the outer rings of holiness bore the brunt of the physical burdens: transporting the implements of the tabernacle and defending the Ark from the first wave of any attack on the holy of holies. The two families in the outer rings of holiness were given the primary burden of transporting the implements of sacrifice, for they lawfully bore the implement of defense: the sword. They were the sanctions-bringers against invaders: Merari first and then Gershon. Twice as many wagons filled with offerings went to Merari as to Gershon (Num. 7:7–8) because Merari had to transport twice as much. Merari served in the outer ring of the three concentric circles of authority.[2] The last line of defense was Kohath. More of the Kohathites would survive an unsuccessful attack than the Gershonites; more of Gershon would survive than Merari. Conversely, God would kill more of the Kohathites than the Gershonites for profane acts, while Gershon was more at risk than Merari.

---

by the priests for subsequent sacrifice.

2. See Chapter 3, above: section on "Hierarchy and Inner Circles," subsection on "Circles of Authority," pp. 60–61.

Equal Tribal Assessments

This offering was the offering for the altar. The earlier offering had been for the construction of the tabernacle (Ex. 36:3). Numbers 7 recounts in detail the same story a dozen times: one day per tribe. It lists what each of the tribal princes placed in the wagons. Each prince represented one tribe; each offering was the same.

> And his offering was one silver charger, the weight thereof was an hundred and thirty shekels, one silver bowl of seventy shekels, after the shekel of the sanctuary; both of them were full of fine flour mingled with oil for a meat offering: One spoon of ten shekels of gold, full of incense: One young bullock, one ram, one lamb of the first year, for a burnt offering: One kid of the goats for a sin offering: And for a sacrifice of peace offerings, two oxen, five rams, five he goats, five lambs of the first year (Num. 7:13–17a).

There was no distinction sacrificially among the 12 tribes in terms of their wealth or population. They all owed four of the five sacrifices: whole burnt offering (point one), meal (tribute, allegiance)[3] offering (point two), peace offering (point three), and sin (purification) offering (point four). They did not owe a guilt (reparation) offering (point five), which has no corporate aspect.[4] The Israelites had not sinned against men; they had sinned against God.

The offering was delivered to the tabernacle by princes, i.e., men who served as civil officers. The text does not say how they had apportioned the required offering among the families. We

---

3. Gary North, *Leviticus: An Economic Commentary* (Tyler, Texas: Institute for Christian Economics, 1994), pp. 63-64.

4. Sacrificial offerings had to be male; personal offerings could be female. The purification offering had to be female (Lev. 4:28, 32). Milgrom, *Numbers*, p. 363. Milgrom neglects to mention that the ruler's reparation offering had to be male (Lev. 4:23). It was the common person's offering that had to be female. Masculinity under the Mosaic covenant was associated in the civil covenant with rulership, femininity with subordination. North, *Leviticus*, p. 93.

know only that they brought an equal offering for each tribe. This means that larger tribes paid less per capita[5] than smaller tribes did. Poorer tribes per capita paid as much as wealthy tribes. The principle of proportional taxation did not apply in this instance, i.e., the principle of the tithe. In this case, the assessment was tribal, not personal. It was not a tax; it was an offering. It had to do with the body of the nation as a called-out body of believers. They were represented by princes, probably not in the latter's legal capacity as civil officers but in their capacity as warrior-priests. The nation had been numbered already, before the building of the tabernacle (Ex. 38:25–26). The holy army was now in service.

In the case of atonement offerings, each fighting man was numbered, and each paid a half shekel of silver (Ex. 38:26). In the case of the altar offering, each tribe paid the assessment owed by every other tribe. In the language of modern economics, these assessments were regressive: they weighed more heavily on the poor than the rich.[6] This was also true of the individual assessments at each national mustering. Of course, because the wealth of the Israelites at this time had been extracted from the Egyptians as their lawful restitution for having been made slaves, we do not know what the original distribution of wealth was. Perhaps it was close to equality. It is extremely important to point out that because these offerings were not civil taxes, they throw no light on proper civil tax policy.[7]

5. Technically, per caput: singular.

6. This analysis assumes that we can make interpersonal comparisons of subjective utility, which we cannot do scientifically; we can only do this as ethicists, which is what economists officially want to avoid at all costs, or at least very high marginal costs. Unofficially, the only way they can make any practical recommendations is to assume that they can make such comparisons. See Gary North, *The Dominion Covenant: Genesis* (2nd ed.; Tyler, Texas: Institute for Christian Economics, 1987), pp. 44–54; North, *Tools of Dominion: The Case Laws of Exodus* (Tyler, Texas: Institute for Christian Economics, 1990), Appendix D: "The Epistemological Problem of Social Cost."

7. Rushdoony's arguments to the contrary have colored the theonomist movement for two decades. He designates as a civil poll tax what was a priestly atonement

Cleansing Before Service Begins

After the gifts were delivered to Moses, he spoke to God. God told him to light the lamps, which Aaron did (Num. 8:1–3). Then came the next step: "And the LORD spake unto Moses, saying, Take the Levites from among the children of Israel, and cleanse them. And thus shalt thou do unto them, to cleanse them: Sprinkle water of purifying upon them, and let them shave all their flesh, and let them wash their clothes, and so make themselves clean" (vv. 5–7). Once they were cleansed, it was time for a meat (meal) offering (v. 8a), the offering associated with priestly authority,[8] and a sin or purification offering (v. 8b). This was to take place in front of the assembly (v. 9), who were the representatives of the congregation.[9] First, however, the transfer of representative authority had to pass from the assembly to the Levites by laying on of hands. "And thou shalt bring the Levites before the LORD: and the children of Israel shall put their hands upon the Levites" (v. 10). This is a very important principle: *biblical authority flows downward from God and upward from the people.* The Levites represented the people before God and represented God before the people. Their authority was mediatorial. God's acceptance of their sacrifices judicially sealed the first; the laying on of hands judicially sealed the second.

Aaron offered the Levites as a tribute offering to God: "And Aaron shall offer the Levites before the LORD for an offering of the children of Israel, that they may execute the service of the LORD" (v. 11). To confirm this sacrificial offering of an entire tribe – the representative firstborn – the Levites transferred their offenses symbolically to the two bullocks: one for the

---

assessment on all members of God's holy army. R. J. Rushdoony, *The Institutes of Biblical Law* (Nutley, New Jersey: Craig Press, 1973), pp. 281–82. Cf. North, *Tools of Dominion*, ch. 32.

8. North, *Leviticus*, ch. 2.

9. *Ibid.*, pp. 91–92.

whole burnt offering (their judicially dead legal status),[10] the other for their sin offering. "And the Levites shall lay their hands upon the heads of the bullocks: and thou shalt offer the one for a sin offering, and the other for a burnt offering, unto the LORD, to make an atonement for the Levites. And thou shalt set the Levites before Aaron, and before his sons, and offer them for an offering unto the LORD" (vv. 12–13). Once cleansed ritually, the Levites were ready to be offered to God:

> Thus shalt thou separate the Levites from among the children of Israel: and the Levites shall be mine. And after that shall the Levites go in to do the service of the tabernacle of the congregation: and thou shalt cleanse them, and offer them for an offering. For they are wholly given unto me from among the children of Israel; instead of such as open every womb, even instead of the firstborn of all the children of Israel, have I taken them unto me. For all the firstborn of the children of Israel are mine, both man and beast: on the day that I smote every firstborn in the land of Egypt I sanctified them for myself. And I have taken the Levites for all the firstborn of the children of Israel. And I have given the Levites as a gift to Aaron and to his sons from among the children of Israel, to do the service of the children of Israel in the tabernacle of the congregation, and to make an atonement for the children of Israel: that there be no plague among the children of Israel, when the children of Israel come nigh unto the sanctuary (vv. 14–19).

First, they washed their clothes (v. 21a); second, Aaron made an atonement offering for them (v. 21b). Only then did they go into full-time service (v. 22).

The Levites had to serve Aaron and his sons for a period of 20 years: from age 30 to age 50.[11] After age 50, they still

10. James Jordan writes: "What the sacrifice removes is not sin but death, the judgment for sin. Death having been removed, it is now possible to live a righteous life." Cited in *ibid.*, p. 49.

11. Numbers 4:3, 23, 30, 35, 39, 43, 47. The reading 25 years appears only in Numbers 8:24. There is no textual reconciliation of this problem; commentators from the rabbis to the present have suggested no convincing answer.

served as assistants, presumably doing lighter physical labor and guard duty.[12] "This is it that belongeth unto the Levites: from twenty and five years old and upward they shall go in to wait upon the service of the tabernacle of the congregation: And from the age of fifty years they shall cease waiting upon the service thereof, and shall serve no more: But shall minister with their brethren in the tabernacle of the congregation, to keep the charge, and shall do no service. Thus shalt thou do unto the Levites touching their charge" (vv. 24–26).

The Levites would have served under the priests during the three major feasts, when there was need for many servants. In other times, they probably served on a rotating basis. The Levitical cities had Levites as residents; they were not all permanent dwellers living close to the Ark of the Covenant.

All of this took place before the second numbering, for the next section states: "And the LORD spake unto Moses in the wilderness of Sinai, in the first month of the second year after they were come out of the land of Egypt, saying, Let the children of Israel also keep the passover at his appointed season." (Num. 9:1–2). The Passover was celebrated that month (v. 5), before the second numbering a month later.

The dedication of the gifts took 12 days. Then came the cleansing and dedication of the Levites. It is not clear whether this took place on day 12 or day 13. It did not take place on day 14, since that was the start of Passover: the 14th day of the first month (Num. 9:5).

The Secondary Passover

It was at this time that the question was raised concerning ritual cleanliness and distant journeys. Certain men came to Moses and asked him regarding their contact with a dead body. They had not been allowed to make an offering associated with

---

12. Gordon J. Wenham, *Numbers: An Introduction and Commentary* (Downers Grove, Illinois: Inter-Varsity Press, 1981), p. 97.

the Passover – presumably, the sacrificial lamb. They were ritually defiled. Moses enquired of God.

> And the LORD spake unto Moses, saying, Speak unto the children of Israel, saying, If any man of you or of your posterity shall be unclean by reason of a dead body, or be in a journey afar off, yet he shall keep the passover unto the LORD. The fourteenth day of the second month at even they shall keep it, and eat it with unleavened bread and bitter herbs. They shall leave none of it unto the morning, nor break any bone of it: according to all the ordinances of the passover they shall keep it. But the man that is clean, and is not in a journey, and forbeareth to keep the passover, even the same soul shall be cut off from among his people: because he brought not the offering of the LORD in his appointed season, that man shall bear his sin (Num. 9:9–13).

This indicates that the Passover was the only mandatory annual feast. In the case of the firstfruits (Pentecost) and tabernacles/booths, a man could stay away if he was on a journey or had been in contact with a dead body. In the case of Passover, however, he was expected to attend. This would have kept journeys from extending too far or too long. It placed commerce under temporal boundaries. Under such strict limits, the only possible justification for a journey that kept a man away from both Passovers would have been a distant missionary journey.[13]

The existence of such a provision in the original law code of Israel indicates that profitable foreign trade was a very real

---

13. To argue that Passover was more important than foreign missions is to misconstrue the importance of ritual in Old Covenant Israel. Righteousness was always more important in God's eyes than ritual when honoring a ritual would have interfered with righteousness. "For a multitude of the people, even many of Ephraim, and Manasseh, Issachar, and Zebulun, had not cleansed themselves, yet did they eat the passover otherwise than it was written. But Hezekiah prayed for them, saying, The good LORD pardon every one that prepareth his heart to seek God, the LORD God of his fathers, though he be not cleansed according to the purification of the sanctuary. And the LORD hearkened to Hezekiah, and healed the people" (II Chron. 30:18-20).

possibility. This in turn points to the existence of foreign trade as a separate occupation, especially for those tribes that had cities on the Mediterranean eastern coast. One modern academic interpretation of the Egyptian, Hittite, and Mesopotamian empires is that these inland empires in the second millennium B.C. did not engage directly in foreign trade, but worked through neutral intermediaries along the Mediterranean's eastern coast.[14] If this interpretation is correct, then this dynastic practice placed Israel in a geographically strategic position, along with the Phoenicians to the south and the trading cities north of Tyre and Sidon, such as Ugarit, which served as a conduit between Greece and the Near Eastern cultures.[15] (Professor Gordon believed that the alphabet went from Ugarit to the Hebrews and Phoenicians to the Greeks.)[16] The costs of land transportation were too high to be profitable except for jewels and other high value commodities, i.e., money assets. This was as true in the ancient world as it was until the invention of the railroad. Not having access to any river that led into the great inland empires, Israel's coastal tribes would have to become world traders in order to prosper. This appears to be what they did.[17]

Conclusion

Sinful men cannot make acceptable offerings to God apart from mediation. In this case, a whole system of intermediaries was in operation. The families gave gifts to the tribal leaders; the tribal leaders delivered them to Moses; Moses delivered

---

14. Robert B. Revere, "'No Man's Coast': Ports of Trade in the Eastern Mediterranean," in *Trade and Market in the Early Empires: Economies in History and Theory*, edited by Karl Polanyi, Conrad M. Arensberg, and Harry W. Peterson (Chicago: Regnery, [1957] 1971), ch. 4.

15. Cyrus H. Gordon, *The Common Background of Greek and Hebrew Civilizations* (New York: Norton, 1965), ch. 5.

16. *Ibid.*, p. 130.

17. See North, *Leviticus*, pp. 23–34.

them to the Levites; the Levites delivered them to Aaron; Aaron delivered them to God as sacrifices for the Levites. The animals and meal were used by Aaron to make an offering in the name of the Levites. The Levites had to be cleansed through washing and sacrificial offerings in order for them to serve as mediatorial substitutes for the nation.

The family of Kohath received none of the altar offerings from the tribal princes. The family of Gershon received half of what the family of Merari received (Num. 7:7–8). Merari had greater responsibilities for transporting the tabernacle's instruments than Gershon had. Merari also had greater responsibility in defending the holy of holies from attackers. Merari was the first line of military defense within the confines of the tabernacle area. Merari was less holy than Gershon; Gershon was less holy than Kohath. The tribe that was most holy received none of the altar offering.

Because the sacrificed animals that were not whole burnt offerings could be eaten by the priests, Gershon and Merari had to share their food offerings with Kohath. The princes had brought no sacrifices for the Kohathites to offer and therefore to participate in a meal. Those who were less holy owed an offering to those who were more holy: from the 12 tribes upward to the Kohathites. The Kohathites were the most holy; so, the other tribes owed sacrifices to them.

7

PROGRESSIVE WHINING AND FINAL ACCOUNTING

And when the people complained, it displeased the LORD: and the LORD heard it; and his anger was kindled; and the fire of the LORD burnt among them, and consumed them that were in the uttermost parts of the camp. And the people cried unto Moses; and when Moses prayed unto the LORD, the fire was quenched. And he called the name of the place Taberah: because the fire of the LORD burnt among them (Num. 11:1–3).

The theocentric reference of this passage is God's impatience with Israel's pattern of behavior. They were without faith in Him as the deliverer. They had substituted complaining for faith. They had found that by complaining to Moses about their external conditions, they could get what they wanted. They did not pray; they complained. They did not exercise patience; they whined. Because of God's grace, they had gotten what they asked for. This time, they got more than they asked for.

The Israelites were not satisfied with what they possessed in the wilderness.[1] But their problem was not the wilderness.

1. The Rolling Stones 1965 song, *Satisfaction*, made them world-famous. It began with and returned to this ungrammatical complaint: "I can't get no satisfaction." They spoke for the quail-feasting twentieth-century West.

Their problem was their fear of responsibility. They feared freedom. This fear had become visible when Moses and Aaron first challenged Pharaoh to allow the people to go. Pharaoh ceased delivering straw to them for brick-making. "And the officers of the children of Israel did see that they were in evil case, after it was said, Ye shall not [di]minish ought from your bricks of your daily task. And they met Moses and Aaron, who stood in the way, as they came forth from Pharaoh: And they said unto them, The LORD look upon you, and judge; because ye have made our savour to be abhorred in the eyes of Pharaoh, and in the eyes of his servants, to put a sword in their hand to slay us" (Ex. 5:19–21).

A List of Priorities

This was only the beginning. When fleeing from Pharaoh's army on Egypt's side of the Red Sea, they complained again. "And when Pharaoh drew nigh, the children of Israel lifted up their eyes, and, behold, the Egyptians marched after them; and they were sore afraid: and the children of Israel cried out unto the LORD. And they said unto Moses, Because there were no graves in Egypt, hast thou taken us away to die in the wilderness? wherefore hast thou dealt thus with us, to carry us forth out of Egypt? Is not this the word that we did tell thee in Egypt, saying, Let us alone, that we may serve the Egyptians? For it had been better for us to serve the Egyptians, than that we should die in the wilderness" (Ex. 14:10–12). God delivered them by the miracle of the divided waters.

Then they faced a food crisis: "And the whole congregation of the children of Israel murmured against Moses and Aaron in the wilderness: And the children of Israel said unto them, Would to God we had died by the hand of the LORD in the land of Egypt, when we sat by the flesh pots, and when we did eat bread to the full; for ye have brought us forth into this wilderness, to kill this whole assembly with hunger. Then said the LORD unto Moses, Behold, I will rain bread from heaven for you; and the people shall go out and gather a certain rate every day, that I may prove them, whether they will walk in my law, or no" (Ex. 16:2–4). God gave them manna.

This pattern pleased them: whining to Moses followed by gifts from God. So, they repeated it. "And all the congregation of the children of Israel journeyed from the wilderness of Sin, after their journeys, according to the commandment of the LORD, and pitched in Rephidim: and there was no water for the people to drink. Wherefore the people did chide with Moses, and said, Give us water that we may drink. And Moses said unto them, Why chide ye with me? wherefore do ye tempt the LORD? And the people thirsted there for water; and the people murmured against Moses, and said, Wherefore is this that thou hast brought us up out of Egypt, to kill us and our children and our cattle with thirst? And Moses cried unto the LORD, saying, What shall I do unto this people? they be almost ready to stone me" (Ex. 17:1–4). God gave them water out of the rock (v. 6).

They were in a situation in which they were totally dependent on God: the wilderness. It should have been clear to them that God was sustaining them. The natural environment surely wasn't. Yet they still complained. They thought they deserved more blessings. They insisted that the blessings in Egypt had been greater than the blessings in the wilderness. But they had been slaves in Egypt. This fact they ignored. They placed liberty low on their personal scale of values; their memory of leeks and onions was high on the list. So, the absence of the leeks and onions loomed large in their consciousness. Their liberty under Moses required God's sustaining grace, best manifested in the manna. This sign of their dependence they resented.

Their problem was not the absence of leeks and onions. Their problem was their list of priorities. Each person makes decisions in terms of his list of priorities. A man exchanges a bit of this for more of that. God had provided them with water from rocks and manna from the ground, and this had cost them nothing: free grace. They should have responded with thanksgiving. But they could not swallow the manna contentedly because they could not enjoy the blessings of liberty under God contentedly. They placed liberty at the bottom of their list of priorities; they placed food at the top. Paul wrote of this mentality: "Whose end is destruction, whose God is their belly, and whose glory is in their shame, who mind earthly things" (Phil. 3:19).

Values and Choice

Modern free market economic theory is individualistic. It begins with the individual's goals, his list of priorities. In theory, there is no way for an economist to speak of a collective list of priorities because there is no scientific way to make comparisons of different people's value scales.[2] Nevertheless, such value scales do exist because men act corporately to achieve corporate goals. This is what social policy is all about.

The covenantalist begins with God's covenant, not with the individual or the collective. God's law provides the value scale. His ethical standards for individual behavior tell us what to place where on our personal scale of values. His ethical standards for corporate behavior tell us what to place where on society's scale of values. The story of the exodus and the wilderness stands as a warning beacon to men through the ages: *the blessing of liberty under God is ethically preferable to the promise of security under man*. The promise of security under man is a trap leading into slavery: an illusion.

We make choices in terms of four things: what we want (a scale of preferences), what we have (capital), how much time we think we have, and what we know about the relationships among them (a plan). This decision-making procedure operates

2. Gary North, *The Dominion Covenant: Genesis* (2nd ed.; Tyler, Texas: Institute for Christian Economics, 1987), ch. 4. This summarizes the debate in the 1930's between Lionel Robbins (an individualist) and Roy Harrod (a Keynesian).

under God's sovereignty. He, too, has a scale of preferences,[3] capital (including mankind),[4] a time scale (history),[5] and a plan (decree).[6] Men choose analogous to God, as creatures. Men act re-creatively, not creatively.

Negative Sanctions Applied

Numbers 11 begins with another complaint. We are not told what it was. We are told that God had finally had enough. He began a series of lessons that never made any lasting impression on the exodus generation. He responded to their complaint with supernatural fire. This sanction matched His emotion:

---

3. "Will the LORD be pleased with thousands of rams, or with ten thousands of rivers of oil? shall I give my firstborn for my transgression, the fruit of my body for the sin of my soul? He hath shewed thee, O man, what is good; and what doth the LORD require of thee, but to do justly, and to love mercy, and to walk humbly with thy God? (Mic. 6:7–8). "Thy kingdom come. Thy will be done in earth, as it is in heaven" (Matt. 6:10). Cf. Matthew 23:23.

4. "The earth is the LORD'S, and the fulness thereof; the world, and they that dwell therein" (Ps. 24:1). "For every beast of the forest is mine, and the cattle upon a thousand hills" (Ps. 50:10).

5. "And I heard the man clothed in linen, which was upon the waters of the river, when he held up his right hand and his left hand unto heaven, and sware by him that liveth for ever that it shall be for a time, times, and an half; and when he shall have accomplished to scatter the power of the holy people, all these things shall be finished" (Dan. 12:7). "Heaven and earth shall pass away, but my words shall not pass away. But of that day and hour knoweth no man, no, not the angels of heaven, but my Father only" (Matt. 24:35–36).

6. "For as the heavens are higher than the earth, so are my ways higher than your ways, and my thoughts than your thoughts. For as the rain cometh down, and the snow from heaven, and returneth not thither, but watereth the earth, and maketh it bring forth and bud, that it may give seed to the sower, and bread to the eater: So shall my word be that goeth forth out of my mouth: it shall not return unto me void, but it shall accomplish that which I please, and it shall prosper in the thing whereto I sent it" (Isa. 55:9–11). "Blessed be the God and Father of our Lord Jesus Christ, who hath blessed us with all spiritual blessings in heavenly places in Christ: According as he hath chosen us in him before the foundation of the world, that we should be holy and without blame before him in love: Having predestinated us unto the adoption of children by Jesus Christ to himself, according to the good pleasure of his will" (Eph. 1:3–5). "For we which have believed do enter into rest, as he said, As I have sworn in my wrath, if they shall enter into my rest: although the works were finished from the foundation of the world" (Heb. 4:3).

"His anger was kindled; and the fire of the LORD burnt among them" (v. 1) The people cried out to Moses for relief. Moses prayed to God, and the fire stopped.

The next verse indicates how little they had learned: "And the mixt multitude that was among them fell a lusting: and the children of Israel also wept again, and said, Who shall give us flesh to eat? We remember the fish, which we did eat in Egypt freely; the cucumbers, and the melons, and the leeks, and the onions, and the garlick: But now our soul is dried away: there is nothing at all, beside this manna, before our eyes" (4–6). God had answered their request for food a year earlier. They had grown bored with this miracle. They wanted more. Moses wanted out:

> Then Moses heard the people weep throughout their families, every man in the door of his tent: and the anger of the LORD was kindled greatly; Moses also was displeased. And Moses said unto the LORD, Wherefore hast thou afflicted thy servant? and wherefore have I not found favour in thy sight, that thou layest the burden of all this people upon me? Have I conceived all this people? have I begotten them, that thou shouldest say unto me, Carry them in thy bosom, as a nursing father beareth the sucking child, unto the land which thou swarest unto their fathers? Whence should I have flesh to give unto all this people? for they weep unto me, saying, Give us flesh, that we may eat. I am not able to bear all this people alone, because it is too heavy for me. And if thou deal thus with me, kill me, I pray thee, out of hand, if I have found favor in thy sight. . . (vv. 10–15a).

God was angry with the people; Moses had a right to be weary. God was patient with Moses. God had Moses bring 70 elders near. "And I will come down and talk with thee there: and I will take of the spirit which is upon thee, and will put it upon them; and they shall bear the burden of the people with thee, that thou bear it not thyself alone" (v. 17). God promised to give the people flesh to eat the next day (v. 18). But this promise of blessing was to be delivered by Moses in the language of cursing: "Ye shall not eat one day, nor two days, nor five days, neither ten days, nor twenty days; But even a whole month, until it come out at your nostrils, and it be loathsome unto you: because that ye have despised the LORD which is among you, and have wept before him, saying, Why came we forth out of Egypt?" (vv. 19–20).

This time, Moses showed the lack of faith that was later to cost him entrance into the Promised Land. He asked God rhetorically where all this flesh would come from. His language was reminiscent of Abraham's response to God's promise of a child at age 99. "Shall the flocks and the herds be slain for them, to suffice them? or shall all the fish of the sea be gathered together for them, to suffice them? (v. 22).[7] God's response was short and to the point: "Is the LORD'S hand waxed short? thou shalt see now whether my word shall come to pass unto thee or not" (v. 23). So, God responded to Moses with a challenge: "See if my word comes true." He thereby announced His own prophetic status. "See if my positive sanctions match my promise."

God brought birds in droves, and more than droves. This was an extension of the nation's experience when the manna first appeared: "And it came to pass, that at even[ing] the quails came up, and covered the camp: and in the morning the dew lay round about the host [camp, NASB]" (Ex. 16:13). Before, they had seen the birds. This time, they would feast on them. Briefly. "And there went forth a wind from the LORD, and brought quails from the sea, and let them fall by the camp, as it were a day's journey on this side, and as it were a day's journey on the other side, round about the camp, and as it were two cubits high upon the face of the earth. And the people stood up all that day, and all that night, and all the next day, and they gathered the quails: he that gathered least gathered

---

7. The phrasing of this seemingly rhetorical question is another piece of evidence that Israel numbered about 2.4 million people. Moses would not have used the rhetoric of all the fish in the sea to describe the requirements of feeding a few thousand people.

ten homers: and they spread them all abroad for themselves round about the camp" (vv. 31–32).[8] They began to eat. They had enough food for a month; they would not enjoy it for an hour. "And while the flesh was yet between their teeth, ere it was chewed, the wrath of the LORD was kindled against the people, and the LORD smote the people with a very great plague" (v. 33). They got more than they had bargained for.

Aaron and Miriam

Moses' brother and sister were not satisfied with their authority. "And they said, Hath the LORD indeed spoken only by Moses? hath he not spoken also by us? And the LORD heard it" (Num. 12:2). God brought the three of them into the cloud at the door of the tabernacle. Then He identified Moses as far more than a prophet: "And he said, Hear now my words: If there be a prophet among you, I the LORD will make myself known unto him in a vision, and will speak unto him in a dream. My servant Moses is not so, who is faithful in all mine house. With him will I speak mouth to mouth, even apparently [openly, NASB], and not in dark speeches; and the similitude [likeness] of the LORD shall he behold: wherefore then were ye not afraid to speak against my servant Moses?" (vv. 6–8).

God removed the cloud. Miriam was now leprous. Biblical leprosy was a disease of God's judgment.[9] God did not strike

---

8. The Hebrew words "cubits face earth" were translated as "two cubits high upon the face of the earth." This translation cannot be correct. A pile of dead quail three feet high in an area in the range of 713 miles would constitute billions of quail. If it was a day's journey across the camp – say, 30 miles – then the radius was 15 miles. The formula pi times r-squared gives 731 miles. The phrase "cubits face earth" should be translated as "cubits above the face of the earth," i.e., the height at which the quail flew into the camp: about three feet, where they could be hit with any heavy implement. This was the interpretation of Rashi: "*This means that* they were flying at a height *of two cubits from the ground* so that they reached just up to a man's breast. . . ." Rashi, *Chumash with Targum Onkelos, Haphtaroth and Rashi's Commentary*, A. M. Silbermann and M. Rosenbaum, translators, 5 vols. (Jerusalem: Silbermann Family, [1934] 1985 [Jewish year: 5745]), IV, p. 58 (Num. 11:31).

9. Gary North, *Leviticus: An Economic Commentary* (Tyler, Texas: Institute for

Aaron, who was a man and had a high office. Miriam was a woman and had no office. Her sin was greater than Aaron's: less justification for demanding authority. Aaron immediately repented before God in both of their names (v. 12). Moses cried to God to heal her, which He did, but not without an additional negative sanction: "And the LORD said unto Moses, If her father had but spit in her face, should she not be ashamed seven days? let her be shut out from the camp seven days, and after that let her be received in again" (v. 14). There is no doubt that the people knew all about this; the camp did not move until her week was over (v. 15).

Send in the Spies

The time had come to test the nation's readiness for the conquest of Canaan. "And the LORD spake unto Moses, saying, Send thou men, that they may search the land of Canaan, which I give unto the children of Israel: of every tribe of their fathers shall ye send a man, every one a ruler among them" (Num. 13:1–2). Men with leadership ability would make the decision about the wisdom of invading Canaan. They would make their decision only after first-hand reconnaissance. They would see with their own eyes the land and its inhabitants. They would calculate with their own minds the risk-reward ratio. Then they would decide. "And Moses sent them to spy out the land of Canaan, and said unto them, Get you up this way southward, and go up into the mountain: And see the land, what it is; and the people that dwelleth therein, whether they be strong or weak, few or many; And what the land is that they dwell in, whether it be good or bad; and what cities they be that they dwell in, whether in tents, or in strong holds; And what the land is, whether it be fat or lean, whether there be wood therein, or not. And be ye of good courage, and bring of

Christian Economics, 1994), ch. 9.

the fruit of the land. Now the time was the time of the firstripe grapes" (vv. 17–20). They searched the land for 40 days (25).

Their report was delivered in the familiar form: "We've got good news and bad news." First, the good news: "And they told him, and said, We came unto the land whither thou sentest us, and surely it floweth with milk and honey; and this is the fruit of it" (v. 27). Then the bad news: "Nevertheless the people be strong that dwell in the land, and the cities are walled, and very great: and moreover we saw the children of Anak there" (v. 28).

Then came Caleb, who proclaimed, in effect, "The bigger they are, the harder they fall." "And Caleb stilled the people before Moses, and said, Let us go up at once, and possess it; for we are well able to overcome it" (v. 30).

Faith, Facts, and Actions

At this point, the spies' story changed. The bad news was all true; worse, even. "And there we saw the giants, the sons of Anak, which come of the giants: and we were in our own sight as grasshoppers, and so we were in their sight" (Num. 13:33). Meanwhile, the good news disappeared. The land was nothing; worse, even. "And they brought up an evil report of the land which they had searched unto the children of Israel, saying, The land, through which we have gone to search it, is a land that eateth up the inhabitants thereof; and all the people that we saw in it are men of a great stature" (v. 32).

Caleb and Joshua believed Israel could win; the others believed they could not. When it looked as though Caleb's report might place them in jeopardy militarily, they revised their report. The potential reward was just not worth the risk. Better to wander; better to eat manna; best of all, to have died. "And all the congregation lifted up their voice, and cried; and the people wept that night. And all the children of Israel murmured against Moses and against Aaron: and the whole congregation said unto them, Would God that we had died in the land of Egypt! or would God we had died in this wilderness!

(Num. 14:1–2). Life was their burden; they feared to lose it in battle. Better to return to slavery: "And wherefore hath the LORD brought us unto this land, to fall by the sword, that our wives and our children should be a prey? were it not better for us to return into Egypt? And they said one to another, Let us make a captain, and let us return into Egypt" (vv. 3–4).

Moses and Aaron fell on their faces before the representative assembly (v. 5). Joshua and Caleb remained on their feet and spoke out. The land is good; God will give it to us if He favors us; do not rebel against God or fear the Canaanites (vv. 7–9). Their words were negative sanctions against the people and the other ten spies. The people were ready to respond with more direct sanctions: "But all the congregation bade stone them with stones" (v. 10a).

At that point, God appeared. He was ready to impose comprehensive negative sanctions: "And the LORD said unto Moses, How long will this people provoke me? and how long will it be ere they believe me, for all the signs which I have shewed among them? I will smite them with the pestilence, and disinherit them, and will make of thee a greater nation and mightier than they" (vv. 11–12). Moses intervened and offered the most effective prayer there is: an appeal to God's reputation. "And Moses said unto the LORD, Then the Egyptians shall hear it, (for thou broughtest up this people in thy might from among them;) And they will tell it to the inhabitants of this land: for they have heard that thou LORD art among this people, that thou LORD art seen face to face, and that thy cloud standeth over them, and that thou goest before them, by daytime in a pillar of a cloud, and in a pillar of fire by night. Now if thou shalt kill all this people as one man, then the nations which have heard the fame of thee will speak, saying, Because the LORD was not able to bring this people into the land which he sware unto them, therefore he hath slain them in the wilderness" (13–16). Be merciful, therefore; pardon their iniquity (vv. 18–19).

So, God did just that (v. 20). Then He announced another negative sanction: "Because all those men which have seen my glory, and my miracles, which I did in Egypt and in the wilderness, and have tempted me now these ten times, and have not hearkened to my voice; Surely they shall not see the land which I sware unto their fathers, neither shall any of them that provoked me see it" (vv. 22–23). He also announced a positive sanction: "But my servant Caleb, because he had another spirit with him, and hath followed me fully, him will I bring into the land whereinto he went; and his seed shall possess it" (v. 24). Then He returned to graphic language: "Your carcases shall fall in this wilderness; and all that were numbered of you, according to your whole number, from twenty years old and upward, which have murmured against me" (v. 29). But Joshua and Caleb will enter the land (v. 30).

The rebels' children would be placed under a great burden. "And your children shall wander in the wilderness forty years, and bear your whoredoms, until your carcases be wasted in the wilderness" (v. 33). The adults would die off during these years, matching their 40 unproductive days in the wilderness (vv. 34). To verify His words, God slew the ten cowardly spies who had slandered the land, thereby slandering God's promise regarding the land: "And the men, which Moses sent to search the land, who returned, and made all the congregation to murmur against him, by bringing up a slander upon the land, Even those men that did bring up the evil report upon the land, died by the plague before the LORD" (vv. 36–37).

Always before, when the people repented, the negative sanctions had stopped. Once again, they made a brief repentance (vv. 39–40). Moses understood their chicanery: they planned to show God wrong, again. They would defeat their enemies on their terms. "And Moses said, Wherefore now do ye transgress the commandment of the LORD? but it shall not prosper. Go not up, for the LORD is not among you; that ye be not smitten before your enemies. For the Amalekites and the Canaanites are there before you, and ye shall fall by the sword: because ye are turned away from the LORD, therefore the LORD will not be with you" (vv. 41–43). They refused to listen. They attacked Amalekites and Canaanites who lived in the area. They were soundly defeated (vv. 43–45).

Israel believed the reports it wanted to hear. When the people heard of the good land filled with big people, they discounted the message of the good land. The spies then revised their initial report: bad land, big people. When God told them they were not able to win a relatively minor battle, they refused to believe Him. They trusted in themselves. They did not trust themselves enough to defeat Canaan. They did trust themselves enough to defeat Amalek. Had they listened to Joshua and Caleb, they would not have had to bother with Amalek; they would have marched straight into Canaan. They lost a minor battle, yet they could have won a major battle. The issue was their faith in God's word, not comparative size of armies. Faith in God's word is what they lacked.

Conclusion

Evaluation is an aspect of point four of the biblical covenant: sanctions/judgment. The people were supposed to evaluate their situation in terms of God's word, as confirmed by His acts of deliverance in recent history. They refused to believe God's word; therefore, they evaluated their situation incorrectly. They interpreted the historical facts in terms of covenant-breaking standards. They did not use God's word as their standard of evaluation. God brought corporate judgments against them because of this open disbelief.

The Israelites had fallen into a bad habit: whining to Moses to get what they wanted from God. By God's grace, this whining initially resulted in positive sanctions. The problem was, they did not recognize that it was God's grace, not their whining, that had gained them the objects of their desires. Their whining was a public testimony of their lack of faith in God's promises. They focused on the negative side of their journey, ignoring or denying the positive. This was reflected in the spies' revised report: bad land, big people.

The land was good; the land was theirs for the taking. It was not theirs for the asking. They had to take risks on the battlefield. God was going to bring negative sanctions against Canaan; this was an inescapable aspect of His original promise: "But in the fourth generation they shall come hither again: for the iniquity of the Amorites is not yet full" (Gen. 15:16). God would bring His judgment when the iniquity of the Amorites was full. The Israelites wanted the positive sanction of the land without the negative sanctions associated with battle. The land was not available on these terms. So, Israel rebelled. They wanted the land on their terms; failing that, they did not want the land at all. So, they did not inherit.

Manna was not good enough; they wanted quail. So, they cried out that manna was bad. The land was not good enough; they wanted it empty of resistance. So, they cried out that the land was bad. What was good they evaluated as bad. They brought formal public judgment against manna and the land. God then brought a covenant lawsuit against them.

They were willing to return to Egypt, thereby disinheriting their children. In reply, God disinherited them, skipping a generation. It was the parents who were disinherited by God, not the children.

God did not intend that they dwell in the wilderness forever. He wanted them in the Promised Land. But to gain their promised inheritance, they had to have faith in God and then bear the risks of warfare. This is why God begins the Book of Numbers (*bemidbar*: "in the wilderness") with a military numbering. It pointed to their present condition (wilderness) and the way to a better condition (warfare). Not willing to bear the burden of the risks of warfare, they forfeited their inheritance. They refused to honor the covenantal principle that underlies godly inheritance: "no pain, no gain." They wanted gain without pain, inheritance without negative sanctions. Anything less than this was not good enough for Israel. They forgot the obvious, which the sacrificial system announced clearly: apart from the means of grace, Israel was not good enough for God.

8

DEFERRED GRATIFICATION

Speak unto the children of Israel, and say unto them, When ye be come into the land of your habitations, which I give unto you, And will make an offering by fire unto the L*ORD*, *a burnt offering, or a sacrifice in performing a vow, or in a freewill offering, or in your solemn feasts, to make a sweet savour unto the* L*ORD*, *of the herd, or of the flock. Then shall he that offereth his offering unto the* L*ORD* *bring a meat offering of a tenth deal of flour mingled with the fourth part of an hin of oil. And the fourth part of an hin of wine for a drink offering shalt thou prepare with the burnt offering or sacrifice, for one lamb (Num. 15:2–5).*

The theocentric focus of this passage is God's ownership of the Promised Land. When making an offering, the Israelite would have to offer oil, bread, and wine to God. This representative or token offering pointed to God's ownership of the source of bread and wine: the land. This law would come into force only after the inheritance had been delivered. The law did not apply in the wilderness.

Who is the giver of gifts? God. He reasserted His claim on Israel by reminding them of the inevitability of the Promised Land. He promised again to give the land to them. It would be the land of their habitation. This means that it would be the land of God's habitation. Obviously, the wilderness was not to be their place of habitation. It was merely a transitional residence for the younger generation. For the exodus generation, it was a permanent residence. They would die and be buried in the wilderness they hated.

This law was therefore aimed at the generation of the conquest. It was given to the exodus generation early in the wilderness experience, yet it did not relate to them. They knew this in Numbers 15. This is why this section of Numbers 15 is a problem passage. It did not relate to the lives of those who were old enough to obey it.

Additional Sacrifices

In Wenham's words, this section of Numbers 15 "baffles commentators."[1] It deals with offerings: burnt offerings, peace offerings, and sin (purification) offerings. God required that meal, oil, and wine accompany these offerings. This requirement did not appear in Leviticus 1–7. Why were these requirements added in Numbers 15?

A fairly simple explanation for this change is the fact that the land would offer benefits that the wilderness did not. There was no way for the Israelites to enjoy wine in the wilderness except by trade with nations that were in nearby lands. There is no record of such trade. Oil was also a problem: no olive trees. The oil offerings in the wilderness were limited. Not so in the Promised Land. There they were required with other sacrifices.

The general principle here is that man sins in the face of an environment that testifies to God. The greater the testimony of God's benefits to man, the greater is man's sin. From that person to whom much has been given, much is expected (Luke 12:48).

The Promised Land was flowing with milk and honey; the wilderness was not. God would be entitled to a share of the fruit of the land when the people entered the land. This ap-

---

1. Gordon J. Wenham, *Numbers: An Introduction and Commentary* (Downers Grove, Illinois: Inter-Varsity Press, 1981), p. 126.

plied not just to tithes and voluntary offerings but also to mandatory offerings to cover sin.

This is additional testimony to the fact that God does not call upon man to make huge sacrifices. He warns men that they must not attempt to buy their way out of God's judgment by means of enormous sacrifices. Man does not possess sufficient assets to placate God. To act as though he does is itself sinful.[2] What God does call man to do is to acknowledge that with greater blessings from God there is greater responsibility to God. Their entrance into the land will be a blessing, God announces in Numbers 15. The people should know that the land will bring blessings because there will be additional requirements for the mandated sacrifices, as well as for the voluntary peace offering (Num. 15:9–10).

The parents had just rebelled against God and had been locked out of the Promised Land. What were they going to miss? A lot, God announced. The new requirements for the various offerings testified to the fact that life would be filled with blessings in the land: meal, wine, and oil. The people had rebelled against God by complaining about the insufficiency of manna. In the Promised Land, there will be far more than manna, God was reminding them here.

There will be a new aspect of the offering. "Speak unto the children of Israel, and say unto them, When ye come into the land whither I bring you, Then it shall be, that, when ye eat of the bread of the land, ye shall offer up an heave offering unto the LORD" (Num. 15:18–19). The heave offering will be of the threshingfloor (v. 20). Previously, the heave offering by the people was animal: "And the right shoulder shall ye give unto the priest for an heave offering of the sacrifices of your peace offerings" (Lev. 7:32; cf. Lev. 10:15). When they have land, they will have farms. A small portion of agricultural output

---

2. Gary North, *Leviticus: An Economic Commentary* (Tyler, Texas: Institute for Christian Economics, 1994), ch. 1.

must go to the heave offering. But not yet – not until they arrive in the land.

Willing to Wait

The promise of land was sanctioned by the requirement of additional offerings. The generation of the conquest had been told from the early days of the wilderness wandering that the land would come to them. Their parents did not sacrifice as their children would eventually sacrifice. Their parents were under lesser requirements because their parents were recipients of reduced blessings. The present and future distinction between the required sacrifices testified to the present and future condition of Israel. God would ask for more in the Promised Land. This was proof that God would fulfill His promise. He would become the beneficiary of His own gift of land: greater sacrifices, more pleasing aromas drifting up to heaven. Why wouldn't the younger generation expect the fulfillment of the promise of land? The God of Israel would be a beneficiary.

Their parents were not patient. The sanction against impatience was appropriate: the imposition of the necessity of deferred gratification. God would teach the younger generation a lesson. He would remain patient, not demanding greater sacrifices in the present; so should members of the younger generation remain patient.

This would pressure them to adopt the mentality of upper-class people. Lower-class people are not patient. They resist any suggestion of deferred gratification in life. In contrast, upper-class people are willing to wait to be gratified.[3] This is why upper-class people are more thrifty, make long-range plans, and remain in school longer than lower-class people. The generation of the exodus was a lower-class generation. Their children were not to imitate them. The very structure of the sacri-

---

3. Edward C. Banfield, *The Unheavenly City: The Nature and Future of Our Urban Crisis* (Boston: Little, Brown, 1970), ch. 3.

fices reminded them that God was willing to wait for His lawful rewards. They were, too.

Planning Ahead

The law of the sabbath was specific: no work was to be done on the sabbath. "Ye shall keep the sabbath therefore; for it is holy unto you: every one that defileth it shall surely be put to death: for whosoever doeth any work therein, that soul shall be cut off from among his people. Six days may work be done; but in the seventh is the sabbath of rest, holy to the LORD: whosoever doeth any work in the sabbath day, he shall surely be put to death" (Ex. 31:14–15; cf. 35:2). The law was specific, but what constituted lawful labor? A case-law application was needed here. Israel soon got one:

> And while the children of Israel were in the wilderness, they found a man that gathered sticks upon the sabbath day. And they that found him gathering sticks brought him unto Moses and Aaron, and unto all the congregation. And they put him in ward, because it was not declared what should be done to him. And the LORD said unto Moses, The man shall be surely put to death: all the congregation shall stone him with stones without the camp. And all the congregation brought him without the camp, and stoned him with stones, and he died; as the LORD commanded Moses (Num. 15:32–36).

The stick-gatherer was working on the sabbath. Perhaps he was planning to start a fire. This was illegal on the sabbath. "Ye shall kindle no fire throughout your habitations upon the sabbath day" (Ex. 35:3). Perhaps he had run low on fuel. This also was no excuse. In fact, running low on fuel was Jesus' model of the well-intentioned soul who does not plan ahead regarding the final judgment: the parable of the ten virgins, half of whom forgot to store up oil for the time when the bridegroom would return (Matt. 25:1–13). Perhaps he was doing this to re-sell the sticks later. In this case, he was working commercially. One thing was sure: the stick-gatherer was working. The judges were not sure if the sabbath death penalty extended to this seemingly minimal daily task. It did.

The stick-gatherer could have gathered sticks on the previous six days. He did not gather a sufficient number. A penalty had to be paid: either a lack of sticks or an excess of stones. He refused to regard as legally binding on him either of these negative sanctions against stick-gathering on the sabbath. God, however, did regard the law as binding on him.

Sabbath and Fuel

The gathering of sticks is a fine example of Hebrew case law as applied in the light of a general requirement of the Decalogue. It shows, perhaps, better than any other instance, the implications of the fourth commandment for the Hebrew nation. Consider the economic implications. What was involved in the gathering of sticks? Sticks could be used for at least four purposes:

1. *Heating* the home
2. *Lighting* the home
3. *Cooking* the meals
4. *Selling* for uses 1–3

As far as actual use was concerned, the case in Numbers 15 applied more to the daily life of Hebrew women than it did to the men of the family. It is more often the man and his work which are the focus of modern sabbatarian concern, but this was not necessarily the case in a rural, pre-industrial community. The gathering of sticks was more likely to be the task of children; women were to use them for household tasks, once gathered. Men were to reap the benefits of both the gathering and actual use of the sticks, but in general they would not have much to do with the actual handling of sticks. There could be a few exceptions, of course, but one exception seems to be far more likely, namely, that of the professional stick-gatherer. His work would be most in demand on the sabbath, precisely the day on which the prohibition against work was enforced. A woman who failed to gather sticks earlier in the week could buy some from a professional.

We are not told that the man in Numbers 15 was such a professional, but the severity of the punishment clearly would have made it far more dangerous for such a class of professionals to have come into existence. There was a need for a harsh penalty, men and women being what they are. There is always a delight in violating God's commandments if one is a sinner; if that violation also brings with it certain superficial benefits above and beyond the mere pleasure of defiance, so much the better. Sabbath prohibitions involved heavy costs for the obedient; enforcement of the sabbath required stiff penalties, thus burdening violators with high costs in the form of high risk.

What were the costs of the sabbath? For the man, it was the forfeiture of all income – monetary (less likely in a rural society), psychological, or in physical property – for that day. But women also paid. They had to gather all sticks earlier in the week. It meant more work during the week, either in longer days or by increasing the intensity of the working day – or both. Had the working day not been lengthened or intensified, then other tasks which it was desirable to accomplish would have to have been foregone, and that, as any wife knows, also involves costs (especially if a husband or a mother-in-law notices the failure in question). There would always be a temptation to forego the gathering of sticks during the week, especially if a professional would come by with a load of wood on the sabbath for a reasonably cheap price. If his price was less than the woman's estimation of the costs involved in gathering the wood earlier in the week, a bargain was to be expected. By imposing a rigorous and permanent form of punishment on the violator, the community was able to force up the price of the sticks; risks would be so high that few professionals could survive. How many women could or would pay the costs? It would be cheaper to buy them or gather them earlier in the week. Stick gathering was made an unlikely source of profitable employment on the sabbath. Since the market for sticks on the sabbath was restricted because of the high prices for the sticks (due to the risks involved), the opportunities for temptation were thereby reduced to a minimum. It did not pay anyone to violate the sabbath, and it was too expensive to hire someone to violate it.

Conclusion

The present-oriented person is less willing to plan ahead than the future-oriented person. The stick-gatherer was obviously present-oriented. He did not plan ahead during the previous week. He acted on the spur of the moment on the sabbath. Short of sticks, he sought more. On the sabbath, he retroactively evaluated the previous week's work and found it lacking. He decided that he could make up for lost time. He was wrong. He lost all remaining time. Time ran out for him.

Time runs out for everyone. That is time's curse in a world under God's negative sanction of final judgment. The goal, then, is to make good use of our allotted time while it is available. The sabbath reminds us of this requirement. To honor it means that we must plan ahead. We must work harder during the week to avoid having to work on the sabbath.

Time orientation is important for distinguishing societies. The biblical concept of history is linear: creation, fall, redemption, and consummation. It has a beginning and an end. Men are told to pay attention to the end of time. While this emphasis is minimal in the Old Testament, the last three verses of Daniel being the main exception, the emphasis on the shortness of man's days is continual. Men are to look ahead to their old age, death, and future generations.

The wilderness experience was designed to teach the younger generation patience, daily trust in God (manna), and faith in the good land to come. They were to acknowledge that all good things come on schedule. So do all bad things. That future era would bring good things to Israel and bad things to Canaanites, whose iniquity would at last be filled (Gen. 15:16). They were to imitate God, who was willing to wait for his extra sacrifices until they entered the Promised Land.

The man who gathered sticks on the sabbath failed to honor the deferred gratification principle of the Old Covenant sabbath: rest at the end of the week. He chose to disparage that future rest by failing to plan ahead. He was present-oriented, and this cost him dearly on the day of rest.

9

EVALUATION AND SANCTIONS

And Moses sent to call Dathan and Abiram, the sons of Eliab: which said, We will not come up: Is it a small thing that thou hast brought us up out of a land that floweth with milk and honey, to kill us in the wilderness, except thou make thyself altogether a prince over us? Moreover thou hast not brought us into a land that floweth with milk and honey, or given us inheritance of fields and vineyards: wilt thou put out the eyes of these men? we will not come up (Num. 16:12–14).

I have already commented on the confrontation between Moses on one hand and Korah and Dathan on the other.[1] Korah, a member of the family of Kohath, was Moses' cousin (Ex. 6:18–21). He was joined by Dathan and Abiram, members of the tribe of Reuben (Num. 16:1). They complained that Moses had arrogated too much authority to himself. There was no distinction among Israelites, they said. All were equally holy (v. 3). Moses called for a test of these democratic claims: a test of fire (v. 18).

The rebels had this complaint: Moses was a false prophet. He had told them that God would lead the nation into a land of milk and honey. But where were they? In the wilderness

1. See above, Chapters 3 and 5.

(*bemidbar*). Everyone could see this: wilderness, wilderness all around them. No milk, no honey. We are not blind, they said. "Wilt thou put out the eyes of these men?"

But the accusers went beyond this. Not only were they not in a land of milk and honey, Moses had led them out of a land of milk and honey. Moses had promised them something better than what they had enjoyed in Egypt. He had lured them out of a good land with the promise of a better land. But now they found themselves in a worse land.

This had been the constant theme of the exodus generation since before the parting of the Red Sea: the positive blessings of Egypt. The nation believed in the message of Korah and Dathan. They had voiced it themselves repeatedly. The people's complaint had not been political, however. It had been economic: Where is our water? Where is our meat? This time, the complaint was more political and ecclesiastical: Where is our authority? But the complaint was supported by an appeal to economic conditions. They were saying to Moses: "Your interpretation of God's plan was incorrect. There is no reason for you to elevate yourself above us."

In Hope of Plenty

Moses had come before Pharaoh with a demand: let the Israelites go three days' journey into the wilderness. Pharaoh rejected this demand. Then came a series of confrontations between Moses and Pharaoh. In none of these was the question of Israel's permanent emigration ever raised. God had told Moses that this was His intention (Ex. 3:8, 17), but not until after the Passover did Moses inform the people about this (Ex. 13:5). They knew they were leaving Egypt, for they spoiled the Egyptians, but they did not know where they were going unless they remembered God's promise to Abraham (Gen. 15:16).

When Moses raised the hope of plenty, it caught their imagination. The early confrontations in the wilderness centered around the disparity between the wilderness and the promise, and between the past and the promise. They wanted to be effortlessly delivered by God into the Promised Land. By the time of the rebellion of Korah, the generation of the exodus knew that they would not enter the Promised Land. Having been denied the fulfillment of their promise, they reinterpreted Egypt as the retroactive Promised Land. They had no sense of inheritance. Egypt, the land of bondage, where their children had been condemned to perpetual servitude to foreigners, became the Promised Land. Since that generation would not inherit the real Promised Land, it was obviously not worth inheriting.

This was their present-orientation in action. They were revisionist historians who, less than two years after the exodus, were re-writing the history of their recent experience in Egypt: not bondage but a golden age. They had short memories in public.

Had these political rebels really forgotten about their lives in Egypt? This seems highly unlikely. Their appeal to revisionist history was rhetorical. It was an appeal to the people regarding the unpleasantness of the present wilderness condition. "Just give us a reformed administration, and the wilderness will become more bearable. We suffer in a wilderness as subordinates; let us suffer the wilderness as equals. Egyptian slavery involved subordination; the wilderness involves subordination; let us put an end to subordination!"

This appeal invoked the hope of plenty. This hope had been thwarted by Israel's sin and their fear of confrontation with Canaan. But Korah made no mention of the true causes for the delay of milk and honey. He only mentioned Moses' original promise. He failed to mention that this promise had been conditional on their obedience. He also failed to mention that their children would inherit. They wanted instant fulfillment of the promise of milk and honey.

Milk and honey: this is a familiar political promise by the politician who seeks authority in the name of equality. Wealth is a valid goal: God gave this goal to Moses; Moses gave it to the people. Milk and honey are aspects of kingdom blessings: *positive sanctions for covenantal faithfulness*. The model is the New Heaven and the New Earth (Isa. 65:17–20). The politician and power-seeker who plans to replace the incumbent finds that an appeal to more milk and more honey is a powerful appeal. "The incumbent has promised to deliver the goods; he has failed to deliver; so, elect me."

Korah could not offer the promised plenty of Canaan. God had been very clear about this. That generation would not inherit. What were the obvious options? First, they could return to Egypt, that other land filled with milk and honey. But Egypt had been wiped out: its firstborn sons were dead. It was probably in chaos – or under the rule of invaders. Second, they could stay in the wilderness under Moses' rule. Third, they could stay in the wilderness under a new system of political and ecclesiastical rulers, but in the name of equality. The rebels recommended the third option. But their appeal was to economics: the absence of milk and honey under Moses' rule. "If we can't get what we had been promised under the old regime, let us establish a new regime."

The judgment of God against the rebels was total. This included their wealth. "And the earth opened her mouth, and swallowed them up, and their houses, and all the men that appertained unto Korah, and all their goods" (Num. 16:32). All of their goods disappeared into the pit. Their assets became as cursed as Jericho's would be in the next generation: total (*hormah*). "And he spake unto the congregation, saying, Depart, I pray you, from the tents of these wicked men, and touch nothing of theirs, lest ye be consumed in all their sins" (Num. 16:26).

Poor Evaluation, Large Losses

Did Israel learn its lesson? No. "But on the morrow all the congregation of the children of Israel murmured against Moses and against Aaron, saying, Ye have killed the people of the LORD" (Num. 16:41). They had seen the fire from heaven consume the 250 who had offered sacrifice (v. 35). This did not make an impression on them. The Israelites interpreted all of this in terms of their desire for equality with Moses and Aaron. Their representatives, who had acted to elevate the people, had been destroyed. It was not God who had done this; it was Moses and Aaron. God's immediate response to this accusation was to send a plague on them (v. 47). Only the active intervention of Aaron saved the nation, but 14,700 of them died (v. 49).

Chapter 17 is really an extension of chapter 16. God established one more test and one more evaluation. He had Moses instruct the tribes to bring one rod per tribe. The name of the prince of the tribe was to be written on the tribe's rod. These men were political representatives, not priests. Then He had Moses write Aaron's name on Levi's rod. When these rods were placed before God in the tabernacle and left overnight, Aaron's rod blossomed (v. 8). The other rods did not. Moses brought each man's rod back to him (v. 9). "And the LORD said unto Moses, Bring Aaron's rod again before the testimony, to be kept for a token against the rebels; and thou shalt quite take away their murmurings from me, that they die not" (v. 10). "And the children of Israel spake unto Moses, saying, Behold, we die, we perish, we all perish. Whosoever cometh any thing near unto the tabernacle of the LORD shall die: shall we be consumed with dying?" (vv. 12–13). This ended the rebellion of the people in seeking to become priests or to send their agents to become priests.

The Basis of Evaluation

The people did not suffer from physical blindness; they suffered from moral blindness. They refused to interpret what they saw by means of what God told them through Moses. They were in revolt against God. They were in revolt against Moses. Moses' words were automatically rejected by them. Thus, his evaluation of reality was also rejected by them. They were consistent. They rejected God, Moses, and the reality imposed by God and explained by Moses.

Reality was what Moses said it was. God's visible sanctions came predictably in terms of Moses' evaluation. The people could ignore their own eyes and ears, and did. After the destruction of the rebels, the people blamed Moses. The true god had been represented by the rebels; Moses must have represented a false God. So, God gave them another dose of reality.

Still, God knew this was not enough. He imposed the test of the blossoming rod. This finally persuaded them. They were now afraid to approach the tabernacle. But it had taken negative sanction after negative sanction to persuade them. Seeing, they would not see. This wilful blindness brought a series of negative sanctions on them, just as it had with Pharaoh. They were not myopic; they were Pharaonic.

They could have avoided the negative sanctions at every step, had they listened to Moses: prior to the golden calf incident, prior to the spies' return, prior to the quail, prior to Korah's rebellion, prior to their attribution of righteousness to the late Rev. Korah. Had they listened to Moses, they would have seen reality. Refusing to listen to Moses, they refused to see reality. This was reaffirmed by Jesus in the parable of Lazarus and Dives: "Then he [Dives] said, I pray thee therefore, father [Abraham], that thou wouldest send him to my father's house: For I have five brethren; that he may testify unto them, lest they also come into this place of torment. Abraham saith unto him, They have Moses and the prophets; let them hear them. And he said, Nay, father Abraham: but if one went unto them from the dead, they will repent. And he said unto him, If they hear not Moses and the prophets, neither will they be persuaded, though one rose from the dead" (Luke 16:27–31). Hell is the ultimate negative sanction, yet not even the testimony of one resurrected from the dead can persuade Moses-rejecting men of hell's reality or of the way of escape. The way of escape from the negative sanctions, Abraham said, was a willingness to listen and conform to Moses and the prophets prior to the imposition of the sanctions. This, the generation of the wilderness steadfastly refused to do. And so the negative sanctions kept coming.

Conclusion

The people had looked at their wilderness condition, had compared it with the promise of milk and honey, and had sanctioned the rebels retroactively. Korah had asked rhetorically, "Wilt thou put out the eyes of these men?" But these men could not see. They were judicially blind. Seeing, they would not see.

The nation saw what they wanted to see. They saw Moses and Aaron as tyrants, despite the fact that it had been, and soon would be again, the active intervention of Moses and Aaron that allowed them to survive. They saw the wilderness, but did not see liberty. They saw their children, but did not see the inheritance, which is why they refused to circumcise their sons (Josh. 5:5). They had seen Egypt's tyranny, but viewed it as a land of plenty.

Evaluation is associated with judgment. To evaluate something is to judge it. The test of what an evaluator says is how closely his words match what God has decreed. As Moses said before God's judgment between Moses and Korah, "Hereby ye shall know that the LORD hath sent me to do all these works; for I have not done them of mine own mind. If these men die the common death of all men, or if they be visited after the visitation of all men; then the LORD hath not sent me. But if the LORD make a new thing, and the earth open her mouth, and swallow them up, with all that appertain unto them, and they go down quick into the pit; then ye shall understand that these men have provoked the LORD" (vv. 28–30). But the people did not understand this; they chose not to understand. So the negative sanctions came on them.

Reality imposes sanctions. Evaluation must match reality in order to be successful. Those who evaluate reality accurately reap rewards. Those whose evaluations fail to match reality suffer losses. This is the great law of entrepreneurship: those who forecast the future accurately and act accordingly prosper; those who do not forecast accurately and act accordingly lose. Assets move from those who evaluate properly to those who evaluate improperly.

10

TITHE AND SANCTIONS

And the Lord *said unto Aaron, Thou and thy sons and thy father's house with thee shall bear the iniquity of the sanctuary: and thou and thy sons with thee shall bear the iniquity of your priesthood. And thy brethren also of the tribe of Levi, the tribe of thy father, bring thou with thee, that they may be joined unto thee, and minister unto thee: but thou and thy sons with thee shall minister before the tabernacle of witness. And they shall keep thy charge, and the charge of all the tabernacle: only they shall not come nigh the vessels of the sanctuary and the altar, that neither they, nor ye also, die. And they shall be joined unto thee, and keep the charge of the tabernacle of the congregation, for all the service of the tabernacle: and a stranger shall not come nigh unto you (Num. 18:1–4).*

The theocentric principle here is God's holiness and man's responsibility. God is set apart from man: holiness.[1] This required the creation of a series of concentric circles of holiness around the Ark of the Covenant, where God dwelt with Israel. Someone had to take personal responsibility for guarding[2] these zones of holiness from trespassers whose very presence would profane the sacred space. So, God transferred to the sons of Aaron the responsibility of guarding the sanctuary. Because

1. Point three: ethics.
2. Point four: sanctions.

of man's sin, any iniquity within the sanctuary's boundaries had to be dealt with ritually. This was the task assigned to Aaron and his sons by God: to guard the sanctuary and cleanse it. They bore the responsibility for any violations of the holiness of the sanctuary's sacred boundaries.

God's goal was the elimination of the effects of sin in Israel. He desired to remove the nation from the judgment of sin. By creating a system of ritual acts of cleansing, God made possible life apart from the imposition of His negative sanctions: "And ye shall keep the charge of the sanctuary, and the charge of the altar: that there be no wrath any more upon the children of Israel" (v. 5).

Boundaries had to be respected in Israel. But boundaries, like law, to which sanctions are not attached are merely opinion. The boundaries of the Ark of the Covenant were not mere opinion. God's sanctions enforced the boundaries associated with His dwelling place. Because it is better to fall into the hands of angry men than an angry God,[3] He appointed defenders. They would impose preliminary sanctions to guard the sacred space associated with the Ark. "And I, behold, I have taken your brethren the Levites from among the children of Israel: to you they are given as a gift for the LORD, to do the service of the tabernacle of the congregation. Therefore thou and thy sons with thee shall keep your priest's office for every thing of the altar, and within the vail; and ye shall serve: I have given your priest's office unto you as a service of gift: and the stranger that cometh nigh shall be put to death" (vv. 6–7).

A Meat-Eating Priesthood

The sons of Aaron could lawfully claim certain offerings as food: "This shall be thine of the most holy things, reserved from the fire: every oblation of theirs, every meat [meal] offer-

---

3. "And fear not them which kill the body, but are not able to kill the soul: but rather fear him which is able to destroy both soul and body in hell" (Matt. 10:28).

ing of theirs, and every sin offering of theirs, and every trespass offering of theirs, which they shall render unto me, shall be most holy for thee and for thy sons. In the most holy place shalt thou eat it; every male shall eat it: it shall be holy unto thee" (vv. 9–10). These sacrifices were not regarded as the care and feeding of God – a common belief among pagan societies.[4] Rather, they served as legal coverings for the donors and as food for the priests. The priests received the heave offerings (v. 11). They received the best, not the dregs: "All the best of the oil, and all the best of the wine, and of the wheat, the firstfruits of them which they shall offer unto the LORD, them have I given thee" (v. 12). But to receive these offerings, the priest had to be clean before God: "And whatsoever is first ripe in the land, which they shall bring unto the LORD, shall be thine; every one that is clean in thine house shall eat of it" (v. 13). The primary goal was holiness; the secondary goal was the support of priests.

"Every thing devoted in Israel shall be thine" (v. 14). A devoted item was the most holy of all. It could not be repurchased by the donor, unlike the dedicated object. The dedicated item could be repurchased by an additional payment of 20 percent (Lev. 27:15); not so the devoted item (Lev. 27:28–29).

Second, the priest received a payment for the firstborn male in every family, as well as firstborn males of unclean beasts (v. 15). The payment was five shekels of the sanctuary (v. 16). The firstborn males of cows, sheep, and goats could not be redeemed; they had to be offered to the priests, who then sacrificed them.

This raises the question of transport. These animals had to be taken to Jerusalem to be sacrificed. They were not the property of the Levites; they belonged to the sons of Aaron. "And

4. Jacob Milgrom, *Leviticus 1-16*, vol. 3 of *The Anchor Bible* (New York: Doubleday, 1991), p. 59. Cf. Gary North, *Leviticus: An Economic Commentary* (Tyler, Texas: Institute for Christian Economics, 1994), pp. 47–48.

the flesh of them shall be thine, as the wave breast and as the right shoulder are thine. All the heave offerings of the holy things, which the children of Israel offer unto the LORD, have I given thee, and thy sons and thy daughters with thee, by a statute for ever: it is a covenant of salt for ever before the LORD unto thee and to thy seed with thee" (vv. 18–19). The costs of transportation were high. Presumably, the animals did not have to be delivered immediately. As they fattened up, they became more valuable as food. The priests would become the owners of more valuable animals. A man with a large herd would have driven the designated animals to Jerusalem at one of the mandatory festivals. This would have made the trip more difficult. It also would have filled the roads with droppings, which presumably would have been collected by farmers whose properties were close to the roads.

Four of the five primary sacrifices (v. 9) had to be eaten in the holy place (v. 10). The first primary offering, the whole burnt offering (Lev. 1), was exclusively God's; the priest retained only the hide (Lev. 7:8). Verse 10 specifies "every oblation" (*corban*), which means every sacrifice. This is comprehensive language: "every oblation" was substituted for the whole burnt offering. This means that the priests alone had access to all of these holy offerings. The question arises: What about the heave offerings (v. 8)? Could they be shared with the other Levites? The language of the texts indicates that the offerings placed on the altar were the exclusive responsibility of the priests and therefore the exclusive property of the priests. These offerings could not be shared, for they had to be consumed in the holy place.

Every firstborn male born of a clean animal had to be brought to Jerusalem. The priests had to eat this meat in the holy place. The other families of Levi therefore could not partake, for they had no access to the innermost part of the tabernacle. Even their wives could not participate: "every male shall eat of it" (v. 10). There must have been a lot of unconsumed meat; the greater Israel's prosperity, the greater the waste. The excess had to be disposed of, presumably outside the camp, as was required of the sin offering for the priesthood (Lev. 4:12; 8:17; 9:11).

God's Law vs. Vegetarian Virtue

This law makes it clear that the priests of Israel were meat-eaters. Eating meat on a regular basis was a mark of their holiness in a society in which meat was a comparative luxury. They represented God, and God is described in the Bible as one who delights in the odor of burning flesh (Ex. 29:18; Lev. 1:9). The tabernacle-temple was a place of mouth-watering odors, where a barbecue was in progress day and night. Those who approached the holy place could not have avoided this smell. It reminded them of God's judgment: either a substitute goes on God's altar or else the person does.

The unconsumed meat was a form of holy waste. God shared the roasted flesh of animals only with the sons of Aaron. They ate their meals in the presence of God. Representatively, they feasted well in the presence of God, just as sin-free man is to feast well in the presence of God. The exclusive nature of this feast pointed to the grace of God in bringing sinful men into His presence.

It is one of the marks of God's blessing in the modern world that an ever-increasing percentage of men are able to afford to eat meat on a regular basis. This fact of free market capitalism is deeply resented by those who can legitimately be described as soybean socialists. They cry out against the sinfulness of the West, and especially the United States, for consuming so much meat. They bring their version of a covenant lawsuit against Americans who enjoy eating beef. Ronald J. Sider's book, *Rich Christians in an Age of Hunger* (1977), is a representative example. This book became a best-seller among neo-evangelical Christians in the late 1970's until I hired David Chilton to write *Productive Christians in an Age of Guilt-Manipulators* (1981), after which Sider's book faded into oblivion, as politically liberal fads generally do.[5]

Sider blamed Third World poverty on the meat-eating West. Residents in the United States consume five times more grain per capita than those living in developing nations, he correctly observed. This blessing he regarded as a moral infraction. It is impoverishing the Third World. "The major reason for this glaring difference is that we eat most of our grain indirectly – via grain-fed livestock and fowl. . . . Why is that important? Because it takes many pounds of grain to produce just one pound of beef. . . . Beef is the cadillac of meat products. . . . It is because of this high level of meat consumption that the rich minority of the world devours such an unfair share of the world's available food."[6] He repeated this accusation, almost word for word, in the ignored and now nearly forgotten third edition of his book.[7] His language of guilt manipulation is evident: "devours," "unfair share." We can almost hear Korah and Dathan railing against Aaron: "You and your sons are eating an unfair share of our beef. You are devouring our fields by your lust for meat, especially beef. You are no more holy than we are. Let us all publicly demonstrate our commitment to equality by eating nothing but grains from now on."

Not only did the priesthood feast on beef and other clean meats, they were required to throw away every ounce that they did not eat. This was holy wastefulness, and it was commanded by God. Any complaining about this procedure on the part of the non-priestly families of Levi, let alone any other tribe, was an assault on the integrity of the sacrificial system. Sinners were to bring their special offerings to God, and the priests alone benefitted directly. It unquestionably paid to be a priest.

---

5. It was co-published by Inter-Varsity Press and the Paulist Press.

6. Ronald J. Sider, *Rich Christians in an Age of Hunger: A Biblical Study* (Downers Grove, Illinois: Inter-Varsity Press, 1977), pp. 42–44.

7. Waco, Texas: Word, 1990, pp. 22–23.

The fat was to go to God: "And the priest shall burn them upon the altar: it is the food of the offering made by fire for a sweet savour: all the fat is the LORD'S. It shall be a perpetual statute for your generations throughout all your dwellings, that ye eat neither fat nor blood" (Lev. 3:16–17). This was a mark of God's sovereignty; it also was a form of dietary protection for the priests. If they did not honor this legal claim by God, and they ate the fat, then there would be negative consequences in their arteries. But the idea that eating meat in large quantities should be universally avoided, irrespective of individual metabolisms and budgets, flies in the face of God's sacrificial system. Was it a curse to be a priest? Did God bring His loyal priesthood under the negative sanction of poor diet and bad health? Did He provide a daily miracle in cleaning the arteries of the priesthood? The texts reveal nothing like this. What they do reveal is a national sacrificial system that mandated an overflow of meat into the tabernacle.

We are no longer under the rules of this system. We can lawfully eat meat or chicken or even tofu burgers, as we see fit. Whether we should eat lots of beef depends on our incomes and our metabolisms. The issue is not to be decided by an appeal to morals; it is a personal matter of taste, cost, and health. Just as the righteous priests' constant feasting on meat was a mark of their position of great responsibility, authority, and blessing, so is the West's abundance of meat.[8]

Implications of This Inheritance

The Levites had no landed inheritance outside of Levitical cities: "And the LORD spake unto Aaron, Thou shalt have no inheritance in their land, neither shalt thou have any part

8. The fact that McDonald's hamburger restaurants have become in our day the most visible sign of America's cultural presence in foreign nations is altogether appropriate. The company's universally recognized corporate representative, Ronald McDonald, is a clown with a smiling face. Theologically speaking, soybean socialists are clowns with angry faces. I prefer the smiling Ronald to the nagging Ronald.

among them: I am thy part and thine inheritance among the children of Israel. And, behold, I have given the children of Levi all the tenth in Israel for an inheritance, for their service which they serve, even the service of the tabernacle of the congregation" (Num. 18:20–21). This law had important implications for both the social order and the political order of Israel.

Social Implications

There is always the problem of envy and jealousy in a society. The jealous person thinks: "You have something I want. I will take it from you." This was the sin of Korah and Dathan. The envious person thinks: "You have something I want. I cannot get it from you. I will destroy it so that neither of us can enjoy it." This had been the sin of the Philistines in regard to Abraham: "For all the wells which his father's servants had digged in the days of Abraham his father, the Philistines had stopped them, and filled them with earth. And Abimelech said unto Isaac, Go from us; for thou art much mightier than we. And Isaac departed thence, and pitched his tent in the valley of Gerar, and dwelt there. And Isaac digged again the wells of water, which they had digged in the days of Abraham his father; for the Philistines had stopped them after the death of Abraham: and he called their names after the names by which his father had called them" (Gen. 26:15–18). The Philistines were envious: better to fill up these wells with dirt rather than retrieve water from them today but risk having Abraham or his heirs claim them later and benefit from them.

The system of Levitical inheritance kept jealousy and envy at a minimum. The Israelites were required to pay tithes to the Levites, but the Levites could not inherit rural land. Only later, if Israel became a predominantly urban society, would this restriction on rural land ownership fade as a major restraint on the wealth of Levi. The Levites had to be supported by the nation, but only in proportion to the prosperity of the nation.

There is no doubt that God deliberately established offsetting inheritances: tithes vs. land. "But the tithes of the children of Israel, which they offer as an heave offering unto the Lord, I have given to the Levites to inherit: therefore I have said unto them, Among the children of Israel they shall have no inheritance" (Num. 18:24). If the Israelites grumbled about the arrangement, this grumbling would be completely illegitimate. The Levites bore the sins of the nation if they did not guard the tabernacle from defilement: "But the Levites shall do the service of the tabernacle of the congregation, and they shall bear their iniquity: it shall be a statute for ever throughout your generations, that among the children of Israel they have no inheritance" (v. 23). The Levites were compensated for the risk they bore. The closer that men drew to the tabernacle, the greater their risk.

Political Implications

The Levites had no inheritance in the land. They lived in 48 designated Levitical cities which were distributed throughout the land (Num. 35:7). This meant that they could serve as legal counsellors and literate specialists. No other tribe had a monopoly claim on these services. The Levites were unlikely to become operational agents of any single tribe, since their sources of prosperity and the locus of their influence were distributed across the nation. If the tribe of the king sought an alliance with the Levites of Jerusalem, there were Levites living inside the boundaries of the other tribes whose interests were local. These Levites of the cities provided counter-weights to Levites living near the king's palace. There might be court priests in Israel, but there would be country Levites to offset their influence.

At the same time, the Levites could not amass landed wealth for their families. This meant that tribal leaders did not have to worry about a political consolidation resulting from economic consolidation for as long as Israel remained predominantly agricultural. Local leaders could seek alliances with the Levites against the central government without feeling threatened. This acted as a restraint on political centralization.

The Levites received their income from local residents. This made them dependent on the prosperity of local populations. If residents in one region had wanted to establish restrictions on the export or import of goods, the local Levites might have approved. But there were Levites in other regions who had different interests. The priests would decide the limits of ecclesiastical interpretation, but there would have been a tendency for the national priesthood to balance the interests of all in order to keep peace in the tribe. This would have tended to favor the development of a national body of legal precedents that did not benefit one region at the expense of another. This would have consolidated legal opinion in ecclesiastical matters, but not on the basis of one regionally dominant tribe's interests. This consolidated body of precedents would have reflected the opinions of all the regions, since Levites resided in each region. The regionalism of the tribes was offset by the nationalism of Levi. At the same time, the potential regionalism of the priesthood in Jerusalem was offset by its economic interests. The priesthood maximized its income and its political independence by maximizing the income of the whole nation, since the priesthood was paid a tithe of the tithes received by the Levites (vv. 26–28).

Fee for Sacred Services Rendered

The Levites were forbidden to cheat the priesthood by sending the dregs of their produce. They had to send the best: "Out of all your gifts ye shall offer every heave offering of the Lord, of all the best thereof, even the hallowed part thereof out of it" (v. 29). The priests were to be well-paid. They were the senior representatives of the nation before God. To cheat them was to cheat God. If the nation did this, God would bring negative sanctions against them: "Will a man rob God? Yet ye have robbed me. But ye say, Wherein have we robbed thee? In tithes and offerings. Ye are cursed with a curse: for ye have robbed me, even this whole nation" (Mal. 3:8–9).

The tithe was the designated system of payment. It was priestly. The tithe burdened every member of society the same. The rich paid ten percent of their net income; so did the poor. There were no exempted classes except the priests themselves. No one was too poor or too rich to escape paying. Had the payment been a fixed quantity of goods or money, the poor would have been burdened excessively, and the rich would have paid a token. The tithe meant that each income group would be equally burdened.

The tithe governed giving to the Lord's priestly representatives. The tithe was a matter of life and death – eternal life and death. In matters of eternal life and death, the tithe principle governs payments. No one is able to buy his salvation; at the same time, no one is able to escape his lawful acknowledgment of his need for an intermediary institution that represents God: a priesthood. Man can be saved apart from such a priesthood, but no saved man is supposed to abandon his biblically mandatory economic support of God's priesthood, i.e., those who possess a lawful monopoly over the administration of the sacraments: God's sanctions in history. Those who guard the sacraments are entitled to a tithe on each covenant-keeper's net income.[9]

The principle of the tithe is not the free market's auction principle of "high bid wins." Salvation is not in fixed supply, to be allocated by a central distributor on the basis of competitive bidding. Salvation is not part of the curse; it is the overcoming of the curse. Salvation is not governed by the law of economic scarcity, i.e., "at zero price, there is greater demand than supply." But the supply of priestly guardians is not infinite. Their

---

9. Gary North, *Tithing and the Church* (Tyler, Texas: Institute for Christian Economics, 1994).

services must be paid for. So, the tither is not buying his salvation; he is supporting the representatives whose task it is to declare the way of salvation and to allocate access to the sacraments. Tithing is therefore a sacramental function; it is a payment for sacred services rendered.

This does not mean that tithing is mandatory in order to receive the sacraments. The sacraments are not for sale for money. They are allocated, however. Those who do not profess faith in the God of the Bible are not allowed access to the sacraments. Also, those who have been excommunicated because of their flagrant sinning do not have lawful access. In Israel, access to Passover was limited to circumcised males and their families. The phrase "cut off from his people" appears regularly in the Mosaic law. This was a judicial cutting off. A judicially consecrated representative of the church must decide who has lawful access to the sacraments. His services must be paid for. The tithe is the mode of payment mandated by God. Those who pay less fall short of God's requirements (Mal. 3:8–9).

The Politics of Plunder

God did not designate this system of equal percentage giving as unfair. Twentieth-century man does. First, his designated sovereign agency is the State, not the church. To cheat the taxman is to cheat the State: the highest relevant court of appeal in history. Second, modern man points to an equal percentage payment system and calls it *regressive*: an excessive burden on the poor. The tithe principle is in fact *proportionate*, but modern man dismisses proportionate taxation as regressive, thereby condemning it in the name of a supposedly higher morality: one opposed to oppressing the poor. Modern man calls for *progressive* taxation, i.e., graduated tax brackets. The rich should pay a greater percentage of their income, we are told. Modern man does not identify what percentage of income taxation constitutes a boundary beyond which the State cannot lawfully go. Establishing such boundaries is understood as wholly arbitrary: a matter of political power. Those who pay a lower percentage of their income, because they constitute a majority, establish the upper limits of taxation.

Modern taxation is justified in terms of a messianic view of the State: the State as healer. The State requires support from the people in order to accomplish its tasks. These tasks are said to be inherently unbounded: as extensive as man's pain and vulnerability. They are defined through political power. One of these tasks is the redistribution of wealth, officially from rich to the poor; in fact from the wealthy and upper middle classes to the middle classes in the name of the poor. The middle classes, like the Mosaic priests, staff the bureaucratic posts that administer the funds and enforce the regulations. They are understood as the agents of healing. They represent the middle class in the name of all the people, and they distribute the funds officially on behalf of the poor. Yet almost every study of government legislation and its tax burdens reveals that the middle class receives the lion's share of the State's benefits.[10] They exercise a majority, and their political representatives do not openly thwart their interests.

In 1945, Beardsley Ruml gave a speech to the American Bar Association (ABA). Ruml was never a well-known man, and he is long forgotten today, even among professional historians, but his influence in the United States for a generation was enormous. In 1922, he was hired to run the Laura Spelman Rockefeller Fund. He had previously been employed as an assistant to the president of the Carnegie Corporation. He was 26 years old.[11] He later served as dean of the Social Sciences Division of the University of Chicago. From 1923 on, he ran the Rocke-

---

10. George J. Stigler, "Director's Law of Public Income Redistribution," *Journal of Law and Economics*, 13 (April 1970). Aaron Director is Milton Friedman's brother-in-law.

11. Don Fisher, *Fundamental Development of the Social Sciences: Rockefeller Philanthropy and the United States Social Science Research Council* (Ann Arbor: University of Michigan Press, 1993), p. 32.

feller-funded Social Science Research Council, assisted by his older academic colleague, University of Chicago political scientist Charles E. Merriam.[12] Through this organization after 1928, Ruml funded large segments of the American social science community to promote the ideology of the government-regulated economy. As Donald Fisher writes: "A bargain was struck between social scientists, Rockefeller philanthropy, and the State that has since become an accepted part of the way we organize social life."[13] In 1954, the Reece Committee investigations on tax-exempt foundations concluded: "The Social Science Research Council is now probably the greatest power in the social science research field."[14] He drafted part of the Social Security Act in 1935, and he was the driving force in 1942 behind the introduction of Federal income tax withholding, which began in 1943.[15] This dramatically increased the collection of individual income taxes: from $3.2 billion in 1942 to $19.7 billion in 1944.[16] Ruml was on the board of the New York Federal Reserve Bank from 1937 to 1947; he served as chairman during the final six years. This is the dominant Federal Reserve Bank among the dozen regional branches of America's central bank. No one reaches this post who is not fully trusted by the highest levels of banking and government.

He announced to the ABA that with the creation of a U.S. central bank (1913) and the suspension of domestic gold pay-

---

12. Barry D. Karl, *Charles E. Merriam and the Study of Politics* (University of Chicago Press, 1974), p. 182.

13. Fisher, Preface.

14. *Tax-Exempt Foundations, Report*, House of Representatives, 83rd Congress, 2nd session, Report 2681, Dec. 16, 1954 (Washington, D.C.: U.S. Government Printing Office, 1954), p. 47. Cf. pages 47–51.

15. Patrick D. Reagan, "The Withholding Tax, Beardsley Ruml, and Modern American Public Policy," *Prologue: Quarterly of the National Archives*, 24 (Spring 1992), p. 23. Cf. Randolph E. Paul, *Taxation in the United States* (Boston: Little, Brown, 1954), pp. 328–36.

16. *Historical Statistics of the United States: Colonial Times to 1970* (Washington, D.C.: Department of Commerce, Bureau of the Census, 1975), p. 1122.

ments in exchange for dollars (1933), the United States no longer needs to levy taxes for revenue purposes. With the power to create money, he said, the ultimate revenue source is the nation's central bank. Taxes have become means of redistributing wealth among groups and to express public policy "in subsidizing or in penalizing various industries and groups."[17] "The second principal purpose of federal taxes is to attain more equality of wealth and of income than would result from economic forces working alone. The taxes which are effective for this purpose are the progressive individual income tax, the progressive estate tax, and the gift tax. What these taxes should be depends on public policy with respect to the distribution of wealth and of income."[18] The mechanism of taxation had become an important means of pursuing national policy objectives, not a means of providing the State with revenue. Put differently, the inflation tax of fiat money creation by the central bank had become the revenue source; other forms of State taxation were means of wealth redistribution. His opinion has not been shared by many officials, but in theory, the distinction could be applied. In practice, the central bank's inflation tax and other forms of State taxation are used as both revenue sources and as social policy tools.

Such a view of the State transforms politics. Politics becomes the politics of plunder rather than the defense of individual liberty, the defense of property rights, and protection against violence. The civil government moves from being an agency that imposes negative sanctions against criminals on behalf of their victims[19] to an agency that provides positive economic sanctions to favored members of the community[20] at the ex-

17. Beardsley Ruml, "Taxes for Revenue Are Obsolete," *American Affairs*, 8 (Jan. 1946), p. 36.

18. *Idem*.

19. Gary North, *Victim's Rights: The Biblical View of Civil Justice* (Tyler, Texas: Institute for Christian Economics, 1990).

20. Or outside the community, e.g., State-to-State foreign aid.

pense of negative economic sanctions imposed on others in the community. Control over taxation and economic regulation has in the twentieth century become a three-fold matter: the exercise of presumed messianic power, the suppression of one's class enemies, and economic self-defense. Jack Douglas has put it well: ". . . the welfare states in the most Christian Western states have strongly emphasized their supposed enactments of the Christian virtues – compassion, charity, forgiveness, kindliness, and so on, even when they have simultaneously been rabidly pursuing the seven deadly sins."[21] In fallen man, power tends to corrupt, and absolute power corrupts absolutely – Lord Acton's famous dictum.[22] This applies to taxation, for the power to tax involves the power to destroy – Chief Justice John Marshall's equally famous dictum.[23]

Israel's priesthood was not to become a battlefield of wealth redistribution among classes. God placed explicit limits on what the Levites could lawfully request in God's name: the tithe. The Levites were under God's law. Men might pay them less than a tithe, but this would bring God's negative sanctions in history. Individuals might pay more, but this extra giving was not called a tithe; it was a voluntary offering.

The Levites were restricted by a boundary, the tithe. The tithe was not a means of income redistribution among classes. The tithe was the inheritance of the Levites. It was owed to them by the tribes. This was not a matter of choice among those who were under the covenant.

---

21. Jack D. Douglas, *The Myth of the Welfare State* (New Brunswick, New Jersey: Transaction, 1991), p. 11.

22. Letter to Mandell Creighton (April 5, 1887); reprinted in *Selected Writings of Lord Acton*, 3 vols. (Indianapolis, Indiana: Liberty*Classics*, 1986), II, p. 383. The context of this remark was his rejection of the authority of the Papacy to use the State to impose physical torture and execution against heretics. Acton was a Roman Catholic.

23. *McCulloch v. Maryland* (1819); reprinted in *John Marshall's Defense of McCulloch v. Maryland* (Stanford, California: Stanford University Press, 1969), p. 46.

Conclusion

The tithe is grounded legally in the sovereignty of ordained officials over the administration of the sacraments. It is the biblically mandated payment for sacramental services rendered. In Mosaic Israel, these services involved animal and other sacrifices. They also involved Passover and the two other mandatory national feasts. The Levites were guardians of the tabernacle area, while the Aaronic priests were the guardians of the Ark of the Covenant. This guardianship had to be paid for. The Levites received a tithe of the net income of the Israelites; the priests received a tithe of the income of the Levites. Income flowed up the chain of ecclesiastical command.[24]

By giving the Levites a tithe rather than rural land as the tribe's inheritance, God balanced both the social order and the political structure of Mosaic Israel. Levites served as legal advisors in every region. They had local allegiances economically, but they also had a national allegiance judicially: the priesthood. Neither the king nor local tribal leaders could exercise primary influence over the Levites as a tribe. Levites owed their allegiance to a different chain of command, ecclesiastical rather than political.

The Israelites were not buying their salvation with their tithes. They were paying for human services associated with the operation of the sacrificial system. The tithe was not a market price, i.e., high bid wins. Rather, it was a priestly price: proportional giving. The poor man and the rich man paid the same proportion. This made sure that the day-to-day administration of the sacrificial system involved an equal economic sacrifice for all. This form of equality was the equality of the percentage of forfeited income, not the equality of price. The equality of price – one price for all men – would have burdened the poor more than the rich. It would also have created the illusion that salva-

24. See Chapter 3, above: section on "The Hierarchical Flow of Funds and Service."

tion was for sale on a competitive market. This would have implied a scarcity of salvation. Unlike a scarce resource, salvation is available to all at zero price. What is scarce is not salvation but rather the guardians of the sacraments.

Priestly pricing is proportional pricing. The closer we get to life-and-death services, the closer we approach priestly pricing. The free market pricing principle of high bid wins does not apply equally to every occupation and service. It specifically does not apply to the guardians of the sacraments.

The law of the sacrifices mandated a flow of meat to the sons of Aaron. There was no vegetarianism in Israel. Most of the sacrifices were clearly meat-based. The sweet savor of soybean cakes and tofu may have impressed Cain, but Abel's sacrifice was accepted by God. Abel's blood-based sacrifice continued as the standard in Mosaic Israel.

11

THE LURE OF MAGIC

And Moses and Aaron gathered the congregation together before the rock, and he said unto them, Hear now, ye rebels; must we fetch you water out of this rock? And Moses lifted up his hand, and with his rod he smote the rock twice: and the water came out abundantly, and the congregation drank, and their beasts also. And the LORD spake unto Moses and Aaron, Because ye believed me not, to sanctify me in the eyes of the children of Israel, therefore ye shall not bring this congregation into the land which I have given them (Num. 20:10–12).

The chapter begins with the death of Miriam (v. 1). It closes with the death of Aaron (v. 28). Aaron died at age 123 (Num. 33:39). This was in the fortieth year after the exodus (Num. 33:38). Moses died at age 120 (Deut. 34:7). He died just before Israel's entry into the land; so, he was 80 years old at the time of the exodus.

The events of this chapter were important for the nation because they mark the late stages of the transfer of inheritance. The generation of the exodus had been told by God that they would not enter the land; they would die in the wilderness (Num. 14:32). Miriam had just died. Moses and Aaron were old men. Time was visibly running out on the few remaining members of the exodus generation. But their legacy of rebellion still survived. The Israelites once again complained to Moses regarding the faithlessness of God.

And there was no water for the congregation: and they gathered themselves together against Moses and against Aaron. And the people chode with Moses, and spake, saying, Would God that we had died when our brethren died before the LORD! And why have ye brought up the congregation of the LORD into this wilderness, that we and our cattle should die there? And wherefore have ye made us to come up out of Egypt, to bring us in unto this evil place? it is no place of seed, or of figs, or of vines, or of pomegranates; neither is there any water to drink (Num. 20:2–5).

Moses and Aaron once again went to God for a solution. "And Moses and Aaron went from the presence of the assembly unto the door of the tabernacle of the congregation, and they fell upon their faces: and the glory of the LORD appeared unto them" (Num. 20:6). This time, God promised another deliverance. He would provide water out of a rock a second time. The first time, shortly after the exodus, God had commanded Moses to strike a rock with his rod. "Behold, I will stand before thee there upon the rock in Horeb; and thou shalt smite the rock, and there shall come water out of it, that the people may drink. And Moses did so in the sight of the elders of Israel" (Ex. 17:6). This time, however, He commanded Moses only to speak to the rock in public: "Take the rod, and gather thou the assembly together, thou, and Aaron thy brother, and speak ye unto the rock before their eyes; and it shall give forth his water, and thou shalt bring forth to them water out of the rock: so thou shalt give the congregation and their beasts drink" (Num. 20:8).

Moses Rebels Against God

Moses took the rod (v. 9), gathered the assembly before the rock (v. 10), spoke a word of condemnation to them (v. 10), and struck it twice (v. 11). The water gushed forth, but so did

God's voice. God told Moses that Moses had not believed Him. His act did not sanctify God before the people (v. 12).

God's prophecy regarding the future of their generation as a result of the false reports of the ten spies had been clear: only Joshua and Caleb would enter the Promised Land as conquerors. Moses and Aaron were not singled out as survivors. But they had not participated in the false reporting. God dealt with Moses subsequently as if he had not been guilty of any terminal infraction. The spies had brought the condemnation on their generation, but apparently not on Moses and Aaron. Nevertheless, Moses and Aaron had not been listed by God as survivors. It should have been clear that something they would do later would keep them out of the Promised Land, because they were neither exempted by God's condemnation nor were they responsible for the false reports. They should have understood this. They should have been better prepared for this final testing of their faith. They should have known that God's prophecies of negative sanctions are both ethical and conditional: "unless you turn from your evil ways and obey me." A prophecy that something negative must happen in history is a warning that the recipient of the bad news must turn from his evil. It is never a prophecy that something must happen irrespective of God's sovereign, initiating grace of redemption and man's subordinate repentance. Jonah learned this after his ministry to Nineveh had been successful. God did not destroy Nineveh.

A Matter of Causation

Moses was familiar with rocks that produce water. God had previously told him to take the rod and strike a rock. He had done as he was told, and this act of obedience was followed by the flow of water. The people had seen this miracle (Ex. 17:6). Nevertheless, this had not changed their hearts. Neither had the subsequent miracles and the plagues. God's negative sanctions had not registered on their ethical consciousness. They were still complainers. They still came before Moses with this complaint: "What has God done for us lately?" They wanted further positive sanctions despite their rebellion.

Moses, deep down inside, remained a man of his generation. He did not fully believe God's prophetic word. He had doubts – not so grave as the people's doubts, but serious enough so that he hesitated to rely on God's word alone. Moses had spoken with God. He had seen God do mighty things through him. What he should have learned from all this was that God's word is true. Men can rely on it. God spoke the world into existence (Gen. 1). When God says that something will come to pass, it will come to pass unless man's repentance intervenes – always an aspect of His negative prophetic word. When God instructed an Old Covenant prophet to speak a positive prophetic word before the people, the prophet could rest assured that whatever God told him to say would come to pass. A negative prophecy was always qualified – "unless you repent" – but a positive word was sure. The people were given the benefit of the doubt. The bad prophetic news was qualified; the good news was not. There is no case of a positive prophetic word's being overturned by man's rebellion.

The Israelites refused to accept this. They kept complaining to Moses that God had promised them an inheritance of milk and honey. They deliberately refused to count: four generations to the conquest (Gen. 15:16); Moses' generation was generation three. But their rebellion in the incident of the spies had been the secondary cause of their disinheritance. The fourth generation had a positive word from God, and it would surely be fulfilled. This prophetic structure should be understood as a promise to the recipients of the promise of landed inheritance that they would not rebel, that God's grace would surely sustain them. A negative prophecy could be overcome by God's grace of redemption, while a positive prophecy could not be overcome by man's rebellion, although it might be postponed, since God would in this case overcome man's natural proclivity to rebel. This structure of prophecy is an aspect of God's grace. Grace tends toward blessings in history.[1]

Moses should have believed God's positive promise unconditionally, but he did not. He did not believe that his mere speaking to the rock would result in a flow of water. God did not tell him to tap the rock. God told him only to take the rod, assemble the people, and speak before the rock. There was a required plan, but it did not involve striking the rock. There was visible cause and effect, but it did not involve striking the rock. The system of cause and effect was supernatural. Speaking to a rock in public was surely not the normal way to provide large quantities of water in a wilderness. To speak water out of a rock is surely a miracle worth recording. But Moses did not believe God to this degree. He wanted two intermediate steps: striking the rock twice.

In Genesis 1, God spoke the world into existence. There was no intermediary causation. God spoke; events consistent with His word immediately took place. The time interval in each step was less than one day. There was no uniformitarian continuity of time, with events taking place slowly in a cosmic process of evolutionary development. God spoke the world into existence. His word was sufficient.

Men do not normally possess such a word of authority. They speak, but only those who hear and understand can bring to pass what is spoken. The tower of Babel is the consummate example. When a breakdown occurred in corporate communication, men ceased to build. Without the cause and effect of the continuity of speech, men cannot work together. The division of labor breaks down.

When a man who possesses authority speaks, his words initiate a process of cause and effect. But man's words have no effect directly on inanimate objects. Mind over matter is God's

---

1. This is an argument against both amillennialism and premillennialism. This argument rests on the covenantal connection between sanctions and inheritance.

prerogative, not man's; so is word over matter. We do not think and grow rich merely by thinking. We do not gain it when we "name it and claim it" merely by speaking. There must be intermediary causation: possibly supernatural, probably natural, but never automatic.

To speak an event into existence apart from human, animal, or electrical-mechanical intermediation is to rely on supernatural causation. A supernatural being who hears and understands what a man has spoken then transforms that realm which is external to both the speaker and the hearer. The speaker's words initiated the transformation; they did not cause it.

Moses recognized the supernatural nature of the event. There was no question that only God could bring it to pass. The question facing Moses was this: On what basis would God bring it to pass? By a publicly spoken word alone? Or by an additional causative step or steps? What was binding: God's word or a ritual act? What were the means of grace: words and taps or merely words?

Moses relied on ritual. He would speak and tap the water out of the rock. The ritual was of his design: not just one tap, as had been the case at Horeb, but two. Why two? The text does not say. But two it had to be, Moses decided. One tap would not do. A spoken word alone would not do.

This reliance on ritual is a familiar pattern in history. Men find that ritual enhances the authority of words. The ritual makes the words more likely to be obeyed. The ritual in fact is thought to invest the words with power. The words are thought to be impotent without an accompanying ritual. The ritual distinguishes authoritative words from non-authoritative words.

In what way does ritual invest words with power? There are three answers, each corresponding to one of the three rival views of causation in history: magical (realism), traditional (nominalism), and judicial (covenantalism). The realist believes that ritual infuses words with power. There is a separate realm of power that can be tapped into by man through a mixture of words and ritual. Ritual is what connects words to power. The nominalist believes that rituals persuade men that words have greater authority. Men are more likely to believe in the words because of the presence of ritual. The judicialist believes that ritual invokes or calls down power when the words are lawfully spoken. It is the judicial legitimacy of the words in the context of historical circumstances that invests the words with power.

Adam's Transgression[2]

The best way biblically to answer this debate over the nature of causation is to consider Adam's transgression. When God announced a judicial boundary around the forbidden tree, did He invest the tree and its fruit with special properties that would automatically produce certain results if touched or eaten? Or was the tree merely symbolic, having no express judicial relationship with God, but only giving Adam an opportunity to prove himself faithful or not? Or was the tree set apart as a unique place of communion, a place declared by God as off-limits to Adam? We need to consider the three views of causation and their respective analyses. The first two answers conform to the philosophical categories of realism and nominalism. Both are incorrect. The third position conforms to the biblical category, covenantalism.

A. Metaphysical Boundary

We know that their eyes were immediately opened after they ate. They recognized their own nakedness and guilt. Was the fruit itself the source of their discontinuous change of perception? Was the tree a gateway to cosmic forces of illumination, a "cosmic tree," to use the language of pagan mythology?[3] Did it

2. This section appeared originally in Gary North, *Boundaries and Dominion: The Economics of Leviticus* (computer edition; Tyler, Texas: Institute for Christian Economics, 1994), ch. 6.

3. The cosmic tree was related to the idea of the cosmic mountain: the *axis mundi*

mark "the center of the world," the supreme sacred space?[4] Could Adam and Eve somehow manipulate these cosmic forces to gain further knowledge or power? Was the forbidden tree a microcosm that offered man power over the macrocosm, analogous to the voodoo doll's supposed power to produce analogous effects in the thing represented by the doll? Could Adam and Eve achieve "unity of being" with the universe through subsequent forbidden feasts? Could they achieve self-transcendence? In short, could they become mini-gods, as the serpent had promised Eve (Gen. 3:5)?

The Genesis account of their transgression informs us that immediately after their eyes were opened, the forbidden tree was no longer the focus of their interest. They did not seek additional fruit. They did not invoke cosmic forces to protect them or do their bidding. They paid no further attention to the tree. They did not act as though they believed the tree possessed any special properties other than its fruit, which was admittedly good to view and good to eat. Even the serpent said nothing further to them. There was no need for him to say anything. His words and work were over. Adam and Eve had performed the profane act. It was an act of judicial transgression: a trespass.

It is clear that their new-found self-awareness was the product of *self-judgment*: they had evaluated their act of rebellion in

---

or axis of the world – the line drawn through the earth which points to the pole star. It was the link between heaven and earth. See Mircea Eliade, *Patterns in Comparative Religion* (New York: Sheed & Ward, 1958), p. 111; cf. 266–67, 271, 273–74. On the *axis mundi*, see the extraordinary, complex, and cryptic book on ancient mathematics, myth, and cosmology, *Hamlet's Mill: An essay on myth and the frame of time*, by Giorgio de Santillana and Hertha von Dechend (Boston: Gambit, 1969). It should be obvious what the source of these cosmic tree and cosmic mountain myths was: the garden of Eden, itself located on a mountain or raised area, for the river flowing through it became four rivers (Gen. 2:10).

4. Eliade writes: "The tree came to express the cosmos fully in itself, by embodying, in apparently static form, its 'force', its life and its quality of periodic regeneration." *Patterns*, p. 271.

the light of their new interpretation of God's word.[5] They did not rush to discover a chemical formula for an antidote to poison fruit. They also did not rush to discover a magical formula to protect themselves from the cosmic forces that the fruit had unleashed. They correctly understood that the fruit was not their problem; God's promised judgment was. The tree had meaning to them only in terms of God's legal boundary around it, which they had transgressed. The fruit was of no further interest or use to them. They referred to it again only under God's subsequent cross-examination.

B. Symbolic Boundary

What about the tree's unique symbolic status? Was the response of Adam and Eve merely the product of an increase in their self-awareness, a perception induced solely by their act of transgression? In other words, was the tree merely a symbolic agency in the transformation of their own self-awareness, something like an ethical mirror? Was the transformational power of the tree merely psychological? In short, had the transformational power of the tree merely been imputed to it by Adam and Eve?

If the tree served solely as a symbol of man's ethical condition, then on what basis did the radical and discontinuous increase of their mutual self-awareness take place? What was it about eating forbidden fruit that produced their perception of nakedness? Their immediate concern was not that they feared that God would bring judgment against them sometime in the future; it was that they were immediately discomforted by their own nakedness. It was not that the now-partially denuded tree pointed symbolically to their completely denuded judicial condition in the eyes of God; it was that they experienced shame in their own eyes as judges. God had assigned a necessarily judi-

5. That it was a new interpretation is seen in their response: sewing fig leaf aprons rather than confessing their sin in prayer and seeking God's forgiveness.

cial task to them when He told Adam to guard the garden.[6] Adam's task was to announce preliminary judgment against Satan, for Satan had testified falsely regarding the character of God. "Hath God said?", the serpent had asked. But Adam and Eve had served instead as false judges, rendering judgment implicitly against God and explicitly against God's word.[7] Immediately, they recognized that they were wearing no "robes" – the mark of lawful judicial authority. They were *judicially uncovered* before each other. Their perceived dilemma had nothing further to do with the tree. Now the primary symbol of their spiritual condition was their own naked flesh. They sought to cover this revelation with fig leaves.

God was not judicially present in the garden immediately after their sin. He did not shout a warning to them: "I said not to touch that!" He gave them time to respond, either as covenant-breakers or covenant-keepers. They responded as covenant-breakers. They knew that His negative sanctions were coming, but their immediate concern was not their nakedness in His eyes; it was nakedness in their own eyes. Later, they hid themselves from God when they heard Him coming; in the meantime, they felt a compulsive need to hide their flesh from each other.

They reacted as though the psychological effects of eating from a merely symbolic tree – their sense of shame regarding their own personal nakedness – could be successfully covered by the leaves of another fruit-bearing tree. A representative of the plant kingdom had been a crucial aspect of this crisis of perception, so they covered themselves with leaves. They did not slay the serpent or some other animal in their quest for a covering. *They dealt with their sin symbolically*: the tree had become to them a symbol of their transgression, and so their

---

6. "And the LORD God took the man, and put him into the garden of Eden to dress it and to keep [*shawmar*: guard] it" (Gen. 2:15).

7. Gary North, *The Dominion Covenant: Genesis* (2nd ed.; Tyler, Texas: Institute for Christian Economics, 1987), Appendix E: "Witnesses and Judges."

required coverings should be of a similar kind. (Their son Cain was to make a similar evaluation of his judicially uncovered condition when he brought a sacrifice of the ground rather than an animal sacrifice [Gen. 4:3].)

They were wrong. Their problem was judicial, not symbolic. They had not transgressed a mere symbol; they had transgressed the boundary surrounding God's restricted property. They had been involved in a *boundary violation*. It is not that some sacred object serves merely as man's ethical mirror; it is instead God's law that serves as the mirror.[8]

C. Judicial Boundary

"And the eyes of them both were opened, and they knew that they were naked" (Gen. 3:7a). The use of the passive voice here is significant. *By whom* were their eyes opened? Either by God directly or by their own consciences as God's image-bearers. We are not told which. What we are told is that prior to their act of transgression, their eyes were not open; afterwards, they were. This must mean that "open eyes" in this sense was *judicial*. They *saw* what they had done. They *evaluated* their new condition in the light of God's warning. They *understood* at least some of the consequences. But, being in sin, they misjudged what would be required to cover the effects of their sin. They twisted their own self-judgment. They made it seem less important than it was, as if it were a sin suitable for self-atonement.

The tree served as a symbol only to the degree that it was *set apart* (sanctified) by God as His exclusive property. The tree did not reflect man or man's psyche; it represented God as sovereign owner of the cosmos. Its status as a visible symbol (i.e.,

---

8. "For if any be a hearer of the word, and not a doer, he is like unto a man beholding his natural face in a glass [mirror]: For he beholdeth himself, and goeth his way, and straightway forgetteth what manner of man he was. But whoso looketh into the perfect law of liberty, and continueth therein, he being not a forgetful hearer, but a doer of the work, this man shall be blessed in his deed" (James 1: 23–25).

judicial evidence) of man's covenant status was relevant only in terms of its own designated status as a sanctified object. It had been judicially and verbally set apart by God. The tree was therefore *sacred*. It was not to be touched or eaten by man until God removed the restriction. To violate this sacred object was to *profane* it. To eat from it meant death, not in the sense of a poison apple, nor in the sense of a prohibited metaphysical doorway to overwhelming cosmic forces, nor in the sense of a means of man's self-realization of his own inherent evil, but in the sense of inevitable historical and eternal sanctions imposed by an absolute personal God. Eating from the tree changed man's judicial status. This was a profane act. Adam became profane: entering the judicial status of God's declaration, "Guilty as charged." He became *sacrilegious*.

As we shall see, so did Moses.

Moses, the Would-Be Magician

Moses was acting as a realist, i.e., as a magician. His ritual act of tapping the rock was a magical act: a power-infusing component of a supernatural pattern of causation. His words supposedly would not stand alone; they required an infusion of supernatural power, which only ritual could supply. Following tradition was surely not the deciding issue here, i.e., nominalism. Speaking to a rock in a traditional manner would not bring forth the water. There was no traditionalist cause-and-effect pattern associated with speaking to a rock. Furthermore, if Moses had been acting as a judicialist, he would not have tapped the rock. The tapping ritual added nothing of substance to his words, and it subtracted from the authority of his words, for God had commanded him only to speak publicly to the rock, not tap it.

Pagan magical religion sees the priest as an intermediary between a realm of supernatural power and the realm of man's daily affairs. This supernatural realm may be personal or impersonal, but selected men access it through defined rituals.

The boundary between supernatural power and natural causation is controlled by the priest because he is the master of ritual. Even his spoken words can take on the character of ritual. They become formulas of power rather than prayers of supplication.

In tapping the rock, Moses acted as a pagan priest. When he relied on the rod as the means of bringing water from the rock, he adopted the mentality of the magician. This rod had served him as an implement of sanctions, both negative (the Nile's cursed water) and positive (Horeb's blessed water).[9] Moses had become psychologically dependent on this rod. In his mind, it became a tool of supernatural power rather than a symbol of supernaturally delegated judicial authority. He did not regard God's word as authoritative; rather, it was God's word *plus*: the rod. As a prophet, Moses was to speak events into existence by repeating God's word. It was God's word that was the basis of Moses' authority, not the visible implement of authority. But because Moses had repeatedly used this visible indicator of his prophetic authority as a means of invoking the predictable historical sanctions associated with the Old Covenant's prophetic office, he adopted the mentality of a pagan priest. He moved from biblical covenantalism to pagan realism. He moved from judicial invocation to magical manipulation.

This move was not absolute. Moses still brought a judicial invocation against Israel: "Hear now, ye rebels; must we fetch you water out of this rock?" (v. 10b). He identified them as rebels who relied on public displays of God's power rather than His promises. But in saying this, he condemned himself, for he, too, relied on public displays of God's power rather than His promises. That was why he tapped the rock. God had promised Moses to bring water in response to Moses' public verbal invo-

9. "And the LORD said unto Moses, Go on before the people, and take with thee of the elders of Israel; and thy rod, wherewith thou smotest the river, take in thine hand, and go" (Ex. 17:5).

cation. Moses and Aaron did not believe Him, which God stated explicitly: ". . . because ye believed me not" (v. 12a).

Negative Sanction: Disinheritance

God announced that Moses and Aaron would not lead the nation into Canaan. This had also been His negative sanction against the generation whose tribal representatives had sought to stone Caleb and Joshua. God had not specifically announced that Moses and Aaron would die in the wilderness, but it had been implied by the fact that he singled out only Caleb and Joshua. God's sanctions are judicially associated with inheritance and disinheritance. The ultimate negative sanction is eternal disinheritance. When God told Moses and Aaron that they would not live to lead the next generation into Canaan, He was bringing a major negative sanction against them.

God in His grace provided water out of the rock. The people in their rebellion would have water to drink. Nevertheless, that generation was doomed to die in the wilderness. God in His grace also allowed Moses and Aaron to live long enough to lead the nation through the wilderness. But their fate would be the same as their sister Miriam's (v. 1): they would die in the wilderness. They would not share in the inheritance.

Moses and the people shared too many presuppositions. This is why they shared the same curse: disinheritance. First, Moses trusted in ritual over God's spoken word. He acted as a magician rather than as a prophet. Similarly, the people expected God's blessings irrespective of His verbal judgments against them. They expected the promised inheritance (v. 5) apart from their covenantal faithfulness to His revealed word.

The Old Covenant prophet's word was ethically conditional. Jonah is the archetype. Jonah announced publicly that Nineveh would perish in 40 days (Jonah 3:4). The nation immediately repented. God spared them for this repentance. The prophecy was conditional: destruction unless you repent. Jonah had not announced the conditional clause, but it was implicit in Jonah's message. It is even possible that Jonah had not understood the conditionality of his message, for he sulked when God did not destroy Nineveh 40 days later (Jonah 4).

The Israelites kept reminding Moses that God's promise to them had not come true. This was the heart of their rebellion. They had not paid attention to the details of His promise to Abraham: the fourth generation would inherit. While some of them would have participated in the inheritance had they not rebelled, their sons would lead the army. When Moses promised to lead them into a land of milk and honey, he meant covenantally: their sons would receive what Abraham had promised. The parents would inherit through the actions of their sons. They forfeited their co-participation through their rebellion in Numbers 14. They had attempted to stone the representatives of the generation of the conquest, Caleb and Joshua.

They viewed the prophetic office as a pagan priesthood: infusing words with power through ritual irrespective of the judicial content of the words. They wanted signs and wonders; Moses provided this for them. By succumbing to the temptation of tapping the rock, he acted as Aaron had in the golden calf incident: pandering to the people. They wanted a magical religion of ritual without ethics, rewards without obedience. God disinherited them for acting consistently with this pagan worldview. God told Moses to remove Aaron's robes of authority and place them on Eleazar, which Moses did (vv. 26–28). Aaron immediately died (v. 28). Chapter 20 begins with Miriam's death; it ends with Aaron's death and the month of national mourning. The sanction of disinheritance had been applied by God in full public view.

Conclusion

When Moses tapped the rock twice in order to coax water out of it, he publicly proclaimed a magical religion. He added a ritual of his own to the word of God. Without this ritual, he decided, either God would not honor His word or the people would not be moved to faith in the God who speaks events into existence. Moses and Aaron displayed a lack of faith in such a God. They therefore suffered the same negative sanction that burdened their generation: disinheritance.

Cause and effect in history are covenantal. God decrees whatever comes to pass. History is governed by God in terms of God's will, both hidden (Deut. 29:29) and revealed. God told Moses to speak His words to the people. God did not tell Moses to add any ritual in order to verify God's words or to infuse power into the supernatural nature of the event that followed: water out of a rock. God's word was sufficient. But Moses did not believe this. His actions publicly testified to his disbelief.

Magic is a religion that substitutes ritual for ethics. It invokes power through ritual acts. Even its words take on the character of ritual: formulas. Magic is a religion of manipulation: ritual acts that supposedly produce predictable changes in the world outside the sacred priestly realm. This is not biblical religion. Biblical religion has rituals, but these rituals are judicial, not magical. They do not enable the priest to tap into a realm of power irrespective of the ethical content of men's acts. Biblical ritual is judicial, bringing men under the terms of God's law and the sanctions attached to it. The sanctions are real, i.e., historical, but they are the outcome of a cause-and-effect system that rests on ethics rather than ritual. "Will the LORD be pleased with thousands of rams, or with ten thousands of rivers of oil? shall I give my firstborn for my transgression, the fruit of my body for the sin of my soul? He hath shewed thee, O man, what is good; and what doth the LORD require of thee, but to do justly, and to love mercy, and to walk humbly with thy God?" (Mic. 6:7–8).

12

THE PSYCHOLOGY OF VICTORY

Wherefore it is said in the book of the wars of the Lord, *What he did in the Red sea, and in the brooks of Arnon (Num. 21:14).*

The book of the wars of the Lord is one of several missing books that are referred to in the Bible. These include the book of Jasher (Josh. 10:13; II Sam. 1:18), the book of the acts of Solomon (I Ki. 11:41), the books of Samuel the seer, Nathan the prophet, and Gad the seer (I Chron. 29:29), the prophecies of Ahijah the Shilonite and Iddo the seer (II Chron. 9:29), the book of Shemaiah the prophet (II Chron. 12:15), and the chronicles of the kings of the Medes and Persians (Esth. 10:2). This is the first biblical reference to a now-missing book.

The text informs us that these wilderness wars began at the border of the wilderness, the Red Sea, where God destroyed the army of Pharaoh. The missing chronicles continued at least until the war listed in this chapter: the war at Arnon, the border of Sihon's kingdom. The victories associated with the defeat of Sihon became part of Israel's folk heritage: proverbs of destruction. "Wherefore they that speak in proverbs say, Come into Heshbon, let the city of Sihon be built and prepared: For there is a fire gone out of Heshbon, a flame from the city of

Sihon: it hath consumed Ar of Moab, and the lords of the high places of Arnon" (Num. 21:27–28).

The question arises: When did this final series of wars begin? Did the generation of the exodus initiate them? Or was it the generation of the conquest? It was the latter. Miriam and Aaron were dead by the time the battles began. They died in the fortieth year after the exodus (Num. 33:38). By this time, all of the older generation had died off except Moses. They had died during the 38 years from the exodus to Israel's arrival at Kadesh-barnea (Deut. 2:14). This took place prior to the journey to Mt. Hor (Num. 33:36–37), where Aaron died.

Moses was old. It was he who would announce the terms of the inheritance to the next generation: the Book of Deuteronomy is a record of these terms. This second giving of the law (*deutero, nomos*) was preparatory to national covenant renewal: the circumcision of the conquest generation (Josh. 5:7). God's prophecy to Abraham regarding the inheritance of the fourth generation (Gen. 15:16) was about to be fulfilled. What we see in this chapter is the manifestation of a new psychology of victory in Israel. There was one final rebellion. After this, open rebellion ended until after the conquest.

Hormah

Hormah was the city where the Israelites had suffered a major military defeat. They had attempted to prove Moses wrong regarding their inability to prosper militarily after their attempted stoning of Joshua and Caleb. "Then the Amalekites came down, and the Canaanites which dwelt in that hill, and smote them, and discomfited them, even unto Hormah" (Num. 14:45). That legacy of defeat would now be reversed.

Chapter 21 is an account of several wilderness wars. The first was the war with king Arad the Canaanite. He lived in the south, outside the borders of Canaan (Josh. 12:6–7, 14). He started a war with Israel, and he took some of them prisoner (Num. 21:1). "And Israel vowed a vow unto the LORD, and said,

If thou wilt indeed deliver this people into my hand, then I will utterly destroy their cities. And the LORD hearkened to the voice of Israel, and delivered up the Canaanites; and they utterly destroyed them and their cities: and he called the name of the place Hormah" (vv. 2–3).

Israel's counter-attack was preceded by a vow. A biblical vow is a promise sworn to God that if God performs a specific act in history, the vow-taker will perform another act or series of acts. This is a lawful oath before God. Such an oath is an aspect of point four of the biblical covenant model: oath/sanctions. The vow implies that God will impose negative sanctions on anyone who takes such a vow and subsequently fails to perform his side of the bargain. "If a man vow a vow unto the LORD, or swear an oath to bind his soul with a bond; he shall not break his word, he shall do according to all that proceedeth out of his mouth" (Num. 30:2). "When thou shalt vow a vow unto the LORD thy God, thou shalt not slack to pay it: for the LORD thy God will surely require it of thee; and it would be sin in thee. But if thou shalt forbear to vow, it shall be no sin in thee" (Deut. 23:21–22). The vow is therefore a self-maledictory oath: calling down God's negative sanctions in history for failing to abide by the terms of the oath.

Israel promised to destroy utterly the cities under Arad's authority. This they did. The area of devastation Israel called Hormah. The word *hormah* is derived from the Hebrew word for "devoted." A thing devoted by a vow to the Lord could not be bought back (Lev. 27:28–29).[1] The *hormah* was the ban.[2] It was the judicial equivalent of a whole burnt offering. All of it belonged to God. It was fit for burning, under a curse, like Jericho: "And the city shall be *accursed*, even it, and all that are therein, to the LORD: only Rahab the harlot shall live, she and

1. Gary North, *Leviticus: An Economic Commentary* (Tyler, Texas: Institute for Christian Economics, 1994), pp. 582–84, 594–95.

2. *Ibid.*, pp. 622–23.

all that are with her in the house, because she hid the messengers that we sent" (Josh. 6:17; emphasis added). The Hebrew root word is the same in both cases: devoted or accursed.

The Serpent as Negative Sanction

After the defeat of Arad and prior to the next phase of the wilderness wars, Israel rebelled one last time. Their complaint was the same old complaint: God had failed to live up to His promise. This had been the complaint of the exodus generation: God supposedly had broken His vow to Israel. As always, that generation failed to acknowledge that the prophecy had been to Joshua's generation. The exodus generation had rebelled against God by rejecting the testimony of Joshua and Caleb, representatives of the fourth generation, and by seeking to impose the sanction of death on them: stoning (Num. 14). The next generation now repeated their complaint. "And they journeyed from mount Hor by the way of the Red sea, to compass the land of Edom: and the soul of the people was much discouraged because of the way. And the people spake against God, and against Moses, Wherefore have ye brought us up out of Egypt to die in the wilderness? for there is no bread, neither is there any water; and our soul loatheth this light bread" (Num 21:4–5).

Early in the wilderness period, God had brought positive sanctions on the nation when they had offered this complaint: manna (Ex. 16) and water from the rock (Ex. 17). But later on, He had brought negative sanctions against them for their complaining: fire (Num. 11:1–2) and plague (Num. 11:33). It should have been clear to them that if they persisted in this complaint – comparing Egypt's bondage conditions favorably with life in the wilderness – He would impose further negative sanctions. They had not learned this lesson, yet they had been wandering for several decades. Like children who repeatedly commit the same infraction, despite previous punishments, so was Israel. They needed another lesson. "And the LORD sent fiery serpents among the people, and they bit the people; and much people of Israel died" (Num. 21:6). The people then repented: "Therefore the people came to Moses, and said, We have sinned, for we have spoken against the LORD, and against thee; pray unto the LORD, that he take away the serpents from us. And Moses prayed for the people" (v. 7).

The Brass Serpent

At this point, an event took place that raises difficult questions regarding symbolism in the ancient Near East, as we shall see. "And the LORD said unto Moses, Make thee a fiery serpent, and set it upon a pole: and it shall come to pass, that every one that is bitten, when he looketh upon it, shall live. And Moses made a serpent of brass, and put it upon a pole, and it came to pass, that if a serpent had bitten any man, when he beheld the serpent of brass, he lived" (vv. 8–9). This took place sometime in the second half of the fifteenth century before the birth of Jesus Christ.

The brass serpent was attached to a pole. This image still marks the guild of physicians: a serpent entwined around a pole. A similar symbol, two serpents entwined around a pole, goes back to Sumeria. The Sumerian god Ninazu was the god of healing. The son of this god, Ningishzida, was represented by the two snakes and pole.[3] This is known today as the caduceus: in Greek mythology, the wand of Hermes. The symbol of a snake on a pole is also associated with Asklepius, the Greek god of healing. This god was the Greek deity most frequently represented in snake form.[4] The Phoenecians' healing god, Eshmun, was represented by a snake.[5] The snake-pole symbol

---

3. E. A. Wallis Budge, *Amulets and Talismans* (New Hyde Park, New York: University Books, [1930?] 1961), pp. 488–89.

4. John Cuthbert Lawson, *Modern Greek Folklore and Ancient Greek Religion: A Study in Survivals* (New Hyde Park, New York: University Books, [1910] 1964), pp. 274–75.

5. Jacob Milgrom, *The JPS Torah Commentary: Numbers* (New York: Jewish Publi-

was part of the crest of the Surgeon General of the United States until 1871. The caduceus replaced it in 1871.[6]

Did God select a symbol familiar as a sign of healing in the pagan Near East in Moses' day? Or was this event the origin of this Near Eastern symbol of healing? The conventional academic dating systems place the events of the exodus late in the second millennium, B.C. The earliest clay tablets containing Sumerian literary history are dated as having been written late in the third millennium. Large numbers of these clay tablets are dated as having been written in the first half of the second millennium.[7] By revising the conventional academic chronologies of the ancient Near East, which insert a mythical Dark Age era, 1200 BC to 700 BC,[8] we may be able to identify the caduceus symbol as contemporary with Israel's wilderness era. To determine which came first, the wilderness event or the Sumerians' caduceus snake-pole symbol, we must first determine the

---

cation Society, 1990), p. 459.

6. "Caduceus," *Grolier Encyclopedia* (1990).

7. Samuel Noah Kramer, *History Begins at Sumer* (Garden City, New York: Anchor, [1956] 1959), p. xix.

8. Gary North, *Moses and Pharaoh: Dominion Religion vs. Power Religion* (Tyler, Texas: Institute for Christian Economics, 1985), Appendix A: "The Reconstruction of Egypt's Chronology." My book appeared in the same year that the authors of *Centuries of Darkness* first met at the London Institute of Archeology. They found that they had all become skeptical regarding chronologies of the ancient Near East, i.e., that "the 'centuries of darkness' inserted into the histories of so many areas between 1200 and 700 BC were largely illusory." Peter James, *Centuries of Darkness: A challenge to the conventional chronology of Old World archeology* (New Brunswick, New Jersey: Rutgers University Press, 1993), p. xviii. The authors believe that the general inflation is more like 250 years than 500 (p. xxi). The modern source of this call for a revised Near Eastern chronology was Immanuel Velikovsky, whose reconstruction proved to be, writes James, "disastrously extreme" (p. xxi). An attempt to revise ancient chronologies was pursued for three decades by Isaac Newton. His book, published without his permission, was *The Chronology of the Ancient Kingdoms Amended* (1725). Cf. Frank Manuel, *Isaac Newton, Historian* (Cambridge, Massachusetts: Harvard University Press, 1963). The most detailed revisionist study I have read on the topic of Egypt's chronology in relation to Israel's is an unpublished, 89-page, single-spaced personal letter sent to me by Brad Sparks in 1986. It should be updated and published, but I no longer know where Sparks is.

date of the earliest appearance of the symbol. This task still lies ahead of us. "Clearly, a colossal amount of work lies ahead in building new detailed chronologies for individual areas," writes revisionist Peter James.[9]

The sanction facing the bitten Israelite was death. To escape it, the victim had to take a ritual step: to look at the elevated symbol of deliverance. This symbol became the archetype of the sinner's access to spiritual healing: "And as Moses lifted up the serpent in the wilderness, even so must the Son of man be lifted up: That whosoever believeth in him should not perish, but have eternal life" (John 3:14–15). These words precede the widely quoted verse, "For God so loved the world, that he gave his only begotten Son, that whosoever believeth in him should not perish, but have everlasting life" (John 3:16). The ultimate negative sanction, the second death (Rev. 20:14), is removed through a man's willingness to acknowledge the reality of the eternal effects of the serpent's sting in his life, and to subordinate himself to God by acceding to the means of grace. The serpent, as the original earthly agent of man's evil and rebellion, symbolizes man's broken covenant with God. What was placed on both the pole and the cross, symbolically and judicially speaking, was sin: "For he hath made him to be sin for us, who knew no sin; that we might be made the righteousness of God in him" (II Cor. 5:21). The pole and the cross represent the sanction of death: God's permanent negative sanction against the serpent and its effects. By lifting up an image of the serpent, Moses identified the agency of the negative sanction against man: sin. The man who failed to acknowledge this means of deliverance was doomed.

This healing by the elevated serpent was the positive sanction that transformed Israel from a nation of psychologically defeated nomads into a nation of pilgrims on the march. This time, Israel at long last learned its lesson. Never again did

9. James, *Centuries of Darkness*, p. xxii.

Israel bring the accusation against Moses that God had brought them into the wilderness to die, and that Egypt had been a better place to live. The only instance even remotely similar to the old complaint was Joshua's prayer to God after Israel's defeat at Ai. He complained that it would have been better to have remained on the far side of the Jordan. But his complaint was not that Israel was better off outside the land. He appealed to the holiness of God's name: "For the Canaanites and all the inhabitants of the land shall hear of it, and shall environ us round, and cut off our name from the earth: and what wilt thou do unto thy great name?" (Josh. 7:9). Israel's defeat would reflect badly on His name. God then told him of the infraction that had polluted Israel: the theft of something from Jericho, which had been placed under the total ban of *hormah*.

Sanctions and Inheritance

Israel's wanderings continued (Num. 21:10–13). They came to Beer. Here the leaders of the nation were instructed by Moses to dig a well. "And from thence they went to Beer: that is the well whereof the LORD spake unto Moses, Gather the people together, and I will give them water. Then Israel sang this song, Spring up, O well; sing ye unto it: The princes digged the well, the nobles of the people digged it, by the direction of the lawgiver, with their staves" (vv. 16–18a). This took place shortly before Israel's initial occupation of the land outside Canaan. When the nation's leaders dug the well, they were visibly serving the needs of those whom they represented judicially. They personally expended scarce resources on behalf of the nation as a whole. The idea of *political leadership as public service* became part of Israel's folklore, encapsulated in the song of the well.

Then Israel journeyed to the border area between the Amorites and Moab. Moab had been born through the incestuous union of Lot and his daughter (Gen. 19:37). Moab and his brother Ammon had always displayed the mark of Sodom:

sinful rebellion. It took ten generations of circumcision and profession of faith for a Moabite or an Ammonite to gain citizenship in Israel (Deut. 23:3), compared to three generations for an Edomite or an Egyptian (Deut. 23:8). The Amorites had conquered Moab and had appropriated much of Moab's land (Num. 21:26). There was a proverb regarding this defeat: "Woe to thee, Moab! thou art undone, O people of Chemosh: he hath given his sons that escaped, and his daughters, into captivity unto Sihon king of the Amorites" (v. 29). The defeat of the Moabite god Chemosh was revealed in his surrender of the Moabites to the Amorites. This was the meaning of a military defeat in pagan antiquity: the surrender of the gods of the defeated army.[10] It was only Israel that renounced this theology of local gods, for God promised to allow their enemies to defeat them if they disobeyed Him (Lev. 26:17, 25, 33). He would remain with them spiritually in any captivity.

Israel asked Sihon, king of the Amorites, to allow Israel to pass through his territory on the king's highway. Sihon not only refused, he assembled his army against Israel. This was an unnecessary act of war. Israel had asked Edom the same thing, and had gone another way when Edom refused (Num. 20:14–21). Edom had assembled an army, but this was a defensive operation (Num. 20:20). Sihon attacked Israel without provocation (Num. 21:23). This led to his complete destruction in battle (v. 24). Israel took possession of all of the Amorite cities (v. 25). "Thus Israel dwelt in the land of the Amorites" (v. 31). This land became the inheritance of two and a half tribes. "And Moses gave unto them, even to the children of Gad, and to the children of Reuben, and unto half the tribe of Manasseh the son of Joseph, the kingdom of Sihon king of the Amorites, and the kingdom of Og king of Bashan, the land, with the cities

---

10. Fustel de Coulanges, *The Ancient City: A Study on the Religion, Laws, and Institutions of Greece and Rome* (Garden City, New York: Doubleday Anchor, [1864] 1955), Bk. III, Ch. XV.

thereof in the coasts, even the cities of the country round about" (Num. 32:33).

Moses had been told by God that by making the request to pass through the cities under Sihon's jurisdiction, he would provoke the king to imitate the Pharaoh and launch a suicidal confrontation. Deuteronomy 2 records in greater detail God's strategy of conquest. "Rise ye up, take your journey, and pass over the river Arnon: behold, I have given into thine hand Sihon the Amorite, king of Heshbon, and his land: begin to possess it, and contend with him in battle. This day will I begin to put the dread of thee and the fear of thee upon the nations that are under the whole heaven, who shall hear report of thee, and shall tremble, and be in anguish because of thee" (Deut. 2:24–25). The war was preceded by Moses' attempt to initiate peace: "And I sent messengers out of the wilderness of Kedemoth unto Sihon king of Heshbon with words of peace. . ." (v. 26). God dealt with Sihon as He had dealt with Pharaoh: He hardened Sihon's heart. "But Sihon king of Heshbon would not let us pass by him: for the LORD thy God hardened his spirit, and made his heart obstinate, that he might deliver him into thy hand, as appeareth this day" (v. 30). This was the beginning of Israel's inheritance: "And the LORD said unto me, Behold, I have begun to give Sihon and his land before thee: begin to possess, that thou mayest inherit his land" (v. 31). Israel also gained the inheritance of Moab by conquering Sihon. In Numbers 22 through 25, we read of Moab's attempts to reclaim this forfeited inheritance: first by a military alliance with Midian and by prophetic cursing by Balaam, then by physical and spiritual seduction.

Moses used this initial conquest to extend Israel's power: "And Moses sent to spy out Jaazer, and they took the villages thereof, and drove out the Amorites that were there" (Num. 21:32). The first group of spies sent out by Moses had returned from Canaan with negative reports (Num. 14). This time, their reports furthered the conquest of Canaan. This was the preliminary series of conquests designed to teach the generation of the conquest that God was faithful, that Israel could win in battle. City by city, the inheritance was built up. Israel began to move from a people on a pilgrimage to a people with roots in the land.

The next confrontation was with Og, king of Bashan. He, too, was utterly defeated (v. 35). Thus did Og join Sihon in the folklore of Israel's conquests.[11]

Conclusion

Numbers 21 records a series of corporate capital sanctions: against Arad the Canaanite, against the people of Israel, against Sihon the Amorite, against the cities of Jaazer, and against Og of Bashan. Negative sanctions against Moab had already been applied by God through Sihon. Arad and his cities did not become part of Israel's inheritance. They became *hormah*: a whole burnt offering to God. This pattern of conquest was repeated by the next generation: Jericho became *hormah*. In neither case was Israel allowed to appropriate the land or property of these cities.

Israel was ethically transformed by the serpent experience. The nation ceased complaining about the wilderness as a promise unfulfilled by God. Shortly thereafter, God began to deliver into their hands parts of the land outside the boundaries of the Jordan. At first, this was the result of an offensive attack by Sihon, but after possessing Sihon's inheritance, Moses began an offensive campaign modeled after the failed campaign of Numbers 13–14. He sent spies out; then Israel conquered a city, Jaazer. Then Og launched a war against them, which he lost.

---

11. Numbers 32:33; Deuteronomy 1:4; 29:7; 31:4; Joshua 2:10; 9:10; Nehemiah 9:22; Psalm 135:11.

Israel's mentality changed as a result of these initial battles. Israel began to occupy defeated nations' land. Israel's psychology of defeat began to change to a psychology of victory. The tribes began to secure an inheritance for themselves and their heirs through a series of military victories. The positive sanction of victory became the basis of Israel's inheritance.

What had produced this change? We can blame the serpents' sanctions, but this is only a minor part of the story. Their complaint was a recapitulation of the sin of the generation of the exodus. This was the same old complaint. The beginning of inheritance began soon after the serpents did their covenantal work. Israel had not occupied king Arad's land, for it was under the ban, as Jericho would be. But the next military victories allowed Israel to cease wandering. These victories changed the psychology of the nation. The old complaint that God had not fulfilled His promise to Israel regarding the Promised Land received a death blow: down payments on the victory to come.

13

THE OFFICE OF COURT PROPHET

And Balak's anger was kindled against Balaam, and he smote his hands together: and Balak said unto Balaam, I called thee to curse mine enemies, and, behold, thou hast altogether blessed them these three times. Therefore now flee thou to thy place: I thought to promote thee unto great honour; but, lo, the LORD hath kept thee back from honour. And Balaam said unto Balak, Spake I not also to thy messengers which thou sentest unto me, saying, If Balak would give me his house full of silver and gold, I cannot go beyond the commandment of the LORD, to do either good or bad of mine own mind; but what the LORD saith, that will I speak? (Num. 24:10–13).

At this stage of his career as a prophet, Balaam was still serving as God's representative. He was still refusing to curse Israel. He understood what God had promised to do for Israel. He also understood that Israel was no longer under the curse of God that had made nomads out of the exodus generation, wandering in circles. "He hath not beheld iniquity in Jacob, neither hath he seen perverseness in Israel: the LORD his God is with him, and the shout of a king is among them" (Num. 23:21). Israel was immune to divination, incantations, and other paraphernalia of magic: "Surely there is no enchantment against Jacob, neither is there any divination against Israel:

according to this time it shall be said of Jacob and of Israel, What hath God wrought!" (Num. 23:23).

"Every Man Has His Price!"

Balak, king of Moab (Num. 22:4), realized that he had a monumental problem on his hands. He had seen the Israelites defeat Sihon and thereby gain the inheritance of Moab that Sihon had collected from Moab (Num. 21:26). The Israelites had then gone on to defeat the city of Jaazer and Og of Bashan. They were no longer the defeated people who had been routed by the Amalekites and Canaanites (Num. 14:45). Their numbers were vast. They were a company, Balak informed the Midianites (Num. 22:4), as in *multitude* (Gen. 28:3).

Balak had formed an alliance with Midian. Moab was the heir of Lot. Midian was the heir of Abraham through Keturah (Gen. 25:1–2). Moses had fled from Egypt to Midian (Ex. 2:15). He had been given an inheritance in Midian through his wife and his children. Now, a generation later, Midian had allied itself with Moab against Moses. Soon, Midian would participate in a joint action with Moab to undermine Israel's faith by worshipping the gods of Moab (Num. 25:1–2, 6). Midian came under negative sanctions because of this (Num. 25:17).

What Balak needed, he decided, was a court prophet who would curse Israel in the name of God. Prophets could be purchased, Balak believed. "He sent messengers therefore unto Balaam the son of Beor to Pethor, which is by the river of the land of the children of his people, to call him, saying, Behold, there is a people come out from Egypt: behold, they cover the face of the earth, and they abide over against me. Come now therefore, I pray thee, curse me this people; for they are too mighty for me: peradventure I shall prevail, that we may smite them, and that I may drive them out of the land: for I wot that he whom thou blessest is blessed, and he whom thou cursest is cursed" (Num. 22:5–6).

Balak believed in the power of verbal curses when delivered by an official representative of God. Negative sanctions in history could be successfully invoked by means of a curse. This required a prophet, whose word was authoritative because what he said would surely take place. A prophet prophesied. For a price, Balak believed, Balaam would prophesy evil against a king's enemies. His curses were for sale. The positive sanction of money could purchase the negative sanction of God's curse in history. Such were the religious convictions of Balak.

"And the elders of Moab and the elders of Midian departed with the rewards of divination in their hand; and they came unto Balaam, and spake unto him the words of Balak" (Num. 22:7). Balaam inquired of God, and God told him not to go with them, for Israel is blessed (v. 12). At first, Balaam refused to appear before the king (v. 13). Balak sent another group, this one even more honorable than the first (v. 15). This indicates that Balak was trying to negotiate a low price; he had not sent his most prestigious representatives the first time. He was persuaded that "every man has his price," but also that it is not shrewd to offer your top price early in the negotiations. Having failed in his first attempt to lure Balaam into his court, he raised his price: "For I will promote thee unto very great honour, and I will do whatsoever thou sayest unto me: come therefore, I pray thee, curse me this people" (v. 17). But Balaam refused again: "And Balaam answered and said unto the servants of Balak, If Balak would give me his house full of silver and gold, I cannot go beyond the word of the LORD my God, to do less or more" (v. 18). He inquired again of God, and this time God told him to go with them.

Balaam's Price

This raises a difficult question: Why did God tell him to go this time? God did not want him to go. Balaam went with them. "And God's anger was kindled because he went: and the angel of the LORD stood in the way for an adversary against him" (v. 22a).

God had already told Balaam that Israel was sacrosanct: beyond negative sanctions. He had also told him not to go with the first group of emissaries (v. 12). For a prophet of God, this revelation should have been sufficient. But Balak knew his man. Balaam had a price. That price was determined in stages. This is why Balaam came to God again (v. 19). Maybe this time God's answer would be different. And so it was: "And God came unto Balaam at night, and said unto him, If the men come to call thee, rise up, and go with them; but yet the word which I shall say unto thee, that shalt thou do" (v. 20). Balaam was like a moth flitting around an open flame. When Balak's price rose, so did Balaam's interest. Perhaps God would give him a new word of knowledge. At some price, maybe God would change His mind.

Balak and Balaam shared the same view of prophecy; they disagreed only regarding the price. Balak believed that the prophet could be bought off. The words of the prophet supposedly had power within themselves; God was either an afterthought or a tool of the prophet. Balak did not want the prophet to serve as an intermediary, speaking God's word as God's representative (point two of the biblical covenant model). What Balak wanted was an invocation of negative sanctions against Israel. God was unwilling to impose these sanctions. He told Balaam to tell this to Balak, which Balaam did: "How shall I curse, whom God hath not cursed? or how shall I defy, whom the LORD hath not defied? For from the top of the rocks I see him, and from the hills I behold him: lo, the people shall dwell alone, and shall not be reckoned among the nations" (Num. 23:8–9). But Balak's response was to recommend a change of perspective: "And Balak said unto him, Come, I pray thee, with me unto another place, from whence thou mayest see them: thou shalt see but the utmost part of them, and shalt not see them all: and curse me them from thence" (Num. 23:13).

Balak was a manipulator. He believed that man, not God, is sovereign. He believed that the prophet's power stemmed from himself or from some impersonal cosmic repository of power. If he could persuade the prophet to declare a word of power, then the cosmos would respond and impose that curse. God had nothing to do with the curse; Balaam was sovereign, not God. And Balaam had a price. The answer Balak wanted to know was what this price was. If he could ascertain Balaam's price and pay it, he would become sovereign over Israel on the battlefield. He might even regain Moab's lost inheritance, which Israel occupied.

Balaam insisted that he was not in a position to deliver what the king wanted. "God is not a man, that he should lie; neither the son of man, that he should repent: hath he said, and shall he not do it? or hath he spoken, and shall he not make it good? Behold, I have received commandment to bless: and he hath blessed; and I cannot reverse it" (Num. 23:19–20). Israel was going to win: "Behold, the people shall rise up as a great lion, and lift up himself as a young lion: he shall not lie down until he eat of the prey, and drink the blood of the slain" (v. 24).

This concerned Balak. He had asked for a prophetic word; he did not like what he heard: a blessing for Israel. He wanted to return to the *status quo ante*: "And Balak said unto Balaam, Neither curse them at all, nor bless them at all" (v. 25). But he was too late: the prophetic word had been spoken. "But Balaam answered and said unto Balak, Told not I thee, saying, All that the LORD speaketh, that I must do?" (v. 26). So, Balak suggested another change of perspective: "And Balak said unto Balaam, Come, I pray thee, I will bring thee unto another place; peradventure it will please God that thou mayest curse me them from thence. And Balak brought Balaam unto the top of Peor, that looketh toward Jeshimon" (vv. 27–28).

This is the classic sign of a manipulator: "Just keep your options open until you see things my way." He wants a particular outcome. If he cannot get what he wants by approaching the evidence from one perspective, he approaches it from another. He is not involved in a search for truth. He is buying a preconceived outcome.

Balaam cooperated again. "And Balak did as Balaam had said, and offered a bullock and a ram on every altar" (v. 30). It was obvious that he was caught between two opposing forces, and he wanted to escape the pressure. He wanted temporal rewards from Balak, but he did not want punishment from God. He kept the process open-ended for as long as he could. He sought God in the wilderness through a trance (Num. 24:1, 4). The revelation was the same, only more so: "How goodly are thy tents, O Jacob, and thy tabernacles, O Israel! As the valleys are they spread forth, as gardens by the river's side, as the trees of lign aloes which the LORD hath planted, and as cedar trees beside the waters. He shall pour the water out of his buckets, and his seed shall be in many waters, and his king shall be higher than Agag, and his kingdom shall be exalted. God brought him forth out of Egypt; he hath as it were the strength of an unicorn [wild bull]: he shall eat up the nations his enemies, and shall break their bones, and pierce them through with his arrows" (vv. 5–8). Then came God's promise of sanctions for Balaam: "He couched, he lay down as a lion, and as a great lion: who shall stir him up? Blessed is he that blesseth thee, and cursed is he that curseth thee" (v. 9).

At this unpleasant news, Balak rejected Balaam and sent him home. He rebuked Balaam for having failed to deliver the curse he wanted (v. 10). It was all God's fault. "Therefore now flee thou to thy place: I thought to promote thee unto great honour; but, lo, the LORD hath kept thee back from honour" (v. 11). Before, Balak had expected Balaam to perform as requested, on Balaam's own authority. Now, however, Balak ridiculed Balaam by pointing out that God had decided to keep Balaam from receiving the honors which the king had planned to bestow on him. God was obviously being vindictive against Balaam; this had nothing to do with Israel's protected covenantal status.

At What Price?

The economist shares Balak's view of pricing. He may not argue that every man has his price, but he argues that *at the decision-making margin*, every man will evaluate a price. The decision-maker will count the cost of saying *no* to the offer. His cost of saying *no* is whatever he might have gained by saying *yes*, minus whatever it would cost him to say yes and fulfill his contract.

If a future-oriented individual believes that God will impose negative sanctions on a scale beyond calculation, he will refuse to say *yes* to an offer that endangers his future. Jesus asked: "For what shall it profit a man, if he shall gain the whole world, and lose his own soul?" (Mark 8:36). By this He meant that the cost-benefit ratio of a soul-threatening decision is overwhelmingly on the side of righteousness. The cost of doing evil is too high. The magnitude of the discrepancy is so great that gaining the whole world would be a bad bargain. This understanding had governed His own response to Satan's temptation: "Again, the devil taketh him up into an exceeding high mountain, and sheweth him all the kingdoms of the world, and the glory of them; And saith unto him, All these things will I give thee, if thou wilt fall down and worship me. Then saith Jesus unto him, Get thee hence, Satan: for it is written, Thou shalt worship the Lord thy God, and him only shalt thou serve" (Matt. 4:8–10).

What this means is that for some decision-makers, the net cost of saying *no* to evil is so minuscule as not to be a factor. The person's fear of God is so great that the price offered does not register on his scale of values. At what price will a mother murder her infant son? For some mothers, no such price exists. For others, it does – a prophetic mark of covenant-breaking.[1]

1. "Then I will walk contrary unto you also in fury; and I, even I, will chastise

If no price is sufficiently high to register on her scale of value, then the price can be said to be economically irrelevant. It is not an economic factor for her. There is no choice to be made. A clever economist can then define the problem out of existence: "Since there can be no choice, there is no trade-off; without a trade-off, there is no economically relevant marginal price." A morally wise economist, however, will say that some people do not have a price.

Sin being what it is, and present-orientation being what it is, in most decisions most men will have a price. The covenant-breaker believes that this area of decision-making is wider than it really is, for there are people who believe that the price of disobedience to God is too high. The economist, rarely being a covenant-keeper, and also a methodological atheist – though usually a self-declared morally neutral agnostic – finds it difficult to believe that there are people who act irrespective of price. He may re-define the array of prices to include men's beliefs in the hereafter, but in practice, the typical economist presumes what Balak presumed: every man has his price. The humanistic economist rejects or ignores the ultimate law of sociology: "Some do; some don't."

Donkey, Prophet, and King

The story of Balaam's journey to meet the king is better known than the circumstances of the event. Balaam was initially told by God not to accompany the two kings' representatives (Num. 22:12). Balaam did not want to take *no* for an answer.

---

you seven times for your sins. And ye shall eat the flesh of your sons, and the flesh of your daughters shall ye eat" (Lev. 26:28–29). "And the king said unto her, What aileth thee? And she answered, This woman said unto me, Give thy son, that we may eat him to day, and we will eat my son to morrow. So we boiled my son, and did eat him: and I said unto her on the next day, Give thy son, that we may eat him: and she hath hid her son. And it came to pass, when the king heard the words of the woman, that he rent his clothes; and he passed by upon the wall, and the people looked, and, behold, he had sackcloth within upon his flesh" (II Ki. 6:28–30).

God knew this. Balaam told the representatives that he would not come with them, but he left a way of escape. This is the classic answer of the bureaucrat: announce a negative at the first request, but leave a way of escape. The bureaucrat who retreats from *yes* to *no* alienates some politician's constituent. A bureaucrat who retreats from *no* to *yes* placates the constituent.

Next, God allowed him to go with the representatives, but God did not want him to go. He knew Balaam's heart, which was evil. On the journey, the angel of the Lord appeared to Balaam's donkey, but Balaam did not see it. Three times the donkey refused to go forward. Three times, Balaam struck the donkey for disobedience. Finally, the angel revealed himself to Balaam, informing him that "I went out to withstand thee, because thy way is perverse before me" (Num. 22:32b). Balaam then offered to turn back (v. 34). "And the angel of the LORD said unto Balaam, Go with the men: but only the word that I shall speak unto thee, that thou shalt speak. So Balaam went with the princes of Balak" (v. 35).

The best-informed participant was the donkey, who saw the angel from the beginning. Less informed was Balaam, who saw the angel only after the donkey did, and only after he had beaten the donkey three times (v. 32). Least informed was Balak, who refused three times to accept God's word through Balaam that God had a special relationship with Israel. "And Balak's anger was kindled against Balaam, and he smote his hands together: and Balak said unto Balaam, I called thee to curse mine enemies, and, behold, thou hast altogether blessed them these three times" (Num. 24:10). Balaam three times had tried to persuade the donkey to do things his way; he used negative sanctions, but these failed. Balak three times had tried to persuade Balaam to do things his way; he used positive sanctions, but these failed. The donkey was a better servant of God than Balaam was; Balaam was a better servant of God than Balak was. The donkey defied Balaam in order to protect Balaam from the angel; Balaam defied Balak in order to protect himself from God. The donkey was not self-interested; Balaam was. This incident reveals that covenant-breakers in their rebellion do not have the common sense of a donkey. A donkey serves its master better than a covenant-breaker serves God (Isa. 1:3). The words of Balaam to the donkey should warn covenant-breakers of the wrath to come: "I would there were a sword in mine hand, for now would I kill thee" (Num. 22:29b). If Balaam was ready to kill his faithful donkey out of personal pride, what is God ready to do with covenant-breakers who resist Him out of this same pride?

Balaam's Motivation

Balaam did not want Balak to have the last word in this matter. He revealed another prophecy that he had been given in the vision (Num. 24:16). He presented the king with a messianic prophecy: "I shall see him, but not now: I shall behold him, but not nigh: there shall come a Star out of Jacob, and a Sceptre shall rise out of Israel, and shall smite the corners of Moab, and destroy all the children of Sheth. And Edom shall be a possession, Seir also shall be a possession for his enemies; and Israel shall do valiantly. Out of Jacob shall come he that shall have dominion, and shall destroy him that remaineth of the city" (vv. 17–19). He prophesied the extinction of the Amalekites and the Kenites (vv. 20–22). Then he departed (v. 25). But as we learn in Numbers 31, Balaam's last word was an incomplete word. He remained the king's agent rather than God's.

The account of Balaam's prophecy indicates that he was weak, hoping that he might profit from his position as a court prophet, but strong enough to resist Balak's request that he utter a curse against Israel in God's name. He refused to say *no* each time that Balak asked him to reconsider or to look at the matter from a new geographical perspective. He played with fire, but he initially avoided getting burned. The problem was, he could not stop playing with fire. His seeming immunity led to his eventual destruction.

He refused to utter a false prophecy against Israel, but he then devised the plan by which the Midianite allies of Moab seduced the Israelites. "Behold, these caused the children of Israel, through the counsel of Balaam, to commit trespass against the LORD in the matter of Peor, and there was a plague among the congregation of the LORD" (Num. 31:16). For this, Moses ordered him executed, after the military defeat of Midian (v. 8).

Balaam's plan involved the use of Moabite and Midianite women as temptresses. "And Israel abode in Shittim, and the people began to commit whoredom with the daughters of Moab. And they called the people unto the sacrifices of their gods: and the people did eat, and bowed down to their gods" (Num. 25:1–2). This was the first time that Israel is said to have openly worshipped foreign gods; it would not be the last. This false worship angered God (v. 3). There is no doubt that this had been Balaam's plan. He believed that God supported Israel because of Israel's righteous behavior. "He hath not beheld iniquity in Jacob, neither hath he seen perverseness in Israel: the LORD his God is with him, and the shout of a king is among them" (Num. 23:21). What he had misunderstood was that God did not see iniquity in Israel because of its absence in Israel. He failed to see it judicially. God looked at the judicial coverings that He had provided Israel: the sacrifices, the system of cleansing, and the other boundaries that separated Israel from the other nations. He had chosen Israel despite Israel's sins. He was building up Israel as His people. Thus, any attempt to undermine Israel's commitment to God would not result in the defeat of Israel but the defeat of the perpetrators. Balaam had prophesied: "Let me die the death of the righteous, and let my last end be like his!" (Num. 23:10b). His words subsequently condemned him. He died the death of the unrighteous.

There is no indication that Balaam was paid for having suggested this strategy of subversion. Paid or not, Balaam wanted to be part of the establishment. He wanted to be an insider, part of the inner ring. As C. S. Lewis remarked before a group of university students: "Of all passions the passion for the Inner Ring is most skillful in making a man who is not yet a very bad man do very bad things."[2] The king of Moab had sent representatives of Moab and Midian to recruit him (Num. 22:7). This was proof of his importance to the leaders of the alliance. Access to power is a strong lure. Balaam would not sell a false prophecy to Balak, though he refused to turn down the king's request definitively at the very beginning of the negotiations. Balak believed that every man has his price. Balaam did have a price, but that price seems not to have been money. The price was access to power, to importance within the inner ring. He thought of himself as a master strategist. He believed that he could undermine the basis of Israel's support by God. This way, he would be able to announce a true prophecy that was favorable to Balak's cause.

Balaam was formally a true prophet. He refused to utter a false prophecy, i.e., a judicially binding curse in God's name. "And Balaam answered and said unto the servants of Balak, If Balak would give me his house full of silver and gold, I cannot go beyond the word of the LORD my God, to do less or more" (Num. 22:18). Ethically, however, he was a false prophet. He used his knowledge of God's covenantal relationship with Israel – a covenant grounded in ethical stipulations – to lure Israel into adultery in the broadest sense. Balaam had a surface understanding of biblical covenantalism. He understood that God's corporate sanctions in history enforce His covenant's stipulations. Balaam believed that if he could lure Israel into the judicial status of a covenant-breaking nation, God would impose negative corporate sanctions on Israel. These, he believed, would weaken Israel, allowing the alliance to defeat Israel. He could then invoke a curse against Israel. He would

---

2. C. S. Lewis, "The Inner Ring" (1944), in Lewis, *The Weight of Glory and Other Addresses* (New York: Macmillan, 1980), p. 103.

thereby establish himself as both a true prophet and a court prophet.

God did impose sanctions on Israel: 24,000 died in a plague (Num. 25:9). More would have died had it not been for the representative judicial action of Phinehas, the son of Eleazar (v. 7), who executed an Israelite man and Midianite woman in their act of debauchery (v. 8). But Israel's sin did not break the covenant permanently. God's grace covered the transgression. God then called Israel to battle Midian (v. 17). It was Midian that lost the war, not Israel (Num. 31).

Conclusion

Balaam was the classic court prophet. The court prophet in Israel served the king, not God. The king paid him to speak the word of the king in the name of God. Whether he declared the future accurately was irrelevant to his status as a court prophet.

Covenant law is intended to lead sinners to repentance. Balaam did not call Balak to repentance before God. Instead, he sought a way to lure Israel into sin. He misused his knowledge of God's covenant. He sought a perverse end by means of the law itself. In this sense, he adopted Satan's strategy with Eve in the garden and Jesus in the wilderness: partial citations of the law in order to undermine the intent of the law, i.e., covenantal faithfulness to God. Balaam announced God's commitment to Israel because of Israel's righteousness, and then he devised a strategy to make Israel unrighteous. For this, God placed him under the negative sanction of execution.

14

DIVIDING THE INHERITANCE

And the LORD spake unto Moses, saying, Unto these the land shall be divided for an inheritance according to the number of names. To many thou shalt give the more inheritance, and to few thou shalt give the less inheritance: to every one shall his inheritance be given according to those that were numbered of him. Notwithstanding the land shall be divided by lot: according to the names of the tribes of their fathers they shall inherit. According to the lot shall the possession thereof be divided between many and few (Num. 26:52–56).

The theocentric focus of this law is the familiar theme of ownership: God was the owner of the Promised Land. He delegated to Israelite tribes and then to families inter-generational stewardship over certain plots of land. He served as the original agent of distribution by means of the casting of lots. Tribes were to serve as the secondary agents of distribution: allocating ownership in terms of family size. The question to be resolved was ethical: To what extent was the allocation of land based on considerations of equity – family size and need – and to what extent on the question of equality of family inheritance? That is, was the allocation based more on family size or tribal inheritance rights? This problem has baffled rabbinic commentators for almost two thousand years.

This command to allocate portions of the land followed the second wilderness numbering of Israel (Num. 26:1–2). The nation had already been involved in a series of defensive wars against Canaanites who dwelt outside the boundaries of the Jordan. Israel did not initiate them. (The conquest of Jazeer may have been an exception.) Israel was victorious over these nations and had begun to occupy large tracts of real estate, but only because the previous holders had attacked Israel rather than allowing Israel access through their lands. This was the down payment on Israel's inheritance, prophesied by Abraham: "But in the fourth generation they shall come hither again: for the iniquity of the Amorites is not yet full" (Gen. 15:16). Now, the iniquity of the Amorites had become full. The Amorite tribes outside of the boundaries of Canaan had launched a pair of offensive campaigns against Israel (Num. 21:23, 33), which they lost. This marked the beginning of the conquest.

By Lot or by Need?

The nation numbered 601,730 men of fighting age (v. 51), which was very close to what it had been a generation earlier. Once this was ascertained, God laid down the law of spoils. First, it was by family size. "To many thou shalt give the more inheritance, and to few thou shalt give the less inheritance: to every one shall his inheritance be given according to those that were numbered of him" (v. 54). Second, it was by lot. "Notwithstanding the land shall be divided by lot: according to the names of the tribes of their fathers they shall inherit" (v. 55). Taken at face value, these two rules are inconsistent. If distribution is strictly by lot, then there is no way to allocate property in terms of "larger families–more land." A plot of land will go to the family selected by lot.

Pre-modern rabbinical commentators were not agreed on a way to resolve this. Some, following Rashi, argued that the Holy Spirit (*Ruach Hakodesh*) allocated unequal portions to the families. "Although the portions were not *of* equal *area* because, *as we have now said*, in all cases they assigned the portions according to the numerousness of the tribe, yet they did so only by aid of the lot, but the lot fell by the utterance of the Holy Spirit, as is explained in Baba Bathra (122a)."[1] The problem here was the text's indication that Israel's leaders had to consider the size of the tribes. If God was in solely in charge of this, why did Moses mention this problem in the rules governing allocation? It seems as though the rules placed this responsibility on the rulers.

Nachmanides rejected this interpretation: ". . . it is explicitly stated in the Gemara [Baba Bathra 117b] that the meaning of [this section] according to the Sages was not to distinguish in any way between [the portion given to] each particular tribe [since they each received an equal portion]. . . . [T]he Rabbis expressly came to the conclusion that the Land was *not* divided according to the heads of men, [i.e., according to the overall population], but it was divided among [all] the tribes [equally]. Thus they divided it into twelve equal parts, and each tribe took that part which was assigned to it by lot."[2] The rabbis debated about whether the inheritance went to the sons at the time of the second wilderness numbering as individual warriors or whether they inherited their shares in terms of what God had allocated at the exodus to their fathers.[3]

Isaac ben Judah Abravanel (1437–1508), an Iberian rabbinic commentator, offered a third possibility. The lots for the tribes identified the region of the nation in which a tribe would ultimately dwell, but the size of these tribal plots was based on tribal population. Some tribes might receive less fertile land, so

---

1. Rashi, *Chumash with Targum Onkelos, Haphtaroth and Rashi's Commentary*, A. M. Silbermann and M. Rosenbaum, translators, 5 vols. (Jerusalem: Silbermann Family, [1934] 1985 [Jewish year: 5745]), IV, p. 129 (comment on verse 53).

2. Nachmanides, *Commentary on the Torah*, 5 vols. (New York: Shilo, [1267?] 1975), III, p. 313.

3. Samson Raphael Hirsch, *The Pentateuch*, 5 vols. (Gateshead, London: Judaica Press, [1875?] 1989), IV, *Numbers*, pp. 446–48.

they would be granted larger territories within the general region. The modern commentator, Jacob Milgrom, thinks that this is the correct approach, with this modification: the families, too, would receive their plots in terms of their size, not by lot.[4] But is he correct?

If allocation was strictly by lot to each family, then the presumption is that the plots allocated were all the same size. But the allocation was not strictly by lot. There was also a consideration of family size. The question is: Which family? Was a family determined on a "one numbered warrior, one family plot" basis? Or was it based on the family name within each tribe? Or was it some sort of mixture?

Individual Plot or Tribal Plot?

In the second Numbers mustering, each tribe's census was broken down into families, and each family was named. In the first Numbers mustering, only Levi's report was broken down by family names (Num. 3:17). The other tribal families were not named. After each tribal name, this phrase occurs: ". . . after their families, by the house of their fathers, according to the number of the names, from twenty years old and upward, all that were able to go forth to war." The distinguishing mark of this earlier numbering is this phrase: "according to the number of the names." In the numbering described in Numbers 26, this phrase does not occur. Instead, the name of each family appears. This points to the importance of family name in the second wilderness numbering. Each family knew that it would be a part of a victorious military campaign. Each knew what the terms of the inheritance were. Each had its name recorded in anticipation of the victory.

By identifying family names, meaning the names of the sons of the twelve patriarchs (Joseph's two sons initially counting as

---

4. Jacob Milgrom, *The JPS Torah Commentary: Numbers* (New York: Jewish Publication Society, 1990), p. 481.

one family), the elders of each tribe knew that larger family units would have to be allocated more land. The question was: More land out of what sized tribal portion?

If this command from God was to be honored, there had to be a fixed reference point. The problem facing the commentator is to identify this fixed reference point. Was it the size of the *family plot*, with the same sized plot distributed by lot to each warrior? Was the *tribal plot* size fixed, with the allocation of plots within this fixed unit determined by the size and number of the families belonging to the tribe? Or was the constant factor the *general geographical location* of the land rather than the size of the allocation? If so, was this confined to the tribes' allocation, or were family plots also governed by the "general location" principle?

First, if each family plot was the same size, with allocation based on the number of holy warriors within each tribe, then the tribes' inheritances would not have been equal in size. Larger tribes would have received larger allocations. This was Rashi's opinion. Second, if each tribal allocation was the same size, then the individual warriors' inheritances would have varied in terms of the number of families in the tribe: members of larger tribes received smaller family inheritance on average. The families would then have been granted larger or smaller plots in terms of their size. This was Nachmanides' opinion, and he cited rabbinical tradition. This would have meant that members of small tribes with few families would have been granted larger plots, on average, than members of populous tribes.

There is a problem with Nachmanides' interpretation: a subsequent clarification of the law. "And ye shall divide the land by lot for an inheritance among your families: and to the more ye shall give the more inheritance, and to the fewer ye shall give the less inheritance: every man's inheritance shall be in the place where his lot falleth; according to the tribes of your fathers ye shall inherit" (Num. 33:54). It appears as though the casting of lots was also used to divide up tribal real estate among each tribe's families: "every man's inheritance shall be in the place where his lot falleth." It also sounds as though larger families received larger portions: "And ye shall divide the land by lot for an inheritance among your families: and to the more ye shall give the more inheritance, and to the fewer ye shall give the less inheritance." What did these phrases mean? Did "allocation by lot" apply both to the tribes and families? Did the "allocation by population" also apply to both? If so, how? How did God's allocation by lot integrate with the rulers' allocation in terms of population and presumed economic need?

Dual Allocations

The language of Numbers 33:54 indicates that both systems of allocation governed the initial allocation, first to tribes and then to families. How might this have worked? Let us consider Abravanel's suggestion. The land was divided up into eleven regions, but initially there were no fixed boundaries assigned to these large plots. Then lots were cast to determine which tribe would live in which region. Variations in the land's productivity would not become matters of inter-tribal conflict except in the tribes' border areas. The falling of the lot would govern the distribution. Then the question of tribal size became an issue. Here the rulers would have to decide. The Levites would probably have played an important role here because they were not given any rural land. Levites would live in cities in all regions. They had no self-interest in favoring one tribe over another. By using the lot method to allocate land regionally, and by using population to establish boundaries, the system reduced tribal conflict over the regional assignments, yet it honored considerations of equity: not favoring the members of small tribes by granting them family plots that were larger on average than the plots inherited by populous tribes.

If this dual allocation system was established as a way to reduce the number of inter-tribal conflicts regarding general location, yet to preserve equity based on family plot size, then the same dual allocation system would have worked in the same way to reduce the number of intra-tribal conflicts. The casting of lots determined each family's legal claim to a piece of property in a region within the tribe's inheritance, but the boundaries of the plots were determined by considerations of family size in relation to the land's expected productivity.

The decision facing the rulers was comparable to the decision facing the parents of several children. They have inherited a piece of property which, for some reason, they cannot legally sell. It is time to build a home. Should they tell the architect to build all of the rooms the same size? If they do, then the older children will complain, "But I need more room. The younger children have rooms as large as ours. It's not fair!" If they build different-sized rooms, the complaint from the younger children will be: "But the older one's rooms are bigger. You're not treating us the same. It's not fair!" What should the parents tell the architect to design? Then there is the additional question of where the rooms are to be placed, given the design of the house. Will one room look out on a lovely back yard, while another room face the blank side of the next door neighbor's house?

The language of Numbers 33:54 governing the distribution of both tribal land and family plots seems to indicate that both principles of allocation had to be honored. If the two systems of allocation were in force, we can better understand how this system worked by using the analogy of the home. Casting lots will determine which part of the home each child will live in: facing the back yard, front yard, or the next door neighbor's house; close to the kitchen or close to the joint bathroom; etc. "Don't complain to us; the lots decided your location." Once this general placement of the children's rooms is decided, the size of the rooms are designed in terms of the needs of older children vs. younger children.

The analogy breaks down in one crucial respect: older children grow up and move out. This leaves their rooms available for younger children who have also grown. In Israel, once a family was assigned its plot of ground, it could not permanently move out or buy more, except to move inside a walled city, where the jubilee land law did not apply.

Joshua's Allocations

Subsequent revelation provides us with additional evidence regarding the actual allocation of tribal land. "And the lot of the children of Joseph fell from Jordan by Jericho, unto the water of Jericho on the east, to the wilderness that goeth up from Jericho throughout mount Bethel, And goeth out from Bethel to Luz, and passeth along unto the borders of Archi to Ataroth, And goeth down westward to the coast of Japhleti, unto the coast of Beth-horon the nether, and to Gezer: and the goings out thereof are at the sea. So the children of Joseph, Manasseh and Ephraim, took their inheritance" (Josh. 16:1–4). The first thing to consider is the highly specific territory described here. The borders of this inheritance were already fixed. This seems to call into question Abravanel's interpretation. But maybe not, as we shall see.

The second point is the singular word: lot. One lot fell to the children of Joseph. There had been an existing unit of land. The lot associated with this unit of land fell to the two tribes of Joseph. This means that the lot was associated with one patriarch. This led to a complaint:

> Yet it came to pass, when the children of Israel were waxen strong, that they put the Canaanites to tribute; but did not utterly drive them out. And the children of Joseph spake unto Joshua, saying, Why hast thou given me but one lot and one portion to inherit, seeing I am a great people, forasmuch as the LORD hath blessed me hitherto? And Joshua answered them, If thou be a great people, then get thee up to the wood country, and cut down for thyself there in the land of the

Perizzites and of the giants, if mount Ephraim be too narrow for thee. And the children of Joseph said, The hill is not enough for us: and all the Canaanites that dwell in the land of the valley have chariots of iron, both they who are of Beth-shean and her towns, and they who are of the valley of Jezreel. And Joshua spake unto the house of Joseph, even to Ephraim and to Manasseh, saying, Thou art a great people, and hast great power: thou shalt not have one lot only: But the mountain shall be thine; for it is a wood, and thou shalt cut it down: and the outgoings of it shall be thine: for thou shalt drive out the Canaanites, though they have iron chariots, and though they be strong (Josh. 17:13–18).

The heirs of the two sons of Joseph believed that they had been short-changed by the lot allocation system. They appealed to their might, i.e., their greater numerical strength, over the other tribal units. They deserved more land because they were in fact two family units, not one. In other words, the two tribes were calling for a revision based on population size. This seems consistent with Abravanel's view: lot first, then reallocation based on population. But the two tribes were also raising a judicial point: they were two tribes. They had obviously been allocated only one tribal unit.[5]

Joshua's response was both clever and critical of their claim. He understood their request as a judicial claim rather than a population claim: "one lot only." They wanted another lot. There were twelve non-Levitical tribes, not eleven. He told them, "You may have more land," he said. "Just go do your job and conquer the Canaanites whom you have allowed to occupy the land. You may claim another tribe's share of the inheri-

5. These two tribes received their inheritance from Jacob one generation later than the other sons did, for they were grandsons of Jacob. So, their population expansion began later, biologically speaking. This would have made a considerable difference in their size at the time of the conquest. They would have been much smaller than the other tribes. Where, then, did they get their extra numbers? From adoptions. The sons of Joseph in the early years would have attracted more volunteers, since Joseph was the Pharaoh's agent. I am indebted to David McCalman for this insight. This is additional evidence for the presence of the adoption process early in Israel's stay in Egypt.

tance by finishing what neither your tribe nor the other tribe has been able to complete: the conquest." In other words, he said: "All right, you self-proclaimed mighty men of war, you tough guys: go out and exterminate some really tough guys who are armed with iron chariots. Mighty is as mighty does. Put your muscle where your mouths are." Did they have a legitimate legal claim? Let them prove their claim on the battlefield.

The heirs of Joseph had a plausible legal case: they were in fact two families. They had been counted as two families in the musterings. Joshua took this into consideration. But he did not grant them their request irrespective of what they would do to enforce their claim. Combined, they were larger than other tribes. But numbers are as numbers do. They had to prove their case by evicting Canaanites. That is, they had to do something extra in order to validate their claim. They could keep any extra ground they conquered. This answer was Joshua's way to head off criticism from the other tribes. The other tribes might come back and complain: "Joseph was entitled to one share, just like the rest of us. He could not lawfully bequest what was not his to give. Let the heirs of his two sons accept this without trying to get their hands on our land." Joshua would have an answer: "They did not take away your land; they took away Canaanites' land. They earned their extra portion on the battlefield. It is only fair that they should share in a larger inheritance."

This was a special case: legal rather than demographic. The next seven cases were not special.

And there remained among the children of Israel seven tribes, which had not yet received their inheritance. And Joshua said unto the children of Israel, How long are ye slack to go to possess the land, which the LORD God of your fathers hath given you? Give out from among you three men for each tribe: and I will send them, and they shall rise, and go through the land, and describe it according to the inheritance of them; and they shall come again to me. And they shall divide it into seven parts: Judah shall abide in their coast on the south, and the house of Joseph shall abide in their coasts on the north. Ye shall therefore describe the land into seven parts, and bring the description hither to me, that I may cast lots for you here before the LORD our God (Josh. 18:2–6).

This indicates that these seven tribes already had received their inheritances. Joshua announced the regions that Judah, Ephraim, and half the tribe of Manasseh would occupy.[6] We know from the previous chapter that Joseph had received his land by lot. This indicates that the tribal lots for all of the tribes had already been cast. Each tribe knew approximately where its land would be. Each tribe would send out surveyors. So far, this is consistent with all three approaches to the allocation problem: Rashi's, Nachmanides', and Abravanel's.

The men were sent out in teams of three with instructions to survey the land. This indicates that the wars of conquest were over. The surveyors were not told to do an extensive survey in terms of the actual numbers of families in their tribes. Upon their return, they were to place before Joshua the descriptions of the boundaries of each of the seven tribal units.[7] The text does not indicate that the seven plots were equal.

He had told them to bring back their descriptions "that I may cast lots for you here before the LORD our God" (v. 6). So, there was still a further allocation of land remaining. This indicates clearly that two separate castings of lots had to take place. The first was tribal. The second applied to clans or smaller family units.

---

6. This indicates that Ephraim and half the tribe of Manasseh had been successful in removing the Canaanites. The text says "their coasts" not "his coast" with respect to the tribe of Joseph.

7. This indicates that the Israelites had learned in Egypt how to survey. The highly sophisticated skills of the Egyptians in this regard are rarely noted in textbooks. See the appendix by Livio Stecchini in Peter Tompkins, *Secrets of the Great Pyramid* (New York: Harper & Row, 1974).

We are not told how the surveyors knew precisely which land belonged to which tribe, nor are we told if there had been, or would be, a demographics-based reallocation after the tribal lots were cast (Abravanel). We are not told whether a post-survey reallocation took place. What we are told is that there had been a previous casting of lots, as indicated by the complaint by the heirs of Joseph, as well as by the fact that the surveyors knew generally where their tribes' inheritances were. We also know that another casting of lots lay ahead.

Rashi argued that God would have decided where the lots fell, with large tribes receiving large inheritances. His view is theologically conceivable, though not very plausible. (Why had Moses brought up the family size issue if God would decide all this?) Nachmanides argued that the tribal plots were equal. Abravanel argued that only the tribal regions were determined by lot.

Nachmanides' position has to be rejected, at least with respect to family plots. His approach assumed tribal plots of equal size and allocated by lot, with family plots that varied in size in terms of family size. But why would there have to be an additional round of lot-casting? If the clan or family allocations were based strictly on need, what role did lot-casting play? With respect to family plots, we are left with some variation of Abravanel's approach: lot-casting to determine general location, plus a subsequent reallocation in terms of family size.

This still does not answer the question: Were the tribal allocations equal in size? Ethically speaking, if it was proper to reallocate land for families after the lots had been cast, then there seems nothing wrong with applying this principle to tribes. This does not mean that this was done.

We are not told whether tribal territorial units were equal in area. We are told that family units were unequal. Joshua's comment indicates that lot-casting in some way applied to the secondary, intra-tribal allocations. What, then, is meant by Numbers 33:54? "And ye shall divide the land by lot for an inheritance among your families: and to the more ye shall give the more inheritance, and to the fewer ye shall give the less inheritance: every man's inheritance shall be in the place where his lot falleth; according to the tribes of your fathers ye shall inherit." The principle seems to be that demographic considerations apply to families. A general allocation principle governed family inheritance: "to the more ye shall give the more inheritance, and to the fewer ye shall give the less inheritance." I conclude that this principle applied to the tribal territories, too. I side with Abravanel, though with this modification: the dual lot-demographics allocation system applied to tribes and families alike, not just to tribes.

How could this allocation system have applied to the Levites? Levi received a portion of the land: 48 walled cities (Num. 35:7), plus suburbs around them for their cattle (Num. 35:4). The height of each of these suburbs was fixed: 2,000 cubits (3,000 feet). "And ye shall measure from without the city on the east side two thousand cubits, and on the south side two thousand cubits, and on the west side two thousand cubits, and on the north side two thousand cubits and the city shall be in the midst: this shall be to them the suburbs of the cities" (Num. 35:5). The diagram suggests one way that this might have been laid out.[8]

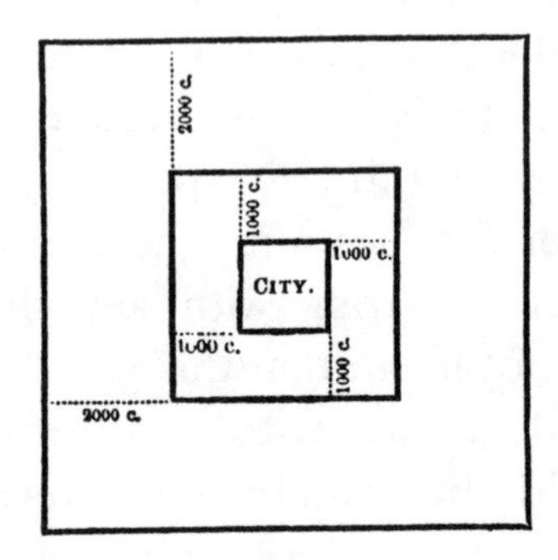

8. C. J. Ellicott, *Numbers* (Grand Rapids, Michigan: Zondervan, 1961 reprint), p. 214.

The size of each city would have been different. The area of a plot with a 2,000-foot side of a city wall would have been larger than a plot with a 1,500-foot side. Thus, the size of the Levites' combined plots would have been different, city by city.

We are not told how each Levitical family was assigned residence in a particular city, but lot-casting would have been an obvious means. The cities, like the tribal plots (if either Rashi or Abravanel was correct, and Nachmanides was wrong), varied in size. Once assigned to a city, a family would have received its plot by lot, but the principle of family size would probably have governed the final allocation.

Conclusion

The second Numbers mustering of Israel was preliminary to the conquest of Canaan. Tribal families were named because they would soon become the recipients of the post-conquest distribution of land. The tribes may have received equal portions of land, but probably there were post-lot reallocations based on the land's productivity and the size of the tribes. This surely was the system governing families.

The tribes had to fight the Canaanites before receiving their land. Even Reuben, Gad, and half the tribe of Manasseh, who had received their inheritance on the far side of the Jordan (Num. 34:14), would not inherit until they and the other tribes had conquered Canaan (Num. 32). Ephraim and half the tribe of Manasseh had to fight in order to claim a two-plot inheritance. There could be no final allocation of the spoils until all the land was conquered. God would reward each tribe according to His good pleasure.

Joshua administered the casting of lots that governed family allocations (Josh. 18:6). He probably left to tribal leaders the final reallocation based on family size and need. There was an equity consideration here: the number of mouths to feed. There was also a military input consideration: the number of warriors provided by each tribal family. It seems unreasonable that a tribe that had contributed large numbers of warriors received an equal share of the spoils. This would have penalized the warriors of the larger tribes: smaller plots, on average. A large family in a small tribe might have received more land than a large family in a large tribe if all tribal territories were equal. This would have constituted an economic penalty on large tribes. Joshua's answer to the heirs of Joseph indicates that the more that a tribe contributed to the victory, the more land it deserved in the post-conquest allocation.

The distribution of family plots was by lot and by post-lot reallocation on the basis of family size. It seems likely that this same system governed the allocation of tribal territory. The lot determined the general region of one's inheritance: tribal territory and family plots. The question of need in relation to population governed the family allocation procedure and probably governed the tribal.

15

BLOODLINE INHERITANCE

And the LORD *spake unto Moses, saying, The daughters of Zelophehad speak right: thou shalt surely give them a possession of an inheritance among their father's brethren; and thou shalt cause the inheritance of their father to pass unto them. And thou shalt speak unto the children of Israel, saying, If a man die, and have no son, then ye shall cause his inheritance to pass unto his daughter. And if he have no daughter, then ye shall give his inheritance unto his brethren. And if he have no brethren, then ye shall give his inheritance unto his father's brethren. And if his father have no brethren, then ye shall give his inheritance unto his kinsman that is next to him of his family, and he shall possess it: and it shall be unto the children of Israel a statute of judgment, as the* LORD *commanded Moses (Num. 27:6–11).*

The theocentric focus of this law is ownership: God was the primary owner of the Promised Land. He would soon delegate to Israelite families the inter-generational secondary ownership of certain plots of land. These families were to serve as stewards in the administration of God's land.

Stewardship is a hierarchical function: point two of the biblical covenant model. The steward is a legal representative of the owner. The steward must apply the owner's principles of administration (point three) to the assets entrusted to him. Stewardship also involves sanctions: profit and loss. If he fails, he will be placed under negative sanctions by the owner. Jesus' parable of the talents is the New Testament summary of this arrangement (Matt. 25:14–30).

Milgrom argues that the case of the daughters of Zelophehad marks off a separate section of the Book of Numbers. The first encounter opens the new section (Num. 27); the second encounter closes it (Num. 36). The chapters that follow the second Numbers mustering (Num. 26) differ sharply with the preceding ones. The earlier chapters display the murmurings of the exodus generation; the second section displays the faithfulness of the conquest generation.[1]

Five daughters of Zelophehad came to Moses with a problem. They had no brothers. Their father had died. They asked a question: "Why should the name of our father be done away from among his family, because he hath no son? Give unto us therefore a possession among the brethren of our father" (v. 4). The judicial issue here was a man's name. The economic issue was inheritance. A righteous man's name was supposed to be preserved in Israel. His inheritance in the land was proof of his righteous status. The daughters were careful to identify their father as having been in the company of the saints: "Our father died in the wilderness, and he was not in the company of them that gathered themselves together against the LORD in the company of Korah; but died in his own sin, and had no sons" (v. 3).

Korah's name had become tainted. His family had forfeited his goods: "And the earth opened her mouth, and swallowed them up, and their houses, and all the men that appertained unto Korah, and all their goods" (Num. 16:32). But his sons must have broken with the sin of their father, for they survived the judgment: "And the earth opened her mouth, and swallowed them up together with Korah, when that company died, what time the fire devoured two hundred and fifty men: and

1. Jacob Milgrom, *The JPS Torah Commentary: Numbers* (New York: Jewish Publication Society, 1990), p. xiii.

they became a sign. Notwithstanding the children of Korah died not" (Num. 26:10–11). They remained active priests. "And Shallum the son of Kore, the son of Ebiasaph, the son of Korah, and his brethren, of the house of his father, the Korahites, were over the work of the service, keepers of the gates of the tabernacle: and their fathers, being over the host of the LORD, were keepers of the entry" (I Chron. 9:19). Zelophehad's daughters seemed to be arguing that if Korah's evil name had not passed to his sons, who retained a priestly inheritance, how much more should five daughters of a righteous man have an inheritance in the land.

The Preservation of the Seed

This inheritance law was an aspect of the seed laws of Israel. The messianic promise set forth by Jacob was that Judah would bear the sword in Israel until Shiloh came (Gen. 49:10). The tribes had to be kept separate until the fulfillment of this prophecy. The seed laws and inheritance laws were an aspect of this separation. I wrote in the Conclusion of *Leviticus*:

> Land laws and seed laws were laws associated with God's covenantal promises to Abraham regarding his offspring (Gen. 15–17). There was a chronological boundary subsequently placed on the seed laws: Jacob's prophecy and promise. "The sceptre shall not depart from Judah, nor a lawgiver from between his feet, until Shiloh come; and unto him shall the gathering of the people be" (Gen. 49:10). After Shiloh came, Jacob said, the scepter would depart from Judah. The unified concept of *scepter and lawgiver* pointed to the civil covenant: physical sanctions and law. Jacob prophesied that the lawful enforcement of the civil covenant would eventually pass to another ruler: Shiloh, the Messiah.
>
> The Levitical land laws were tied covenantally to the Abrahamic promise regarding a place of residence for the Israelites (Gen. 15: 13–16). These land laws were also tied to the Abrahamic promise of the seed. "In the same day the LORD made a covenant with Abram, saying, Unto thy seed have I given this land, from the river of Egypt unto the great river, the river Euphrates" (Gen. 15:18). The mark of those

included under the boundaries of these seed laws was the covenantal sign of circumcision (Gen. 17:9–14). Circumcision established a personal covenantal boundary. There were also family and tribal boundaries tied to the laws of inheritance. The ultimate inheritance law was above all a land law: the jubilee law (Lev. 25).[2]

In Numbers 36, the case of the daughters of Zelophehad reappeared. Given two facts – the jubilee law and the judicial status of a wife as an adoptee into her husband's family and tribe – the daughters' land would pass into the tribes of their husbands if they inherited land and then married men who were outside their tribe (Num. 36:3). This would have created a parcel of one tribe's land within the boundaries of another tribe. Moses then announced a modification of the jubilee law: "This is the thing which the LORD doth command concerning the daughters of Zelophehad, saying, Let them marry to whom they think best; only to the family of the tribe of their father shall they marry. So shall not the inheritance of the children of Israel remove from tribe to tribe: for every one of the children of Israel shall keep himself to the inheritance of the tribe of his fathers" (vv. 6–7). The landed inheritance was tied more to the tribe than to the family. Upon marrying into another tribe, a daughter surrendered her inheritance to her sisters. Each tribe had a legal claim to the land within its borders. This claim was exercised through judicial representatives: families. Each family was under the jurisdiction of its tribe. It gained its lawful authority over its land through the tribe.

This modification of the jubilee land inheritance law was designed to keep the tribes geographically separated. This prevented any tribe from becoming dominant outside its own sphere of geographical authority. Loyalty would be to the tribe, region by region. This tribal decentralization would restrain the development of nationalism except as an aspect of Israel's

2. Gary North, *Leviticus: An Economic Commentary* (Tyler, Texas: Institute for Christian Economics, 1994), pp. 637–38.

priesthood. Even a king would be restricted from amassing rural land and houses for his heirs. For all the evil that Ahab did, it was his theft of Naboth's vineyard that brought God's final sanction against him. God told Elijah: "And thou shalt speak unto him, saying, Thus saith the LORD, Hast thou killed, and also taken possession? And thou shalt speak unto him, saying, Thus saith the LORD, In the place where dogs licked the blood of Naboth shall dogs lick thy blood, even thine" (I Ki. 21:19).[3]

The land inheritance law elevated family name over economic productivity, love, or power. The land owner could not disinherit his family by selling his rural inheritance to the highest bidder. The tribal name was elevated over family name. To preserve each family's name in a specific tribe, and to preserve the numerical strength of each tribe, God established a land inheritance system for rural property that subsidized the heirs of the conquest generation.

Old Covenant Inheritance-Disinheritance

There was covenantal disinheritance in Israel: civil, ecclesiastical, or familial. A father was not allowed unilaterally to disinherit just one son. A father had to follow strict rules of inheritance. "If a man have two wives, one beloved, and another hated, and they have born him children, both the beloved and the hated; and if the firstborn son be hers that was hated: Then it shall be, when he maketh his sons to inherit that which he hath, that he may not make the son of the beloved firstborn before the son of the hated, which is indeed the firstborn: But he shall acknowledge the son of the hated for the firstborn, by

---

3. This was fulfilled in I Kings 22:38. For Jezebel, who had planned the evil act (I Ki. 21:5–9), it would be worse: the dogs would actually eat her. "And of Jezebel also spake the LORD, saying, The dogs shall eat Jezebel by the wall of Jezreel" (I Ki. 21:23). This was fulfilled in II Kings 9:35.

giving him a double portion of all that he hath: for he is the beginning of his strength; the right of the firstborn is his" (Deut. 21:15–17).

The eldest son received a double portion. The question is: Why? There are two reasons: judicial and economic. Judicially, the eldest son was the first son to bear his father's name. He was a testimony from God to the man that God had decided to bless the man's name in Israel. The son would have a place in the national covenant in the next generation. He would rule over his brothers until they departed from the family's land. Isaac blessed Jacob, thinking that Jacob was Esau, his firstborn: "Let people serve thee, and nations bow down to thee: be lord over thy brethren, and let thy mother's sons bow down to thee: cursed be every one that curseth thee, and blessed be he that blesseth thee" (Gen. 27:29). This was a matter of judicial authority. The firstborn normally replaced his father's rule over the family. Second, economic: with greater blessings come greater responsibilities. This is a basic biblical principle of personal responsibility. The eldest son presumably had to bear the primary responsibility in supporting his feeble parents in their old age. The Bible does not say this explicitly; it is a conclusion based on the fact of the double portion. This conclusion is consistent with the principle announced by Christ: "For unto whomsoever much is given, of him shall be much required: and to whom men have committed much, of him they will ask the more" (Luke 12:48b).

The only way that a man could unilaterally disinherit a son was to disinherit all of his children: to cut off his family's name in the tribe. He could do this by pledging his land to a priest and then breaking the pledge by remaining in control of the land and its income. At the jubilee, the land went to the priest if the man failed to redeem the land from the priest (Lev. 27:19–21).[4] This was the only way that a priest could become

4. North, *Leviticus*, pp. 608–11.

a land owner in rural Israel. It was also the only time that a tribe forfeited its legal claim over rural land, and then only to a member of the one tribe that was scattered throughout the nation and had no tribal landed inheritance. This tribe's authority was not dependent on its possession of rural land, nor would its sporadic inheritance of scattered plots provide it with a means of extending its influence. Its national influence was tied to its very inability to extend power through the accumulation of land. So was its financing: the tithe.

Geographically, disinherited sons were cut off from their tribe. They could reside in a city or rent land in the country, but the family's name ceased to be a permanent legacy in the tribe except by adoption into a city. The elders of a city could reverse any son's loss of tribal connection, but they could not reclaim his forfeited land. That had passed permanently to a priest.

How could just one evil son be disinherited under the Mosaic Covenant? First, by civil execution. "If a man have a stubborn and rebellious son, which will not obey the voice of his father, or the voice of his mother, and that, when they have chastened him, will not hearken unto them: Then shall his father and his mother lay hold on him, and bring him out unto the elders of his city, and unto the gate of his place; And they shall say unto the elders of his city, This our son is stubborn and rebellious, he will not obey our voice; he is a glutton, and a drunkard. And all the men of his city shall stone him with stones, that he die: so shalt thou put evil away from among you; and all Israel shall hear, and fear" (Deut. 21:18–21). Second, by ecclesiastical excommunication. If a priest excommunicated a man, he could not inherit from his father.[5] He was "cut off from his people." In both cases, the father could not unilaterally disinherit just

5. Gary North, *Tools of Dominion: The Case Laws of Exodus* (Tyler, Texas: Institute for Christian Economics, 1990), pp. 836–37.

one son. Either the elders or a priest would have to take formal action to validate the disinheritance.

New Covenant Inheritance-Disinheritance

With the transfer of the kingdom from Israel to the church (Matt. 21:43), the laws of inheritance were transformed. With a new priesthood came a new legal order. This biblical principle of judicial transformation was announced by the author of the epistle to the Hebrews: "For the priesthood being changed, there is made of necessity a change also of the law. For he of whom these things are spoken pertaineth to another tribe, of which no man gave attendance at the altar. For it is evident that our Lord sprang out of Juda; of which tribe Moses spake nothing concerning priesthood. And it is yet far more evident: for that after the similitude of Melchisedec there ariseth another priest, Who is made, not after the law of a carnal commandment, but after the power of an endless life. For he testifieth, Thou art a priest for ever after the order of Melchisedec" (Heb. 7:12–17). The Mosaic land inheritance laws ceased with the advent of the new priesthood. There was no longer any need to keep the tribes geographically separate. The church recognized this, of course, but so did the Jews. After the fall of Jerusalem and the burning of the temple, Judaism replaced the Old Covenant religion. Judaism is not the religion of Old Covenant Israel, a fact that Jews who are familiar with their tradition readily admit.[6]

In Mosaic Israel, a father could not unilaterally disinherit his son; under New Covenant law, he is allowed to. This transfers economic authority to the father. The threat of economic disinheritance is a hammer that he holds over wayward children. He is not compelled by New Covenant law to subsidize evil. He was not compelled by law to subsidize evil under the Mosaic law,

---

6. Jacob Neusner, *Judaism and Scripture: The Evidence of Leviticus Rabbah* (University of Chicago Press, 1986), Preface.

but his authority to make this assessment was shared with civil or ecclesiastical authorities.

The law of the double inheritance of the eldest son no longer binds anyone biblically. Younger sons no longer are expected to reside on the land of their fathers under the authority of the eldest brother. This is why the law of the levirate marriage no longer applies: an unmarried brother who lives on his father's land with his brother is no longer required to marry his dead brother's widow if he died without children (Deut. 25:5–6). Neither land ownership nor family name confers covenantal status in the New Covenant. There are no tribes, so inheritance has nothing to do with tribal boundaries. A family's name in Israel is no longer judicially relevant. When Shiloh came, any prophetic function of a family's name ceased. Through adoption into God's family, His name alone remains covenantally relevant (John 1:12; Eph. 1:5). Daughters receive the covenant sign of baptism as a binding judicial mark of this adoption; they can lawfully inherit with sons.

A father is allowed to establish other systems of hierarchical authority over the family's inheritance: trustees, general partners, and so forth. He is allowed to choose the best person for the job of administering the family's assets. Ethics and competence count for more than family name. Any attempt to elevate family name above Christian confession is cultic. Biblical familism was relevant only with respect to the prophecies regarding the coming Messiah. Biblical familism under the Mosaic law was tied to the tribes. When tribal authority disappeared with the fall of Jerusalem, so did biblical familism. Any attempt to revive familism in the name of Old Covenant law is therefore cultic. This is seen most clearly in the British Israelite movement, which self-consciously ties familism to tribalism. Familism is a traditional alternative to covenantalism, especially in politically conservative circles.[7] Jesus warned against familism in no un-

7. Gary North, *Baptized Patriarchalism: The Cult of the Family* (Tyler, Texas: Ins-

certain terms: "For I am come to set a man at variance against his father, and the daughter against her mother, and the daughter in law against her mother in law. And a man's foes shall be they of his own household. He that loveth father or mother more than me is not worthy of me: and he that loveth son or daughter more than me is not worthy of me" (Matt. 10:35–37). He never said anything so harsh as this against the State.

New Covenant biblical inheritance and disinheritance rest on formal confession and ethics. The true son is the son who confesses and then obeys God the Father by conforming himself to God's Son, Jesus Christ. He is entitled to a double portion or more if his brothers and sisters are less faithful than he is. The New Covenant goal is to build up the kingdom of God in history by multiplying the inheritance over time. "And every one that hath forsaken houses, or brethren, or sisters, or father, or mother, or wife, or children, or lands, for my name's sake, shall receive an hundredfold, and shall inherit everlasting life" (Matt. 19:29). Entry into the family of God is established by confession, as manifested in baptism: a self-maledictory oath taken under God, which incorporates a person into God's family. Family membership is maintained by outward obedience to God's moral law and by regular covenant renewal, as manifested in the sacrament of the Lord's Supper. The New Covenant's extension of family inheritance in history has visibly shifted from tribalism to confessionalism. Shiloh has come.

Conclusion

Bloodline inheritance had a political function in pre-exilic Mosaic Israel: the separation of families within the tribes and also of tribes within the nation. This was to insure that no family or tribe was able to centralize power or wealth by means of land purchases. The jubilee law returned a family's rural land

titute for Christian Economics, 1994).

to the heirs of the conquest generation. Tribal decentralization preserved liberty in Mosaic Israel prior to the exile. After the exile, those who returned to Israel were a handful compared to the numbers that inherited at the time of the conquest. Israel became a captive nation. National preservation, not decentralization, became the primary political goal. This became a priestly function rather than a tribal function.

After the exile, the land inheritance law changed. Inheritance was still governed by the jubilee, but this was to include pagans who resided in the land at the time of Israel's return. "Thus saith the Lord GOD; This shall be the border, whereby ye shall inherit the land according to the twelve tribes of Israel: Joseph shall have two portions. And ye shall inherit it, one as well as another: concerning the which I lifted up mine hand to give it unto your fathers: and this land shall fall unto you for inheritance" (Ezek. 47:13–14). "So shall ye divide this land unto you according to the tribes of Israel. And it shall come to pass, that ye shall divide it by lot for an inheritance unto you, and to the strangers that sojourn among you, which shall beget children among you: and they shall be unto you as born in the country among the children of Israel; they shall have inheritance with you among the tribes of Israel. And it shall come to pass, that in what tribe the stranger sojourneth, there shall ye give him his inheritance, saith the Lord GOD" (Ezek. 47:21–23). If the jubilee was actually honored, which we do not know, it was to be honored in a new way. Gentiles were to be given access to the land. Genocide was no longer part of the Old Covenant order. This post-exilic law was to serve as a herald of a New Covenant order to come, where Jews and gentiles would inherit the kingdom together in terms of confession and ethics, not blood.

16

OATH AND SANCTIONS

If a man vow a vow unto the Lord, *or swear an oath to bind his soul with a bond; he shall not break his word, he shall do according to all that proceedeth out of his mouth (Num. 30:2).*

The oath constitutes point four of the biblical covenant model: oath/sanctions.[1] Oath and sanctions are linked judicially. A covenantal oath is a *self-maledictory* oath. It formally invokes God's negative sanctions in advance, should the oath-taker not perform the details of his oath. Without the threat of God's negative sanctions, there is no valid covenantal oath. Putting this another way, where it is not valid to invoke such sanctions, a biblical oath is not valid. Putting it even more specifically, a self-maledictory oath is valid only when sworn under the judicial authority of an institution that has been authorized by God to impose or accept such an oath. There are three such institutions: church, family, and State. This is the reason why secret societies misuse the power of the oath when they impose initiatory oaths of secrecy that invoke negative sanctions. Such oaths are not valid, nor are the unsanctioned institutions that require

1. Ray R. Sutton, *That You May Prosper: Dominion By Covenant* (2nd ed.; Tyler, Texas: Institute for Christian Economics, 1992), ch. 4.

such oaths of their members. Those who have bound themselves by such an oath are formally part of a covenantal order that seeks to replace God's kingdom.

A biblical oath is made to God. It may be made to God directly, such as a promise to obey Him, or through the authority of others who have been designated by God as His covenantal agents. The oath is secured by taking it officially under the authority and sanctions of God. This authority must not be invoked haphazardly. God's name is not to be misused. It is not some sort of universal judicial seal for every conceivable personal promise. It is limited to those uses and those institutions that God has authorized. "Thou shalt not take the name of the LORD thy God in vain; for the LORD will not hold him guiltless that taketh his name in vain" (Ex. 20:7).

Laws Governing Biblical Oaths

The Mosaic laws governing vows to God were rigorous. The man who made a personal vow to God could do so in private. The vow's details were between him and God. In contrast, the person who made a vow to a covenantal institution did so in some public ceremony. His oath was a matter of public record. God noted it; other men noted it. This oath was enforceable by the institution administering it. It was a vow which proceeded out of a person's mouth. A mute person presumably wrote down the details of his oath if he could write. If he could not write, he must have made some other visible response to specific questions.

A Woman's Vow

Most of chapter 30 deals with vows made by women. The Mosaic law allowed women to make vows, but with the exception of the widow or the unmarried daughter of a deceased man, her vows did not become valid if vetoed by the head of her household: either her husband or her father. A woman was under masculine authority, and this authority had the right to annul her vow. God did not recognize as judicially binding the unilateral vow of a woman who was under masculine authority.

> If a woman also vow a vow unto the LORD, and bind herself by a bond, being in her father's house in her youth; And her father hear her vow, and her bond wherewith she hath bound her soul, and her father shall hold his peace at her: then all her vows shall stand, and every bond wherewith she hath bound her soul shall stand. But if her father disallow her in the day that he heareth; not any of her vows, or of her bonds wherewith she hath bound her soul, shall stand: and the LORD shall forgive her, because her father disallowed her. And if she had at all an husband, when she vowed, or uttered ought out of her lips, wherewith she bound her soul; And her husband heard it, and held his peace at her in the day that he heard it: then her vows shall stand, and her bonds wherewith she bound her soul shall stand. But if her husband disallowed her on the day that he heard it; then he shall make her vow which she vowed, and that which she uttered with her lips, wherewith she bound her soul, of none effect: and the LORD shall forgive her. But every vow of a widow, and of her that is divorced, wherewith they have bound their souls, shall stand against her. And if she vowed in her husband's house, or bound her soul by a bond with an oath; And her husband heard it, and held his peace at her, and disallowed her not: then all her vows shall stand, and every bond wherewith she bound her soul shall stand. But if her husband hath utterly made them void on the day he heard them; then whatsoever proceeded out of her lips concerning her vows, or concerning the bond of her soul, shall not stand: her husband hath made them void; and the LORD shall forgive her. Every vow, and every binding oath to afflict the soul, her husband may establish it, or her husband may make it void. But if her husband altogether hold his peace at her from day to day; then he establisheth all her vows, or all her bonds, which are upon her: he confirmeth them, because he held his peace at her in the day that he heard them. But if he shall any ways make them void after that he hath heard them; then he shall bear her iniquity. These are the statutes, which the LORD commanded Moses, between a man and his wife, between the father and his daughter, being yet in her youth in her father's house (Num. 30:3–16).

The head of the household had to be informed of the woman's vow in order for it to become operational. The vow did not become binding until one day after he heard it and allowed it to stand. The head of household exercised veto power. As a legal intermediary between God and a woman, the male head of the household bore the responsibility of authorizing her vow. This was the judicial issue. The economic issue was that the resources required for her to fulfill her vow would come out of the family's resource base. For every minute that it cost her to fulfill her vow, that minute could not be allocated to assisting her husband, which was her assigned task as a wife or daughter. The head of the household would have to estimate in advance whether this additional cost was too high.

The fact that a widow's vow required no further authorization indicates that a vow was an act of the head of a household. The widow did not have an intermediary. With her marriage, she had substituted a new head of household for her father. With the death of her husband, she was elevated to his office as household head. This office possessed God-given authority independent of the gender of the holder. Her vow before God required no intermediary to confirm it. Judicially, her word was binding; economically, she had to make the authoritative estimate regarding the family cost of fulfilling it.

Except for a widow, a woman was represented judicially by a man. The representative had to validate the oath of the person represented. Presumably, such an arrangement also extended to male children under age 20. A young man could take an oath, but it had to be confirmed. The hierarchical nature of covenantal representation governed the invocation of oaths.

New Testament Alterations

Has this masculine-dominant hierarchical structure changed in the New Testament? Regarding the ecclesiastical oath, there has been a fundamental change. Baptism is a covenant oath-sign.[2] Females are baptized. They are allowed to take an oath of allegiance to God through membership in His church without asking permission from their husbands or fathers. In fact, they are required to make such a covenant in defiance of this authority. "Think not that I am come to send peace on earth: I came not to send peace, but a sword. For I am come to set a man at variance against his father, and the daughter against her mother, and the daughter in law against her mother in law. And a man's foes shall be they of his own household. He that loveth father or mother more than me is not worthy of me: and he that loveth son or daughter more than me is not worthy of me" (Matt. 10:34–37).

Has a woman's access to baptism changed anything in family authority? The New Testament does not indicate any major change in the family other than the elimination of the Mosaic law's easy divorce (Deut. 24:1; Matt. 5:31–32). The husband is still the head of his household (I Tim. 3). Yet the story of Jael indicates that a wife could lawfully break the vow of her husband when his vow was illegitimate. Her husband had sworn peace with Sisera (Judg. 4:17). She killed Sisera anyway. She did this under the general authority of Deborah, who was a national judge in Israel and under whose leadership the Israelite army was bringing sanctions against Sisera. Jael did not violate her husband's oath on her own authority; she did so under a superior covenantal civil authority. She respected the civil hierarchy by disobeying a subordinate hierarchy. Her rebellion against her husband was part of Israel's rebellion against Sisera, and is so celebrated in Deborah's song. She was promoted in honor among women. "Blessed above women shall Jael the wife of Heber the Kenite be, blessed shall she be above women in the tent" (Judg. 5:24).

---

2. Meredith G. Kline, *By Oath Consigned: A Reinterpretation of the Covenant Signs of Circumcision and Baptism* (Grand Rapids, Michigan: Eerdmans, 1968), ch. 5.

The Civil Oath

In the area of civil government, women are not under any biblical restrictions regarding oath-taking. They may lawfully become citizens; they may swear and then testify in a court of law. They may also vote: the imposition of judicial sanctions, a form of covenant renewal. What was an historically unique case with Deborah has become common in the twentieth century: female judgeship. In no area of life has there been a more fundamental break with classical civilization, where women had no role to play in civil government because they had no role to play in the rites of the city, which were the legal basis of citizenship. The legacy of Greece and Rome was one of exclusion of women from all things civil. Kitto writes of Athens: "Women were not enfranchised: that is, they could not attend the Assembly, still less hold office. They could not own property: they could not conduct legal business: every female, from the day of her birth to the day of her death, had to be the ward, so to speak, of her nearest male relative or her husband, and only through him did she enjoy any legal protection."[3] Women in the late Roman Republic were far more emancipated socially than their Athenian predecessors had been,[4] but they could not vote.[5] They could not appear in court as witnesses.[6] They were not even answerable to the State; their families alone had the right to judge them.[7] "Among the ancients," writes Fustel, "and especially at Rome, the idea of law was inseparably connected with certain sacramental words. . . . [W]hat placed a man under obligation in the ancient law was not conscience, or

---

3. H. D. F. Kitto, *The Greeks* (Baltimore, Maryland: Penguin, 1951), p. 221.

4. F. R. Crowell, *Cicero and the Roman Republic* (Baltimore, Maryland: Penguin, [1948] 1964), pp. 280–82.

5. *Ibid.*, p. 187.

6. Fustel de Coulanges, *The Ancient City: A Study on the Religion, Laws, and Institutions of Greece and Rome* (Garden City, New York: Doubleday Anchor, [1864] 1955), Bk. II, Ch. VIII, p. 92.

7. *Ibid.*, p. 93.

the sentiment of justice; it was the sacred formula."[8] Women, not having access to the religious rites of the city, could not lawfully invoke this formula.

It took over three millennia for the Bible's principle of the oath-bound female judge to be honored on a widespread basis in society. Women in the West received the civil franchise in the years following the First World War (1914–18), the war that also ended kingship in the West. Kingship was allowed by the Mosaic Covenant (Deut. 17), but it was a less preferred judicial order than rule by judges (I Sam. 8). A female judge was in general preferable to a king under the Mosaic system, but it took the enormous social disruption of World War I for the West to acknowledge this politically by driving out its kings and giving women the vote. Bible-believing churches resisted this political development. Pagan suffragettes – freethinkers and Spiritualists[9] – and their masculine, liberal, and radical political allies first promoted it on a national level in England and the United States. The women's suffrage movement in the United States was secular.[10] In the United States in the late nineteenth century, there was an alliance in the North and West between anti-liquor temperance societies, dominated by women and including Protestant evangelicals, and the women's suffrage movement, but the national leaders of the evangelical churches did not support women's right to vote. In the American South, the suggestion was resisted strongly.[11]

When the church and Christians refuse to extend God's kingdom principles in history, covenant-breakers may decide to

---

8. *Ibid.*, III:xi, p. 191.

9. Richard J. Carwardine, *Evangelicals and Politics in Antebellum America* (New Haven, Connecticut: Yale University Press, 1993), p. 32. He cites Anne Braude, *Radical Spirits: Spiritualism and Women's Rights in Nineteenth-Century America* (Boston: Beacon, 1989).

10. Eleanor Flexner, *Century of Struggle: The Woman's Rights Movement in the United States* (rev. ed.; Cambridge, Massachusetts: Harvard University Press, 1975).

11. Robert T. Handy, *A Christian America: Protestant Hopes and Historical Realities* (2nd ed.; New York: Oxford University Press, 1984), pp. 80–81.

do so. When they do, they will gain authority over the Christians for a time. God brings positive sanctions to those who uphold His law, even at the expense of His covenant people's authority. While covenant-breakers cannot indefinitely uphold God's law, since it testifies against them, during the period when they do uphold it, they gain external blessings.[12]

Paying Off a Vow

The payment of a vow could not be made out of a person's second-best capital, unlike a voluntary offering to which no promise was attached. "And whosoever offereth a sacrifice of peace offerings unto the LORD to accomplish his vow, or a freewill offering in beeves or sheep, it shall be perfect to be accepted; there shall be no blemish therein. Blind, or broken, or maimed, or having a wen, or scurvy, or scabbed, ye shall not offer these unto the LORD, nor make an offering by fire of them upon the altar unto the LORD. Either a bullock or a lamb that hath any thing superfluous or lacking in his parts, that mayest thou offer for a freewill offering; but for a vow it shall not be accepted" (Lev. 22:21–23). A person could lawfully give a priest an animal that was not suitable for the altar, but when it came to an animal to be sacrificed on the altar, its blemish-free condition was required.

This rule governed all vow payments. It extended back to the economic source of the asset: "Thou shalt not bring the hire of a whore, or the price of a dog, into the house of the LORD thy God for any vow: for even both these are abomination unto the LORD thy God" (Deut. 23:18). This is why prostitutes were not citizens of Israel. They had the legal status of uncircumcised strangers. They could not bring their tithes and offerings to God, so they could not be members of the church. This separated them from citizenship in the holy commonwealth.

12. Gary North, *Dominion and Common Grace: The Biblical Basis of Progress* (Tyler, Texas: Institute for Christian Economics, 1987), ch. 6.

They could not serve as judges, as Deborah did. But they were not threatened with civil sanctions so long as they did not consort with married men, and so long as they were not daughters of a priest.[13] Polluting a priest's household brought pollution into God's presence. This was a sacred boundary violation: profaning the temple. This violation of household authority was a capital crime. "And the daughter of any priest, if she profane herself by playing the whore, she profaneth her father: she shall be burnt with fire" (Lev. 21:9). Her harlotry put the nation at risk of God's negative sanctions.

Voluntary but Irrevocable

"When thou shalt vow a vow unto the LORD thy God, thou shalt not slack to pay it: for the LORD thy God will surely require it of thee; and it would be sin in thee. But if thou shalt forbear to vow, it shall be no sin in thee. That which is gone out of thy lips thou shalt keep and perform; even a freewill offering, according as thou hast vowed unto the LORD thy God, which thou hast promised with thy mouth" (Deut. 23:21–23). A personal vow is not required by God, although in order to gain lawful access to judicial authority in church, family, and State, a vow is required. When a person swears a vow to God, or to other men who are allowed by God to accept such a vow, he must fulfill the terms of his vow. God does not hold him guiltless who breaks his vow. God also does not relegate to second-class status a person who does not swear a vow.

A publicly sworn vow had to be paid publicly. "I will pay my vows unto the LORD now in the presence of all his people" (Ps. 116:14). So vowed David. This is especially true for men who hold public office. They must set a judicial example, as David understood. He repeated this vow four verses later. His son Solomon also understood the importance of adhering to the

13. A non-virgin who married a man without informing him of her status risked stoning as a whore (Deut. 22:21).

vow's stipulations: "When thou vowest a vow unto God, defer not to pay it; for he hath no pleasure in fools: pay that which thou hast vowed. Better is it that thou shouldest not vow, than that thou shouldest vow and not pay. Suffer not thy mouth to cause thy flesh to sin; neither say thou before the angel, that it was an error: wherefore should God be angry at thy voice, and destroy the work of thine hands?" (Eccl. 5:4–6).

Why take a vow? One reason is to ask for positive sanctions from God. "And Jacob rose up early in the morning, and took the stone that he had put for his pillows, and set it up for a pillar, and poured oil upon the top of it. And he called the name of that place Bethel: but the name of that city was called Luz at the first. And Jacob vowed a vow, saying, If God will be with me, and will keep me in this way that I go, and will give me bread to eat, and raiment to put on, So that I come again to my father's house in peace; then shall the LORD be my God: And this stone, which I have set for a pillar, shall be God's house: and of all that thou shalt give me I will surely give the tenth unto thee" (Gen. 28:18–22). This act of dedication invoked God's name, and God later identified Himself to Jacob by referring back to this event: "I am the God of Bethel, where thou anointedst the pillar, and where thou vowedst a vow unto me: now arise, get thee out from this land, and return unto the land of thy kindred" (Gen. 31:13).

The vow could be corporate as well as personal: "And when king Arad the Canaanite, which dwelt in the south, heard tell that Israel came by the way of the spies; then he fought against Israel, and took some of them prisoners. And Israel vowed a vow unto the LORD, and said, If thou wilt indeed deliver this people into my hand, then I will utterly destroy their cities. And the LORD hearkened to the voice of Israel, and delivered up the Canaanites; and they utterly destroyed them and their cities: and he called the name of the place Hormah" (Num. 21:1–3).

A vow that called down God's positive sanctions in exchange for the payment of a future vow is easy to understand. God was expected to pay in advance. If He did not deliver what the vow-taker had asked for, the oath was not inaugurated. But the vow-taker could show thanks to God, and devotion to God, by taking a vow after a deliverance by God. The crew of the boat on which Jonah was travelling made such a post-deliverance vow: "Wherefore they cried unto the LORD, and said, We beseech thee, O LORD, we beseech thee, let us not perish for this man's life, and lay not upon us innocent blood: for thou, O LORD, hast done as it pleased thee. So they took up Jonah, and cast him forth into the sea: and the sea ceased from her raging. Then the men feared the LORD exceedingly, and offered a sacrifice unto the LORD, and made vows" (Jonah 1:14–16). These vows were made by men who were not formally covenanted to God – a biblical example of common grace in operation.

The stranger could lawfully invoke a vow. The priests were required to participate in the fulfillment of a vow that involved priestly activities. "Speak unto Aaron, and to his sons, and unto all the children of Israel, and say unto them, Whatsoever he be of the house of Israel, or of the strangers in Israel, that will offer his oblation for all his vows, and for all his freewill offerings, which they will offer unto the LORD for a burnt offering" (Lev. 22:18).

New Testament Oaths

Hierarchy is still part of every covenantal institution. Oaths are still valid. No covenant can be ratified apart from the invocation of the member's oath. The oath is the required means for a person to establish a lawful judicial claim on the benefits – positive sanctions – of membership in the covenant institution. There has to be formal subordination to the covenant in order for the sanctions to become operative. There is nothing in the New Testament that indicates that an oath to join a church, establish a new family through marriage, or receive citizenship from a civil government are invalid. On the contrary, there can be no binding covenantal membership apart from such a oath. It is the oath that seals the covenant judicially. For example, the difference between fornication and marital sexual union is not physical; it is judicial. The presence of a judicially binding public oath differentiates the latter from the former.

The New Testament sometimes seems to be hostile to oaths, but the context of these passages indicates that public oaths of covenant ratification and renewal were not an issue. Oaths invoked in non-covenantal relationships were the issue. Jesus said:

> Again, ye have heard that it hath been said by them of old time, Thou shalt not forswear thyself, but shalt perform unto the Lord thine oaths: But I say unto you, Swear not at all; neither by heaven; for it is God's throne: Nor by the earth; for it is his footstool: neither by Jerusalem; for it is the city of the great King. Neither shalt thou swear by thy head, because thou canst not make one hair white or black. But let your communication be, Yea, yea; Nay, nay: for whatsoever is more than these cometh of evil (Matt. 5:33–37).

Jesus referred here to a traditional practice of publicly promising to perform some act and covering his promise with the veneer of additional authority invoking supernatural authority. This practice was never valid. There are lawful public oaths taken to covenantal institutions; there are lawful private oaths to God; but there are never private oaths to other men that are lawfully invoked by an appeal to God or the supernatural. A person who seeks to establish a unique degree of authority for his promise to another person by invoking supernatural hierarchy and supernatural negative sanctions is misusing the oath. He is covering his personal testimony with the aura of covenantal authority. This is a violation of the commandment not to take God's name in vain. It is a boundary violation: profanation.[14] The New Testament Greek word for oath is *horkos*: fence.[15]

There was an example of such an oath in the persecution of Paul by a group of Jewish fanatics. "Then the chief captain took him by the hand, and went with him aside privately, and asked him, What is that thou hast to tell me? And he said, The Jews have agreed to desire thee that thou wouldest bring down Paul to morrow into the council, as though they would enquire somewhat of him more perfectly. But do not thou yield unto them: for there lie in wait for him of them more than forty men, which have bound themselves with an oath, that they will neither eat nor drink till they have killed him: and now are they ready, looking for a promise from thee" (Acts 23:19–21). The Greek word for "oath" in this case meant anathematizing, i.e., self-maledictory. It was an invalid oath, and those who took it either broke it or starved themselves to death. They did not kill Paul.

The Christian's word is so bounded by authority that his words should be trusted apart from any invocation of supernatural hierarchy. The Pharisees did this on a regular basis. They also adopted peculiar rules regarding what words constituted a valid invocation.

> Woe unto you, ye blind guides, which say, Whosoever shall swear by the temple, it is nothing; but whosoever shall swear by the gold of the temple, he is a debtor! Ye fools and blind: for whether is greater, the gold, or the temple that sanctifieth the gold? And, Whosoever shall swear by the altar, it is nothing; but whosoever sweareth by the gift that is upon it, he is guilty. Ye fools and blind: for whether is greater, the gift, or the altar that sanctifieth the gift? Whoso therefore shall swear by the altar, sweareth by it, and by all things thereon. And whoso shall

---

14. Gary North, *Leviticus: An Economic Commentary* (Tyler, Texas: Institute for Christian Economics, 1994), ch. 6.

15. The third commandment relates to boundaries: point three of the biblical covenant model. It parallels the eighth commandment, which prohibits theft.

swear by the temple, sweareth by it, and by him that dwelleth therein. And he that shall swear by heaven, sweareth by the throne of God, and by him that sitteth thereon (Matt. 23:16–22).

Jesus challenged all such man-made rules. The word of a covenant-keeper should be simple and direct. There must be no verbal tricks, no counterfeit oaths subsequently declared null and void because of an imprecise formula. James repeated this warning: "But above all things, my brethren, swear not, neither by heaven, neither by the earth, neither by any other oath: but let your yea be yea; and your nay, nay; lest ye fall into condemnation" (James 5:12).

A covenant oath does not invoke surrogate phrases for heaven. It invokes God's name. This oath is a direct verbal appeal to God because it is taken under a unique institution that has been authorized by God to impose sanctions in His name: church, family, or State. This authority to impose God's sanctions in history is what identifies the institution as covenantal.

Social Contract Theory

The four biblical covenants – personal, ecclesiastical, familial, and civil – have served as models for other relationships and institutions. The corporate covenants linking God, man, and other men have been imitated by atheistic contracts. A contract is analogous to a covenant, but with God's name removed from the formal agreement. It does not invoke God's name or His sanctions in enforcing the agreement's stipulations.

The civil covenant under God has become a civil contract among men. There is no historical evidence that such an act of contracting ever took place. This historical event is completely hypothetical. This was well understood by Rousseau, whose *Social Contract* (1762) was preceded by his earlier study of the subject, his dissertation on inequality. In that essay, he wrote of the state of nature, the hypothetical pre-contractual judicial condition: "Let us begin then by laying facts aside, as they do not affect the question."[16] Enlightenment political theory, both right wing (Whig) and left wing (Rousseau) operated on the assumption that this hypothetical social contract is the judicial foundation of civil government's assertion of a right to inflict violence in defense of civil law. The State created by this contract then becomes the enforcer of its implicit stipulations: natural law. There is no appeal beyond the State. Covenantalism under God becomes contractualism: a man-created, man-based social order.

The family covenant under God then becomes the marriage contract under the State. The justification of divorce becomes social: what is good for society as interpreted by the State. So does the justification for disciplining children. The family then comes under the jurisdiction of the State because God is no longer taken seriously as one of the participants in the arrangement. The State replaces God as the supreme sanctioning agent.

Economic contracts are also analogous to the covenant. The State becomes the ultimate guarantor of a contract's stipulations. The contract's participants agree to perform certain duties in exchange for money or other assets. The mutuality of the contract brings benefits to both signers. The State threatens negative sanctions for a violation of the contract, thereby increasing the likelihood of performance. Contractualism had been an aspect of Western political theory since the late Middle Ages.[17] The Scholasticism of Thomas Aquinas was the major source.[18] Contractualism was developed as a comprehensive social philosophy – not just for civil government but for society – by Enlightenment thinkers of the eighteenth century. The

---

16. Rousseau, "A Dissertation on the Origin and Foundation of the Inequality of Mankind" (1754), in Jean Jacques Rousseau, *The Social Contract and Discourses*, Everyman's Library (New York: Dutton, [1913] 1966), p. 161.

17. Sir Ernest Barker, "Introduction," in Barker (ed.), *Social Contract: Essays by Locke, Hume, and Rousseau* (New York: Oxford University Press, 1962), p. vii.

18. *Ibid.*, pp. viii–ix.

Scottish Enlightenment was decentralist, emphasizing the bonds of society before and more comprehensive than the State. The European Enlightenment tended to reverse this; its focus was statist, with the State as the organizing principle of society. The Scottish Enlightenment's outlook became the social philosophy of English Whiggism. Scottish Enlightenment political thought was a deistic version of seventeenth-century Scottish Presbyterianism's covenant theology: government as an appeals court system that intervenes when all other human governments and associations fail to settle a dispute. Continental Enlightenment political thought was a deistic version of the Jesuit order's hierarchy: civil government as centrally directed, highly disciplined social order. "Citizen" became for the French Revolutionaries what "brother" was for the Jesuits. (Among Communists a century later, "comrade" replaced "citizen.")

Nineteenth-century English liberalism abandoned even the weak deistic elements of Whiggism.[19] Nothing substantive remained except the stipulations of the two contracts: private and civil. The sanctions upholding the stipulations of the contract were said to be exclusively secular. Nineteenth-century Continental liberalism also abandoned the doctrine of God. Anticlericalism became a new religion.[20]

Darwinism and the State

Darwinism had a transforming impact on both Anglo-American and Continental social thought. In the two decades after the publication of *The Origin of Species* (1859), Darwinism was used by the disciples of Herbert Spencer to bolster the free market by asserting the legitimacy of unguided economic competition as the means of the survival of the fittest individuals and businesses. Over the next two decades, intellectual opinion

---

19. Owen Chadwick, *The Secularization of the European Mind in the 19th Century* (New York: Cambridge University Press, 1975), ch. 2.

20. *Ibid.*, ch. 5.

shifted dramatically: Darwinism was increasingly used to support statism, in which State economic planning was invoked by Darwinists to defend the survival of the fittest society through scientific planning. Rather than viewing society as analogous to nature – red in tooth and claw – the new social Darwinism viewed society as analogous to a plant breeder's greenhouse, with the scientific elite serving as the breeder. The directionless, anti-teleological free market was dismissed as anachronistic, even as a directionless, anti-teleological nature was also dismissed. Both were understood as having been superseded by planning, teleological man, meaning a scientific elite acting in the name of mankind. The primary theorist who announced this new social Darwinism was Lester Frank Ward.[21]

Darwinism undermined Whiggism by undermining Newtonianism. Whiggism had been undergirded by a Newtonian view of the universe: mathematical and mechanical. Newton's Unitarian god supposedly created it and sustained it. By 1850, such a god was no longer regarded as necessary to social theory, but the social fruits of that god's authority still lingered: faith in the coherence of a social system established through a myriad of voluntary contracts. Society was believed to be the result of human action but not of human design – Scottish Enlightenment theorist Adam Ferguson's worldview a century earlier.[22]

The Newtonian worldview was essentially mechanical. In Newtonianism, mathematics rules the cosmos. To the extent that physics became the ideal model for men's social theories, the quest for social order became the quest for the mathematically fixed laws of society.[23] Natural law was understood as

---

21. Gary North, *The Dominion Covenant: Genesis* (2nd ed.; Tyler, Texas: Institute for Christian Economics, 1987), Appendix A.

22. F. A. Hayek, "The Results of Human Action but not of Human Design," in Hayek, *Studies in Philosophy, Politics and Economics* (University of Chicago Press, 1967), ch. 6.

23. Louis I. Bredvold, *Brave New World of the Enlightenment* (Ann Arbor: University of Michigan Press, 1961), ch. 2.

governing historical processes, bringing order to these processes. This worldview collapsed under the weight of a reforming social Darwinism, which relied increasingly on the State as an agent of social change, scientific planning, and ethical action. In Europe, this new social outlook was called social democracy. In the United States, it was called Progressivism.

No better statement of the transformation can be found than liberal Presbyterian elder Woodrow Wilson's 1908 book, *Constitutional Government of the United States*. In 1907, Wilson openly moved from laissez-faire Jeffersonianism to Progressivism. He was the president of Princeton University at the time. He wrote *Constitutional Government* as a thinly disguised fat campaign tract for the Democratic Party's 1908 nomination for the Presidency. The book was published in the year of the Presidential election. Fundamentalist Presbyterian elder and radical political populist William Jennings Bryan received the nomination for the third time; Wilson had to wait four more years to attain his goal. He was elected President in 1912 and again in 1916.

His book praised the Presidency as the central political office: head of the party. This was a self-conscious break from the U.S. Constitution's view of the office. The Constitution does not mention political parties, and the Framers had hated political factions in 1787. They also hated big government (Hamilton excepted). They inserted checks and balances into the Constitution in order to prevent the growth of a large central government. Wilson, having switched to Progressivism, had to undermine this older political faith. He turned to Darwin for the solution. The Framers had been Whigs because they had been Newtonians, he correctly argued. This Newtonian Whig worldview is incorrect, he insisted, and so is the Constitutional order that assumes it. "The government of the United States was constructed upon the Whig theory of political dynamics, which was a sort of unconscious copy of the Newtonian theory of the universe. In our own day, whenever we discuss the structure or development of anything, whether in nature or in society, we consciously or unconsciously follow Mr. Darwin; but before Mr. Darwin, they followed Newton. Some single law, like the law of gravitation, swung each system of thought and gave it its principle of unity."[24] This shift in outlook from Newtonianism to Darwinism in social theory was basic to the American Progressivism. It justified the creation of a planned economy.

The checks and balances built into the federal government by the Constitution had become a hindrance to effective political action, he said. This language of balances reflects mechanism. We need to overcome this mechanical way of thinking, Wilson insisted: "The trouble with the theory is that government is not a machine, but a living thing. It falls, not under the theory of the universe, but under the theory of organic life. It is accountable to Darwin, not to Newton. It is modified by its environment, necessitated by its tasks, shaped to its functions by the sheer pressure of life. No living thing can have its organs offset against each other as checks, and live. On the contrary, its life is dependent upon their quick cooperation, their ready response to the commands of instinct or intelligence, their amicable community of purpose. Government is not a body of blind forces; it is a body of men, with highly differentiated functions, no doubt, in our modern day of specialization, but with a common task and purpose. Their cooperation is indispensable, their warfare fatal. There can be no successful government without leadership or without the intimate, almost instinctive, coordination of the organs of life and action. This is not theory, but fact, and displays its force as fact, whatever theories may be thrown across its track. Living political constitutions must be Darwinian in structure and in practice."[25]

This was the Progressives' worldview: the State as a centralized agency of reform in which sufficient political power is

---

24. Woodrow Wilson, *The Constitutional Government of the United States* (New York: Columbia University Press, [1908] 1961), pp. 54–55.

25. *Ibid.*, pp. 56–57.

concentrated to overcome the economic power of large corporations. The State becomes society's coordinator, like the central nervous system-brain connection: organic.

Three Choices

The biblical view of society is neither mechanistic nor organic. It is covenantal. It is based on the binding nature of covenants established by oaths under God – oaths that invoke sanctions in history. Covenant theology is personalistic, for God created the universe and sustains it by His sovereign power. Covenant theology is also judicial. It insists on broad historical predictability in terms of Bible-revealed covenantal laws to which are attached corporate sanctions. It is the predictability of these corporate sanctions that make possible a distinctly Christian social theory. Without predictable corporate sanctions, there cannot be social theory. When Christians deny the predictability of God's corporate historical sanctions in terms of covenant law, they necessarily place themselves under the rule of humanist law and a humanist social order. They must then choose between 1) the individualistic contractualism of a social order sustained by faith in Darwinian competition or 2) the statist contractualism of a social order sustained by faith in Darwinian central planning.

The statist offers these criticisms of contractualism. First, there is no comprehensive ethical basis for contractualism other than individual self-interest, which can be radically anti-ethical. Second, the predictable, socially beneficial results of the free market's sanctions – profit and loss – are suspect. Market profitability at best reflects the producer's performance in meeting the temporary desires of economically successful buyers, not the economic system's performance in meeting the true needs of the broad mass of citizens. Third, the contractualist social system evolves over time without rational direction or predictability. Who is to say that it will not evolve into socialism? So, why wait? Adopt socialism now.

The contractualist offers these criticisms of statism. First, the ethics of power-seeking politicians and bureaucrats are highly suspect. In any case, these ethics will evolve over time; Darwinism offers no permanent ethics. Any appeal to social ethics as superior to individual ethics is a smoke screen for the self-interested plans of power-seekers. Second, the predictable results of unchecked, monopolistic political power over other men's decisions are evil. "All power tends to corrupt, and absolute power corrupts absolutely." Third, the economic system behaves irrationally under central planning because central planners have no rational success indicators in a socialistic economy: prices that reflect the true state of supply and demand. From the late seventeenth century until the present, Christian social theorists have chosen between these two broad social theories: statist and individualist. They have not offered an outspokenly biblical alternative. They have baptized one or another of humanism's theories. The suggestion that Christianity offers a separate social theory superior to humanistic theories is inherently theocratic, and Protestantism since 1700 has been anti-theocratic.

With each revolution in Western epistemology – from Platonism to Aristotelianism to Cartesianism to Newtonianism to Darwinism – there has been a corresponding revision of operational Christian social theory. The church has played catch-up, following a generation or two later, dutifully repeating its formula: "Yes, the Bible is consistent with that. Forget what Christians said back then."

Conclusion

Taking a vow is a serious matter. It is always sworn to God. It may be sworn directly, but it also may be sworn to a covenantal agency lawfully representing God. Because it necessarily invokes God's negative sanctions for failure to perform its stipulations, a covenant oath is called self-maledictory. Because the invocation of negative sanctions brings a special judicial authority to the oath, the use of it is restricted by God. His name may not lawfully be invoked to authenticate a personal oath in public unless there is a covenantal agency empowered by God to bring negative sanctions against the oath-taker: church, family, or State. A personal oath to God apart from a sanctioning agency must not be sworn in public. It must be sworn in private.

Under the Mosaic covenant, a wife or daughter had to have her oath confirmed by her husband or father in order for it to be binding, unless she governed her own household. The widow was the representative independent woman: head of her own household. In New Covenant times, because of baptism's lawful application to both sexes, adult daughters are legally independent; so, they possess this covenantal authority. When a judicially independent woman pays for the fulfillment of her oath, she can lawfully take a vow. God will hold her to it.

A promise that does not invoke God's name or sanctions is a contract. The presence of a self-maledictory oath distinguishes a covenant from a contract. A contract does not possess the sanctified status of a covenant. Breaking a contract that results in harm to another person is a sin, but it is not of the same magnitude as breaking an oath-invoked covenant. Contracts are not to be elevated to the status of covenants. Covenants are not to be debased to the level of contracts. Covenantalism is the biblical basis of contractualism, not the other way around. Whig political theory since Adam Smith has failed to understand this crucial aspect of causality: from covenant to contract. Whig social theory places contractualism at the center.

The civil government is a covenantal institution. While contractualism is valid for explaining economic relationships – the quest for mutual self-interest by means of the division of labor – it is not valid as a form of political theory, despite the presence of personal self-interest and the division of labor in political affairs. Civil government has the God-given monopolistic authority to impose physical sanctions on evil-doers: the sword. The free market does not legitimately authorize any agency to impose physical sanctions. Its sanctions are not lawfully invoked by covenant oath.

The focus of political theory should be the proper imposition of negative sanctions: suppressing evil, not increasing net economic productivity. The biblical goal of civil government is the suppression of evil. Any increase in economic productivity is a positive effect of suppressing evil.

17

WAR BRIDES

And they warred against the Midianites, as the Lord commanded Moses; and they slew all the males. And they slew the kings of Midian, beside the rest of them that were slain; namely, Evi, and Rekem, and Zur, and Hur, and Reba, five kings of Midian: Balaam also the son of Beor they slew with the sword. And the children of Israel took all the women of Midian captives, and their little ones, and took the spoil of all their cattle, and all their flocks, and all their goods. And they burnt all their cities wherein they dwelt, and all their goodly castles [fortresses], with fire. And they took all the spoil, and all the prey, both of men and of beasts (Num. 31:7–11).

Midian had tempted Israel by sending women to marry them and then lure them into the worship of false gods. "And the Lord spake unto Moses, saying, Vex the Midianites, and smite them: For they vex you with their wiles, wherewith they have beguiled you in the matter of Peor, and in the matter of Cozbi, the daughter of a prince of Midian, their sister, which was slain in the day of the plague for Peor's sake" (Num. 25:16–18). Yet in this passage, Moses allowed the Israelites to marry Midianite women. Why the apparent discrepancy?

Marriage is a covenantal institution. It is governed by laws of the covenant. The Mosaic law established laws for the marrying of foreign women. These laws were explicit. The only foreign women who could lawfully be married by an Israelite were survivors of a military conflict in which Israel annihilated a foreign city outside the Promised Land (Deut. 20:14), or converts to the faith (e.g., Rahab, Ruth).

The Destruction of Midian

The destruction of Midian was now covenantally complete. The cities were burned. All the males were slain. But this was not *hormah*. The unmarried young women and girls were lawfully taken captive as spoils; so were animals and precious metals. "And Moses said unto them, Have ye saved all the women alive? Behold, these caused the children of Israel, through the counsel of Balaam, to commit trespass against the LORD in the matter of Peor, and there was a plague among the congregation of the LORD. Now therefore kill every male among the little ones, and kill every woman that hath known man by lying with him. But all the women children, that have not known a man by lying with him, keep alive for yourselves" (Num. 31:15–18).

This sanction of mass execution was in accord with the law of foreign warfare that God subsequently revealed to Israel. "And if it will make no peace with thee, but will make war against thee, then thou shalt besiege it: And when the LORD thy God hath delivered it into thine hands, thou shalt smite every male thereof with the edge of the sword: But the women, and the little ones, and the cattle, and all that is in the city, even all the spoil thereof, shalt thou take unto thyself; and thou shalt eat the spoil of thine enemies, which the LORD thy God hath given thee. Thus shalt thou do unto all the cities which are very far off from thee, which are not of the cities of these nations" (Deut. 20:12–15).

The women were legal as spoils; the Israelites were allowed to marry them. But first the women had to go through a rite of covenantal transition, of purification.

When thou goest forth to war against thine enemies, and the LORD thy God hath delivered them into thine hands, and thou hast taken them captive, And seest among the captives a beautiful woman, and hast a desire unto her, that thou wouldest have her to thy wife; Then thou shalt bring her home to thine house; and she shall shave her head, and pare her nails; And she shall put the raiment of her captivity from off her, and shall remain in thine house, and bewail her father and her mother a full month: and after that thou shalt go in unto her, and be her husband, and she shall be thy wife. And it shall be, if thou have no delight in her, then thou shalt let her go whither she will; but thou shalt not sell her at all for money, thou shalt not make merchandise of her, because thou hast humbled her (Deut. 21:10–14).

The Israelite could not marry a foreign woman until she had shaved her head. This was a visible mark of her new covenantal subordination. She had been under another culture's authority before; now she was under a new authority. The removal of the mark of her subordination, her hair,[1] and its re-growth in a new household testified to her new legal condition. She was also to bewail her father and mother for a month. This was a ritual break with the old conditions of her existence: the authority of her parents' household. Clearly, this woman had not been anyone's wife. She would not be a woman seeking revenge against her new husband for having killed her first husband. She would not bring the children of another man into her new household.

This is another reason why Israel was required to kill the sons, including infant sons, of the defeated nation. There would be no warriors or sons of warriors of a defeated culture inside the gates of Israel. The survival of the young women was a positive sanction – grace – for the defeated culture. The negative sanction of annihilation was normative. Moses made it clear

1. "But every woman that prayeth or prophesieth with her head uncovered dishonoureth her head: for that is even all one as if she were shaven. For if the woman be not covered, let her also be shorn: but if it be a shame for a woman to be shorn or shaven, let her be covered" (I Cor. 11:5–6).

that there was to be mercy shown to some and none to others: "Now therefore kill every male among the little ones, and kill every woman that hath known man by lying with him. But all the women children, that have not known a man by lying with him, keep alive for yourselves" (Num. 31:17–18).

The Defeat of Paganism's Gods

These women were pagans by profession of faith and life-style, yet they were eligible to become wives. How could the purity of marriage be maintained? Because these women were captives who were no longer under the covenantal authority of pagan gods. The gods of the pagan world were local gods, gods of the city-state. When a city was defeated, so were its gods. When a city was utterly wiped out, so were its gods. These captive women now had no ritual connection with the gods of their city.[2] Those gods had been wiped off the face of the earth. Israel was instructed to destroy foreign cities and every male inside its walls. This was the proof of the defeat of the city's local gods.

When the gods of a pagan city outside of Canaan fell to Israel, Israel was to have no fear of them again. In contrast, the gods of Canaan were a continuing threat, since they were tied to the land itself. To spare anyone in those cities in which Israel intended to dwell was not allowed. "But of the cities of these people, which the LORD thy God doth give thee for an inheritance, thou shalt save alive nothing that breatheth: But thou shalt utterly destroy them; namely, the Hittites, and the Amorites, the Canaanites, and the Perizzites, the Hivites, and the Jebusites; as the LORD thy God hath commanded thee: That they teach you not to do after all their abominations, which

2. They may not have had any connection before, except through their fathers. This was the case in Greece and Rome. Women did not participate in the rites of the city, only in household rites.

they have done unto their gods; so should ye sin against the LORD your God" (Deut. 20:16–18).

The virgin who had been taken from her city, which was then burned to the ground, had been stripped of her covenant. This did not make her a covenant-keeper, but it placed her under the covenantal jurisdiction of an Israelite. Mosaic law did not recognize the necessity of a captive wife to confess faith in Israel's God. There was no rite of covenantal access for women. Circumcision was for males only. For that matter, males who were purchased from abroad had to be circumcised and then given access to Passover, even if they made no confession of faith. "He that is born in thy house, and he that is bought with thy money, must needs be circumcised: and my covenant shall be in your flesh for an everlasting covenant" (Gen. 17:13). The judicial issue was not their confession; rather, it was the confession of the head of the household that was determinative.

The judicial issue was sanctions. The head of the household imposed family sanctions. Those under his authority were counted as covenant-keepers because they were under the authority of a covenant-keeper. These subordinates could not lawfully recruit household members into idolatry. To do so was a capital crime.

> If thy brother, the son of thy mother, or thy son, or thy daughter, or the wife of thy bosom, or thy friend, which is as thine own soul, entice thee secretly, saying, Let us go and serve other gods, which thou hast not known, thou, nor thy fathers; Namely, of the gods of the people which are round about you, nigh unto thee, or far off from thee, from the one end of the earth even unto the other end of the earth; Thou shalt not consent unto him, nor hearken unto him; neither shall thine eye pity him, neither shalt thou spare, neither shalt thou conceal him: But thou shalt surely kill him; thine hand shall be first upon him to put him to death, and afterwards the hand of all the people. And thou shalt stone him with stones, that he die; because he hath sought to thrust thee away from the LORD thy God, which brought thee out of the land of Egypt, from the house of bondage. And all

Israel shall hear, and fear, and shall do no more any such wickedness as this is among you (Deut. 13:6–11).

The threat of this civil sanction was regarded by the Mosaic law as sufficient to warrant marriage to a female survivor of an annihilated foreign culture.

Two Forms of Liberating Subordination

Forcible covenantal subordination of foreigners was possible in two ways: by purchase (slavery) and by captive marriage. The covenantal goal in both cases was the servant's separation from bondage to pagan gods. Slavery was a form of evangelism: when successful, far better than eternity spent in hell. The captive woman who entered a household by marriage was not to be treated as a slave. She could not be sold by her husband. She had been humbled once by the shaving of her head, the paring of her nails, and her physical status as a wife. She could not lawfully be humbled a second time by the same man. She had made the transition out of paganism through marriage; she therefore could not be made a slave by the man who had brought her out of paganism. This indicates that the covenantal purpose of both the permanent servitude of, and marriage to, captive women was liberation out of paganism. A pagan could be liberated in either way, but not both. Liberation was a one-time act.

This means that an ex-pagan wife could not become a permanent slave in Israel unless she was divorced by her husband and later married a permanent slave or a pagan who then became a permanent slave through crime or debt. Her status as a free woman had been guaranteed by her first husband. She could give up this status through marriage to a man who did not possess it, but it could not be removed from her by law without her consent unless she was excommunicated for cause and then committed a crime whose restitution payment required her sale into slavery. Even this limit to her status is implied; it is nowhere stated. It is implied because being cut off from the covenant was a judicial sanction against an Israelite male who broke a major law, including a public denial of God. Biblical law does not subsidize evil. It does not create a class of criminals beyond the law's negative sanctions. But for a rejected captive wife to be subjected to the threat of permanent servitude, she either had to commit a crime as an excommunicant or else subordinate herself to a pagan, who was, or who later became, a permanent slave.

Land Laws and Civil Jurisdiction

The law governing the marriage of captive women was a land law. We know this because the parallel law governing warfare within the boundaries of Canaan was different: every human resident of Canaan was to be killed.

The Mosaic covenant was a geographical covenant. It established judicial differences between Jew and Greek, as well as between male and female. Circumcision was the physical mark of the difference between Jew and Greek, as well as between men and women.

The threat to Israel came from the gods of Canaan. Because the gods of paganism were geographically based, and because God's dwelling place was inside the boundaries of Israel, the threat of distant foreign gods was reduced. This is why God established in His law the negative sanction of national captivity for Israel (Deut. 28:41). Captivity to gods outside of the Promised Land would not destroy Israel because Israel would seek to escape this bondage and return to the Promised Land. After their return from the exile, Israel did not again worship the gods of Canaan. But Israel also did not again go out to conquer foreign cities. Israel remained under political bondage to foreign empires.

The Mosaic laws of conquest no longer apply today in the area of religion. We are not told to execute every male inside the gates of another city. The universality of the gospel transcends political groupings. It crosses borders. This was true in the post-exilic era, too. Jews spread throughout the empires of the Near East, residing under the civil rule of many gods. The Mosaic laws of warfare ended with the end of Israel as a separate civil jurisdiction. The total annihilation of Canaan was a one-time genocidal requirement. The Mosaic laws of near-annihilation also ended when the boundaries of Israel no longer served to identify the monopolistic civil jurisdiction of God within the confines of a single nation.

Conclusion

The destruction of Midian involved the capture of virgin girls. These women were marriageable. Their eligibility for marriage was what authorized Israel to spare their lives. They were no longer seen as a threat to Israel's covenant. The gods of their cities were covenantally dead. The captives recognized this. They had no covenantally significant religion to invoke against Israel.

18

THE SPOILS OF HOLY WARFARE

Take the sum of the prey [booty: v. 32] that was taken, both of man and of beast, thou, and Eleazar the priest, and the chief fathers of the congregation: And divide the prey into two parts; between them that took the war upon them, who went out to battle, and between all the congregation (Num. 31:26–27).

The 12,000 warriors (v. 5) who battled Midian were at greater risk, statistically speaking, than those who had not been selected to fight. Actually, the combatants were at zero risk: every one of them survived, a miraculous result (v. 49). But they did not know this outcome prior to the war. The post-war division of the spoils reflected the fact that the warriors had placed themselves at greater risk. They kept half of the booty.

From their half was taken a small payment: one out of 500 of the living captives, women and animals (v. 28). This portion was given to Eleazar the priest as a representative of the Aaronic priesthood (v. 29). This was booty for all of the priesthood. Eleazar had no need for 32 new wives (v. 40). From the half of the proceeds given to the congregation, one out of 50 of the living captives was given to the Levites (v. 30).

The Israelites who did not participate in the war were required to pay ten times the quantity of goods paid by the warriors who did fight: one out of 50 vs. one out of 500. This means that those who had not been at risk had to pay ten times the tribute of those who had been at risk. This payment was only 20 percent of a tithe: one in 50 vs. one in 10. It was more like a firstfruits offering than a tithe: a token payment. The tithe would have been owed after the distribution of the booty, when each recipient knew exactly what he had received. But because the required tithe on living animals was paid only on the net increase in the herd, with the tenth animal owed to God when it passed under the rod (Lev. 27:32), it was possible that God would not receive a tithe on the booty. The net increase of each herd might not have been ten beasts that year. If nine or fewer animals had been added to a herd during the year, the herd's owner owed nothing. This was a likely situation in the wilderness. So, God's priestly tribe did get paid something "off the top" prior to receiving tithes from individuals.

Taxes vs. Spoils

The fact that those who were at risk paid one-tenth of the tribute owed by those who were not at risk seems to indicate that the modern principle of graduated taxation is anti-biblical. Those who receive more income, i.e., entrepreneurs who are at greater risk of losing their wealth, are today required to pay to the State a higher percentage of their income than those who earn less income. In the case of the spoils of Midian, those at risk paid only ten percent of what was required from those who were not at risk. Those who had been at risk forfeited half of the spoils to those who had not been at risk. This was not a tax. It was not paid to the State.

Tribal warriors had been chosen as covenantal representatives of Israel to wage holy war against a national foe. The war's outcome was predetermined. God would surely destroy Midian. This war had been initiated by God, not by Israel (v. 3). Military spoils were therefore part of the nation's judicial-covenantal system. This was not a case where a man was working on behalf of his family, seeking a private return on his labor. On such an increase, he would have owed firstfruits plus a tithe – nothing more. He would not have been required to share half of his income with other Israelites. In contrast, a man chosen to fight Midian was working as a national covenantal agent. He was bringing destruction to a military enemy. He was wielding the sword on behalf of God: a bringer of God's negative corporate sanctions. This was a priestly act and also a military act. It was holy warfare. The laws governing the allocation of military booty were different from the laws governing the tithe.

A Voluntary Offering

This had been a miraculous victory. "And they said unto Moses, Thy servants have taken the sum of the men of war which are under our charge, and there lacketh not one man of us" (v. 49). Their enemies had been completely wiped out, yet not one warrior had died. This, concluded the captains, required a special payment to God. "We have therefore brought an oblation for the LORD, what every man hath gotten, of jewels of gold, chains, and bracelets, rings, earrings, and tablets, to make an atonement for our souls before the LORD" (v. 50).

Each of the warriors had taken booty on his own behalf (v. 53). This was legitimate. They violated no law. They had divided the living goods with the other Israelites, but they were not required to share their inanimate booty. Nevertheless, the captains decided to give all of the inanimate booty to God. This was an act of devotion: economically meaningful thanks for having been protected as an army. It was also a kind of life insurance premium. If they publicly acknowledged by such sacrificial giving that they had received miraculous protection from God, they might receive similar protection in the upcoming battles in Canaan. This battle was a kind of military exercise in preparation for the conquest. If word spread to Canaan that not one Israelite had perished in the victory over a large, rich nation like Midian, fear would also spread in Canaan. Fear was already spreading there, as Rahab testified later to the spies. "For we have heard how the LORD dried up the water of the Red sea for you, when ye came out of Egypt; and what ye did unto the two kings of the Amorites, that were on the other side Jordan, Sihon and Og, whom ye utterly destroyed. And as soon as we had heard these things, our hearts did melt, neither did there remain any more courage in any man, because of you: for the LORD your God, he is God in heaven above, and in earth beneath" (Josh. 2:10–11). This was surely to the advantage of Israelite warriors.

Normally, this atonement money would have been paid prior to the battle at the time of the numbering (Ex. 30:13). This had not been required because the nation had already been numbered in preparation for the conquest of Canaan (Num. 26:2–51). Immediately after this, God revealed a system for allocating the land (vv. 52–56). Because the battle over Midian was preparatory for the conquest, God did not require them to be numbered again. They did not pay the half shekel of silver to the Levites. But when it became clear in retrospect that they had not really been at risk during the battle, they decided to forfeit any personal economic gains they had made as individuals. They concluded: "No pain, no gain."

Their payment of atonement money was voluntary. It was a public admission that this had not been a normal military encounter. They paid the atonement money, not as a judicial covering for having killed Midianites, but as an acknowledgment that they had been physically covered by God during the battle. They did not keep the booty as a personal reward for having put their own lives at risk when their lives had not been at risk.

Moses and Eleazar accepted this payment on behalf of God. "And Moses and Eleazar the priest took the gold of the captains of thousands and of hundreds, and brought it into the tabernacle of the congregation, for a memorial for the children of Israel before the LORD" (v. 54). This memorial would remain as a testimony to the protecting hand of God in battle, but also as a public acknowledgment that the men who had received God's special protection had acknowledged this by a voluntary gift.

Conclusion

The military spoils of Midian were unique. The whole nation had not been directly involved in the battle. Only a small, covenantally representative force had been chosen to fight. This would not be the case in Canaan. This was a preliminary campaign designed to prove to Israel that God was with them in a special, miraculous way. Not one Israelite died in battle.

The representative character of this force was manifested in the requirement that the participating warriors forfeit half of their animate spoils to the nation. The nation made a small tribute payment to the Levites; the warriors paid a tenth of this tribute to the Aaronic priests through Eleazar. Those who had entered the battle at greater risk statistically paid less than those who remained behind.

The miraculous outcome of the battle – no Israelite deaths – so impressed the warriors that they voluntarily gave their inanimate booty to Moses and Eleazar. They had not in fact been at risk, so they decided not to keep the booty that was normally the reward of any soldier who could take it in battle. The risk-reward ratio of normal combat had been overcome in this battle by God's intervention. The statistical improbability of the campaign testified to God's special presence among them. The combatants publicly acknowledged that there had been no risk by surrendering their personal rewards to the covenantal representatives of the God who had removed the risk.

19

LAND TO MATCH MEN'S SKILLS

Now the children of Reuben and the children of Gad had a very great multitude of cattle: and when they saw the land of Jazer, and the land of Gilead, that, behold, the place was a place for cattle (Num. 32:1).

Where did the Reubenites and the Gadites get their cattle? Israel had been wandering in the wilderness for almost four decades. What kind of wilderness was it? Was it a place where cattle multiplied? Or were these cattle the spoils of war? Or were they the fruit of trade?

Some of these cattle could have come from Egypt, for the Israelites took cattle out of Egypt (Ex. 12:38). This raises the question: Where did the Egyptians get these cattle? Hadn't their flocks been depleted by the hail and then by the death of the firstborn (Ex. 12:29)? It seems clear that before the hail, many Egyptians feared Moses' words: "Send therefore now, and gather thy cattle, and all that thou hast in the field; for upon every man and beast which shall be found in the field, and shall not be brought home, the hail shall come down upon them, and they shall die. He that feared the word of the LORD among the servants of Pharaoh made his servants and his cattle flee into the houses: And he that regarded not the word of the

LORD left his servants and his cattle in the field" (Ex. 9:19–21). Obviously, a lot of people brought in their cattle and stayed inside themselves. Second, the Israelites, though slaves, did own cattle in Egypt. "Our cattle also shall go with us; there shall not an hoof be left behind; for thereof must we take to serve the LORD our God; and we know not with what we must serve the LORD, until we come thither" (Ex. 10:26). Conclusion: there must have been grass in the wilderness.

Some of these cattle came from the victory over Bashan. "But all the cattle, and the spoil of the cities, we took for a prey to ourselves" (Deut. 3:7). Previously, the Israelites had destroyed the cities of King Arad. These cities were called *hormah* (Num. 21:3), which implies total destruction. There is no indication that they took spoils from Arad's cities. This military victory was more like a whole burnt offering comparable to the subsequent total destruction of Jericho. So, the cattle did not come from Arad. We know that Israel confiscated Sihon's cattle (Deut. 2:35). The Israelites collected considerable cattle from Midian (Num. 31:33, 44). Some of the cattle may have come from the another Amorite nation: Jaazer (Num. 21:32).

All of the tribes also participated in the spoils. These two tribes may have traded their inanimate wealth to members of the other tribes in exchange for cattle. These two tribes must have had special interest in cattle and special skills related to herding. They viewed the ownership of cattle as of greater value to them than the ownership of other forms of wealth that they possessed. A profitable exchange was possible if the cattle owners in the other eleven tribes wanted what the two tribes possessed.

Capitalizing One's Productivity

The leaders of the two tribes approached Moses and Eleazar with a proposition: an exchange. They were willing to give up any legal claim on the land inside Canaan's borders in exchange for the land that Israel had already conquered beyond the Jordan. "Even the country which the LORD smote before the congregation of Israel, is a land for cattle, and thy servants have cattle" (Num. 32:4). They sought a match between the land and their preferred form of capital: cattle. They believed that they would possess greater wealth if this specialized land became theirs rather than the agricultural land of Canaan.

This was an economic decision which acknowledged the reality of the division of labor. The output of land varies. The output of people varies. If land and labor match, the result is greater wealth for those who own the land. That is, those people who have skills associated with a certain type of productivity can capitalize the value of these skills by owning the land through which these skills can maximize economic output. As the value of their output rises, in part as a result of their control over land with special characteristics, the value of the land also rises. But ownership and control are different. A man may rent land and thereby control it, but any increased value that his actions impart to the land may later be claimed by the land's owner. So, if a person possesses the specialized skills and knowledge to make a certain plot of land rise in value, he would be wise to purchase this land before the land's existing owner recognizes the producer's ability to raise the value of the land's output, and therefore before the owner can respond to this information by raising the land's price. In other words, by purchasing the land, the producer appropriates the value of his future productivity. He capitalizes his productivity by owning the land that appreciates because of this productivity.

Probably the best examples of this capitalization process in the second half of the twentieth century are Disneyland and Disney World, the world-famous amusement parks. In the early 1950's, when Walt Disney's company built Disneyland, he bought up enough land to build the park in what was then a less sparsely populated area in Southern California: before the regional freeway system was completed. Neither he nor anyone else knew if this venture would be successful. No one had ever built a family theme park before. The result was successful beyond anyone's wildest imagination. The tourists streamed into the city of Anaheim. The price of land located close to Disneyland skyrocketed. Others bought it, built hotels and other businesses on it, and reaped the reward. Disneyland made them rich.

Disney did not make the same mistake twice. Disney World is located on a huge tract of land near Orlando, Florida: 27,000 acres,[1] or 42 square miles. The Disney organization has drained the swamps and built hotels on the property, as well as two other theme parks: Epcot Center and the MGM movie theme park. The company's goal is to get tourists to come there for a week and spend every penny within the confines of the Disney theme park system. Nevertheless, successful rival theme parks have been built in Orlando, which became the major year-round vacation city in the world, 1971 to 1996. Land in the Orlando area has continued to rise in value for a quarter of a century. It is the only city in the United States that never suffers from economic recession. But the lion's share of the increase in land value located close to Disney World has gone to the Disney organization, which capitalized its knowledge and its name by buying up the surrounding land before it became expensive. Disney locked in ownership of land needed for future expansion. He bought it at a pre-Disney World price. He bought it more cheaply per acre because he bought so much land at one time. The Disney company received a discount for volume. Disney believed that the total return on this investment would be greater than the forfeited interest return on the money the company tied up in buying and holding the land. The appreciation of the price of Disney stock since 1965 indicates that Disney was correct.

The two tribes saw an opportunity. They were cattlemen. If they could gain ownership of recently conquered land that was

---

1. This is 10,800 hectares.

more suitable for cattle ranching than farming, they would reap an entrepreneurial reward. Because they knew that members of the tribes legally would not be allowed to buy or sell land to non-members – the jubilee land law (Lev. 25) – they understood that capitalization in their case would go from the land to their cattle ranching skills. Land ownership in Israel would be less mobile than cattle ownership. To maximize the value of their skills in cattle ranching, they needed ownership of specialized land. They would not be allowed to buy comparably specialized land after the conquest. This land's highest valued use, they believed, was for cattle ranching. Anyway, for their purposes, this was its highest valued use. They could best capitalize their cattle raising skills by owning this land rather than tracts of land across the Jordan. So, they made their offer to Moses.

The subsequent land distribution indicates that the two tribes represented half the tribe of Manasseh. "And Moses gave unto them, even to the children of Gad, and to the children of Reuben, and unto half the tribe of Manasseh the son of Joseph, the kingdom of Sihon king of the Amorites, and the kingdom of Og king of Bashan, the land, with the cities thereof in the coasts, even the cities of the country round about" (Num. 32:33). Thus, we should conclude that half of Manasseh also had reasons for preferring Gilead. They may have been cattle specialists. They may have had another reason. In any case, they preferred to join their brethren on the wilderness side of the Jordan.

Covenant Before Contract

Moses had a ready reply. It was the reply of a military commander. "And Moses said unto the children of Gad and to the children of Reuben, Shall your brethren go to war, and shall ye sit here? And wherefore discourage ye the heart of the children of Israel from going over into the land which the LORD hath given them?" (vv. 6–7). He understood that the cost of conquest was the shedding of blood. God had given the Israelites their assignment: to impose the maximum sanction in history, i.e., genocide. "And thou shalt consume all the people which the LORD thy God shall deliver thee; thine eye shall have no pity upon them: neither shalt thou serve their gods; for that will be a snare unto thee" (Deut. 7:16). He knew that there would be negative effects on the morale of the other tribes if these two tribes were given the land before the conquest. The whole nation had defeated the tribes beyond the Jordan. Why should just two tribes reap the entire nation's present spoils without putting themselves at further risk?

The tribal leaders had a reasonable solution to Moses' concern: "We will build sheepfolds here for our cattle, and cities for our little ones: But we ourselves will go ready armed before[2] the children of Israel, until we have brought them unto their place: and our little ones shall dwell in the fenced cities because of the inhabitants of the land. We will not return unto our houses, until the children of Israel have inherited every man his inheritance. For we will not inherit with them on yonder side Jordan, or forward; because our inheritance is fallen to us on this side Jordan eastward" (Num. 32:16b–19). In other words, they would more than place themselves at risk alongside of the other tribes; they would serve as the advance guard. The negative sanctions of death and injury would place them at risk. They would receive no economic reward until the risks of warfare were behind them.

Moses agreed to these terms: "And Moses said unto them, If ye will do this thing, if ye will go armed before the LORD to war, And will go all of you armed over Jordan before the LORD, until he hath driven out his enemies from before him, And the land be subdued before the LORD: then afterward ye shall return, and be guiltless before the LORD, and before Israel; and this land shall be your possession before the LORD" (Num. 32:20–

2. Hebrew word: *paniym*. It can be translated many ways, but among these are "face," "forefront."

22). He made no mention of their offer to serve as an advance guard, which had been their original offer, which demonstrated that fear of combat was not the issue. He reduced their required level of commitment. If they broke the terms of this less rigorous covenant, Moses said, there would be negative sanctions: "But if ye will not do so, behold, ye have sinned against the LORD: and be sure your sin will find you out" (v. 23). We know this agreement was a covenant rather than a contract because of the threat of God's negative sanctions.

Was their offer sincere? The layout of the nation's military formation indicates that it was. Reuben and Gad marched side by side. Manasseh was on the right flank.[3]

If the nation subsequently marched into battle with the "south" quadrant leading the attack, Gad and Reuben would take the brunt of the initial resistance. Simeon would also be exposed. Manasseh would be on the right flank. If half the tribe of Manasseh joined Simeon's ranks, Simeon would receive additional support, thereby compensating for its increased risk.

To accept this offer, Moses would have had to sacrifice Judah's role as the "point man" of the nation, the primary swordbearer in battle, a position consistent with Jacob's prophecy: "The sceptre shall not depart from Judah, nor a lawgiver from

3. James B. Jordan, *Through New Eyes: Developing a Biblical View of the World* (Brentwood, Tennessee: Wolgemuth & Hyatt, 1988), p. 205.

between his feet, until Shiloh come; and unto him shall the gathering of the people be" (Gen. 49:10). Judah had led the nation during the wilderness wanderings. "In the first place went the standard of the camp of the children of Judah according to their armies: and over his host was Nahshon the son of Amminadab" (Num. 10:14). Milgrom calls the army's eastern flank the choicest position, since Moses and Aaron camped at the entrance of the tabernacle.[4] So, in this sense, the offer was an offer by the eldest brother (Reuben) to replace Judah in the conquest. This was in fact the way the tribes marched into Canaan. Reuben, Gad, and half the tribe of Manasseh crossed the Jordan before their brethren (Josh. 4:12).

The curse of Jacob against Reuben was that he was unstable. "Reuben, thou art my firstborn, my might, and the beginning of my strength, the excellency of dignity, and the excellency of power: Unstable as water, thou shalt not excel; because thou wentest up to thy father's bed; then defiledst thou it: he went up to my couch" (Gen. 49:3–4). By becoming one of the point tribes in the conquest, Reuben removed this curse, even as Levi had removed his curse by bearing the sword against the tribes after the golden calf incident. In Joshua 22, the last section of the book, we read of the suspected idolatry of the trans-Jordan tribes, which turned out not to be idolatry but an affirmation of the covenant. In Judges, we read of Reuben's presence with Deborah and Barak in the war against Sisera, when other tribes were absent (Judg. 5:15–16). Reuben obviously had become stable in his ways.

---

4. Jacob Milgrom, *The JPS Torah Commentary: Numbers* (New York: Jewish Publication Society, 1990), p. 340. He cites Numbers 3:38: "But those that encamp before the tabernacle toward the east, even before the tabernacle of the congregation eastward, shall be Moses, and Aaron and his sons, keeping the charge of the sanctuary for the charge of the children of Israel; and the stranger that cometh nigh shall be put to death." He says that the southern flank (Reuben, Gad, Simeon) was the next most important position when the army was marching east, since the rotation was to the right. *Ibid.*, p. 341.

Structuring a Persuasive Offer

Moses then assembled representatives of the other tribes to announce the terms of this covenant (v. 28). He told them the options. He structured the options in such a way that the other tribes could hardly refuse. "And Moses said unto them, If the children of Gad and the children of Reuben will pass with you over Jordan, every man armed to battle, before the LORD, and the land shall be subdued before you; then ye shall give them the land of Gilead for a possession: But if they will not pass over with you armed, they shall have possessions among you in the land of Canaan" (vv. 29–30). If the two tribes fought alongside the other ten non-Levitical tribes, they would surrender their share of the Promised Land to the other ten tribes. This was clearly a benefit to the other tribes. The other tribes would trade any future claims on the land of Gilead to the two tribes and half the tribe of Manasseh (v. 33). On the other hand, if the two tribes refused to fight, they would still inherit their share of the land of Canaan.

Was this fair? Why should these two and a half tribes receive part of the spoils of war if they refused to fight? Because of the promise to Abraham: his seed would inherit the land. This promise was qualified in only one way: circumcision. Without this covenantal mark, this seed and land prophecy would not come to pass. This is why the sons of Israel had to be circumcised after they crossed the Jordan but before they conquered Jericho (Josh. 5:7). The two and a half tribes could not be kept out of the land if they agreed to fight. In fact, it seemed impossible to keep them out even if they refused to fight. They were entitled to their share of the land.

So, the offer was structured in such a way that the positive sanctions of the two and a half tribes' participation favored the other tribes: their forfeiting of any claims to land inside the Jordan River's boundaries. Reinforcing this offer was the fact that a negative sanction would be imposed on the other tribes if the two and a half tribes refused to cross over: sharing equal portions in the division of the lands. Every tribe would receive 26 percent more land if the two and half tribes fought. The other tribes would give up this benefit if they refused to agree to the arrangement, and the two and a half tribes then sat on their hands in Gilead. There was no legal way to keep the non-participants out of the spoils.

Moses knew he had a problem. The two and a half tribes were strongly committed to the idea that they should inherit Gilead. If he rejected their offer, they might refuse to cross over the Jordan out of spite. Because of their cattle, they had a special desire to possess Gilead – a desire not shared equally by the other tribes. If they refused to cross over, this might start a mass defection among the other tribes. In any case, some tribes might experience defections. Militarily, it was Moses' task to keep the tribes together. They had marched out of Egypt in military array (Ex. 13:18: NASB).[5] They were supposed to march into Canaan the same way. So, Moses structured the sanctions in such a way that the other tribes were unlikely to reject the offer.

Free Riders

There was a risk accompanying this offer. It resulted from what economists call the free-rider problem. If the nature of a goal is inherently collective – a successful military campaign is such a goal – but not all participants are required to provide working capital in order to receive the benefits, then it pays some people to sit on the sidelines. They ride free of charge alongside paying customers. This creates a shortage of the scarce service, i.e., a shortage at a price that most people would be willing to pay if everyone were required to pay the same price. If no one is going to be penalized for not paying his fair

---

5. Literally, five in a rank. James B. Jordan, *The Sociology of the Church: Essays in Reconstruction* (Tyler, Texas: Geneva Ministries, 1986), p. 215. The root word is derived from the Hebrew word for five (II Sam. 2:23; 3:27; 4:6; 20:10).

share – whatever other participants regard as fair[6] – why should anyone participate? If no one participates, the collective goal cannot be achieved.

This is the logical justification for the imposition of civil compulsion in certain collective efforts. This free rider argument lies behind the creation of an analytic economic category called public goods. Economist Edwin Dolan describes public goods as "goods or services having the properties that (1) they cannot be provided to one citizen without being supplied also to that citizen's neighbors, and (2) once provided for one citizen, the cost of providing them to others is zero. Perhaps the best example of a public good is national defense."[7] A missile-defense system protects everyone in the region whether or not one person pays. But if anyone so protected can legally escape paying, then the missile-defense system will probably not be built.

The free market offers a solution in most areas of resource allocation: no participation in the end result for those who refused to participate in the effort – "no pain, no gain." A legal boundary is placed around the end product, i.e., a property right is established. The legal system authorizes property owners to exclude free riders. But exclusion from God's covenant with Israel was not allowed merely for failure to participate in military service. Deborah could not legally force Barak to lead the army against Sisera (Judg. 4:8). Similarly, she could not force the tribes to participate. This is why she included ridicule against some non-participating tribes in her song of victory

6. In a collective effort, there is no scientific way of determining a fair share. This is another application of a central dilemma for theoretical economics: the impossibility of making interpersonal comparisons of subjective utility. See Gary North, *The Dominion Covenant: Genesis* (2nd ed.; Tyler, Texas: Institute for Christian Economics, 1987), ch. 4; North, *Tools of Dominion: The Case Laws of Exodus* (Tyler, Texas: Institute for Christian Economics, 1990), Appendix D: "The Epistemological Problem of Social Cost."

7. Edwin G. Dolan, *Basic Economics* (2nd ed.; Hinsdale, Illinois: Dryden, 1980), p. 56.

(Judg. 5:16–17, 23). She used the negative sanction of retroactive ridicule because she had no civil negative sanction at her disposal. Moses also refused to establish an extra-biblical legal basis of exclusion from the covenant of Israel.

If other tribes demanded some sort of additional reward for their participation in the conquest, they might defect if Moses refused to grant it. The army of Israel might be depleted. So, Moses took a risk. Announcing a negative sanction against the other tribes – sharing their inheritance in Canaan with these non-combatants if they refused to accept the two tribes' offer – might backfire on him. He had two counter positions: one stated, the other implied. First, he offered a positive sanction: a 26 percent increase in post-war land allocation for the other nine and a half tribes. They would receive a larger percentage of land that was more suitable for farming than Gilead, which was presumably what the other tribes preferred. They were not cattlemen. Second, he implied a negative sanction. He would call off the invasion. He did not say this, but if there were mass defections – too many free riders sitting on the sidelines – this was the implication. This would have meant dividing up Gilead among all twelve tribes: a major reduction in tribal spoils.

The representatives of the other tribes assessed the offer and decided to accept it. The rewards outweighed the costs. By consenting to the offer, they would gain the military cooperation of the two and a half tribes. They would also gain a significant increase in the post-war land distribution inside Canaan by forfeiting land outside Canaan that was more beneficial to cattlemen than to other agricultural producers. This land would probably be even less valuable after the conquest, for it would be more distant from whatever city God would choose inside Canaan as the city of the tabernacle. This would mean longer and more expensive journeys to attend the three annual feasts. It is not surprising that they agreed to the offer.

It is also not surprising that the Israelites had trouble displacing all of the Canaanites. The inability of Joshua to transfer any of the inheritance of one tribe to another because of the former's military non-participation or its failure to overcome the Canaanites probably hampered his overall military campaign. It took six years for Israel to conquer the land of Canaan,[8] and the task was never fully completed (Josh. 15:63; 17:12–13). There was one period in which the inheritance was delayed for seven tribes: "And there remained among the children of Israel seven tribes, which had not yet received their inheritance. And Joshua said unto the children of Israel, How long are ye slack to go to possess the land, which the LORD God of your fathers hath given you?" (Josh. 18:2–3). He may have had a free-rider problem.

Conclusion

Reuben and Gad possessed lots of cattle. The land of Gilead outside of Canaan was better suited to cattle raising than Canaan. These tribes realized that Gilead was better suited to their occupations than anything they might conquer in Canaan. They wanted to capitalize the value that they would bring to the land as cattlemen. They approached Moses with an offer: an inheritance in Gilead in exchange for an inheritance in Canaan. This was a contract.

Moses made sure that the covenant came first: the inheritance of Israel as promised to Abraham by God. They would have to put their lives on the line in the national war effort inside Canaan before they could inherit outside Canaan. They had to stake their claim to Canaan before they could stake their claim to Gilead. Moses also invoked God's negative sanctions against the two tribes if they failed to participate. They apparently took this covenantal threat seriously (v. 23). Once every-

---

8. Israel wandered 40 years in the wilderness (Josh. 5:6). The first numbering in Numbers took place in the second year after the exodus (Num. 1:1). Moses sent in the spies shortly after this numbering. Caleb was age 40 at the time Moses sent in the spies; he was 85 when he began his final campaign in Canaan (Josh. 14:6–7, 10). Thus, Caleb was victorious in year six of the conquest, 46 years after the exodus.

one had inherited his property in Canaan, they would be allowed to return to their land in Gilead. They agreed.

Moses made a persuasive offer to the other ten tribes: inherit the land of two and a half tribes in exchange for land outside the Promised Land that the nine and a half tribes did not really want, plus gain the military support of these tribes, or else (unstated) forfeit this additional land in Canaan and maybe not get aid from the two and a half tribes. This offer was strong enough to keep defectors from refusing to invade Canaan, even though a person, family, or tribe could not be excluded from inheritance inside Canaan for non-participation in the conquest.

20

SANCTIONS AND INHERITANCE

Speak unto the children of Israel, and say unto them, When ye are passed over Jordan into the land of Canaan; Then ye shall drive out all the inhabitants of the land from before you, and destroy all their pictures, and destroy all their molten images, and quite pluck down all their high places: And ye shall dispossess the inhabitants of the land, and dwell therein: for I have given you the land to possess it (Num. 33:51–53).

God instructed Moses to repeat the command given to the generation of the exodus: exterminate the Canaanites. This work of extermination was to mark them as a covenant people.

And he said, Behold, I make a covenant: before all thy people I will do marvels, such as have not been done in all the earth, nor in any nation: and all the people among which thou art shall see the work of the LORD: for it is a terrible thing that I will do with thee. Observe thou that which I command thee this day: behold, I drive out before thee the Amorite, and the Canaanite, and the Hittite, and the Perizzite, and the Hivite, and the Jebusite. Take heed to thyself, lest thou make a covenant with the inhabitants of the land whither thou goest, lest it be for a snare in the midst of thee: But ye shall destroy their altars, break their images, and cut down their groves: For thou shalt worship no other god: for the LORD, whose name is Jealous, is a jealous God: Lest thou make a covenant with the inhabitants of the land, and they go a whoring after their gods, and do sacrifice unto their gods, and one call thee, and thou eat of his sacrifice; And thou take of their daughters unto thy sons, and their daughters go a whoring after their gods, and make thy sons go a whoring after their gods (Ex. 34:10–16).

The exodus generation did not honor God's command. They preferred to wander in the wilderness, hoping against hope to be allowed to return to Egypt. They believed that God would not impose the same kinds of negative sanctions on Canaan that He had imposed on Egypt. They did not want to become the military agents who would impose His negative sanctions, any more than they had wanted Moses to impose negative sanctions against Pharaoh (Ex. 5:20–23).

The next generation of Israelites was ready to play the role of sanctions-bringer. They had recently imposed negative sanctions on Arad, Og, Sihon, and Midian. God had upheld them miraculously in the war on Midian: not one life lost (Num. 31:49). They had wielded the sword effectively. They had experienced the taste of victory. They liked it. They wanted more.

The Spoils of War

Moses offered them positive sanctions: land. "And ye shall divide the land by lot for an inheritance among your families: and to the more ye shall give the more inheritance, and to the fewer ye shall give the less inheritance: every man's inheritance shall be in the place where his lot falleth; according to the tribes of your fathers ye shall inherit" (Num. 33:54). Their tribes' general location would be established by lot, i.e., not by politicians or priests. God would give each tribe its due. The actual boundaries were probably decided in terms of tribal size, as with family allocations. But the rulers would allocate the actual parcels in terms of the size of the families.[1] This way, those who had better fulfilled the dominion covenant mandat-

1. See Chapter 14, above.

ing large families (Gen. 1:28) would not be initially penalized by less land per family member.[2]

God also cautioned them regarding negative sanctions if they refused to impose total annihilation against the Canaanites. "But if ye will not drive out the inhabitants of the land from before you; then it shall come to pass, that those which ye let remain of them shall be pricks in your eyes, and thorns in your sides, and shall vex you in the land wherein ye dwell. Moreover it shall come to pass, that I shall do unto you, as I thought to do unto them" (Num. 33:55–56). The Israelites were not immune from God's negative sanctions in history. To the degree that they adopted the religion of Canaan, they would be treated analogously. The judicial issue was therefore not bloodline but confession of faith and obedience to the terms of the covenant. The sanctions were covenantal.

First War, Then Peace

The pattern of victory over Canaan was Old Covenant sabbatical: first work, then rest. The sabbath commandment is the fourth commandment.[3] It has to do with the negative sanction of work and the positive sanction of rest. Israel had to wage war for six years before gaining its rest.[4]

Israel was not told in advance that the removal of the Canaanites would take six years. God did tell them that it would not be an overnight process, since the animals of Canaan were not to be allowed to escape from the domination of mankind. "I will not drive them out from before thee in one year; lest the land become desolate, and the beast of the field multiply

2. Over time, large families would mean smaller plots of land. This is why the jubilee land law tended toward urbanization, where the jubilee inheritance law did not apply. See Gary North, *Leviticus: An Economic Commentary* (Tyler, Texas: Institute for Christian Economics, 1994), pp. 416–22.

3. Gary North, *The Sinai Strategy: Economics and the Ten Commandments* (Tyler, Texas: Institute for Christian Economics, 1986), ch. 4.

4. See Chapter 19, footnote 8.

against thee. By little and little I will drive them out from before thee, until thou be increased, and inherit the land" (Ex. 23:29–30).

Moses began his public presentation to the conquest generation by listing the places where Israel had rested along the way. They had wandered, rested, and wandered again. They had found no permanent rest. They had moved 33 times from the time of the exodus to the death of Aaron on Mt. Hor (Num. 33:5–38). Aaron's death occurred in the fortieth year after the exodus (v. 38). Then they began a final series of wanderings: eight resting places in less than one year (vv. 41–49).

These final wanderings were different: Israel defeated major enemies. This time, they were not driven out; rather, they drove out others. They were able to build up both their confidence and their land holdings through force of arms. They had been attacked repeatedly; they had won repeatedly. This began a psychological transformation of the nation: from a defensive to an offensive mentality. They had not initiated these wars, but they had won them. This was in preparation for their crossing of the Jordan River: the move to total offense.

The exodus generation had maintained the peace by fleeing whenever challenged. Their solution to an external challenge was a retreat. They had been told by Moses that God was not going to give them a definitive victory in their lifetimes. This made them defensive. They did not want trouble. Their inheritance was cut off. They had no intention of placing their lives at risk for the sake of the inheritance of their children. They demonstrated this one-generation time perspective by refusing to circumcise their children (Josh. 5:7). The mark of a legal claim on the inheritance that had been promised to Abraham was circumcision. The exodus generation refused to impose the mark of the covenant on their heirs. They were saying, in effect, "If we cannot inherit, then why should our sons inherit?"

The generation of the conquest had lived as wanderers because of their parents' rebellion and cowardice. They had seen the consequences of rebellion and cowardice. They had lived all of their adult lives under negative sanctions. They had grown tired of this pattern of behavior. They wanted their inheritance, and they were willing to pay for it on God's terms: military conquest. This was risky, but it was better than living as wanderers.

God warned them that if they refused to drive out the Canaanites, they would fall under the same negative sanctions that Canaan was about to experience. The threat of negative historical sanctions is inherent in the biblical covenant. Canaan was about to learn this first-hand. So was Israel. But Israel had gained positive sanctions – land – by becoming God's agency of negative sanctions: a holy army.

This army was being taught a lesson: the trustworthiness of God's promises. This was an important lesson for the nation prior to the conquest. The victors' positive sanctions in warfare were gained through the losers' negative sanctions. Positive and negative sanctions are military corollaries. Warfare is a zero-sum activity: losers supply the winnings of the winners. This makes warfare different from the free market, where both trading partners expect to gain through a voluntary exchange.

Conclusion

Moses made it clear to the conquest generation that the terms of success in history are judicial. The Israelites were required to maintain their commitment to God's law. This included the one-time law of annihilation. The gods of Canaan were local gods who exercised their authority within the geographical boundaries of the promised inheritance. This is why the nations of Canaan had to be destroyed. Military conquest alone would destroy the authority and jurisdiction of the gods of Canaan. The defeat of those gods would mark the victory of God. The historical issue was sanctions.

God announced: "I have given you the land to possess it" (Num. 33:53). But to collect what He had already given, they had to dispossess the Canaanites and their gods. Israel's inheritance was not delivered on a silver platter. They had to earn it. Yet it had been promised to Abraham (Gen. 15:16). There was a promise; there were also conditions. One of these conditions was circumcision. The other was military conquest. There was promise; there was also deliverance. To collect on the promise, Israel had to impose negative sanctions against Canaan. The iniquity of the Amorites was at long last full (Gen. 15:16). Their day of reckoning had come. Israel was God's designated agent for this imposition of God's judgment in history.

God's promise to Abraham looked forward to the day of judgment on Canaan. This promise was eschatological with respect to Canaan: last things. The victory of Israel involved the imposition of negative sanctions on Canaan. These sanctions were necessary conditions for the fulfillment of the promise. Moses told the leaders of Reuben and Gad that they had to participate in the war in order to receive their inheritance on the wilderness side of the Jordan: no warfare–no inheritance. They had already benefited from the victories of the holy army of Israel; they would have to contribute to the victory within Canaan's boundaries.

With respect to the eschatology of Canaan and the inheritance of Israel, sanctions were a necessary part of the fulfillment of God's prophecy: "But in the fourth generation they shall come hither again: for the iniquity of the Amorites is not yet full" (Gen. 15:16). It was not possible for Israel to separate sanctions from the inheritance. Similarly, it was not possible for Israel to separate sanctions from eschatology, i.e., Canaan's eschatology. The victory of Israel over Canaan involved the imposition of negative sanctions. Israel's victory was Canaan's defeat. More to the point, the visible victory of Israel's God was the visible defeat of Canaan's gods. The covenantal victory of God was the necessary corollary of the covenantal defeat of Canaan's gods. It is not covenantally legitimate to discuss eschatology apart from sanctions, any more than it is to discuss God's law apart from the law's specified sanctions. They are a covenantal unit: law, sanctions, and eschatology. Modern Christian theology denies this unbreakable covenantal unity. So did the exodus generation.

21

CITIES OF REFUGE

And the LORD *spake unto Moses, saying, Speak unto the children of Israel, and say unto them, When ye be come over Jordan into the land of Canaan; Then ye shall appoint you cities to be cities of refuge for you; that the slayer may flee thither, which killeth any person at unawares. And they shall be unto you cities for refuge from the avenger; that the manslayer die not, until he stand before the congregation in judgment. And of these cities which ye shall give six cities shall ye have for refuge (Num. 35:9–13).*

This law rested on the theocentric principle of God as the provider of sanctuaries in history for innocent people who are suspected of wrongdoing. The parallel principle is that the accused person who chooses to dwell outside of these safe havens is totally at risk in a world of imperfect knowledge and imperfect justice.

God gave Levi an inheritance: 48 cities (Num. 35:7). Of these 48 cities, six were designated as cities of refuge (v. 6). God told Israel that three of these cities were to be located inside the boundaries of Canaan; the other three were to be across the Jordan in the lands allocated to Reuben, Gad, and half the tribe of Manasseh (v. 14). After the conquest, "they appointed Kedesh in Galilee in mount Naphtali, and Shechem in mount Ephraim, and Kirjath-arba, which is Hebron, in the mountain of

Judah. And on the other side Jordan by Jericho eastward, they assigned Bezer in the wilderness upon the plain out of the tribe of Reuben, and Ramoth in Gilead out of the tribe of Gad, and Golan in Bashan out of the tribe of Manasseh" (Josh. 20:7–8).

Murder or Accidental Death

These cities of refuge were unique. They offered protection to anyone who innocently caused the death of another.

> Thou shalt prepare thee a way, and divide the coasts of thy land, which the LORD thy God giveth thee to inherit, into three parts, that every slayer may flee thither. And this is the case of the slayer, which shall flee thither, that he may live: Whoso killeth his neighbour ignorantly, whom he hated not in time past; As when a man goeth into the wood with his neighbour to hew wood, and his hand fetcheth a stroke with the axe to cut down the tree, and the head slippeth from the helve, and lighteth upon his neighbour, that he die; he shall flee unto one of those cities, and live: Lest the avenger of the blood pursue the slayer, while his heart is hot, and overtake him, because the way is long, and slay him; whereas he was not worthy of death, inasmuch as he hated him not in time past (Deut. 19:3–6).

This grant of protection to the suspect did not relieve judges from the responsibility of trying him. Murder was a capital crime. The elders in the city of refuge did not subsidize murder. They offered a cooling-off period. The congregation in the suspect's community retained primary jurisdiction. "But if he thrust him suddenly without enmity, or have cast upon him any thing without laying of wait, Or with any stone, wherewith a man may die, seeing him not, and cast it upon him, that he die, and was not his enemy, neither sought his harm: Then the congregation shall judge between the slayer and the revenger of blood according to these judgments" (Num. 35:22–24). The question was: Where should the suspect remain in protective custody before the trial? Israel had no prison system. The city of refuge served as a kind of prison for the man: it kept him in, but it kept the blood avenger out. The city did not enforce his functional incarceration; the blood avenger did.

The civil court in the suspect's jurisdiction had primary authority after the suspect had fled to the city of refuge. It could seek his extradition into its protective custody. The elders of his home community would send someone to escort him home. These escorts would protect him from the blood avenger until after the trial. If the local court then declared him innocent, it would send him back to the city of refuge. "Then the congregation shall judge between the slayer and the revenger of blood according to these judgments: And the congregation shall deliver the slayer out of the hand of the revenger of blood, and the congregation shall restore him to the city of his refuge, whither he was fled: and he shall abide in it unto the death of the high priest, which was anointed with the holy oil" (Num. 35:24–25). This congregation must have been located in his home town, for the text required the congregation to restore him to his city of refuge. Obviously, he was not in his city of refuge during the trial. If declared innocent, he would not live among the relatives of the victim until after the death of the high priest. Again, this served as a cooling-off measure.

The local congregation might declare him guilty. It would then turn him over to the blood avenger. "But if any man hate his neighbour, and lie in wait for him, and rise up against him, and smite him mortally that he die, and fleeth into one of these cities: Then the elders of his city shall send and fetch him thence, and deliver him into the hand of the avenger of blood, that he may die. Thine eye shall not pity him, but thou shalt put away the guilt of innocent blood from Israel, that it may go well with thee" (Deut. 19:11–13). The blood avenger would execute the sentence.

Degrees of Protection

The city of refuge tried the person initially. The judges listened to his story. If they believed it, he could remain inside the city until his home court demanded his extradition and arranged protective custody for him. Until his community demanded his extradition, he was allowed to remain in the city of refuge, safe from the blood avenger.

> That the slayer that killeth any person unawares and unwittingly may flee thither: and they shall be your refuge from the avenger of blood. And when he that doth flee unto one of those cities shall stand at the entering of the gate of the city, and shall declare his cause in the ears of the elders of that city, they shall take him into the city unto them, and give him a place, that he may dwell among them. And if the avenger of blood pursue after him, then they shall not deliver the slayer up into his hand; because he smote his neighbour unwittingly, and hated him not beforetime. And he shall dwell in that city, until he stand before the congregation for judgment, and until the death of the high priest that shall be in those days: then shall the slayer return, and come unto his own city, and unto his own house, unto the city from whence he fled (Josh. 20:3–6).

The civil court in a city of refuge had jurisdiction only within the boundaries of its city. The city was comparable to a modern embassy. Inside its four walls, no other nation exercises jurisdiction. Outside, the laws governing the foreign nation or city are sovereign. Inside the city of refuge, a man was legally immune from attack by the blood avenger. Outside, he was not immune.

It was a matter of jurisdiction. The civil court in a city of refuge possessed a geographically limited jurisdiction in the case of accidental manslaughter. The blood avenger had the primary jurisdiction outside of the city's walls prior to the suspect's trial back home. The suspect's local civil court had jurisdiction, but it had to demand extradition in order to enforce it. When it did so, jurisdiction shifted from both the city of refuge and the blood avenger.

Today, a civil court decides finally who is to blame. In Mosaic Israel, the local court assessed guilt or innocence. But to try the person, the local community had to wait until the city of refuge took him. The avenger of blood – the *go'el* or *ga'al*– had the authority to execute the suspect on sight prior to his arrival in a city of refuge.

Blood Avenger, Kinsman-Redeemer

Mosaic law devotes considerable space to this family office. The kinsman-redeemer was the closest relative. Boaz was Naomi's kinsman-redeemer (Ruth 2:20). God is spoken of as Israel's kinsman-redeemer. "Thus saith the LORD, your redeemer, the Holy One of Israel; For your sake I have sent to Babylon, and have brought down all their nobles, and the Chaldeans, whose cry is in the ships" (Isa. 43:14). David spoke of God as his kinsman-redeemer: "Let the words of my mouth, and the meditation of my heart, be acceptable in thy sight, O LORD, my strength, and my redeemer" (Ps. 19:14). Job viewed God as the final judge: "For I know that my redeemer liveth, and that he shall stand at the latter day upon the earth" (Job 19:25).

Yet this redeemer, this deliverer, was also the judge who had the authority to execute a man who had killed the redeemer's nearest of kin. Until the man arrived in a city of refuge, the blood avenger served as jury, judge, and executioner. In Israel, where a death was involved, there was swift justice. This sanction was permanent.

Sanctions and Incentives

The death penalty is the limit of any civil sanction. The State is to be neither bloodthirsty, imposing torture or mass executions, nor soft-hearted, imposing a lesser sanction. The incentive either to exceed or avoid imposing God's law is always very great. The Mosaic law had two major methods of assigning the responsibility for executing the capital sanction: shared responsibility and unitary responsibility. Shared responsibility removed the full responsibility from the citizen. The method of execution, stoning, made it impossible for any participant to know if his blow had killed the criminal. Unitary responsibility fell to the blood avenger. The blood avenger knew that his act would kill the suspect. He was the nearest of kin, and he had the incentive to execute judgment. But there was only one blood avenger. Everyone else in the community had to restrain himself. *There were to be neither mobs nor clan feuds in Israel.* Both shared responsibility and unitary responsibility were under God's law and his restraints. The restraint in this case was geographical: a city of refuge.

The office of blood avenger was designed to reduce the threat of clan or family feuds. One person was designated as a lawful agent of the State. His lethal action kept the violence from spreading. When a family member was killed, the family as a unit did not seek vengeance. One member did. In fact, the other members of the family were not allowed to restrain the suspect from fleeing to a city of refuge. No family could assign the task of hunting down the suspect to the fastest runner in the family. The office was held strictly on a next-of-kin basis.

The tribes could more easily restrict bloodshed from spreading by keeping the roads open. To give the suspect a better opportunity to reach a court, the tribes made sure that easy access was possible. The Mosaic law also allowed travellers to eat a handful of food free of charge (Deut. 23:24–25; Matt. 12:1). The man who was killed by a blood avenger had been given an opportunity to escape. His family had less incentive to retaliate against a member of another family, since the same legal protection was available to all. To exact vengeance against the blood avenger in such a case, let alone against other family members of the deceased victim, was to remove the protection that the city of refuge offered to everyone.

Open roads were therefore a life-and-death issue. Everyone had an incentive to support the maintenance of open roads leading to one or more cities of refuge. The Bible does not establish who has jurisdiction over roads, but the system of refuge cities indicates that for roads connecting to, or feeding into, these cities of refuge, the State had an obligation to build and maintain them as part of the judicial system. There would have been no toll roads into these cities. To have established tolls would have been to sell access to justice. The Bible does not authorize such a system of justice.

The Presumption of Guilt and Innocence

The man who accidentally killed his neighbor was automatically presumed guilty by the blood avenger. This means that the slain victim, who could not speak on his own behalf, was automatically presumed innocent. The suspect was not allowed to defend himself physically against the blood avenger; to have done so would have been assault or murder. In the latter case, the State would have imposed the death penalty. The innocent man would have forfeited his innocence by killing his lawful pursuer. The courts recognized the right of the blood avenger to execute the suspect. Had they not done so, powerful suspects could have disposed of speedy but ineffective avengers.

With respect to everyone else in Israel, the suspect was not considered guilty. He had the right of protection if he reached a city of refuge. He could not be killed by the blood avenger within the walls of that city. At the death of the high priest, he returned home in safety: innocent for life.

This reduced the cost of murder trials in Israel. The suspect bore the cost of fleeing to a city of refuge. He would have started running as soon as he recognized that his victim was dead. This surely would have increased the likelihood that he would have done his best to save the victim's life if he appeared as though he could be saved. But once the victim was dead, there was no time to waste.

The blood avenger, who was probably biased in favor of the victim, would bear the cost of pursuing the suspect. No one else would. The judges in a city of refuge, presumably with no bias against the suspect, would conduct the preliminary hearing. If the suspect wanted to bring witnesses on his behalf, he or the witnesses would have borne the expense of travel. The city of refuge supplied only the judges. This would have taken place only when the suspect managed to make it to the city. This means that the bulk of the cost of prosecuting murder suspects would have been borne by the blood avenger. The defense cost would have been borne mostly by the suspect. This system allocated the costs of murder to those with the greatest incentive to gain a settlement.

The system also forced a suspect to identify himself publicly. Running away did not imply his guilt. He headed for a city of refuge where he could publicly protest his innocence. The blood avenger knew where to find him. The cost of tracing the suspect was low. If he was innocent, the refuge city's judges might protect him. If he was guilty, the blood avenger knew where to plead his case. There would be fewer unsolved murders in Israel because of this system. An unsolved murder was a major problem in Israel because of bloodguilt. This is why there was a formal system of public expiation for unsolved deaths (Deut. 21:1–9). "So shalt thou put away the guilt of innocent blood from among you, when thou shalt do that which is right in the sight of the LORD" (Deut. 21:9).

The dead man could not speak on his own behalf. This is why the suspect was presumed guilty by the victim's family, but only one person could lawfully apply the appropriate sanction apart from a trial: the kinsman redeemer, who acted judicially on behalf of the victim. The refuge city system increased the incentive for a suspect to prove his case in a civil court. He had to identify himself as a suspect to the authorities.

Personal Boundaries and Defensive Jurisdiction

Not every death was under the jurisdiction of the blood avenger. The blood avenger gained jurisdiction over suspects who had been involved in what appeared to be an unrelated activity, such as work, where what could have been an accident caused a death. There were certain situations in which circumstances indicated that the victim had initiated the violence. In this case, a blood avenger had no jurisdiction.

A deceased intruder was retroactively presumed guilty. When a householder killed an unknown thief or intruder inside the boundaries of his house when it was obvious that the intruder had no legitimate reason to be inside, there was no question of the householder's liability (Ex. 22:2–4). He was innocent. An intruder who came into the house at night had no legal rights. The blood avenger had no jurisdiction. The house's boundaries testified against the intruder.

If a man attacked another man in front of witnesses, and the defender killed him, the blood avenger had no jurisdiction. The slayer's boundaries had been violated. He was presumed innocent; only a local court could declare him guilty.

The case laws indicate that the victim had not initiated violence against the slayer. The slayer's rock or axe head had caused the fatal injury. The victim had done nothing to bring on the response of the slayer. He had violated no boundaries. The witnesses, if any, could not speak definitively on behalf of the slayer or the slain. In such a case, the victim was presumed innocent. The blood avenger then had lawful jurisdiction until the suspect could place himself inside the walls of a city of refuge.

The refuge city system was designed to overcome two crucial features of Israelite society: the limits of knowledge and the tendency of clan societies to develop blood feuds. The limits of knowledge are universal; clan societies are not. Israel was a tribal society. A tribal society is a usually clan-based society, for families, including extended families, possess their civil jurisdiction through a tribal council or court. The legal hierarchy is tribal. The civil sanctions are imposed tribally: in Israel's case, corporate stoning. Thus, families within a tribal society are tempted to seek analogous authority to impose final sanctions, since the judicial system appears to be based on bloodlines. This is the sociological basis of clan feuds.

Israel established limits on such a development. The Levites were one limit: counsel from outside the tribe's regional authority. The cities of refuge, which were all Levitical cities, were another limitation. The blood avenger seems to be a clannish office, but it operated to limit the spread of clan feuds. In fact, the blood avenger was an agent of the State who received his office through the family. His authority to impose lawful sanctions was limited by the civil congregation of his own city and by the mortality of the high priest.

The Death of the High Priest

We are not told why the high priest had to die in order for the innocent man to be released. The high priest's death had preeminence over the civil government of the innocent man's local community as well as over the blood avenger. The "blood feud," i.e., the family or clan feud, had to be eliminated. There had to be a healing judicial act which would overcome the blood lust of the avenger. It was not enough for a local court to declare the suspect innocent. There had to be a death. The death of the high priest was a substitutionary atonement. The dead man had been presumed the victim of foul play by his family. The local court had overturned this judgment on the basis of incomplete evidence, but the case was not settled permanently until the high priest died. The suspect then had his name cleared in history. No further act of violence against him was legal. The blood avenger had no further jurisdiction.

There has to be a way to bring disputes to a peaceful end. The costs of perpetual warfare are too high. Such conflicts undermine peace. Too many resources must otherwise be expended to reduce violence. The death of the high priest ended all defense costs for the suspect. The high priest's death called into session the court of highest earthly appeal, which automatically handed down a verdict of "innocent." The authority of the court of the city of refuge was thereby extended beyond the jurisdiction of the city.

This law is no longer in force. It cannot be; there is no earthly high priest. Without a mortal high priest, there would be no way for an innocent man ever to return to his home. There would be no prospect of full liberty for the innocent man. This law was operationally annulled with the exile, when Israel lost jurisdiction over civil justice inside its boundaries. It was definitively annulled with the death of the true high priest, Jesus Christ.

Conclusion

The cities of refuge were designed to reduce conflict, especially family feuds. The initial burden of proof was on the suspect. If he was fleet of foot, he might escape judgment by the blood avenger. If he could plead his case to the judges of the city of refuge, he could live. If he subsequently persuaded his local court, he would have been returned to the city of refuge that had sheltered him. If he outlived the high priest, he could lawfully return to his community.

Blood had been shed, and it had to be atoned for. The judicial issue here was expiation: cleansing bloodguilt for the land and for the victim's family. The refuge city system reduced the number of unsolved cases of murder. This protected the land. The death of the high priest provided the final expiation for the original bloody act. This protected the local community from the heavy costs of family feuds.

To protect themselves, communities had to keep the roads open. Roads in Israel were both judicial and sacramental: judicial with respect to the cities of refuge; sacramental with respect to the festivals and required sacrifices at the central city. There is no biblical evidence that State highway construction was justified on the basis of its positive economic effects, although the roads surely had positive economic effects. What the roads were intended to provide was access to justice and access to expiation. Both justice and expiation were geographically based. "Speak ye comfortably to Jerusalem, and cry unto her, that her warfare is accomplished, that her iniquity is pardoned: for she hath received of the LORD'S hand double for all her sins. The voice of him that crieth in the wilderness, Prepare ye the way of the LORD, make straight in the desert a highway for our God. Every valley shall be exalted, and every mountain and hill shall be made low: and the crooked shall be made straight, and the rough places plain: And the glory of the LORD shall be revealed, and all flesh shall see it together: for the mouth of the LORD hath spoken it" (Isa. 40:2–5).

Having to dwell inside the boundaries of a city of refuge until the high priest died was a negative sanction. The person so condemned probably would have had to change occupations. He would have had to learn to compete in a completely different environment. This no doubt was an incentive for those working in jobs that involved imposing risk on others to take care of their equipment.

The odd thing is that the Mosaic law was silent about what family sanctions there were against accidental manslaughter inside a city of refuge. Presumably, the kinsman-redeemer did not possess the power of enforcement against anyone who lived inside a city of refuge. If so, then the city of refuge would have been a more risky place to work: less care regarding the repair of the tools of one's trade. The threat of living inside the confines of a city of refuge would have weighed less heavily on someone who already lived in one.

The fact that the victim's family received nothing from the person who had caused the death but escaped to a city of refuge indicates that Mosaic civil law did not rest on the doctrine of strict liability. Strict liability requires the person who inflicts an injury to compensate the victim, no matter what the circumstances. Mosaic law rested on a much less rigorous concept of liability. If a damage-producer could not reasonably have foreseen it, the State allowed him a way to avoid making full compensation on an eye-for-eye basis. Men are not omniscient; biblical law acknowledges this fact in its concept of liability.

22

TRIBAL INHERITANCE

This is the thing which the LORD *doth command concerning the daughters of Zelophehad, saying, Let them marry to whom they think best; only to the family of the tribe of their father shall they marry. So shall not the inheritance of the children of Israel remove from tribe to tribe: for every one of the children of Israel shall keep himself to the inheritance of the tribe of his fathers. And every daughter, that possesseth an inheritance in any tribe of the children of Israel, shall be wife unto one of the family of the tribe of her father, that the children of Israel may enjoy every man the inheritance of his fathers. Neither shall the inheritance remove from one tribe to another tribe; but every one of the tribes of the children of Israel shall keep himself to his own inheritance (Num. 36:6–9).*

The tribe of Manasseh was divided. Half of the tribe lived in Gilead, that section of Israel which lay beyond the Jordan. The chief rulers of this part of the tribe approached Moses with a question: What about the jubilee year?

And they said, The LORD commanded my lord to give the land for an inheritance by lot to the children of Israel: and my lord was commanded by the LORD to give the inheritance of Zelophehad our brother unto his daughters. And if they be married to any of the sons of the other tribes of the children of Israel, then shall their inheritance be taken from the inheritance of our fathers, and shall be put to the inheritance of the tribe whereunto they are received: so shall it be taken from the lot of our inheritance. And when the jubile of the children of Israel shall be, then shall their inheritance be put unto the inheritance of the tribe whereunto they are received: so shall their inheritance be taken away from the inheritance of the tribe of our fathers (vv. 2–4).

The five daughters of Zelophehad had previously come to Moses with a question: What about their inheritance? More to the point, what about the survival of their father's name in Israel? "Our father died in the wilderness, and he was not in the company of them that gathered themselves together against the LORD in the company of Korah; but died in his own sin, and had no sons. Why should the name of our father be done away from among his family, because he hath no son? Give unto us therefore a possession among the brethren of our father" (Num 27:3–4). The law was silent on this matter. The daughters did not want to lose their land, but the Mosaic law weighed heavily on the side of masculine authority. They sought a clear-cut ruling from God: Did God place the preservation of masculine authority above feminine authority to the extent of removing a man's inheritance from his exclusively female progeny? "And Moses brought their cause before the LORD. And the LORD spake unto Moses, saying, The daughters of Zelophehad speak right: thou shalt surely give them a possession of an inheritance among their father's brethren; and thou shalt cause the inheritance of their father to pass unto them. And thou shalt speak unto the children of Israel, saying, If a man die, and have no son, then ye shall cause his inheritance to pass unto his daughter" (Num. 27:5–8).

Household authority rather than gender was primary in Israel. Like the widow who became the head of her household, and who thereby gained the right to declare a vow independently of a man (Num. 30), so were the daughters of a man who died without sons. His name was to be preserved in Israel through his offspring. Daughters rather than brothers were the means of preserving his name.

Adoption Through Marriage

A problem still remained: What about marriage? When a man married, his wife brought a dowry into the marriage. The dowry was what distinguished a wife from a concubine. The dowry was generally provided by the bridegroom: a bride price. This is why Saul established the terms of his daughter's dowry for David: the foreskins of a hundred Philistines (I Sam. 18:25). Because the bridegroom provided the bride price, a daughter was not an economic burden on her brothers. Her dowry did not cost them part of their inheritance. A sister was not a source of negative economic sanctions in the family.[1] In contrast, a son inherited a portion of his father's land. This capitalized his branch of the family. This is how a man's name was normally preserved in Israel.

Then what about marriage? If the daughter inherited a portion of her father's land, and her husband was outside the tribe, would the tribe's inheritance be reduced? The jubilee law as written indicated that this was the case. The issue was judicial: adoption. The bride was adopted into her husband's family. We know this because of the response of the tribal leaders. If the wife had not become a member of her husband's family, which could take place only through adoption, then the problem the leaders brought before Moses would never have arisen. But the husband was under the authority of another tribe. Through his authority over his wife, based on her adoption into his household, his tribe would gain authority over the legacy of the man who died without sons.

The judicial solution was tribal. If a daughter married a man who was a member of her tribe, she inherited her father's land.

---

1. Gary North, *Tools of Dominion: The Case Laws of Exodus* (Tyler, Texas: Institute for Christian Economics, 1990), ch. 21.

If he was outside her tribe, she forfeited her inheritance. This inheritance was part of her tribe's inheritance. It was located within the legal boundaries established by lot (Num. 36:2). The tribe's judicial authority extended to its borders. The enforcement of God's civil law was tribal. Each tribe would apply God's law locally as it saw fit. This judicial decentralization was a major source of liberty in pre-exilic Israel. The central civil government could not impose its will over the tribes apart from an appeals system (Ex. 18).

The creation of geographical zones exempt from local tribal law would have undermined this decentralized system of rule. If one tribe could extend its authority by means of marriage, this would have subsidized a form of inter-tribal imperialism. The power of one tribe could have been extended through a program of seeking out brotherless virgins in another tribe. These women, already vulnerable, would have become pawns in a game of inter-tribal politics. To protect them, and to protect the regional authority of each tribe, God revealed a solution: the forfeiture of landed inheritance by a woman adopted into the family of a rival tribe. Landed inheritance was not strictly individualistic. "If a man have two wives, one beloved, and another hated, and they have born him children, both the beloved and the hated; and if the firstborn son be hers that was hated: Then it shall be, when he maketh his sons to inherit that which he hath, that he may not make the son of the beloved firstborn before the son of the hated, which is indeed the firstborn: But he shall acknowledge the son of the hated for the firstborn, by giving him a double portion of all that he hath: for he is the beginning of his strength; the right of the firstborn is his" (Deut. 21:15–17). It was also not strictly familistic, as the case law of Zelophehad's daughters indicates. It was partially tribal. "Neither shall the inheritance remove from one tribe to another tribe; but every one of the tribes of the children of Israel shall keep himself to his own inheritance" (Num. 36:9). The preservation of a man's name mandated the preservation of his tribe's name. The preservation of a man's inheritance mandated the preservation of his tribe's authority over his land. Only with the defeat of Israel by Assyria and the defeat of Judah by Babylon did this system of tribal authority end. It ended because the hierarchy of civil authority was transferred by God from Israel to a series of pagan empires.

Progressive Revelation and Eschatology

Perhaps more than any other incident in Scripture, the story of Zelophehad's daughters reveals the progressive nature of God's revelation in biblical history. The jubilee land law was incomplete. It did not answer the question: What if an Israelite dies without sons? This question was raised by the five daughters in Numbers 27. Moses asked God; God replied: daughters should inherit, not the man's brothers or his uncles. But this answer raised another question: What if a daughter marries a man from outside her tribe? This was a problem because of a judicial issue that is never directly raised in the Mosaic law but which is the most fundamental of all judicial issues: adoption. Ultimately, this is the issue of redemption: the transition from wrath to grace. While the Mosaic law does not discuss it, this issue underlies the entire system: adoption into a tribe through a family or a city (citizenship); adoption into a family through marriage (inheritance); adoption of one family's inter-generational slave into another Israelite family (liberation).

God did not reveal the details of all this at one point in time. He revealed it over time. The jubilee law did not answer all of the problems of inheritance. Neither did God's initial revelation to Moses regarding the daughters of Zelophehad. He waited for the appearance of the moral discipline that used to be called casuistry – the systematic application of God's law to specific cases – to reveal new problems. Then He revealed the answers through Moses.

With the closing of the canon of Scripture, progressive revelation ceased. No new revelation comes to man that has authority equal to that of the Bible. A claim of judicial equality is in fact a claim of judicial superiority, for that which lawfully interprets past judgments is judicially superior to the past. God's revelation in Numbers 36 was superior to what He revealed in Numbers 27. That which He revealed in Numbers 27 was superior to what He had revealed in Leviticus 25.

Casuistry did not cease with the closing of the canon of Scripture. Casuistry is basic to every legal system. In the West, casuistry ceased to be practiced by Protestants around the year 1700.[2] The demise of Protestant casuistry was part of a larger social transformation: the replacement of Puritanism's theocratic ideal by Newtonian rationalism, Enlightenment speculation, and political secularism. The kingdom of God was progressively restricted to heart, hearth, and church. This was a denial of the comprehensive claims of God on man and his institutions.[3] The revelation of the Bible was assumed to be irrelevant to civil affairs. The revealed law of God was assumed to be subordinate to both natural law and common law because natural law is supposedly more universal than biblical law, and common law is second in authority after natural law. The categories of space and time were invoked against biblical law. They still are, although the category of time is generally given precedence: the doctrine of evolution. Cultural relativism has generally replaced natural law theory in academic circles.

This raises the issue of eschatology. If God's law can never extend to the four corners of the earth through mass evangelism and conversion, then the common-ground categories of space and time will continue to supersede the category of biblical law in the thinking of the vast majority of Christians. That is, if progressive sanctification is eschatologically impossible outside the boundaries of heart, hearth, and church, the king-

---

2. Kenneth E. Kirk, *Conscience and Its Problems: An Introduction to Casuistry* (new ed.; London: Longmans, Green, 1948), pp. 206–207.

3. Kenneth L. Gentry, Jr., *The Greatness of the Great Commission: The Christian Enterprise in a Fallen World* (Tyler, Texas: Institute for Christian Economics, 1990).

dom of God must remain confined in history to cultural ghettos. The revealed law of God loses its operational authority because it supposedly was circumscribed spatially and temporally. This ignores the existence of God's specially revealed cross-boundary laws.[4] Their existence was manifested in the ministry of Jonah, who prophesied God's corporate negative sanctions against Nineveh. Cross-boundary laws are geographically universal. They are also temporally binding.

Only with a restoration of biblical casuistry can the kingdom of God be consummated in history.[5] But until there is widespread belief in the triumph of the gospel in history, casuistry will remain, at best, the hobby of a handful of Christian academics with a lot of time on their hands.

Conclusion

The case law application of the jubilee law which we find in Numbers 36 ends the Book of Numbers. There is no question what the issue was: inheritance. This is the issue of continuity in history. In the context of Mosaic Israel, this issue was the preservation of a man's name. But it also involved his tribe's name. It had to do with the messianic prophecy of Jacob regarding the coming of Shiloh. "The sceptre shall not depart from Judah, nor a lawgiver from between his feet, until Shiloh come; and unto him shall the gathering of the people be" (Gen. 49:10). This was a seed law. It was also a land law: the preservation of the judicial authority of the tribes in a decentralized holy commonwealth. This judicial commonwealth ceased in the realm of civil government with the exile. So did the land laws in their original form.

---

4. Gary North, *Leviticus: An Economic Commentary* (Tyler, Texas: Institute for Christian Economics, 1994), pp. 6, 180, 256, 324, 455, 629, 631–32, 643–45.

5. North, *Tools of Dominion*, ch. 1.

CONCLUSION

Harden not your heart, as in the provocation, and as in the day of temptation in the wilderness: When your fathers tempted me, proved me, and saw my work. Forty years long was I grieved with this generation, and said, It is a people that do err in their heart, and they have not known my ways: Unto whom I sware in my wrath that they should not enter into my rest (Ps. 95:8–11).

The Book of Numbers is the Pentateuch's book of sanctions: the fourth book in the Pentateuch. Oath/sanctions is point four of the five-point biblical covenant model.[1] The Book of Numbers is an integral part of the five books of Moses. Its theme – sanctions – is integral to the five-point biblical covenant model.

The book begins with the mustering of the holy army of God. This was the second mustering. The first had taken place about seven months earlier (Ex. 38:26). The third and final mustering took place just before the conquest of Canaan (Num. 26). A numbering required the payment of atonement money for the blood to be shed in the subsequent battles of the army (Ex. 30:12, 15).[2]

---

1. Ray R. Sutton, *That You May Prosper: Dominion By Covenant* (2nd ed.; Tyler, Texas: Institute for Christian Economics, 1992), ch. 4.

2. Gary North, *Tools of Dominion: The Case Laws of Exodus* (Tyler, Texas: Institute for Christian Economics, 1990), ch. 32.

The Slave's Mentality

The Israelites had spent their lives as slaves. Through their leaders, they had resisted Moses and Aaron after the two had confronted Pharaoh (Ex. 5:20–21). In refusing to heed this request by Israel's elders, Moses and Aaron replaced them as national leaders by the time of the exodus. Each of God's ten negative sanctions against the Egyptians followed a confrontation between Moses and Pharaoh. These sanctions publicly ratified God's sovereignty over Pharaoh.[3] They also ratified the transfer of civil and ecclesiastical authority from the existing rulers of Israel to Moses and Aaron. The exodus, which culminated in Israel's crossing of the Red Sea (positive sanction) and the drowning of Pharaoh and his charioteers (negative sanction), was the final ratification of this transfer of authority. But as the Book of Numbers reveals, these foundational sanctions in the history of Israel did not completely persuade the ex-slaves. They repeatedly lost faith in Moses' leadership, which meant that they repeatedly lost faith in the God whom Moses represented, and who consistently brought visible sanctions in response to Moses' words. Moses' ability to forecast God's immediate sanctions identified him as a prophet, yet the people resisted Moses' words and God's ratification of them. In this sense, they were like their former master, Pharaoh. They would promise to obey, but then they refused.

Slaves depend on masters. The master first makes plans; he then works to carry them out. He gathers resources, which includes slaves. He owns both the raw materials and the slaves. The model for the office of master is God the Creator, who created raw materials and then created Adam. God owned all of these resources because He created them. He delegated responsibility to Adam to administer His resources in terms of a goal: Adam's judicially representative dominion over the earth (Gen.

---

3. Gary North, *Moses and Pharaoh: Dominion Religion vs. Power Religion* (Tyler, Texas: Institute for Christian Economics, 1985).

1:26–28). To one degree or other, the master delegates responsibility to his slaves; if he did not, he would have to do the work himself. Of what economic use would such unemployed slaves be? They would be little more than adornments for the master: consumer goods.

Representation

A good slave must learn to think his master's thoughts representatively. He should think to himself, "How would my master want me to do this?" This is why Christ warned: "No servant can serve two masters: for either he will hate the one, and love the other; or else he will hold to the one, and despise the other. Ye cannot serve God and mammon" (Luke 16:13). A good slave will not do things the way his evil master would. He therefore becomes unfaithful to his master, even if his acts increase his master's wealth. He becomes a representative of another, higher master, the heavenly master who lays down the law in history and enforces it in history. This is why bad masters lose control over good slaves in history. The good master eventually delivers good slaves from their intermediary bad masters. He does this in history. The nineteenth century is proof.

The Israelites had lived in Egypt under two masters: God and the supposedly divine Pharaoh. As time went on, and as deliverance seemed to be delayed, they took on the moral characteristics of their earthly master, Pharaoh. We see this in the first confrontation between Moses and Pharaoh: Moses' slaying of the cruel taskmaster. The Israelites were envious of him. They preferred to see him torn down from his position of authority rather than have him rule over them. "And when he went out the second day, behold, two men of the Hebrews strove together: and he said to him that did the wrong, Wherefore smitest thou thy fellow? And he said, Who made thee a prince and a judge over us? intendest thou to kill me, as thou killedst the Egyptian? And Moses feared, and said, Surely this thing is known" (Ex. 2:13–14). That phrase, "Who made thee a prince and a judge over us?" was to become the constant refrain of the Israelites in the wilderness. The answer was obvious: God had. In rejecting the leadership of Moses, they were rejecting the authority of God. This was God's testimony to Samuel half a millennium later: "And the LORD said unto Samuel, Hearken unto the voice of the people in all that they say unto thee: for they have not rejected thee, but they have rejected me, that I should not reign over them. According to all the works which they have done since the day that I brought them up out of Egypt even unto this day, wherewith they have forsaken me, and served other gods, so do they also unto thee" (I Sam. 8:7–8). They wanted a leader like the other nations had, which meant that they wanted gods like the other nations had. They preferred Pharaoh to Moses. They preferred the golden calf to God.

Time Preference

The Israelites were marked by impatience. In their years in Egypt, they had grown impatient with God. They looked to Pharaoh as the ultimate sanctions-bringer in history. Yet God operated on a very strict timetable. "And it came to pass at the end of the four hundred and thirty years, even the selfsame day it came to pass, that all the hosts of the LORD went out from the land of Egypt" (Ex. 12:41).[4] This impatience is a familiar theme in the Book of Numbers. The golden calf incident was typical of Israel's entire wilderness experience: with Moses absent, the people played with idols.

This short time frame is common to lower-class people, who are present-oriented.[5] They are slaves to the present. The Bi-

4. The actual time they spent inside Egypt's national borders was 215 years; the time they spent under Egypt's kingdom authority, which extended to Canaan, was 430 years. See North, *Moses and Pharaoh*, pp. 14–17.

5. Edward C. Banfield, *The Unheavenly City: The Nature and Future of Our Urban Crisis* (Boston: Little, Brown, 1970), pp. 47–48, 53–54.

ble says that we must be slaves to the future.[6] God rules the future as absolutely as He rules the present and the past. An important mark of His people's faithfulness is their confidence in the future, for it is governed by God's eternal decree. This is seen through faith, since we cannot see the future. But God's reliability has been revealed in the Bible through the prophets' accurate predictions of future events.[7] The mark of the true prophet was two-fold: accurate predictions regarding the future (Deut. 18:22) and faithful theological testimony regarding the one true God (Deut. 13:1–5).

A person who is future-oriented is upper class, no matter what his present income is. His thinking is characterized by long-range planning, thrift, and a willingness to defer gratification. Mises calls this phenomenon low time-preference. The future-oriented person is willing to lend at comparatively low rates of interest. He is unwilling to borrow at high rates of interest in order to fund present consumption.[8]

The generation of the exodus could not plan for the future successfully. They were trapped by their own present-orientation. They could not see beyond the present. They were therefore blind to the reality of the past. They kept crying out to Moses to take them back to Egypt. They remembered the past in terms of the low-risk immobility of slavery. The past deliverances of God did not persuade them to accept His promise of future protection because they had no confidence in history.

---

6. North, *Moses and Pharaoh*, pp. 259–60.

7. This is why higher critics of the Old Testament invariably conclude that prophetic passages that demonstrably came true, most notably those in Daniel forecasting three future empires, were written after the fact. The suggestion that some men can know the future in detail is an implicit affirmation of teleology: a future that is fixed, i.e., not open-ended in terms of the present. It affirms predestination. Only man is allowed by humanists to seek to predestine the future, and even he is not acknowledged as being capable of achieving this goal.

8. On time-preference and the rate of interest, see Ludwig von Mises, *Human Action: A Treatise on Economics* (New Haven, Connecticut: Yale University Press, 1949), ch. 19.

They did not believe that the events of the exodus testified to the reliability of God's covenant with them. They did not believe Moses when he prophesied the positive sanction of future victory. They demanded constant reassurance. "What have you done for us lately?" was their constant rhetorical question to Moses, and therefore to God.

In this sense, they were radical empiricists: spiritual forefathers of David Hume and modern existentialists. For the radical empiricist, there is no continuity of law in history. Patterns of cause and effect that individuals believe they have observed in the past do not prove the continuing existence of the same fixed patterns in their observations, let alone in the world beyond their observations, whether in the present or the future. The fact that a radical empiricist remembers that when he stuck his finger into boiling water, it hurt, does not prove to him that it will hurt the next time he does this. The mother's warning to her small child who is about to touch a hot stove – "Hot! Hot!" – may persuade the small child not to touch it after a few painful experiences, or even after one, but this does not persuade the radical empiricist to change his theory of causation and perception.[9] The small child possesses greater epistemological clarity and more common sense than the radical empiricist. Similarly, the children of the exodus generation had more sense than their parents. They, unlike their parents, learned from experience.

Sanctions and Inheritance

The Israelites departed from Egypt bearing spoils. The sons of Israel survived the corporate negative sanction of the death of the firstborn. All of Egypt's firstborn sons perished on the

9. I think this has something to do with Jesus' warning about hell: "Hot! Hot!" Rebellious children do not listen. They prefer to remain radical empiricists rather than become Christians. "Show me!" they cry. Jesus rose from the dead to ratify the reliability of His warning. The radical empiricist then cries: "Show me again!" He refuses to accept God's testimony (Luke 16:30–31).

night of the Passover. Their inheritance went to the departing Israelites. The positive sanction of inheritance was based on the negative sanction of disinheritance. There was a biblical principle at work here: "A good man leaveth an inheritance to his children's children: and the wealth of the sinner is laid up for the just" (Prov. 13:22). The Book of Proverbs extends this principle: "The curse of the LORD is in the house of the wicked: but he blesseth the habitation of the just" (3:33). "The memory of the just is blessed: but the name of the wicked shall rot" (10:7).

The status of the Levites as the tribe in charge of the sacrifices also reveals this relationship between sanctions and inheritance. The sacrificial system was a system of negative sanctions applied to judicial representatives (animals) by judicial representatives (priests). The priesthood represented the firstborn sons of Israel. They had achieved this lofty status because they had shed the blood of 3,000 Israelites after the golden calf incident.[10] But the status of the firstborn was ultimately not lofty, for the firstborn son was under a curse: a representative of Adam, God's firstborn. Only because God accepted an animal substitute did the firstborn sons of Israel survive Passover night. Had there not been a sacrifice, the firstborn sons of Israel would have perished as surely as the firstborn sons of Egypt did. Because the Passover lambs were disinherited, the firstborn sons of Israel inherited. Because the 3,000 sons of Israel were disinherited by the Levites, the Levites inherited the unique judicial status of the nation's priestly tribe. But this judicial status involved great risk: life lived within the sacred boundaries of the tabernacle-temple. Violations of sacred space and sacred ritual could bring death (Lev. 10:1–2). The inheritance of Eleazar and Ithamar was based on the disinheritance of Nadab and Abihu (v. 6).

---

10. See Chapter 4.

Canaan was supposed to be disinherited by Israel. This disinheritance would be the basis of Israel's inheritance. This transfer of wealth was based on ethics, not power. God had told Abraham: "But in the fourth generation they shall come hither again: for the iniquity of the Amorites is not yet full" (Gen. 15:16). Corporate, national iniquity was the covenantal basis of the disinheritance of the Amorites. The progressive rebellion of the Amorites was cumulative. It moved toward eschatological fulfillment.

Sanctions and Eschatology

Israel had been given an eschatology: guaranteed inheritance through military conquest. The exodus generation had not believed this eschatology. Or, more to the point, that generation refused to believe that the eschatological fulfillment of the promise of a land flowing with milk and honey was in any way associated with Israel's prophetic role as a sanctions-bringer in Canaan. Israel rejected the specified terms of the inheritance: military conquest. So, the next generation would inherit. This meant that each of Israel's holy warriors would have to accept both the obligation and threat of personal military sanctions in battle. Israel's national inheritance was tied to the presence of these sanctions.

This leads us to a theological conclusion. Point four of the biblical covenant model is sanctions. It is as tied judicially to point five, inheritance, as it is to point three: law. God imposes historical sanctions, positive and negative, in terms of His covenant law. These sanctions result in inheritance by His covenant people and the disinheritance of covenant-breakers. This is why theonomy is inescapably and indissolubly tied to eschatology. Theonomy is inherently postmillennial because theonomy is biblical law, and biblical law is indissolubly linked to God's covenant sanctions in history. Law without sanctions is mere opinion. Theonomy without predictable historical sanctions is mere opinion – one not widely shared. Theonomy without postmillennialism is God's law without predictable sanctions – sanctions that lead to the victory of God's kingdom, in time and on earth.

The New Covenant has not annulled the covenantal structure of inheritance. On the contrary, the New Covenant reaffirms it. "Blessed are the meek: for they shall inherit the earth" (Matt. 5:5). The New Covenant was marked by a transfer of inheritance from Israel to the church. "Therefore say I unto you, The kingdom of God shall be taken from you, and given to a nation bringing forth the fruits thereof" (Matt. 21:43). This transfer was visibly imposed by God through Rome's destruction of the temple in A.D. 70.[11]

Like the generation of the exodus, the vast majority of today's Christians steadfastly maintain that the covenantal structure of inheritance no longer applies in history. Amillennialism and premillennialism march arm in arm on this point. Amillennialists insist that God will progressively impose corporate negative sanctions against the church. Christendom as a civilization will be suppressed, if it has not already been consigned by God to the ash can of history. Not only that, antinomian amillennialists insist, the very idea of Christendom is a perverse legacy of Old Covenant Israel. They dismiss the ideal of Christendom as "Constantinian."

Meanwhile, premillennialists are divided. Historic premillennialists, whose ranks are thin, agree with the amillennialists: until Christ returns to set up His earthly kingdom, things will get worse for God's people. The dispensationalists insist that things would get worse were it not for the rapture. The church will be delivered out of history. Both of these eschatologies agree: the covenantal structure of history has been reversed by God. Covenant-keepers will be progressively disinherited, which covenant-breakers will inherit the earth. Only the cessation of

11. David Chilton, *The Days of Vengeance: An Exposition of the Book of Revelation* (Ft. Worth, Texas: Dominion Press, 1987).

history – by either the final judgment or the rapture – can bring back the covenantal structure of history as it existed under the Old Covenant.

The New Covenant is, to this extent, a burden of cosmic proportions for God's people compared to the Old Covenant. The death, resurrection, and ascension of Jesus Christ in history brought a harsh legacy into history, we are assured by pessimillennialists: the reversal of the covenant's basis of inheritance. Their eschatologies are consistent with their view of sanctions, i.e., that covenant-breakers will progressively impose historical sanctions on covenant-keepers. Pessimillennialists have a consistent theology of historical sanctions and inheritance: covenant-breakers will inevitably inherit in history because God has predestinated them to impose historical sanctions on the church. This was the operational eschatology of all those who sought to stone Caleb and Joshua.

The suggestion that all three eschatological views can coexist indefinitely inside the same ecclesiastical organization is necessarily a suggestion that neither covenant theology nor eschatology matters decisively in the life of the church. Both doctrines are to this extent *adiaphora*: things indifferent to the Christian faith. Ultimately, this suggestion of eschatological pluralism is highly partisan. It favors the worldview and anti-Christendom agendas of both amillennialism and premillennialism, for these outlooks are united in their opposition to the covenantal structure of inheritance and disinheritance in the New Testament era. In the name of eschatological neutrality, amillennialists and premillennialists come to postmillennialists and ask them to agree that covenantal postmillennialism's view of the past and the future is, historically speaking, a moot point. Moot points are mute points. This is an ancient lure: the myth of neutrality. It is offered in the name of peace and growth. It is the myth that undergirds all forms of confessional pluralism.

This is why a consistent theonomist must reject eschatological pluralism as an ideal for the creeds and confessions of the churches. There is no eschatological neutrality in the Bible. Premillennialism, amillennialism, and postmillennialism cannot all be true. If they are said to be judicially equal, then eschatology is necessarily reduced to the status of *adiaphora*. A church that is not postmillennial is like the generation of the exodus: fearful of judicial and cultural victory, committed to wilderness wandering as a way of cultural life, and hostile to those who, like Caleb and Joshua, predict inevitable victory in history.

To discuss eschatology apart from a consideration of God's law and historical sanctions is to ignore the covenant's structure. The covenant is a unified system. It cannot be broken analytically and still retain its authority. Any consideration of inheritance, either in eternity or in history, has to include the doctrines of sanctions, law, authority, and the sovereignty of God. A discussion of eschatology apart from historical sanctions is as misleading as a discussion of prophecy apart from the sovereignty of God. To say that something must happen in the future while asserting that man is totally free to choose a different future is covenantally absurd. It is equally absurd covenantally to discuss eschatology without discussing sanctions: covenantal cause and effect. It is also covenantally absurd to discuss God's historical sanctions without discussing God's law. The covenant is a unit. It cannot be broken.

Postmillennialists can afford to be patient. They understand that the future will bring victory for Christ's church in history. Christendom will be established in history. So, they can afford to do the work of dominion inside the boundaries of eschatologically pluralist churches. They know that when victory becomes visible over time, the defenders of pessimillennialism will face a much smaller audience. Most people prefer success to failure, dominion to martyrdom. They understand and believe the economist's dictum: "It is better to be rich and healthy than it is to be poor and sick (other things being equal)." Pessimillennialism is popular when things are going badly for the church and kingdom. It offers deliverance out of history: rapture or second coming. But when things start going better, and keep going better, Christians will at long last understand that the establishment of the kingdom of God on earth and in history is what is mandated by the Great Commission.[12] Then will be the time to revise the eschatological portions of various ecclesiastical confessions of faith.

Conclusion

The Book of Numbers is the Pentateuch's book of sanctions. It ends with the story of Zelophehad's daughters. The leaders of the tribe of Manasseh wanted to know about a specific application of the jubilee's laws of inheritance. Would a tribe's land pass to another tribe if an inheriting daughter married a man from the other tribe? The answer was *no*. This is a fitting conclusion to the book of sanctions. It leads to the fifth book of the Pentateuch, Deuteronomy: the book of inheritance.

---

12. Kenneth L. Gentry, Jr., *The Greatness of the Great Commission: The Christian Enterprise in a Fallen World* (Tyler, Texas: Institute for Christian Economics, 1990).

Appendix

HOW LARGE WAS ISRAEL'S POPULATION?

So were all those that were numbered of the children of Israel, by the house of their fathers, from twenty years old and upward, all that were able to go forth to war in Israel; Even all they that were numbered were six hundred thousand and three thousand and five hundred and fifty (Num. 1:45–46).

And all the firstborn males by the number of names, from a month old and upward, of those that were numbered of them, were twenty and two thousand two hundred and threescore and thirteen (Num. 3:43).

Commentators have argued for over a century about the size of Israel's population. Liberals and those influenced by them want to downsize it. Conservatives are at a loss explaining how it got as large as the biblical texts say that it did. There are a whole series of problems in assessing the demographics of Mosaic Israel.

Conservative Bible commentator Gordon Wenham provides several arguments as to why the texts' population figures are wrong – perhaps by as much as a factor of 100 to one. His arguments reveal the extent to which modern evangelical Bible commentators have mimicked higher critics in their ready acceptance of the hypothesis of extensive textual corruption.

Jacob Milgrom's solution is even worse. He suggests that the original author of Numbers lied: ". . . the tendency of ancient epics to inflate numbers is well attested."[1] Despite the fact that multiple texts assert the same demographic picture, thereby reinforcing each other, commentators are ready to substitute their own speculations when these texts do not describe events that conform to present-day scientific or historical theories. This raises the issue of biblical interpretation.

Liberals and the Bible

There are many examples of this methodology in the literature of academic biblical studies. A common example is this one: higher critics of the Bible have sought to re-define the Red Sea. It has become in retrospect the Sea of Reeds, through which the Israelites safely walked across dry land (Ex. 14:21).[2] Just imagine: people actually walked across relatively dried-up marshes! The very thought of this stupendous event paralyzed the Canaanites with fear: "For we have heard how the LORD dried up the water of the Red [Reed] sea for you" (Josh. 2:10a). This escape across the marshes was followed by an unprecedented miracle: Pharaoh's army, hot in pursuit, drowned in this sea of reeds. (The word for "reed" can also be translated "papyrus." Perhaps the Israelites used the reeds to create papyrus to create environmental impact statement forms, and drowned the Egyptians in them. Just a suggestion.) All that is missing from this Red Sea revision is a comparable creek to substitute for the Jordan River: "For the LORD your God dried up the waters of Jordan from before you, until ye were passed

---

1. Jacob Milgrom, *The JPS Torah Commentary: Numbers* (New York: Jewish Publication Society, 1990), p. 339.

2. James King West, *Introduction to the Old Testament: "Hear, O Israel"* (New York: Macmillan, 1971), p. 133. The word "red" (*supf*) can be translated reed or weed, as in: "The waters compassed me about, even to the soul: the depth closed me round about, the weeds were wrapped about my head" (Jonah 2:5). The presence of weeds did not mandate the presence of marshes.

over, as the LORD your God did to the Red sea, which he dried up from before us, until we were gone over" (Josh. 4:23). Perhaps the Jordan was running seasonally low at the time of Israel's crossing.

Another miracle was the manna, which has retroactively become insect dung. And what a miracle it was! Two different species of insects provided it: same color, same texture, same naturally sweet, honey-like flavor – "No preservatives added!" (Ex. 16:31). One insect species was located in the mountains, the other in the lowlands.[3] But the miracle had only just begun: both varieties of insects excreted double loads on the day before the sabbath but nothing on the sabbath (Ex. 16:22, 26–27) – truly strict sabbatarian insects! So, the Israelites feasted on insect dung daily for 39 years. Yet they were also required by God to break a jar if a dead insect was found inside it (Lev. 11:32–33). We might ask rhetorically: Who are we, or who was Moses, or who was God, to blame the murmurers for having preferred eating quail to insect dung (Num. 11:6)?

My conclusion: theological liberalism does a strange thing to people. It turns their brains into manna (lowland variety).

"The Numbers in Numbers Don't Add Up!"

Wenham argues that the wilderness could not have supported such a large population, even with manna, i.e., the heavenly kind. After all, "The bedouin population of modern Sinai amounts to only a few thousand; . . ."[4] Noördtzij agrees: Sinai could not have fed all those people; it was a wilderness. But the whole point of the manna was to sustain the Israelites *miraculously* in the wilderness. The manna was a miracle, as was their

3. F. S. Bodenheimer, "The Manna of Sinai," *The Biblical Archeologist Reader*, X (Feb. 1947); reprinted in G. Ernest Wright and David Noel Freedman, editors, *The Biblical Archeologist Reader* (Garden City, New York: Doubleday Anchor, 1961), p. 79.

4. Gordon J. Wenham, *Numbers: An Introduction and Commentary* (Downers Grove, Illinois: Inter-Varsity Press, 1981), p. 61.

clothing that did not wear out. Moses described both of these as related miracles (Deut. 8:3–4).

Furthermore, Wenham says, archeological evidence points to much smaller population centers: a few thousand people per Canaanite city.[5] God said that it would take years for the invading Israelites to overcome the existing population in Canaan (Ex. 23:29). If the Israelite population was large, there could have been only brief resistance by tiny Canaanite villages.[6] This indicates that the number of Israelites was small. Wenham does not mention another possibility, namely, that today's archeological evidence is incomplete and has been misinterpreted by extrapolating from a handful of discoveries. The same criticism can be leveled at modern chronologies of the ancient Near East prior to the eighth century B.C. Archaeologists therefore date the strata incorrectly. Wenham's failure to mention the possibility that modern archeological scholarship has made crucial errors is also representative of the higher critic's mind-set. When the latest scientific evidence, which he can be confident will eventually be superseded and made obsolete, tells him that the Bible's account is false, he accepts the new evidence and rejects the Bible's account.

Wenham cites a 1906 book by Flinders Petrie,[7] an archeologist, who argued that the word translated thousand (*'eleph*) could mean either "thousand" or "family." Recording the population of Reuben, the text says 46,500 men (Num. 1:21). Not so, said Petrie: the tribe of Reuben really consisted of 46 families (*'eleph*) plus 500 men. Wenham cites his own father's study, which allowed 45 Reubenite leaders and 1,500 men.[8] Noordtzij insists that *'eleph* means "clan."[9] Other estimates of Israel's total population range from 140,000 to as few as 20,000. Petrie

---

5. Wenham, *Numbers*, p. 62.
6. *Ibid.*, p. 61.
7. Petrie, *Researches in Sinai* (London: Murray, 1906).
8. Wenham, *Numbers*, p. 63.
9. Noordtzij, *Numbers*, pp. 24–25.

allowed no more than 5,600.[10] He was being generous; G. Ernest Wright allows no more than 5,000; the Israelites may have been as few as 3,000.[11] This is a reduction from about 2.4 million (men, women, and children). The Bible's account, we are informed, may be off by 800 to one. Not too reliable! But this isn't the half of it. Harrison says that one estimate places the number as low as 100 people.[12]

Ashley simply capitulates: "In short, we lack the materials in the text to solve this problem," i.e., the problem of large numbers.[13] He is exaggerating. We have enough materials in the text to begin to solve the problem. We must use these materials to guide us in our search for the answer.

Whose Numbers Should We Accept?

That the number of Israelites was huge can be seen from the despair of Balak the Moabite in seeking an alliance with the Midianites. "And Moab said unto the elders of Midian, Now shall this company[14] lick up all that are round about us, as the ox licketh up the grass of the field. And Balak the son of Zippor was king of the Moabites at that time. He sent messengers therefore unto Balaam the son of Beor to Pethor, which is by the river of the land of the children of his people, to call him, saying, Behold, there is a people come out from Egypt: behold, they cover the face of the earth, and they abide over against me: Come now therefore, I pray thee, curse me this people; for they are too mighty for me: peradventure I shall prevail, that

10. Wenham, *Numbers*, p. 64.

11. G. Ernest Wright, *Biblical Archaeology* (rev. ed.; Philadelphia: Westminster Press, 1962), p. 66.

12. R. K. Harrison, *Numbers: An Exegetical Commentary* (Grand Rapids, Michigan: Baker, 1992), p. 436.

13. Timothy R. Ashley, *The Book of Numbers* (Grand Rapids, Michigan: Eerdmans, 1993), p. 66.

14. "And God Almighty bless thee, and make thee fruitful, and multiply thee, that thou mayest be a **multitude** of people" (Gen. 28:3).

we may smite them, and that I may drive them out of the land: for I wot that he whom thou blessest is blessed, and he whom thou cursest is cursed" (Num. 22:4–6). I find it difficult to believe that fewer than 5,000 people covered the face of the earth. That about 1,000 warriors terrified Balak seems even less probable. Balaam's prayer is even more revealing: "Who can count the dust of Jacob, and the number of the fourth part of Israel? Let me die the death of the righteous, and let my last end be like his!" (Num. 23:10). But the scholars think Balak and Balaam were grossly exaggerating, that they were terrified of a handful of ex-slaves who somehow had recently conquered King Sihon, the city of Jaazer, and King Og (Num. 21:24–35).

We have a tally of the booty taken from Midian by 12,000 Israelite warriors in the period immediately prior to the invasion of Canaan:

> And the booty, being the rest of the prey which the men of war had caught, was six hundred thousand and seventy thousand and five thousand sheep, And threescore and twelve thousand beeves, And threescore and one thousand asses, And thirty and two thousand persons in all, of women that had not known man by lying with him. And the half, which was the portion of them that went out to war, was in number three hundred thousand and seven and thirty thousand and five hundred sheep: And the LORD'S tribute of the sheep was six hundred and threescore and fifteen. And the beeves were thirty and six thousand; of which the LORD'S tribute was threescore and twelve. And the asses were thirty thousand and five hundred; of which the LORD'S tribute was threescore and one. And the persons were sixteen thousand; of which the LORD'S tribute was thirty and two persons (Num. 31:32–40).

The Bible testifies clearly to the size of at least one city-state in the wilderness. Thirty-two thousand young women and girls were taken captive. This was no village. This was a separate culture that possessed a great deal of wealth.

The degree of honesty of Petrie's argument is more readily assessed when we read the account in Numbers of the size of the families of Levi: Gershon, seven *'eleph*, five hundred (Num. 3:22); Kohath, eight *'eleph*, six hundred (v. 28); Merari, six *'eleph*, two hundred (v. 34). Total number of Levites if *'eleph* means *thousand*: 22,300. This corresponds closely with the summary total of 22,000: "All that were numbered of the Levites, which Moses and Aaron numbered at the commandment of the LORD, throughout their families, all the males from a month old and upward, were twenty and two thousand [*'eleph*]" (Num. 3:39).[15]

Petrie knew he had a problem.[16] In Numbers 3, there can be no confusion over the meaning of *'eleph*. Levi had three family groups; each family had a specific number of males above one month old. This number corresponded closely to the number of Israel's firstborn: "And all the firstborn males by the number of names, from a month old and upward, of those that were numbered of them, were twenty and two thousand [*'eleph*] two hundred and threescore and thirteen" (Num. 3:43). So, the number of Levite males in Numbers 3 – judicial surrogates for Israel's firstborn (Num. 3:12–13) – matched almost perfectly the number of Israel's firstborn males, counted in thousands. We cannot escape the grammar of the numerical account in Numbers 3.

But Petrie sought to evade the plain language of the texts. He argued that the Levites' numbers in Numbers 3 were inserted into the text in a later period. What later period in Israel's history would have imagined that there were 22,000 Levites? Only a period in which there were a lot of Levites. Where did all these Levites come from? If there were only 5,600 adult male Israelites at the time of the numbering, how many adult

---

15. Here there could have been an error in copying: the Hebrew word for 6 – the Kohathites' 8,600 – is similar to the word for 3. If the figure was 8,300, the total was 22,000. Wenham, *Numbers*, p. 71.

16. *Ibid.*, p. 63.

male Levites were there? Four hundred, perhaps? How, and how fast, did this Levite population grow from 400 to so many that 22,000 seemed reasonable to the forger (sorry: "redactor")? Was the redactor so confused that he inserted numbers for the tribe of Levi that totaled four times larger than the number of all the other 12 tribes combined (using Petrie's estimate of 5,600)? Translating *'eleph* in Numbers 1 as "family" rather than "thousand" leads to a dead end. It was an obvious dead end on the day it was proposed in 1906.

Counting the firstborn was required because there had to be a substitute for them: the Levites. The Levites as a tribe would substitute for the firstborn on a one-to-one basis. If there were more firstborn sons than Levite males, someone would have to pay the Levites five shekels per extra firstborn. The Bible does not say who would have to pay. The allocational question was this: Which families had born the "excess" 273 children? If all of the families were counted, and the comparison was made, on what basis would a particular tribe or family be assessed the five shekels? Would it be those families whose firstborn were born later than the others, i.e., families of those firstborn who constituted the excess? This would seem to be fair, but we are not told.

The ratio of firstborn sons to adult males constitutes a long-recognized problem. There were 603,550 adult males (Num. 1:46). There were 22,273 firstborn (Num. 3:43). Wenham writes: "This means that out of 27 men in Israel only 1 was the first-born son in his family. In other words, an average family consisted of 27 sons, and presumably an equal number of daughters."[17] Milgrom also cites this ratio.[18] The firstborn were not adults – age one month and older. The ratio is clearly impossible demographically. Because this dilemma is based on biblical texts, it requires a solution consistent with the texts.

17. Wenham, *Numbers*, p. 61.

18. Milgrom, *Numbers*, p. 339.

Wenham sees none. I see three possible explanations. But before considering them, we must understand the demographics of Israel in Egypt.

Population Growth: Jacob to Moses

There were only four generations from the generation born after the descent into Egypt until the conquest (Gen. 15:16). The time Israel spent in Egypt was 215 years. I discussed in *Moses and Pharaoh* why the 215-year figure is correct, and why the 430 years included the time that Abraham and Isaac spent in Canaan, which was formally under Egyptian sovereignty.[19] Paul was clear on this point: it was 430 years from the promise given to Abraham until the giving of the law to Moses at Mt. Sinai. "And this I say, that the covenant, that was confirmed before of God in Christ, the law, which was four hundred and thirty years after, cannot disannul, that it should make the promise of none effect" (Gal. 3:17). We also know that this stay in Egypt took four generations: the text regarding Jochebed (Num. 26:59).

If a woman bore a child every two years, and if she lived to 120 years old, and if her menopause came at, say, age 80 (Sarah was beyond menopause at age 90), then theoretically she could have borne 30 children in a 60-year reproductive period: age 20 to 80. (A figure of 54 children per family was impossible. This would have required almost one child per year from every woman for her six decades of fertility.)

Let us assume that each of the 70 wives produced 30 children, and all of her children survived, married, and repeated the process. Half of these children would have been sons. The average number of children in Jochebed's generation would

19. On 215 years rather than 430, see North, Gary North, *Moses and Pharaoh: Dominion Religion vs. Power Religion* (Tyler, Texas: Institute for Christian Economics, 1985), pp. 14–17. Cf. Josephus, *Antiquities of the Jews*, Book II, Chapter XV, Section 2, in *Josephus: Complete Works*, William Whiston, trans. (Grand Rapids, Michigan: Kregel, 1960), p. 62.

have been 30 X 70 = 2,100. Of these, 1,050 were sons. Repeating this performance, Moses' generation would have totaled 15,750 men (15 X 1,050). Assuming no retarding effects demographically from the persecution of the Pharaoh, Moses' generation would have produced 236,250 sons (15 X 15,750). If all of Moses' generation had been alive at the time of the first numbering, and all of Joshua's generation, the total would have been 252,000 men. But there were over 600,000 men. Even with the preposterous assumption of 30 children per family, the numbers do not add up.

Relating to the second mustering in the Book of Numbers, we read: "And the name of Amram's wife was Jochebed, the daughter of Levi, whom her mother bare to Levi in Egypt: and she bare unto Amram Aaron and Moses, and Miriam their sister" (Num. 26:59). It appears that Israelite mothers had far fewer than 30 children unless Jochebed missed the mark by a factor of ten to one. Israel's descent into Egypt took place when Jacob was an old man: age 130 (Gen. 47:9). Jochebed's birth occurred after Levi had come down with his father into Egypt. There were no other intervening generations. Moses' generation was the second after the descent. This left only two until the conquest of Canaan (Gen. 15:16).[20]

Adopted Household Servants

Seventy male family members arrived in Egypt: "All the souls that came with Jacob into Egypt, which came out of his loins, besides Jacob's sons' wives, all the souls were threescore and six; And the sons of Joseph, which were born him in Egypt, were two souls: all the souls of the house of Jacob, which came into Egypt, were threescore and ten" (Gen. 46:26–27). Jacob plus

---

20. The children of Joshua's generation did have children, and presumably some of them were over age 20 at the second Numbers mustering. But the leaders were the sons of Joshua's generation, and so are regarded as heirs of God's promise to Abram.

the 66 sons and grandsons plus Joseph plus his two sons equalled 70. They could have brought several thousand servants into Egypt with them: *servants adopted into their families.* Recall that Abraham had 318 household servants (Gen. 14:14).

Only by adopting their servants or other residents of Egypt could the Israelites have reached large numbers by the time of the exodus. If there were 1,500 men who came down with Levi's generation, and each had seven sons, in Jochebed's generation there were 10,500; Moses' generation had 73,500; Joshua's had 514,500. Together, this totalled 588,000 men, which was close to 600,000. So, this would have been biologically possible, but highly unlikely: 14 children per family, all of whom survived and repeated the process.

Then there is the problem of the effect of high birth rates. If Joshua's generation continued to reproduce at these rates, the 600,000 men would have had something like six million children at the exodus, at least 90 percent of whom died in the wilderness. An even higher percentage of them died if any of them had children, since the nation was in zero growth mode in the wilderness. Covenantally, this is an unacceptable scenario: God's judgment against the fourth generation rather than the third. To avoid it, we must conclude that the overwhelming majority of Joshua's generation had two children: replacement rate. From 14 children per family to two children in a single generation: this is simply unheard of in history. Living in slavery did not stop Aaron from having four sons. So, this 14-children-per-family scenario is totally implausible.

It takes such a series of demographic assumptions that are not directly revealed in the texts to solve the problem of the 600,000 adult males, beginning with the assumption of 1,500 (or more) men who were counted as Israelites. We can play with the numbers by assuming that even more servants came down, or that they had lower reproduction rates, or that more residents of Egypt were adopted in Joseph's era, but this does not avoid the adoption issue. There had to be adoptions at some point: either early in the process or at the very end, and possibly all along the way. The larger the number of adoptees early in the process, the smaller the families could be in order to reach 600,000, assuming that most of these 600,000 were not themselves very late adoptees (post-exodus).

The nation experienced zero population growth in the wilderness. The number of adult males at the beginning was the same as the number of adult males at the end. The nation supposedly grew to a huge size during the years of servitude; then, in freedom, its population growth ended. This is not easy to explain. A fast-growing population is characterized by large numbers of children, not the small families that appeared in the wilderness. A fast-growing population rarely reaches zero growth in one generation unless there is a catastrophe, either biological or political, that produces less-than-replacement-rate births or else wipes out children before they reach maturity. Normally, there is a population "echo" of the children who have already been born, even if these children reproduce only at the replacement rate. So many of them are marrying and having children that the population keeps growing even though this generation is only producing two children (replacement rate) per family. The smaller the families were before the exodus, the less of an echo effect in the wilderness. There was no echo in Israel's wilderness experience. The nation reached population stagnation in one generation. There has to be a reason. The death of the bulk of the fourth generation in the wilderness is not a covenantally likely solution: they were the heirs of God's promise to Abraham. Also unlikely is the possibility that they failed to reproduce at all during the wilderness era. Then what happened? This lengthy chapter is my attempt to suggest a plausible explanation. As far as I am aware, no previous commentator has even raised the question.

I see no exegetical escape from the presupposition of adoption: adoption into the original 70 families of Jacob's era and/or after they settled in Egypt, and (as I shall suggest) again before the numbering mentioned in Exodus 38.[21] Adoption came early because the 70 males who came down to Egypt, including sons and grandsons (Kohath's generation),[22] would not have multiplied fast enough to have constituted a numerical challenge to Pharaoh: "And the children of Israel were fruitful, and increased abundantly, and multiplied, and waxed exceeding mighty; and the land was filled with them. . . . And he said unto his people, Behold, the people of the children of Israel are more and mightier than we" (Ex. 1:7, 9). There had to be adoptions by Jacob and his sons in order for the population to have multiplied this much by the time of Moses' infancy. The base of 70 families was not large enough to have provided such a threat in a single generation.

What Seems Reasonable?

Moses had a brother and a sister (Num. 26:59). Was his family abnormally small? Small, but not abnormally small. Aaron had four sons (Num. 26:60). He may have had daughters, but the text does not say so. There were few families with 16 children. This means that there must have been many families for the population to have reached 600,000 men, unless there was a last-minute mass adoption of gentiles just prior to the Exodus mustering. These families must have been the families of the adoptees in Egypt.

The case for adoption is exegetically inescapable. The texts demand it. The only question is: When did the bulk of these adoptions take place? We know that Israel's population was large and growing in the days of Moses' infancy. This indicates

---

21. If someone were to ask me if I think I have ever made an exegetical breakthrough of real significance, one never before suggested by any commentator, this would be my choice. See *Moses and Pharaoh*, ch. 1.

22. Kohath and Jochebed were brother and sister (Num. 26:59). She married her nephew Amram (Ex. 6:20). Presumably, she was born much later than Kohath: the Numbers text says she was born in Egypt. Her birth in Egypt established her as part of the first of the four generations prophesied in Genesis 15:16.

that a significant number of adoptions had already taken place, either before they came down into Egypt or shortly thereafter in the days of Joseph's rulership. There was insufficient time for biological reproduction to have produced such a military threat from the loins of 69 men (Jacob was beyond fatherhood).

The problem is this: Did the adoptees of the early years reach 600,000 adult men at the time of the exodus? We can only speculate; the texts do not tell us authoritatively.

The Meaning of *Firstborn* at Passover

Because of the problem of the 27-to-one ratio, Bible-believing commentators who understand the nature of the demographic problem have frequently dealt with it by altering the definition of *firstborn* in Numbers 3. They employ a different definition for the Passover. We shall see why this is the case in the sections on the proposed solutions.

Numbers 3:40 reads: "And the LORD said unto Moses, Number all the firstborn of the males of the children of Israel from a month old and upward, and take the number of their names." This is the same language that is used in the previous verse: "All that were numbered of the Levites, which Moses and Aaron numbered at the commandment of the LORD, throughout their families, all the males from a month old and upward, were twenty and two thousand." *All* of the male Levites were numbered. The parallel language for the firstborn seems to exclude the possibility that *firstborn* was limited to those sons under age 20.[23] But is this conclusion correct?

On the other hand, is it possible that *firstborn* only referred to males under age 20? Consider the survival of the Egyptian army. The death of the firstborn in Egypt did not seem to afflict adults. "And it came to pass, that at midnight the LORD smote all the firstborn in the land of Egypt, from the firstborn

---

23. Or under age five, if James Jordan is correct. See below: "First Proposed Solution: Firstborn as Young Minors."

of Pharaoh that sat on his throne unto the firstborn of the captive that was in the dungeon; and all the firstborn of cattle. And Pharaoh rose up in the night, he, and all his servants, and all the Egyptians; and there was a great cry in Egypt; for there was not a house where there was not one dead" (Ex. 12:29–30).

Pharaoh survived; so did the captive in prison. The phrase, "the captive," is a representative term: a head of household. So, the adult head of household survived *if he had a firstborn son living at home*. Egypt's firstborn male offspring, at least minors living at home, did not survive. All of Pharaoh's servants arose. All of the Egyptians arose. What can this mean? It means that the adults under Pharaoh's command survived, but their firstborn sons did not. One male was dead in a family, but not two, i.e., both father (if he was a firstborn son) and son.

Pharaoh still commanded an army. Were the survivors all younger sons? This seems unreasonable. The whole command structure would have been destroyed if firstborn officers all died. Furthermore, unless Pharaoh was a second-born son whose older brother had died, he would have perished if death had taken every firstborn son irrespective of his age or his status as household head. If this was true in Egypt, then it may have been true – probably was true – of Israel. After all, the threat of death had been given to both the Egyptians and Israelites. Only the Passover lambs saved Israel from the same negative sanction that afflicted Egypt.

If the sanction of death struck every firstborn son in Egypt, fathers and sons, which I think is unlikely, then the Pharaoh of the Passover was either a second-born son (his older brother had previously died without leaving a son to inherit the throne) or else he was replaced by his younger brother after the Passover, who then pursued Israel. Moses must have been dealing with a Pharaoh who was a surviving brother if *firstborn* for Egyptians meant all firstborn adult males. On the other hand, if *firstborn* meant the *firstborn dwelling in a household*, then Pharaoh could have been biologically a firstborn. His resident son died in his place.

Some Egyptian households would have seen their firstborn sons depart years before. Yet every household had a death. If my view is correct, then those firstborn fathers whose firstborn sons had left home came under the sanction of death. I conclude this because: 1) every household had a death; 2) there were still many adult males left alive in Egypt. This indicates that not every firstborn son died. Those who still lived in their fathers' households did die. For a firstborn son who had left home, and who had a son of his own who died, there also was a death back home: the firstborn head the household, i.e., his firstborn father. There was a death in every household.[24] Only two things could save a firstborn father: the death of his resident firstborn son or the death of a lamb.

Was the threat against Israel the same? Was every male at risk, or were only their sons at risk? The text seems to indicate that the same threat applied to the Israelites that applied to the Egyptians. I conclude that the definition of the term *firstborn* applied equally to both nations: the firstborn son in a household.

We now return to the problem of the 27-to-one ratio between adult males and firstborn sons.

First Proposed Solution: Firstborn as Young Minors

James Jordan asks us to assume that firstborn sons were young minors in a household, i.e., that only minors under the age of five were counted as firstborn sons.[25] Why should we assume this? Why should we assume that they could have had

---

24. No younger brothers headed households in which their firstborn sons had departed. If every household was headed by a firstborn son, then Egypt was in replacement-rate mode: zero population growth.

25. James Jordan: "Who Were the Firstborn Sons?" *Biblical Horizons*, No. 73 (May 1995), p. 4.

older brothers? Textually, the one reason is the size of money payment required by God. The payment to the Levites was five sanctuary shekels per firstborn (Num. 3:47). This was also the size of the payment to the Levites which was required for buying entry through adoption into the family of Levi of a male child, age one month to five years (Lev. 27:6).[26] The second reason is practical: to reduce the number of firstborn in Numbers 3 compared to the number at the Passover. If judicially we can reduce this number, then the biological anomaly disappears.

This approach requires a redefinition of *firstborn*. Jordan at first did not think it does. He wrote that "the original Passover was designed to save, directly, the firstborn sons between the ages of one month and five years; indirectly, everyone else." But in speaking to him about this problem, I learned that he now says that the Numbers 3 definition serves to reduce the number of biological firstborn.

There is a problem with this solution: the echo effect. If *firstborn* means any son under age five, irrespective of older brothers, then his older brothers become a covenantal sanctions problem. If he has, say, three older brothers – one in each five-year age bracket – then Joshua's generation had very large families: at least eight children per family. To avoid the conclusion that large numbers of the fourth generation died in the wilderness, we must assume that the 400,000 fathers produced only one son. This means that the typical firstborn son was also the last-born son. If the 22,273 firstborn sons had older brothers who had been counted at the Passover by means of an earlier definition, then the echo problem appears: 400,000 fathers times eight children, or 3.2 million children. Some 2.8 million died in the wilderness, hopefully before they had their own children, most of whom would also have died.

---

26. Gary North, *Leviticus: An Economic Commentary* (Tyler, Texas: Institute for Christian Economics, 1994), ch. 36.

Joshua's generation was at the end of its peak childbearing years: on average, probably about age 35 or 40. All but two of them were dead 39 years later. If the 22,273 sons had been born over the preceding four years, then the average number of male births was about 5,600 a year. But the replacement rate for 400,000 men was closer to 20,000 a year for two decades. This raises the obvious question: Where did the 600,000 men in Numbers 26 come from? Were most of the other 380,000 sons bunched together demographically from age five up? Were they born over a 16-year period at a rate of 23,000 a year, followed by a sharp drop in the birth rate? (If we were to adopt the definition for *firstborn* as "under age five," applying both to Passover and Numbers 3, then not many firstborn sons were actually at risk at Passover: maybe 25,000 out of 375,000. This may be why Jordan adopts his defiinition only for Numbers 3.) The demographics of this scenario are uncomfortable to a Bible-believing expositor. It may be possible to put all of the seemingly conflicting pieces together, but it is not an easy task.

Jordan's definition of *firstborn* reduces the number of sons in Numbers 3 compared with the Passover. A century ago, C. F. Keil adopted a similar strategy, but with a different way of shrinking the number of numbered firstborn. His solution has the benefit of minimizing the echo problem.

Second Proposed Solution: Births Since Passover

According to this scenario, firstborn sons who were alive at the first Passover had already been atoned for by the blood on the doorposts. Thus, no further payment was necessary. The law governing the money payment to the priests for the first-born was given in the wilderness, after the first Numbers mustering. It did not apply retroactively to those children whose lives had been spared during the Passover, who were not in need of further substitutes; the Passover lambs had served that function. The money payments were due only for those sons who had been born in the wilderness during the 12 months from the Passover in Egypt to a month before the first Numbers mustering.[27] This amounted to 22,273 sons. So, the 27-to-one ratio cannot be taken as applying to all the firstborn in Israel. It applied only to those born in the 12-month interim period.[28]

The demographic question is this: Could 600,000 families have produced 22,273 firstborn sons and approximately the same number of firstborn daughters in 12 months? Conception took place beginning nine months prior to Passover and continuing for another three months. Moses' generation was beyond the normal childbearing years; certainly firstborn children for any of them would have been abnormal. We know that Israel was about to experience a drastic reduction of lifespans, from around age 120 for Moses and Aaron to about 70 to 80 for Joshua's generation (Ps. 90:10). Joshua's generation died of old age in the wilderness; therefore, very few of them were above age 40 at the early musterings.

Let us assume for the sake of argument that there were 400,000 mustered men in Joshua's generation, ages 20 to about 70. Ages 20 to 40 are the prime reproduction years. Could, say, 175,000 families have produced 22,273 firstborn sons? Theoretically, yes, especially if the parents were recently married as a result of the exodus liberation, which perhaps a third of them were. But did this really happen? How many of these 175,000 families had never produced a son? Most of them had, which is why Keil adopted his narrowly circumscribed definition of *firstborn* as a solution to the 27-to-one problem. There is no solid reason to say that his scenario was biologically impossible.

---

27. This eliminated all but the prematurely born sons who were born as a result of the debauchery of the golden calf incident, which took place as Moses was returning from Mt. Sinai. Israel arrived at Sinai in the third month, probably toward the end of the month (if the Jews are correct about dating the arrival at firstfruits/Pentecost). Moses was with God for 40 days. This placed the rebellion at less than nine months prior to the Numbers numbering.

28. C. F. Keil and F. Delitzsch, *Biblical Commentary on the Old Testament* (Grand Rapids, Michigan: Eerdmans, [English translation, 1872–84], n.d.), III, pp. 11–13.

To reproduce themselves, Joshua's generation required 400,000 sons. (Their grandsons could supply the 200,000 replacements for Moses' generation.) The 400,000 sons meant replacement-rate mode: one son per household. So, about 22,000 sons born in one year seems reasonable. If this birth rate had continued for two decades (ages 20 to 40), this would have produced a little over 400,000 sons.

Yet even if all this did happen, it does not solve the more fundamental problem: Where did the 400,000 men of Joshua's generation come from?

In every plausible scenario, the expositor has to rely on the adoption argument to make sense of the numbers. Bible-believing expositors have generally avoided dealing with this demographic problem. Jordan accepts this with respect to the original families, but Keil did not mention it. Biological reproduction rates do not allow the kind of population growth required to get from the 70 males who came down to Egypt in the famine to the 600,000 who were numbered. The texts indicate that Joshua's was the third generation: Kohath, Moses, Joshua. Conclusion: servants must have been adopted into the original families. Israel then spread out through the land of Goshen.

Could Keil's thesis be modified to include prior adoptions? Yes. This would not change his basic point regarding the meaning of *firstborn* in Numbers 3. But to adopt this solution, we must assume a drastic reduction of births, i.e., a drastic reversal of the previous experience of growing families. There was no population echo in the wilderness. This means that Joshua's generation either suffered drastically lower birth rates than their parents or else more of their children died before reaching maturity. A decreased birth rate could have been the effect of the persecution.

The main problem with Keil's thesis is the language that God used to explain His substitution of the Levites for the firstborn: "And I, behold, I have taken the Levites from among the children of Israel instead of all the firstborn that openeth the matrix among the children of Israel: therefore the Levites shall be mine; Because all the firstborn are mine; for on the day that I smote all the firstborn in the land of Egypt I hallowed unto me all the firstborn in Israel, both man and beast: mine shall they be: I am the LORD" (Num. 3:12–13). It sounds as though God was setting apart (hallowing) the Levites because of the previous hallowing of the firstborn. He placed His claim on them. All of this is in the context of the payment of five shekels per firstborn.

The problem with the solutions offered by Jordan and Keil is that they both define *firstborn* in a way that the plain reading of the text seems to deny: *firstborn* as under age five or as a son who was born after Passover. Is there any solution that preserves the normal meaning of the word: a firstborn son of Israel? Yes, but it invokes a scenario that is surely not intuitive, just as the early adoption scenario is not intuitive, though mandatory.

While I devote considerable space to a third scenario, my instincts tell me that Keil's approach creates the fewest problems. But for those who are suspicious about tampering with the plain meaning of words, I offer a thesis that adheres to the definition of *firstborn* as the firstborn son of a household. It also solves the 27-to-one problem and the zero growth problem. It may do this, however, at too high a speculative price. What the reader must understand is that the texts do not offer solutions to these problems in a straightforward manner. You must decide how much "creative explaining" you can tolerate.

Third Proposed Solution: Mass Adoption

If adoption early in Israel's stay in Egypt is the only way to solve the problem of the source of the 600,000, why not follow through on this approach? What about the possibility of later adoptions? What about a mass adoption after the exodus?

I present the following scenario in order to consider the possibility that there is a legitimate alternative to Keil's definition of *firstborn*, which is the heart of his solution to the 27-to-one problem.

Before we study the problem in greater detail, I must present a new definition for Numbers 3: *a firstborn son who was not old enough to be mustered*. He was under age 20. At the Passover, the deciding factor had been the presence of the firstborn son in the household. This changed in Numbers 3. Jordan has one explanation; Keil had another. I tentatively suggest a third: *mustering removed him judicially from his father's household*. With the addition of a new institution, God's holy army, which was assembled through mustering and which required an atonement payment, the definition of a firstborn son changed. Judicially, a soldier in God's holy army was no longer under the same degree of family jurisdiction as he had been prior to his military eligibility. Judicially speaking, he had moved out of his father's household. So, at the time of the Exodus mustering, the criterion of *firstborn* shifted: from a household resident in Egypt to a man under 20 years old.

Recall that I am dealing with three problems: 1) how the 27-to-one ratio could have existed; 2) how a relatively small population of sons became the 600,000 fighting males that invaded Canaan; 3) how Israel grew to 600,000 adult males in three generations: Kohath's (Amram's), Moses', and Joshua's. If *firstborn* means something significantly different in Numbers 3 from what it means in Exodus 12, there ought to be a reason for the change. I think the reason may have been judicial: the presence of the army of the Lord. The following presentation is structured by this definition of *firstborn*. If neither Jordan's nor Keil's definition seems legitimate, then consider the implications of a third.

At the exodus, the Israelites were joined by others who were fleeing the tyranny of Egypt. What if most of them subsequently covenanted with the Israelites? When word spread that the Israelites were about to depart, not to mention the spoils they were carrying with them, others in Egypt saw their opportunity and took it. They had two options: they could go out of Egypt into the wilderness or into Philistia on their own, or they could link up to the nation whose God had just smashed the Egyptian social order. Add to this the miracle of the manna: nearly free food[29] until the conquest (Ex. 16).

A lot of them could have chosen the latter option: to stay with the Israelites. This explains the presence of the mixed multitude with the Israelites (Ex. 12:38). It is possible that some of these people were adopted into the families of Israel as full members. For the sake of argument, let us consider the possibility that the bulk of the mustered Israelites were recent adoptees, and the firstborn sons were biological sons, not adoptees. If true, this would solve the 27-to-one demographic problem.

Biological Sons vs. Adopted Sons

The firstborn sons were biological sons of Israel (Num. 3:12). They were the minor sons of Joshua's generation. Let us assume that this strictly biological definition of *firstborn* governed the mustering process. Those who were subsequently ingrafted into the nation through adoption were not counted as firstborn sons retroactively back to Passover, nor were their children, who had not been born under the covenant. These pre-mustering adoptees added to the number of fighting-age males, but they and their children were not counted as firstborn. *Firstborn* was biological, not judicial: "opens the matrix" (Ex. 13:15).

After the completion of the tabernacle, the Levites were set apart by God as a separate tribal offering in place of biological firstborn sons, as we have seen (Num. 3:12–13). This revelation came after the other tribes were mustered and just before Levi was numbered. This judicial substitution of Levites for firstborn minor sons was a one-time event that took place four months after the mustering in Exodus.

29. There had to be grinding and cooking.

We might assume that the foreign adoptees were grafted into Israel covenantally through circumcision, but this may not have been the case. Those who came out of Egypt were circumcised (Josh. 5:5), but this presumably refers only to Israelites at the time of the crossing of the Red Sea. This great miracle allowed everyone accompanying them to escape, including the mixed multitude. There is no reason to believe that the passage in Joshua refers to the mixed multitude, who would not have been circumcised. This miracle of dry passage must have persuaded the mixed multitude, just as it persuaded the Canaanites, that God was with Israel. At this point – after the Red Sea exodus – some would have asked to be adopted into Israel. Perhaps Israel circumcised these newcomers, but perhaps not. Israel did not circumcise those sons who were born in the wilderness. If adoption did take place without circumcision, a lot more of the mixed multitude males would have consented to be adopted.

Why would Israel have agreed to this mass adoption? Because of their graciousness? Perhaps, but the thought of adding a huge number of potential fighting men to the army would surely have been a major motivation. This decision would soon cost the Israelites a lot of money: the payment of silver at the first mustering and presumably also at the second and third. The adopters had to fund the adoptees' payments. The mixed multitudes had not received the inheritance of the Egyptians.[30] Perhaps they had some silver, but if they were escaping slaves, this is doubtful. The immense number of adoptees in comparison with the number of biological Israelites meant that this adoption into the army of the Lord must have been extremely expensive for each Israelite family. Each family would have had to fund the atonement payment of its adoptees. Expanding the army of the Lord was a costly venture for each

30. See Chapter 4, above: section on "Passover, Sanctions, and Succession," subsection on "Sanctions and Inheritance," pp. 86–88.

original Israelite family. It made economic sense only if they actually planned to invade Canaan. The only way for the economics of adoption to have paid off for the exodus generation was for the nation to have invaded Canaan immediately, thereby receiving its inheritance. The cost of two atonement payments could have been recovered only through military conquest. But after two numberings, the nation suffered a failure of nerve. The inheritance was delayed for another generation.

What if the mixed multitude had been adopted on the day after the death of Egypt's firstborn? They were not part of the original Passover, but perhaps they participated in the spoiling of the Egyptians.[31] This is difficult to imagine: a mass adoption of foreigners followed that very day by a shared inheritance. This would have meant that the adoptees paid their own atonement money, and also that the per capita wealth extracted by the spoiling was vastly smaller. But this does not change the economics of the mustering process. The adoptees were supplied with the atonement money they needed to pay the Levites. Either the Egyptians gave it to them directly or the Israelites did. In either case, the original Israelite families, other than the Levites, wound up with far less wealth than if there had been no adoption.

The mandated payment enforced a huge transfer of wealth from the 12 tribes to the priests and the tabernacle. This also indicates that the Israelites had stripped Egypt of an immense treasure: large enough to fund the payment of three wilderness numberings of mostly adopted foreigners, plus the voluntary offering prior to the building of the tabernacle.

Because of the number of Israelites slain by the Levites after the golden calf incident, I believe that the mass adoption may

31. We say "the Egyptians," but we mean something more circumscribed: those Egyptians living close to the Pharaoh's court. These were the leaders of the nation. It was they who supplied the enormous quantity of gold and silver used later by Israel to build a golden calf, build the tabernacle, and pay for three musterings. To say that these Egyptians had been rich is not putting it strongly enough.

have came after this event. The 3,000 slain men were a significant percentage of the original Israelite population of about 35,000 men.[32] The magnitude of the loss of population was consistent with the magnitude of the crime against God. The loss of one-half of one percent of 600,000 adult males does not seem sufficiently burdensome. But to take this position, I must assume that the mixed multitude had no part in the rebellion, nor would they have participated in the covenant oath at Sinai. This may be too much to assume. If they were adopted earlier, then God was being very lenient with the nation.

In the third numbering (Num. 26), the text is silent with respect to firstborn sons. This is because there was no longer any need to number them as a group. The ratio of biological firstborn sons to the total number of Levite males was established after the initial numbering of the tribes; so, this ratio was no longer judicially relevant except for individual families. From the day of the one-time numbering of the Levites (Num. 3), each non-Levitical family had to pay money to the Aaronic priesthood for each firstborn male under its authority, whether of man or beast (Num. 18:15–16). Numbering the firstborn corporately was no longer necessary.

The Number of Levites

The number of Levites almost perfectly matched the number of biological firstborn minor sons of the other 12 tribes. This was God's doing, not man's. The adoptions took place before Exodus 38:25. Moses did not yet know about the substitution of Levites for firstborn sons. It does not appear that Moses deliberately assigned to Levi a number of adoptees that closely matched the number of firstborn. Presumably, each tribe was assigned a proportional share of new members. As the other tribes' total number of adopted members grew, though not the total number of biologically firstborn sons, the Levites' number

32. See below: "The Number of Levites."

of adopted sons also grew. Moses numbered all of the males of Levi above one month old, not just firstborn sons (Num. 3:39).

Given the mass adoption theory, a relatively small Israelite population existed on Passover night. We know that there were about 22,000 biologically firstborn males one year after the exodus. This was every firstborn male above one month old (Num. 3:40). If the definition of *firstborn* was common to both Israel and Egypt on Passover night, which I think was the case, and only household-resident firstborn Egyptian sons died, which I also think was the case, then the firstborn Israelites were unmarried sons living in their fathers' households. For reasons already offered, I argue that *firstborn* in Numbers meant firstborn males under age 20. I use the 22,000 figure as a marker. There would also have been somewhere in the range of 22,000 firstborn females. But bear in mind that what constituted a firstborn son in Numbers was not exactly the same as at Passover. The definition had changed: males under age 20.

If Israel's population prior to the exodus had been at the replacement rate level, there would have been a one-to-one ratio between firstborn and the total population of each gender: every person a firstborn. This would mean that the number of children of Joshua's generation was about 45,000. There were 45,000 parents and possibly even 45,000 grandparents. Israel's population would have been somewhere in the range of 135,000 people. Again, this assumes zero population growth. But if Aaron's family size was typical – four sons – then there was actually considerable population growth. This means that there were fewer grandparents (Moses' generation) than parents (Joshua's generation).

If Aaron's family and Zelophehad's wilderness family of five daughters (Num. 26:33) were typical, then the Israelites were multiplying above the replacement rate by a factor of two.[33]

33. Zelophehad's family was not typical in the wilderness. It was abnormally large. Replacement-rate demographics were dominant. Perhaps he kept trying for a

We know that the nation had been growing rapidly prior to the Pharaoh of the persecution (Ex. 1:7). Because of the relatively small size of the families in Aaron's day, I believe that the bulk of the adoptions took place prior to the persecution, probably under Jacob. We do not know what happened to the birth rate in Moses' generation, although the examples we have indicate that there may have been growth. If the persecution and slavery that were specifically designed by the Pharaoh to slow the Israelites' rate of growth actually worked, then Moses' generation suffered a reduced rate of increase compared to the previous one. We do not know that this was the case. Aaron had a brother and a sister (Num. 26:59), but he had four sons. There is no way that 70 biological Israelites could have multiplied to 22,000 firstborn sons in three generations without adoptions.

Let us assume that population was doubling every generation. Something in the range of 22,000 firstborn sons were residing in their fathers' households. Let us assume that each of them had a brother, although this is probably too high an estimate for the Passover. Eventually there would have been two brothers per household: doubling. So, there were about 22,000 fathers in Joshua's generation, and 11,000 grandfathers, if all were still alive. So, the adult males of Israel probably totalled fewer than 40,000, perhaps as low as 33,000.

How did this small group reach 600,000 adult males one year after the Passover? The solution has to be mass adoption, sometime after the Passover, or after the exodus, or after the golden calf incident. This influx also provided the males that brought Levi's numbers up to 22,000 males – not firstborn[34] – at the time of the Numbers 3 numbering.

---

son. Perhaps he was an Israelite rather than an adoptee. He may have been operating in terms of an earlier dominion outlook. Or maybe God just blessed him with a lot of children.

34. Because the number of Levite firstborn sons was judicially irrelevant in the substitution process, they were not numbered separately.

The other tribes were mustered first (Num. 1). The Levites were not numbered at this point, by God's command (Num. 1:49). God then announced that the Levites would serve as judicial substitutes for the total number of firstborn males in the other tribes (Num. 3:12–13). As it turned out, the number of biologically firstborn Israelite males was close to the number of Levite males as augmented by the recently adopted recruits. This does not seem to have been the result of planning by the Israelites. This information regarding the substitution had not been known prior to Numbers 3.

Leviticus 27:2–8 referred to an entry price for entering the tribe of Levi. This was a very large amount of money per family, which is why the system served as a barrier to entry.[35] This law was given in Leviticus, which was revealed to Moses after the completion of the tabernacle (Lev. 1:1). But the mass adoption took place prior to the Exodus numbering, i.e., prior to the construction of the tabernacle. The law requiring an entry payment to the Levites had not yet been revealed to Moses. Thus, the other tribes did not have to fund the adoption of thousands of gentiles by the tribe of Levi. The barrier to entry came only after Book of Leviticus was revealed.

If I am incorrect about the Leviticus prices being entry prices into the tribe of Levi, then some other explanation of what those prices were is necessary. I do not see a reasonable alternative. So, I conclude: 1) the bulk of those Israelites who were counted in the Exodus numbering were Israelites by post-Passover adoption; 2) the prices in Leviticus 27:2–8 were priestly adoption prices paid by those who wanted to be adopted into the tribe; 3) the entry fee was not imposed on future adoptees until after the mass adoption had taken place.

After the numbering of the 12 tribes was finished, God told Moses to number the Levites (Num. 3:15). After this counting was completed (v. 34), God ordered a precise counting of the

35. North, *Leviticus*, ch. 36.

firstborn of the other tribes (vv. 44–45). There were an additional 273 biologically firstborn sons in the overall population, for whom ransom money was paid to Aaron (Num. 3:46–51).

Adoption into a Tribe

I am assuming here that adoption was by family or tribe, not by the nation as a whole. Israelites had membership in the congregation through their families, clans, and tribes. Thus, when the mass adoption took place, each family, clan, and tribe received its share of the newcomers. In any case, each tribe did. The newcomers were not citizens in general; they were citizens of tribes. Levi would not have been left out of this initial distribution of new members.

Amram's small family, like Aaron's, indicates that at the time of the exodus, Israel's nuclear families were not large. The question is: How many families were there in each clan? If families were small, there would have had to be many families for Israel's adult male population to have been 600,000 by the Exodus numbering. That is, prior adoptions would have had to multiply the number of nuclear families.

Is the mass adoption of the mixed multitude the likely scenario, with stable population in the wilderness based on a less-than-replacement-rate stagnation, but without a population catastrophe? If so, then the firstborn sons had been born of Israelite mothers; the adoptees were the mixed multitude.

If Israelite fathers adopted gentile sons, then the bulk of these adoptees were probably younger men who were of fighting age. They would have been adopted by Moses' generation. Thus, the bulk of the population was in Joshua's generation. These adults were replaced by the conquest generation. The sons of Joshua came from the loins of Joshua's brothers by adoption. Replacing Moses' generation was statistically incidental; it had not been large compared to the 600,000. Thus, the population moved into replacement-rate mode during the wilderness. Joshua's generation was much larger than Moses' through adoption. Their sons and grandsons did not quite replace the adult males of Moses' generation and Joshua's combined.

So, most of the 600,000 males were probably members of Joshua's generation. If so, then each family bore fewer than two children who reached maturity, for the 600,000 men a generation later included grandsons of Joshua's generation. My conclusion is that their birth rates were low or else the mortality rate for children was high. The first possibility seems more likely. God brought them under a curse in the wilderness: very low birth rates. But He did not kill off large numbers of the fourth generation.

The 22,273 non-Levite, biological (matrix-issued), firstborn sons of Israel, from one month old to age 19, constituted four percent of the fighting-age male population of 603,550. To be in replacement-rate mode, there had to be approximately 22,000 fathers. Some fathers might have been childless; others might have two sons; but nationally, the 22,273 firstborn testified to an upper limit on the number of men in Joshua's generation. Again, to maintain the replacement rate, there could have been no more than about the same number of men in Moses' generation. If there was growth, however, then the number of Moses' generation was less: fathers producing more than one son. If the growth rate was doubling, as Aaron's four children testified to, there were 22,000 fathers and 11,000 grandfathers. This indicates how thoroughly gentile, genetically speaking, Israel's army was at the time of the first mustering, and how important covenantal adoption was in Israel's founding as a nation. Most of the 603,550 were ex-gentiles. This is why they were numbered separately from the biological firstborn. This was serious covenantal evangelism.

There is a weak link in this scenario. I regard it as the major weak link. If the maximum number of men in the third generation was in the range of 22,000 – no higher than 30,000 – then there probably were not this many men at the beginning of the oppression, two generations earlier. For growth to have taken place, there would have been fewer than 22,000 men when the oppression began. The faster the growth, the fewer the men. I believe there was growth: the blessing of God. This was the testimony of the Israelite midwives. What threat would fewer than 22,000 men have posed to the Pharaoh of the oppression? Perhaps he was looking ahead at what might be if he refused to restrict their growth, but in a society that had enough slaves to construct the pyramids, there would not have been a great threat from 10,000 men, let alone 5,000.

My theory of mass adoption and a subsequent tribal membership re-distribution to the Levites is textually speculative. The texts say nothing about either event. But something like this is consistent with the tribal population numbers recorded so exactly and repeatedly in the texts. The adoption scenario may seem far-fetched. But adoption into Israel had been going on from the time of the descent into Egypt, and maybe earlier.

The Mixed Multitude at Passover

There is another important question: Did the firstborn sons of the mixed multitude die on Passover night? Not necessarily. The confrontation was between the God of Israel and the gods of Egypt, who were represented judicially by Pharaoh. Gentile slaves and other residents of Egypt are not mentioned prior to the exodus itself (Ex. 12:38). God had not brought a covenant lawsuit against them.

Let us consider three possible scenarios. *First*, it may be that God spared their sons without blood on their doorposts. The Bible does not say that the homes of the mixed multitude were visited with death; only the homes of the Egyptians: ". . . It is the sacrifice of the LORD'S passover, who passed over the houses of the children of Israel in Egypt, when he smote the Egyptians, and delivered our houses. . . ." (Ex. 12:27). The comprehensive language of Exodus 12:29–30 may indicate otherwise, but Exodus 12:27 may be the dominant theme: Israel vs. Egypt.

Second, it is possible that they believed the Israelites and put blood on their doorposts. To this extent, they covenanted with God: a common-grace, non-adoptive covenanting. Problem: Where did this many of them get the lambs? Or did they use some other form of blood, e.g., the blood of human fathers? Did God accept a substitute form of blood in an emergency? He might have. He wants obedience, not the blood of animals. "The sacrifices of God are a broken spirit: a broken and a contrite heart, O God, thou wilt not despise" (Ps. 51:17). *Third*, it is possible that their firstborn died. This possibility seems unlikely, for the adoption scenario rests on the assumption of the presence of a large population of non-Israelite males. If their firstborn sons did die, who subsequently married all of their firstborn daughters? How did demographic stability occur in the wilderness era, i.e., one wife, one husband, one son, and one daughter?

I think the second possibility is most likely. I reject the first scenario – grace without bloodshed – because of the comprehensive nature of the death of the firstborn in Numbers 8:17: "For all the firstborn of the children of Israel are mine, both man and beast: on the day that I smote every firstborn in the land of Egypt I sanctified them for myself." The firstborn sons and animals of the mixed multitude survived because the parents smeared blood on their doorposts. They believed the God of Israel with respect to the coming sanction. They had seen the other nine plagues. In smearing their doorposts with blood, they did not covenant with God in a special grace sense but in a common grace[36] sense: a visible acknowledgment that He is sovereign and the source of visible covenantal sanctions in history. They broke covenant with the gods of Egypt, but they did not formally covenant with the God of Israel. They only acknowledged that in order to avoid the negative sanction of

36. Gary North, *Dominion and Common Grace: The Biblical Basis of Progress* (Tyler, Texas: Institute for Christian Economics, 1987).

death, they had to obey God and place blood on their doorposts. If they could not locate a lamb, they substituted some other form of blood. They were not held to so strict an honoring of the Passover rites as the Israelites were because they were breaking covenant with Egypt, not establishing a covenant with God. They did not eat a Passover meal, but they did avoid the death of their firstborn. When it came time to leave, they left alongside of Israel because they had broken covenant with Egypt. This did not make them part of Israel; it did separate them from Egypt. Only adoption could make them part of Israel. But their firstborn sons did survive Passover night. These sons provided the next generation of God's holy army.

Not All Were Adopted

Later in Numbers, we read about the mixed multitude. "And the mixt multitude that was among them fell a lusting: and the children of Israel also wept again, and said, Who shall give us flesh to eat?" (Num. 11:4). Where did these people come from? There are two possible answers. First, not all the mixed multitude had covenanted with Israel. Second, these new converts were still regarded as a separate group culturally. They were not yet assimilated into Israel's covenantal life. I think the first answer is the correct one. There were many among the escaping masses who did not want to suffer circumcision (assuming they were to be circumcised) and subordination to the God of the Bible, but they saw the advantages of remaining with the Israelites. For a time, manna had seemed to them to be one of these blessings. They had not been asked to depart from the camp of the faithful.

The mixed multitude served as contrasts to covenant-keepers, and they also served as sources of temptation, as was the case in Numbers 11. They still had an independent voice. The Israelites listened to their complaints against God and then voiced these complaints themselves. Judgment came swiftly: the positive sanction of quail and the negative sanction of plague (Num. 11:31–33).

Objections

There are several plausible objections to my scenario. The main one is that no revelation of such a mass adoption appears in the Bible. But neither does the suggestion of prior adoptions, yet these are necessary to make sense of Israel's demographics.

Second, why would a small nation adopt a lot of questionable pagans? Wouldn't the newcomers swamp the adopters? One reason is that the pagans asked to be adopted, even as the Gibeonites later were willing to become servants (Josh. 9). How could Israel reject such a request and still adhere to God's covenant? If a small local church is approached by 500 local college students who ask to join, what is the church to do? Tell them to go elsewhere? But there was no "elsewhere" in the Old Covenant. Another reason is military. Cowards like large numbers, hoping to reinforce their weak position. Here was a nation that feared marching into Canaan with an army of 600,000 men (even though not all of them could serve). How brave would they have been if there were, say, only 35,000 of them, with a third of these being old men?

Third, what language would have been used to communicate? Probably whatever language the Egyptians used to command these people. Then how was Hebrew ever to become the nation's common language? Perhaps through the same means that Hebrew has become the common language of the modern state of Israel: by conducting worship, civil law, education, and business in Hebrew.

Fourth, one which I have already mentioned: the small size of the population in Kohath's day. In my opinion, this is the strongest objection. It calls into question the reason for the oppression, which ultimately decided Israel's fate in Egypt.

Conclusion

Here are the three problems that are raised by this passage: 1) how the 27-to-one ratio between adult males and firstborn sons could have existed biologically; 2) how a relatively small population of sons became the 600,000 fighting males that invaded Canaan; 3) how Israel grew to 600,000 adult males in three generations.

The third problem can be answered in only one way: through adoption into the nation of Israel. Because the theme of adoption is so central to the issue of God's kingdom in history, I used this theological model to approach the other two problems. I asked: Could the 27-to-one ratio have had something to do with the relationship between biologically firstborn sons and newly adopted adults? Second, could the disparity between the birth rates of the Passover's Israelites and the newly adopted gentiles explain the seemingly overnight appearance of zero population growth during the wilderness era?

Something took place in Israel's wilderness experience which reversed the high population growth rates that had prevailed since their descent into Egypt. I suggest the following: God's imposition of low birth rates on rebels. My solution to the echo problem does not require the death of fourth generation members who were born prior to the exodus. It also allows high birth rates for Joshua's generation: more than firstborn sons.

Jordan's solution, that the firstborn sons were under age five, suffers from the problem of redefining the meaning of *firstborn*. The evidence for five years or younger comes from the adoption price of Leviticus 27:6. It is indirect, at best. This solution creates problems regarding the birth rates of Joshua's generation in Egypt: either below the replacement rate or skewered very strangely during the last four years in Egypt.

Keil's thesis of the numbered firstborn as only those born after the exodus, if coupled with some variant of the early adoption scenario, is plausible, but only at the expense of radically redefining *firstborn* so as to eliminate the Passover's sons from the numbering.

For the person who resists a major redefinition, mine is technically possible though speculative: mass adoption. The enormous number of adult male Israelites at the time of the first numbering, if compared to the small number of firstborn sons, indicates that the Israelites had adopted huge numbers of fleeing gentiles into the nation sometime during the year following the exodus.

This places adoption at the very center of Israel's history as a nation. There must have been prior adoptions: surely of the household servants who came into Israel; probably of residents of Egypt in the years prior to the oppression. But the ratio of adult males to firstborn sons – 27 to one – can be explained in terms of a mass adoption out of the mixed multitude, either at the time of the exodus or in the months that followed, but before the Exodus numbering.

One thing is certain: *Israel was a nation of recruits*. From God's recruiting of Noah, then Abram, then Jacob's servants, and perhaps at the exodus, Israel had been a nation of adopted recruits. This was Ezekiel's clear testimony to the nation: "And say, Thus saith the Lord GOD unto Jerusalem; Thy birth and thy nativity is of the land of Canaan; thy father was an Amorite, and thy mother an Hittite. And as for thy nativity, in the day thou wast born thy navel was not cut, neither wast thou washed in water to supple thee; thou wast not salted at all, nor swaddled at all. None eye pitied thee, to do any of these unto thee, to have compassion upon thee; but thou wast cast out in the open field, to the lothing of thy person, in the day that thou wast born. And when I passed by thee, and saw thee polluted in thine own blood, I said unto thee when thou wast in thy blood, Live; yea, I said unto thee when thou wast in thy blood, Live. I have caused thee to multiply as the bud of the field, and thou hast increased and waxen great" (Ezek. 16:3–7a).

What I have deduced from the texts is based on the data in the texts. This means that the Jews of Jesus' day should have known about the many adoptions of gentiles in Egypt. But the teachers of Israel did not teach this. Even the Jews who believed Jesus (John 8:31) were unaware of it. "They answered him, We be Abraham's seed, and were never in bondage to any man: how sayest thou, Ye shall be made free?" (John 8:33). They were incorrect on both counts. First, they were obviously in civil bondage to Rome, and had been in bondage to pagan empires ever since the exile. Second, they were heirs of the adopted sons of Abraham's heirs.

Any hope in a blood covenant through Abraham was a false hope. The Abrahamic covenant had itself been adoptive. Jesus on another occasion warned the Pharisees and Sadducees: "And think not to say within yourselves, We have Abraham to our father: for I say unto you, that God is able of these stones to raise up children unto Abraham" (Matt. 3:9). The context of that challenge was John's baptism. Jesus employed rhetorical language – stones into sons – to proclaim the message of adoption. The vast majority of those who called themselves Abraham's sons were heirs of adoptees. If they believed otherwise, they had not paid close attention to Moses' accounts of the population explosion in his youth and the post-exodus adult to firstborn ratio.

If Jordan's thesis is correct, namely, that the firstborn sons in Numbers 3 were under age five, then my suggestion regarding Israel's having adopted large segments of the mixed multitude is incorrect, or at least not necessary to make sense of the texts. We could legitimately conclude that adoptions of gentiles into Israel took place earlier in Israel's history, but not necessarily after the exodus Passover.

My objection to his interpretation is based on my view of what a firstborn son was judicially in Egypt: any firstborn son, no matter how old, who had no firstborn son in his own household who would bear the sanction of death. There was no age limit on this judicial status. *The deciding covenantal issue was household residence*. This was why blood had to be smeared on the doorposts, and everyone had to remain inside his house.

This definition changed in the musterings. The firstborn son in Numbers 3 was any firstborn son who was not eligible for mustering because he was under age 20. Judicially speaking, a mustered son had left his father's household. The deciding covenantal issue of household status moved from physical residence to military status: a new hierarchy. But if my thesis concerning late adoptions is wrong, then so is my definition of *firstborn*.

Like Jordan, Keil wants the number of firstborn sons in Numbers 3 to be smaller than the number at Passover, so as to reduce the 27-to-one ratio. He accomplishes this by limiting the time horizon of what constituted a firstborn son in Numbers 3. There were far more firstborn sons, biologically speaking, than those recorded in Numbers 3. How many, we cannot know, but as many as we need to make the ratio believable! This is one way to handle the problem. It does require the addition of the assumption of prior adoptions. By extending the number of births that persisted from the exodus to the Numbers numbering, we discover that Joshua's generation was close to replacement-rate mode. This implies extensive adoptions very early in Israel's sojourn in Egypt: slower growth late in the process; therefore, a minimal echo effect.

In contrast, my thesis of late adoptions allows approximately the same number of firstborn in Numbers 3 as at the Passover. It solves the 27-to-one problem by dramatically increasing the number of biologically unrelated adults numbered. This makes the ratio acceptable by removing it from the realm of biology.

I prefer Keil's thesis to Jordan's. It gives a theological reason for the shift in definition: the atonement of the Passover's firstborn by the lambs. But is Keil's solution superior to my thesis of a post-exodus mass adoption? His explanation is surely less complicated. It raises fewer questions about the problems of assimilating a huge number of foreigners. But to make it plausible, we must make the assumption of extensive early adoptions, probably in Joseph's era, in order to avoid the implications of a monumental demographic echo effect: either a dramatic reduction in the birth rate of Joshua's generation or the deaths of most of the fourth generation in the wilderness.

I have suggested a third possibility: the mass adoption of the mixed multitude. It is the only way I can imagine that the 27-to-one problem can be solved without radically redefining *firstborn* in Numbers 3. Yet I have redefined it slightly: defining the son's departure from his father's household as judicial rather than strictly physical. To answer the 27-to-one problem, there must be two different definitions.

Having made the strongest case I can for the mass adoption thesis, I think it is weaker than Keil's. Yet it is the only substitute for Keil's that I think comes close to solving the three problems. It raises so many questions, however, that it is safer to go with Keil's definition of the firstborn: a firstborn son who was born after the Passover but no less than one month before the second numbering. But in either scenario, there is no escape from the conclusion that Israel was a nation of adoptees.

SCRIPTURE INDEX

INDEX

Backward, Christian Soldiers?
An Action Manual for Christian Reconstruction
by Gary North

Jesus said to "Occupy till I come." But if Christians don't control the territory, they can't occupy it. They get tossed out into cultural "outer darkness," which is just exactly what the secular humanists have done to Christians in the 20th century: in education, in the arts, in entertainment, in politics, and certainly in the mainline churches and seminaries. Today, the humanists are "occupying." But they won't be for long. This book shows why.

For the first time in over a century, Christians are beginning to proclaim a seemingly new doctrine, yet the original doctrine was given to man by God: *dominion* (Genesis 1:28). But this doctrine implies another: *victory*. That's what this book is all about: *a strategy for victory*.

Satan may be alive on planet earth, but he's not well. He's in the biggest trouble he's been in since Calvary. If Christians adopt a *vision of victory* and a *program of Christian reconstruction*, we will see the beginning of a new era on earth: the kingdom of God manifested in every area of life. When Christ returns, Christians will be occupying, not hiding in the shadows, not sitting in the back of humanism's bus.

This book shows where to begin.

290 pp., indexed, paperback, $5.95
Institute for Christian Economics, P.O. Box 8000, Tyler, Texas 75711

Order *all* eleven of the books advertised here for 40% off and pay no shipping costs. Make a check payable to I.C.E. for $121.00 (a $201.00 value!)

Productive Christians in an Age of Guilt Manipulators
by David Chilton

One of the most insidious attacks upon orthodox Christianity has come from the so-called "Christian Left." This book answers the "bible" of that movement, *Rich Christians in an Age of Hunger,* by Ronald Sider.

David Chilton demonstrates that the "Christian Socialism" advocated by Sider is nothing more than baptized humanism — the goal of which is not charity, but raw, police-state power.

The debate between Sider and Chilton centers on one central issue: *Does the Bible have clear guidelines for every area of life?* Sider claims that the Bible does not contain "blueprints" for a social and economic order. The catch, of course, is that Sider then provides *his own* "blueprints" for society, calling for a taxation system which is completely condemned by God's infallible word. Chilton answers that the socialist "cure" is worse than the disease, for socialism actually *increases* poverty. Even when motivated by good intentions, unbiblical "charity" programs will damage the very people they seek to help.

Combining incisive satire with hard-hitting argumentation and extensive biblical references, Chilton shows that the Bible *does* have clear, forthright, and workable answers to the problem of poverty. *Productive Christians* is most importantly a major introduction to the system of Christian Economics, with chapters on biblical law, welfare, poverty, the third world, overpopulation, foreign aid, advertising, profits, and economic growth.

439 pp., indexed, bibliography, paperback, $12.50
Institute for Christian Economics, P.O. Box 8000, Tyler, TX 75711

Order *all* eleven of the books advertised here for 40% off and pay no shipping costs. Make a check payable to I.C.E. for $121.00 (a $201.00 value!)

The Greatness of the Great Commission: The Christian Enterprise in a Fallen World
by Rev. Kenneth L. Gentry

"Save Souls, Not Cultures!" This has been the motto of twentieth-century evangelism. Having encountered heavy resistance to the prophets' message of comprehensive revival and restoration in history, modern evangelical Christianity has abandoned the prophets. Unlike Jonah, who grew weary of life in the belly of a whale, modern evangelicalism has not only grown accustomed to the Church's cultural irrelevance today, it has actually proclaimed this pathetic condition as God's plan for the "Church Age." But is it? Not according to Jesus' instructions to His Church: the discipling (putting under God's discipline) of all nations (Matthew 28:19-20).

Paul makes it clear that the progressive expansion of Jesus' kingdom in history will continue until all things are under His dominion, on earth, before He returns physically to judge the world (I Corinthians 15:25-26). This was David's message, too (Psalm 110:1-2).

This book presents a biblical case for God's salvation and restoration in history. Sin is comprehensive; God's healing grace is no less comprehensive. Wherever sin reigns today, there God speaks to sinful man and offers a way of escape (I Corinthians 10-13). To argue that the Great Commission does not include every aspect of today's cultures — all of Satan's kingdom — is to argue that there is no way of escape in many areas of life.

The war between God's kingdom (civilization) on earth and Satan's kingdom (civilization) on earth is total, encompassing every aspect of life. The Great Commission calls the Church (in this "Church Age") to make a full-scale attack on modern humanist civilization, but always in terms of a positive message and practical program: a better way of life in every area of life. This is the greatness of the Great Commission. It must not be narrowed to exclude culture from God's special grace.

184 pp., indexed, paperback, $9.95; hardback, $25.00
Institute for Christian Economics, P.O. Box 8000, Tyler, Texas 75711

Order *all* eleven of the books advertised here for 40% off and pay no shipping costs. Make a check payable to I.C.E. for $121.00 (a $201.00 value!)

That You May Prosper: Dominion By Covenant
by Rev. Ray R. Sutton

In the history of Christianity there has never been a theologian who has explained to anyone's satisfaction just what the Biblical covenant is. We have heard about "covenant theology" since Calvin's day, but can anyone tell us just what Calvin said the covenant is, how it works, and what common features are found in every Biblical covenant? Can anyone describe just exactly what the seventeenth-century Puritans had in mind when they used the word? They couldn't.

Have you read anywhere that the covenant is an inescapable concept, that it is never a question of "covenant vs. no covenant," that it is always a question of whose covenant? Has anyone explained how all societies have imitated the Bible's covenant model, or how Satan has adapted a crude imitation of the Biblical covenant?

Until Ray Sutton cracked the code of the Bible's covenant structure in late 1985, no one had gone into print with a clear, Biblically verifiable model of the covenant – or if anyone did, no trace of his work has survived. Covenant theologians have never adopted it.

You can check this for yourself. Read any book dealing with the Biblical covenant. See if it explains: (1) the structure of the covenant; (2) the uses of the covenant model in Bible history; (3) the application of the same covenant model in Bible texts, Old and New Testaments; (4) the history of the covenant's impact in the West; and (5) the continuing authority and importance of the Biblical covenant in modern life: church, state, family, business, etc.

Utilizing careful and detailed Biblical exposition, and practical and lucid Biblical application, Sutton shows just how God desires for us to obtain our promised victory. But he not only shows us all the hows of the covenant, he shows us all the whats, whens, wheres, and whys as well.

Whether your interest is theological or practical, philosophical of personal, sociological or devotional, *That You May Prosper* is certain to be an eye-opening contribution to your Christian walk.

347 pp., indexed, bibliography, hardback, $15.95
Institute for Christian Economics, P.O. Box 8000, Tyler, Texas 75711.

Order *all* eleven of the books advertised here for 40% off and pay no shipping costs. Make a check payable to I.C.E. for $121.00 (a $201.00 value!)

He Shall Have Dominion: A Postmillennialism Eschatology

by Rev. Kenneth L. Gentry

The vast majority of those who call themselves evangelical Christians believe that the Church of Jesus Christ has been predestinated by God to fail in history. "It cannot possibly succeed!" Millions of Christians believe that the Church will be "raptured" soon, removing Christians from the turmoils and responsibilities of this life.

Ken Gentry argues otherwise in *He Shall Have Dominion.* He shows that Christians have many great things to accomplish for Christ before He returns bodily to earth.

Two centuries ago, Protestant Christians believed that they would die before Jesus came back to earth. This affected the way they thought, prayed, worked and saved. They built for the future. They were future-oriented. They were upper class. Today, many Protestants believe that Jesus is coming back soon, so they will not have to die. This belief affects the way they think, pray, work, and save. They are present-oriented. They are lower-class. Ken Gentry refutes this outlook, verse by verse.

He Shall Have Dominion is a positive book: positive about the future of the Church. It teaches that Christians will exercise dominion in history. It therefore teaches responsibility. This is why its message is hated. Today's Christians have been taught that they must flee responsibility, for Jesus' sake. They would rather believe that God has predestined His Church to failure than believe that they are personally responsible for transforming society. This is why the Church is so weak in our day.

584 pp., indexed, bibliography, hardback, $19.95
Institute for Christian Economics, P.O. Box 8000, Tyler, TX 75711

Order all eleven of the books advertised here for 40% off and pay no shipping costs. Make a check payable to I.C.E. for $121.00 (a $201.00 value!)

The Sinai Strategy: Economics and the Ten Commandments

by Gary North

There can be little doubt that the Ten Commandments made possible the development of Western Civilization. There is almost equally little doubt that Western Civilization made possible the development of free market capitalism. The question must then be raised: What was it about the Ten Commandments which made possible the development of capitalism in the West, and nowhere (else except in cultures influenced by an already capitalistic West)?

It was not some hypothetical (and non-existent) universal natural law, or "natural law rightly understood," which made possible the development of the free market, but rather biblical law and a biblical concept of linear time. It was Western man's confidence in the validity of the Ten Commandments which alone created free market institutions in world history.

Is it therefore not sufficient to ask: Is capitalism Christian? It is not sufficient to appeal to natural law in the Christian West as the foundation of capitalism. What must be asked is a far more controversial question: Is orthodox, Bible-based Christianity inherently capitalistic? In other words, in cultures where the Bible is preached from Genesis to Revelation, will there be an innate tendency for that culture to adopt a free market economy? Therefore, is socialism inherently heretical biblically? Gary North answers "yes".

The Sinai Strategy is a detailed look at the Ten Commandments and their social, political, and, especially, economic implications. These commandments set forth a strategy of dominion. The war between capitalism and socialism is ultimately a war between God and Satan. Far too many compromised Christians have not recognized the nature of this ethical and institutional war, and they have sided with the socialists. Dr. North has drawn the dividing line between the humanists and the Christians themselves. Will it be God's law or Satan's, Christ's New World Order (inaugurated at Calvary) or Satan's New World Order (scheduled for the year 2000)?

368 pp., indexed, paperback, $12.50
Institute for Christian Economics, P.O. Box 8000, Tyler, TX 75711

Order all eleven of the books advertised here for 40% off and pay no shipping costs. Make a check payable to I.C.E. for $121.00 (a $201.00 value!)

Leviticus: An Economic Commentary

By Gary North

The book of Leviticus is a foreboding book for most readers. The first seven chapters deal with five sacrifices, none of which survived beyond the fall of Jerusalem and the destruction of the temple in A.D. 70. Why should the modern reader immerse himself in all that detail? Other parts of the book are filled with laws of cleanliness. Then there are the incredibly detailed dietary laws. Are all these laws still binding or not? Most churches think not.

Then of what relevance is this difficult book? The church has long answered: "Not much." so, it has remained a closed book for most Christians.

This is a mistake. The book of Leviticus is the third book of the Pentateuch, the book of the moral law. It is also the book of the holy land, i.e., private property. Leviticus sets forth the fundamental economic principle of ownership: God first, then those to whom He has delegated subordinate ownership.

For example, consider Leviticus 19:15. "Ye shall do no unrighteousness in judgment: thou shalt not respect the person of the poor, nor honour the person of the mighty: but in righteousness shalt thou judge they neighbour." This verse provided God's people with two crucial principles, one economic and one judicial.

The economic principle affirms the legitimacy of inequality. The judicial principle affirms the local court system. These two principles — inequality and judicial localism — are fundamental for the creation of a free society. Modern socialism and its supposed replacement, the much-heralded bureaucratic New World Order, are equally hostile to such a view of civil law.

The economic laws of Leviticus are neglected at our peril. But which ones? Not all of them are still in force. *Leviticus: An Economic Commentary* identifies which ones are, and provides a principle of biblical interpretation to prove it.

732 pp., indexed, bibliography, hardback, $29.95
The Institute for Christian Economics, P.O. Box 8000, Tyler, TX 75711

Order all eleven of the books advertised here for 40% off and pay no shipping costs. Make a check payable to I.C.E. for $121.00 (a $201.00 value!)